CLASSROOM ASSESSMENT

SEVENTH EDITION

CLASSROOM ASSESSMENT

CONCEPTS AND APPLICATIONS

MICHAEL K. RUSSELL
Boston College

PETER W. AIRASIAN
Boston College

Mc Graw Hill

*Connect
Learn
Succeed*™

The McGraw·Hill Companies

Mc Graw Hill)

Connect
Learn
Succeed™

CLASSROOM ASSESSMENT, SEVENTH EDITION

Published by McGraw-Hill, a business unit of The McGraw-Hill Companies, Inc., 1221 Avenue of the Americas, New York, NY 10020. Copyright © 2012 by The McGraw-Hill Companies, Inc. All rights reserved. Previous editions © 2008, 2005, and 2001. No part of this publication may be reproduced or distributed in any form or by any means, or stored in a database or retrieval system, without the prior written consent of The McGraw-Hill Companies, Inc., including, but not limited to, in any network or other electronic storage or transmission, or broadcast for distance learning.

Some ancillaries, including electronic and print components, may not be available to customers outside the United States.

This book is printed on acid-free paper.

1 2 3 4 5 6 7 8 9 0 DOC/DOC 1 0 9 8 7 6 5 4 3 2 1

ISBN   978-0-07-811021-4
MHID   0-07-811021-1

Vice President & Editor-in-Chief: *Michael Ryan*
Vice President & Director of Specialized Publishing: *Janice M. Roerig-Blong*
Editorial Director: *Beth Mejia*
Publisher: *Michael Sugarman*
Director of Marketing & Sales: *Jennifer J. Lewis*
Senior Sponsoring Editor: *Debra B. Hash*
Project Manager: *Robin A. Reed*
Design Coordinator: *Margarite Reynolds*
Cover Designer: *Studio Montage, St. Louis, Missouri*
Cover Images: *Upper:* © *Creatas; Lower: Royalty-Free/CORBIS*
Buyer: *Nicole Baumgartner*
Media Project Manager: *Sridevi Palani*
Compositor: *Aptara®, Inc.*
Typeface: *10/12 Veljovic*
Printer: *R.R. Donnelley*

All credits appearing on page or at the end of the book are considered to be an extension of the copyright page.

Library of Congress Cataloging-in-Publication Data

Russell, Michael K., 1967–
    Classroom assessment : concepts and applications / Michael K. Russell,
    Peter W. Airasian.—7th ed.
        p. cm.
    Rev. ed. of: Classroom assessment / Peter W. Airasian, Michael Russell. ©2008.
    ISBN-13: 978-0-07-811021-4 (pbk.)
    ISBN-10: 0-07-811021-1 (hb)
    1. Educational tests and measurements—United States. 2. Academic
achievement—United States—Testing. 3. Education—United States—Evaluation. I. Airasian, Peter W.
II. Airasian, Peter W. Classroom assessment. III. Title.

LB3051.A5627 2012
371.260973—dc22   2011000602

www.mhhe.com

This book is dedicated to Liana, Darius, and Micayla.

ABOUT THE AUTHORS

Michael K. Russell is Associate Professor of Education at Boston College's Lynch School of Education, where he directs the Technology and Assessment Study Collaborative. His research and teaching interests lie at the intersection of assessment and technology. He teaches classroom assessment for pre-service students and courses that focus on issues in testing, assessment, and evaluation to graduate students. Professor Russell has conducted several studies that focus on the use of computer-based technologies to increase test validity. These research issues include computers and writing, computer-based test accommodations for students with special needs, development of diagnostic tests for teachers to use in the classroom, and improvement of the instructional utility of large-scale tests. He is the author of *Technology and Assessment: The Tale of Two Interpretations.*

Peter W. Airasian is Professor of Education at Boston College, where he is Chair of the Department of Counseling, Developmental Psychology, and Research Methods. His main teaching responsibilities are instructing pre- and in-service teachers in classroom assessment. He received his PhD from the University of Chicago, with a concentration in assessment and evaluation. He is a former high school chemistry and biology teacher. Professor Airasian is coauthor of *Minimal Competency Testing* (1979), *School Effectiveness: A Reassessment of the Evidence* (1980), *The Effects of Standardized Testing* (1982), *Assessment in the Classroom* (1996), *Teacher Self-Evaluation Tool Kit* (2001), *Taxonomy for Learning, Teaching, and Assessing: A Revision of Bloom's Taxonomy of Educational Objectives* (2001), and *Educational Research: Competencies for Analysis and Applications* (2002), as well as many articles on classroom assessment and testing.

BRIEF CONTENTS

CONTENTS

CHAPTER 7

UNIVERSAL DESIGN FOR ASSESSMENT   176

CHAPTER 8
PERFORMANCE ASSESSMENTS 200

CHAPTER 9
GRADING 249

CHAPTER 10
COMMERCIAL STANDARDIZED ACHIEVEMENT TESTS   300

HOW COMMERCIAL ACHIEVEMENT TESTS ARE CREATED   303

Test Construction   304

CHAPTER 11
COMPUTER-BASED TECHNOLOGY AND CLASSROOM ASSESSMENT   332

PREFACE

A Conceptual and Applied Approach

This textbook was written for preservice teachers taking a first course in classroom assessment. As students in K-12 schools, preservice teachers participated in a variety of assessments. Memories of assessment activities conjure images of weekly quizzes, homework, unit tests, extended projects, classroom presentations, and standardized multiple-choice tests. The goal of the seventh edition of *Classroom Assessment: Concepts and Applications* is to show that classroom assessment is a key component of all aspects of the instructional process. We also introduce new tools and approaches to classroom assessment that result from the infusion of computer-based technologies into schools.

The text begins with an overview of essential concepts and principles of classroom assessment and explores recent changes in assessment that have grown out of new state and national educational policies. We then examine how assessment applies to each phase of the instructional process—from organizing the classroom as a social setting, to planning and conducting instruction based on sound objectives, to formal assessment of student learning, to grading students, and finally to interpreting standardized tests and statewide assessments. We pay particular attention to developing the ability of preservice teachers to create and employ a variety of assessment methods and tools that are designed to meet specific purposes. The validity of inferences and decisions based on assessment information is examined within each phase of instruction. The goal is to demonstrate that assessment is an integral part of teaching that should not be separated from daily classroom practices.

New to the Seventh Edition

In response to several recent developments and innovations, the seventh edition of *Classroom Assessment* has been expanded in significant ways.

Universal Design for Assessment: The concept of universal design has become a driving force for improving student access to learning materials. It is also essential that assessment tasks be designed to be as accessible as possible for all students. A new chapter examines many ways in which principles of universal design can be applied to classroom assessment.

Formative Assessment: A new chapter focuses on informal and formal methods and techniques that are useful for collecting information that can be used immediately to inform instruction.

Common Assessments and the Race to the Top Program: Recent federal initiatives are likely to rapidly change state assessment programs. Sections have been added that explore these looming changes and discuss the increasing role that technology will play for all types of assessment.

Proven Features and Content

This edition includes features proven useful in prior editions. These features are described below.

Realistic Assessment: The focus throughout is on the realities of classrooms and how assessments can serve these realities.

Validity and Reliability: These central assessment concepts are introduced in the first chapter and then linked in later chapters to each specific type of assessment information. The validity and reliability issues of informal assessment, planning and delivering instruction, grading, using paper-and-pencil tests, performance assessments, and standardized testing are identified. Practical strategies to improve the validity and reliability of varied assessment approaches are presented in each chapter.

Practical Guidelines: A significant portion of each chapter focuses on practical guidelines to follow and common errors to avoid when using the type of assessment being presented. The implications of ignoring the recommendations are also described. Key Assessment Tools boxes, at least two per chapter, highlight practical resources and tools to use in the assessment process.

Teacher Thinking: Throughout the text, excerpts from teachers' comments about assessment add the wisdom of day-to-day practice to assessment situations. A "Thinking about Teaching" question at the opening of each chapter prompts students to put chapter topics into the context of the classroom.

Student-Friendly Writing Style: The text is written with a clear, friendly, and accessible style and is amply supplied with examples and tables to thoroughly engage students. Case studies, referenced in the margins and accessible through the Online Learning Center, bring chapter topics to life.

Online Learning Center: Located at www.mhhe.com/russell7e, this resource includes a student study guide with practice quizzes, case studies, and Web links.

Online Learning Center

An Online Learning Center for instructors and students using *Classroom Assessment* **is available at www.mhhe.com/russell7e.**

For the instructor:

Instructor's Manual: An updated and expanded instructor's manual, including instructional strategies for key concepts and terms, online activities, and more!

Test Bank: An updated test bank in Microsoft Word that includes multiple choice, true/false, short answer, and essay questions for quick and easy test creation.

PowerPoint Slides: PowerPoint lecture slides that outline key points of each chapter.

Instructors can contact their sales representative for access to the instructor's side of the Online Learning Center.

For the student:

The online Learning Center includes case studies that demonstrate chapter concepts using real classroom scenarios.

Acknowledgments

With appreciation for their efforts to improve this work, we acknowledge the following reviewers whose frank and detailed suggestions added much to this revision:

Kathy Lee Alvoid, Southern Methodist University
Bruce F. Brodney, Saint Petersburg College, Gibbs Campus
Cindy M. Casebeer, University of Texas–Pan American
Amy Dombach Connelly, Felician College
Karen Eifler, University of Portland
Dennis M. Holt, University of North Florida
Jerrie Jackson, Our Lady of the Lake University
Beth Nason Quick, Tennessee State University
Gene Schwarting, Fontbonne University
Bruce A. Shields, Daemen College

CourseSmart eTextbooks

This text is available as an eTextbook from CourseSmart, a new way for faculty to find and review eTextbooks. It's also a great option for students who are interested in accessing their course materials digitally and saving money. CourseSmart offers thousands of the most commonly adopted text-books across hundreds of courses from a wide variety of higher-education publishers. It is the only place for faculty to review and compare the full text of a textbook online, providing immediate access without the environmental impact of requesting a print exam copy. At CourseSmart, students can save up to 50 percent off the cost of a print book, reduce their impact on the environment, and gain access to powerful Web tools for learning including full text search, notes and highlighting, and e-mail tools for sharing notes between classmates. For further details contact your sales representative or go to www.coursesmart.com.

McGraw-Hill Create

www.mcgrawhillcreate.com
Craft your teaching resources to match the way you teach! With McGraw-Hill Create you can easily rearrange chapters, combine material from other content sources, and quickly upload content you have written such as your course syllabus or teaching notes. Find the content you need in Create by searching through thousands of leading McGraw-Hill textbooks. Arrange your book to fit your teaching style. Create even allows you to personalize your book's appearance by selecting the cover and adding your name, school, and course information. Order a Create book and you'll receive a complimentary print review copy in 3–5 business days or a complimentary electronic review copy (eComp) via e-mail in about one hour. Go to www.mcgrawhillcreate.com today and register. Experience how McGraw-Hill Create empowers you to teach *your* students *your* way.

CHAPTER 1

THE BREADTH OF CLASSROOM ASSESSMENT

KEY TOPICS

- *The Importance of Assessment: How Has Assessment Changed in Recent Years?*

- *Purposes of Classroom Assessment*

- *Phases of Classroom Assessment*

- *Assessment, Testing, Measurement, and Evaluation*

- *Three General Ways to Collect Data: Student Products, Observations, and Oral Questioning*

- *Standardized and Nonstandardized Assessments*

- *Appropriate Assessments: Valid and Reliable*

- *Ethical Issues and Responsibilities*

CHAPTER OBJECTIVES

After reading this chapter, you will be able to:

- Define *assessment, measurement, test, educational standards, standardized test, validity, reliability,* and other basic terms
- Describe the various purposes of assessment
- Contrast the three main methods of collecting assessment information, and give examples of each
- Explain what validity and reliability are and how they are related to student assessment
- Define three types of educational standards and describe how they influence classroom instruction
- State examples of teachers' ethical responsibilities in collecting or using assessment information

THE IMPORTANCE OF ASSESSMENT: HOW HAS EMPHASIS ON ASSESSMENT CHANGED IN RECENT YEARS?

Assessment is an essential component of teaching. In recent years, however, the importance of assessment has increased even further. Ten years ago, teachers used tests to assess student achievement and determine grades. Quizzes were given to motivate students to study and to help teachers determine how well students were learning new skills and knowledge. Assignments were used to provide opportunities for students to develop knowledge and skills, and to provide teachers with insight into challenges students were encountering. During instruction, teachers asked questions and had students engage in specific activities to gather information about what students understood and what ideas and skills they were struggling with. Occasionally, teachers also administered standardized tests, the results of which were used to provide an external indicator of how well students were developing skills and knowledge. While the decisions made based on each of these types of assessment were important, their stakes were relatively low.

All of these forms of assessment are still important parts of classroom teaching. What is very different is the importance of standardized tests and the high-stakes decisions that are made based on student performance on these tests. Federal laws, such as the No Child Left Behind Act, now require every student in grades 3–8 and in at least one grade in high school to be tested every year in mathematics and language arts. Unlike standardized tests administered 10 years ago, these tests are used to make high-stakes decisions about the quality of schools, teachers, and principals. In some cases, schools that have persistently low test scores may be placed into receivership or closed. Teachers and principals can be

Every student in grades 3–8 and in at least one high school grade must be tested in mathematics and language arts.

dismissed if the test scores of their students are persistently low. And, in some cases, students are denied diplomas or are not allowed to advance to the next grade if their test scores are too low. An even newer federal program, called Race to the Top Assessment, provides up to $350 million to develop tests to be administered to students across several states so that the performance of students can be compared between states. Some national leaders want to use these comparisons to determine how much federal support each state is provided.

Many experts have debated the merits of this increased emphasis on standardized tests. There is considerable disagreement about whether these policies are improving the quality of our educational system. However, one thing is for certain: the importance of and focus on assessment is at an all-time high.

While standardized tests are now an important component of education, teaching and assessment in the classroom involve much more than preparing students for standardized tests. As we explore throughout this book, classroom assessment takes many forms and is a continuous process that helps teachers make decisions about classroom management, instruction, and students.

Classroom assessment takes many forms and helps teachers make many types of decisions.

THINKING ABOUT TEACHING

Why might teachers think of assessment as a continuous process that happens throughout the school day?

C**lassroom assessment** is the process of collecting, synthesizing, and interpreting information to aid in classroom decision making. Throughout the school day, teachers continuously gather and use information to make decisions about classroom management, instruction, student learning, and planning. This book explores a broad range of assessment strategies teachers use when assessing in the classroom. Chapter 1 lays out a general scheme of types of assessments and their uses that will be covered more deeply in later chapters. It also introduces three types of educational standards that are playing an increasingly important role in shaping instruction and assessment in the classroom. It explains how validity and reliability are the keys to effective assessment. It ends with some thoughts about ethical issues related to classroom assessment.

Assessment is the process of collecting, synthesizing, and interpreting information to aid in decision making. Assessment is a continuous part of classroom life.

Every day in every classroom, teachers make decisions about their students, the success of their instruction, and the classroom climate. Today was a typical day in Ms. Lopez's classroom. In addition to preparing the room for the day's activities, putting the work schedule on the chalkboard, reviewing her lesson plans, greeting students as they entered the classroom, taking attendance, distributing supplies, reminding students of next

Saturday's school fair, and monitoring the lunchroom, Ms. Lopez also performed the following tasks:

- Assigned grades to her students' science tests on the planets
- Referred Aaron to the Special Education Department to be screened for poor gross motor skills
- Completed the monthly school progress report on each student in the class
- Moved Tamika from the middle to the high reading group
- Selected Rosa, not Sarah, to deliver a note to Mr. Brown, the school principal
- Decided on topics to cover in next Monday's math lesson
- Met with the special education teacher to review the accommodations Mauricio needed when taking a multiple-choice test
- Stopped the planned language lesson halfway through the period in order to review the previous day's lesson
- Formed a reading group for three students who were progressing more slowly than their classmates
- Rearranged the class seating plan to separate Jamar and Ramon and to move Claudia to the front of the room so she could see the chalkboard better
- Called on Kim twice even though her hand was not raised
- Studied the statewide writing standards to determine what topics to emphasize in instruction
- Switched social studies instruction from discussion to seatwork when the class became bored and unruly
- Encouraged Jing to redraft his English composition to correct spelling and grammar errors
- Decided to construct her own test for the social studies unit rather than using the textbook test
- Sent Antonio to the school nurse when he complained of a headache
- Judged that Tabitha's constant interruptions and speaking out in class warranted a note to her parents about the problem
- Assigned homework in science and social studies, but not in math and language arts
- Checked with the school counselor regarding possible reasons for Miguel's increasingly inattentive class behavior
- Paired Kim, a class isolate, with Aretha, a class leader, for the project in social studies
- Sent Ralph to the principal because he swore at a teacher and threatened a classmate
- Held a parent-teacher conference with Ivan's parents in which she told them that he was a capable student who could produce better work than he had thus far
- Consulted last year's standardized test scores to determine whether the class needed a review of the basic rules of capitalization

As you can see, Ms. Lopez's day in the classroom, like those of all teachers, was filled with situations in which she had to make decisions. Some of these decisions concerned individual students and some concerned the class as a whole. Some were about instructional matters, some about classroom climate, some about student personalities, and some about student learning. Some, like the decision to change Tamika's reading group, were infrequently made decisions. Others, like planning topics for instruction, calling on students during class, and assigning grades to students, were made many times each day. All of Ms. Lopez's actions resulted from decisions she made, and all of her decisions were based on some type of evidence. Like other good teachers, she continually observes, monitors, and reviews student behaviors and performances to obtain evidence for decision making. Taken together, these decisions serve to establish, organize, and monitor classroom qualities such as student learning, interpersonal relations, social adjustment, instructional content, and classroom climate.

Teachers must continually observe, monitor, and review student behavior and performance in order to make informed decisions.

Classroom decisions must be reflective and thoughtful, not impulsive and erratic. The decisions Ms. Lopez made were based on many different kinds of evidence. How did Ms. Lopez know that the way to settle her bored and unruly social studies class was to switch from discussion to seatwork, when there were many other things she might have done to settle the class? What made her decide to move Tamika to the high reading group? Why did she think pairing Kim with Aretha for the social studies project was better than pairing Kim with someone else? Why was Rosa, but not Sarah, trusted to deliver a note to Principal Brown? All of these choices were based on information that helped Ms. Lopez choose a course of action when confronted by the need to make a decision. Think of all the possible sources of evidence Ms. Lopez might have used to help her make these decisions. Notice also that many of the decisions she made were fast paced, practically oriented, and focused on both instructional and social factors. Others involved more thoughtful, lengthy consideration.

PURPOSES OF CLASSROOM ASSESSMENT

Teachers assess for many purposes because they must make many decisions throughout the school day. If we review Ms. Lopez's decisions during her classroom day, we get a sense of the many purposes teachers have for assessment. These purposes include establishing classroom equilibrium, planning and conducting instruction, placing students, providing feedback and incentives, diagnosing student problems and disabilities, and judging and grading academic learning and progress.

Many people think of tests when they hear the term *assessment.* As we can see from Ms. Lopez's decisions, however, classroom assessment encompasses much more than tests and quizzes. Assessment in the classroom occurs for three major domains. The **cognitive domain** encompasses intellectual activities such as memorizing, interpreting, applying knowledge, solving problems, and critical thinking. The **affective domain** involves feelings, attitudes, values, interests, and emotions. The **psychomotor domain** includes physical activities and actions in which students must manipulate objects such as a pen, a keyboard, or a zipper. When Ms. Lopez assigned grades for her students' science tests, she was making an assessment decision in the cognitive domain. When Ms. Lopez switched social studies instruction from discussion to seatwork when the class became bored, her decision related to the affective domain. And when she referred Aaron to the Special Education Department to be screened for poor gross motor skills, Ms. Lopez's assessment decision focused on the psychomotor domain. Although the cognitive domain tends to receive more attention, teachers make assessment decisions for all three domains throughout the school year.

Establishing a Classroom That Supports Learning

An often overlooked purpose of assessment is to establish and maintain the classroom society.

One purpose of assessment is to establish and maintain a classroom environment that supports student learning. Classrooms are complex social settings in which people interact with one another in a multitude of ways. For classrooms to be positive social and learning environments, respect, self-monitoring, and cooperation must be present. Thus, helping students to learn well and maintaining rules for respect in the classroom are closely related. To help students develop comfort in the classroom and anticipate when various activities are likely to occur and how long they will last, routines must be established. When Ms. Lopez selected Rosa instead of Sarah to deliver a note to Principal Brown, and when she changed the class seating plan to move Jamar and Ramon farther apart, she was making decisions to preserve a supportive classroom environment. That she allowed Antonio to go alone to the school nurse indicated her trust in him. On the other hand, Tabitha's constant interruptions and speaking out necessitated sending a note to her parents, and Ralph's swearing and fighting led to his being removed from the classroom. Ms. Lopez's efforts to make Kim a part of the classroom society by calling on her even though her hand was not raised was another attempt to create and maintain a viable social and learning environment.

Planning and Conducting Instruction

Many of the decisions that Ms. Lopez made were focused on planning and conducting classroom instruction. This should not be surprising, since instruction is a central classroom activity. The instructional decisions that

Ms. Lopez made can be divided into two types: planning decisions and teaching decisions. When Ms. Lopez reviewed the statewide writing standards, consulted last year's standardized test scores, selected topics for next Monday's math lesson, and assigned homework in one subject but not another, she was planning future instructional activities.

In addition to planning decisions, the actual process of teaching a class requires constant assessment and decision making. At two points during the day, Ms. Lopez altered her instruction in the middle of the lesson because her students were confused. Once she stopped her language lesson to review the prior day's lesson because student responses to her questions indicated that the class did not understand its content. Another time she switched her method of instruction from discussion to seatwork when the students became bored and off-task.

Assessment information is used to organize students into a functioning classroom society, plan and carry out instruction, and monitor student learning. Assessment is much more than giving formal paper-and-pencil tests to students.

Placing Students

Classroom teachers also make decisions about placements of students. Teachers divide students into reading or math groups, organize students into cooperative learning groups, pair or group students for class projects, or recommend that a particular student be placed with a particular teacher next year. Assessment is a critical component for making sound placement decisions. Ms. Lopez made a placement decision when she moved Tamika from the middle reading group to the high reading group. She made another placement decision when she formed a special reading group for students who were progressing more slowly than their classmates. Finally, when she paired Kim, the class isolate, with Aretha for the social studies project, she made another placement decision. Note that Ms. Lopez's placement decisions were made for both academic and social reasons.

Providing Feedback

Young learners and their caregivers need feedback in order to help improve students' learning and behavior. Observations and feedback intended to alter and improve students' learning are called **formative assessment.** To provide such feedback, teachers must constantly assess student learning and behavior. For example, Ms. Lopez used assessment information from Jing's first-draft book report to suggest ways to improve his writing. She held a parent-teacher conference with Ivan's parents to provide them with information about his progress so that they could better support his learning at home. In both examples of formative assessment, information about academic performance was used to provide feedback to students or parents with the aim of improving performance.

Diagnosing Student Problems and Disabilities

Much of the assessment data that teachers gather is used to identify, understand, and address students' misconceptions and learning difficulties. Teachers are always on the lookout for students who are having learning, emotional, or social problems in the classroom. Having identified such problems, the teacher can sometimes carry out supplemental learning activities or make accommodations, but at other times the student must be referred for more specialized diagnosis and intervention outside the classroom. Thus, Ms. Lopez set up her own in-class group for basic skill remediation, but she recommended that a specialist screen Aaron for his apparent gross motor skill challenge. Referring Aaron to the Special Education Department for screening was another diagnostic decision. Chapter 2 examines disabilities and accommodations in greater detail.

Summarizing and Grading Academic Learning and Progress

The task of grading or making final decisions about students' learning at the end of instruction is termed **summative assessment.** A number of Ms. Lopez's decisions involved summarizing students' academic learning and progress. She assigned grades to her students' science tests, completed a monthly progress report on each student, and decided to construct her own test for the social studies unit rather than use the test provided in her textbook. Much of a teacher's time is spent collecting information that will be used to grade students or summarize their academic progress.

PHASES OF CLASSROOM ASSESSMENT

The types of decisions teachers make based on assessment information can be categorized into three general phases of classroom assessment. Table 1.1 describes and compares these three phases of assessment.

The first phase of classroom assessment occurs early in the school year and is undertaken to learn about students' social, academic, and behavioral characteristics. Based on this information, teachers make decisions about students' academic, social, and behavioral needs in order to create a classroom environment that is supportive of student learning. These **early assessments** help teachers make decisions that

Teachers perform three types of assessment: early assessments, instructional assessments, and summative assessments.

TABLE 1.1   COMPARISON OF THREE PHASES OF CLASSROOM ASSESSMENTS

	Early Assessments	Instructional Assessments	Summative Assessments
Purpose	Provide teacher with a quick perception and practical knowledge of students' characteristics	Plan instructional activities and monitor the progress of instruction	Carry out the bureaucratic aspects of teaching, such as grading, grouping, and placing
Timing	During the first week or two of school	Daily throughout the school year	Periodically during the school year
Evidence-gathering method	Largely informal observation	Formal observation and student papers for planning; informal observation for monitoring	Formal tests, papers, reports, quizzes, and assignments
Type of evidence gathered	Cognitive, affective, and psychomotor	Largely cognitive and affective	Mainly cognitive
Record keeping	Information kept in teacher's mind; few written records	Written lesson plans; monitoring information not written down	Formal records kept in teacher's grade book or school files

enhance instruction, communication, and cooperation in the classroom. A second phase of assessment is used to plan and deliver instruction and includes decisions about what will be taught, how and when it will be taught, what materials will be used, how a lesson is progressing, and what changes in planned activities must be made. These are **instructional assessments.** The final phase of classroom assessment helps teachers make formal decisions and recommendations about student achievement and placement. Decisions such as grading, summarizing progress, interpreting test results, identifying students for special needs placement, and making promotion recommendations are all based on systematic information about a student that is often collected over a period of time. These are **summative assessments.** While there is some overlap between these three phases of assessment, in general early assessments precede instructional assessments and summative assessments follow instructional assessments. Succeeding chapters describe these three phases of assessment in greater detail.

While teachers depend heavily on assessment to inform decisions about shaping the classroom environment, instruction, and student development, other groups with important stakes in education also rely on assessment information collected within the classroom. These groups include national and state policy makers, school administrators, and parents. See Table 1.2.

Instructional assessments are used to help plan and deliver instruction.

Teachers study their students in the first weeks of school so that they can organize their classrooms into social and learning communities.

TABLE 1.2   VARIED PERSPECTIVES AND USES OF CLASSROOM ASSESSMENTS

National and State Policy Makers
- Setting state and national standards
- Complying with the No Child Left Behind Act
- Developing policies based on assessment
- Tracking the progress of national and state achievements
- Providing resources to improve learning
- Providing rewards or sanctions for student, school, and state achievements

School Administrators
- Identifying program strengths and weaknesses
- Using assessment to plan and improve instruction
- Monitoring classroom teachers
- Identifying instructional needs and programs
- Monitoring student achievements over time

Teachers
- Monitoring student progress
- Judging and altering classroom curriculum
- Identifying students with special needs
- Motivating students to do well
- Placing students in groups
- Providing feedback to teachers and students

Parents
- Judging student strengths and weaknesses
- Monitoring student progress
- Meeting with teachers to discuss students' classroom performance
- Judging teacher quality

ASSESSMENT, TESTING, MEASUREMENT, AND EVALUATION

This book is about the process teachers use to gather, evaluate, and use information to make appropriate decisions in the classroom. As you learn about each phase of assessment and the variety of ways in which teachers collect information, keep in mind that **assessment** is a process of collecting, synthesizing and interpreting information in order to make a decision. Depending on the decision being made and the information a teacher needs in order to inform that decision, *testing, measurement,* and *evaluation* often contribute to the process of assessment.

When people hear the word *assessment,* they often think of tests. A **test** is a formal, systematic procedure used to gather information about students' achievement or other cognitive skills. While tests are one important tool for gathering assessment information, the preceding list of Ms. Lopez's decisions makes clear that there are many other information-gathering tools, including projects, portfolios, and observations. Shortly, we'll say more about written tests, as well as techniques of observation and oral questioning.

A test is a formal, systematic procedure for gathering information.

Measurement is the process of quantifying or assigning a number to a performance or trait. The most common example of measurement in the classroom is when a teacher scores a quiz or test. Scoring produces a numerical description of performance: Jackie got 17 out of 20 items correct on the biology test; Dennis got a score of 65 percent on his math test; Rhonda's score on the IQ test was 115. In each example, a numerical score is used to represent the individual's performance or trait.

Measurement is the process of quantifying or assigning a number to a performance or trait.

Once assessment information is collected, teachers use it to make decisions about students, instruction, or classroom climate. **Evaluation** is the process of making judgments about what is good or desirable. For example, judging whether a student is performing at a high enough level to move on to the next reading level or whether to carry out a particular instructional activity requires evaluation. An evaluation is the product of assessment that produces a decision about the value or worth of a performance or activity based on information that has been collected, synthesized, and reflected on.

Evaluation is the process of judging the quality or value of a performance or a course of action.

It is important to recognize that not all assessment decisions require the use of tests or measurement. In addition, not all assessment decisions result in an evaluation or the judging of a student. As we saw in the wide variety of decisions made by Ms. Lopez, classroom assessment can rely on many different types of information and can result in many different types of decisions.

Imagine a teacher at the start of the year who wants to *assess* the mathematics readiness of her students in order to decide where to start instruction. Notice that the reason for assessing is that a decision must be made. First, the teacher gives a grade-appropriate paper-and-pencil *test* of mathematics readiness. The students' scores on the test provide a *measurement* of their math readiness. Of course the teacher uses other methods to collect information to determine readiness. She talks to the students about math, watches them while they do math exercises, and checks prior grades and test scores in their school record files. The teacher then thinks about all the assessment information she has collected. She *evaluates,* or makes a judgment about, the students' current stage of readiness in math. Her final decision, based on her assessment and evaluation, is to review last year's math before beginning this year's topics.

olc

CHAPTER CASE STUDY

Visit the text Online Learning Center (OLC) to read the case of Gina Shrader, a student teacher who learns about the complexities of a typical teaching day as she observes a second-grade teacher and her class.

www.mhhe.com/ russell7e

THREE GENERAL WAYS TO COLLECT DATA: STUDENT PRODUCTS, OBSERVATIONS, AND ORAL QUESTIONING

Teachers gather most of their assessment information using student products, observation techniques, and oral questioning techniques.

Teachers rely on three primary methods to gather assessment information for classroom decisions: student products, observation techniques, and oral questioning techniques.

Student Products

Selection techniques require students to select an answer from choices that are provided; supply techniques require students to construct a response to a question or problem.

Students spend a great deal of time creating products or artifacts. Among the many products students produce are homework, written assignments completed in class, worksheets, essays, book reports, science projects, lab reports, artwork, and portfolios, as well as tests and quizzes. Student products include anything that students are asked to produce or complete by the teacher. Student products generally take one of three forms: selection, supply, and performance. Multiple-choice, true-false, and matching questions on a test are called **selection items,** or selected-response items. As the name implies, the student responds to each question by selecting an answer from choices provided. **Supply items,** or production items, require the student to construct a response to a question or prompt. The length of the response can vary substantially. For example, an essay question requires the student to construct a lengthy, detailed response, while a short-answer or "fill-in-the-blank" question may require only a word or phrase. Performances are an extended form of supply items that often require a substantial amount of time to produce. Examples of **performance tasks** include book reports, journal entries, portfolios, science experiments, and class projects. Whether student products are the result of selection items, supply items, or performance tasks, they provide teachers with concrete samples of student work that can yield valuable information about students' cognitive skills and knowledge.

Observation Techniques

Observation techniques are applied to student activities and to student products.

Observation is a second major method classroom teachers use to collect assessment data. As the term suggests, **observation** involves watching or listening to students carry out a specific activity or respond in a given situation. Through observation, teachers are made aware of such student behaviors as mispronouncing words in oral reading, interacting in groups, speaking out in class, bullying other students, losing concentration, having puzzled looks on their faces, patiently waiting their turn, raising their hands in class, and failing to sit still for more than 3 minutes.

During the school day, teachers often spend substantial amounts of time facing their students and working closely with individual students or small groups of students. Because teachers and their classes are located in a confined space, facing and interacting with one another from one to six hours a day, teachers can observe a great deal of their students' behavior and reactions.

Some observations are formal and planned in advance. In such situations, the teacher purposefully observes a particular set of student behaviors. For example, teachers assess students when they read aloud in a reading group. The teacher might be watching and listening for clear pronunciation of words, changing voice tone to emphasize important points, periodically looking up from the book while reading, and so forth. Because such observations are planned, the teacher has time to prepare the students and identify in advance the particular behaviors that will be observed.

Some teacher observations are formal and planned in advance, while others are informal and spontaneous.

Other teacher observations are unplanned and informal, as when the teacher sees students talking when they should be listening, notices the pained expression on a student's face when a classmate makes fun of his clothes, or observes students fidgeting and looking out the window during a science lesson. Such spontaneous observations reflect momentary unplanned happenings that the teacher observes, mentally records, and interprets. Both formal and informal teacher observations are important information-gathering techniques in classrooms.

Oral Questioning Techniques

Asking oral questions is the third major method teachers use to collect information for assessment. "Why do you think the author ended her story that way?" "Explain to me in your own words what an improper fraction is." "Jack, did you call Ron a mean name?" "Raise your hand if you can tell me why this answer is incorrect." "Who can summarize yesterday's discussion about the water cycle?" "Why don't you have your homework today?" These are all questions teachers use to collect information from students during and at the end of a lesson. Questioning students is very useful during instruction, when it can be used to review a prior topic, brainstorm a new one, find out how the lesson is being understood by students, and engage a student who is not paying attention. The teacher can gather the information he or she requires without breaking the momentum of a lesson to have students work on a more formal quiz, worksheet, or written assignment. Formal oral examinations are used in subject areas such as foreign language, speech, and vocal music.

Oral questioning provides a great deal of formal and informal information about students. Questioning is especially useful during instruction.

The full range of data-gathering methods is needed to collect all the information required for classroom assessment.

Student products, observations, and oral questioning complement one another in the classroom. Imagine having to make classroom decisions without being able to observe students' reactions, performances, answers to questions, and interactions. Now imagine what it would be like if information from student products could not be obtained in classrooms, and imagine what it would be like if teachers could not ask oral questions of their students. Each type of information is needed to carry out the rich and meaningful assessments that occur in classrooms. As a result, teachers need to master all of these evidence-gathering approaches.

STANDARDIZED AND NONSTANDARDIZED ASSESSMENTS

The information teachers collect and use in their classrooms comes from assessment procedures that are either standardized or nonstandardized.

Standardized Assessments

Standardized assessments are intended to be administered, scored, and interpreted in the same way for all test takers.

A **standardized assessment** is administered, scored, and interpreted in the same way for all students, regardless of where or when they are assessed. Standardized assessments are meant to be administered in many classrooms across a school, district, state, or nation. Standardized assessments are intended to be administered to students in many different classrooms, but always under the same conditions, with the same directions, and in the same amount of time as all other students who are taking the test at that time. Moreover, the results of the test will be scored and interpreted the same way for all students. The main reason for standardizing assessment procedures is to ensure that the testing conditions and scoring procedures have a similar effect on the performance of students in different schools and states.

The tests that the No Child Left Behind Act requires states to administer to all students are standardized tests. The Scholastic Assessment Test (SAT) and the American College Testing Program Test (ACT) are also examples of standardized tests. So are national achievement tests such as the Iowa Tests of Basic Skills and the Stanford, Metropolitan, California, and SRA Achievement tests. In some cases, district or school readiness, placement, or achievement tests can also be classified as standardized tests. When Ms. Lopez consulted the previous year's test scores to determine if the class needed a review of capitalization rules, she was examining information from standardized assessment instruments.

Nonstandardized Assessments

Nonstandardized assessments are constructed for use in a single classroom with a single group of students. Most reflect the particular areas of instruction focused on in that single classroom.

When Ms. Lopez decided to construct her own test for the science unit and assigned grades to her students based on the test, she was relying on assessment information that was not standardized. Many of Ms. Lopez's unplanned observations of her students' behavior also are classified as nonstandardized assessments. These fleeting, infrequently occurring, seldom-repeated classroom observations represent a rich and important, though nonstandardized, form of assessment data. Teachers use these idiosyncratic observations to make decisions about individual students and the class as a group.

It is important to note that standardized tests are not necessarily better than nonstandardized ones. Standardization is important when information from an assessment instrument is to be used for the same purpose across many different classrooms and locations. If the decision that results from assessment does not extend beyond a single classroom, rigorous standardization is not as important.

Nonstandardized (teacher-made) tests are developed for a single classroom with a single group of students and are not used for comparison with other groups.

Standardization is important when information from an assessment instrument is to be used for the same purpose across many different classrooms and locations.

Administration in Groups

Traditionally, virtually all group-administered tests relied on paper-and-pencil. Increasingly, however, computers are being used to administer and, in some cases, score tests. In some cases, group-administered computer-based tests are also used to assess oral reading, find solutions to complex problems, and perform simulations of such tasks as assembling equipment or building computer networks. When the task to be assessed involves giving a speech, creating artwork, or performing a play, group-administered procedures are not useful.

Informal group assessment occurs often in the classroom, primarily through teacher observation. When Ms. Lopez watched the class become bored and off-task during a lesson, she was performing group assessment. Similarly, when her students had difficulty answering her questions during the language lesson, she stopped what she was doing to review the previous day's lesson. This is another example of informal, group-based assessment.

Administering group assessments saves time but provides less insight and information about individual students.

Standards-Based Testing

Since the mid-1980s, momentum has grown to develop **educational standards.** The aim of educational standards is to set common goals for instruction and criteria for performance to which all schools and students are held. Today, nearly all states have developed **content standards** and have implemented **performance standards.** Content standards, which sometimes are called curriculum frameworks or standards of learning, define the knowledge and skills students are expected to develop in a given subject area and grade level. Performance standards define how well students are expected to know the content knowledge and how well they are expected to perform the skills included in the content standards. In most cases, performance standards are measured by **standards-based tests** administered by the state. A third type of educational standard focuses on the quality of teachers, the availability of resources such as textbooks and computers, and the condition of facilities in which students are expected to learn. This type of educational standard is referred to as **opportunity to learn standards.** With the passage of the federal No Child Left Behind Act in 2002, all states are expected to develop and meet content, performance, and, to a lesser extent, opportunity to learn standards.

Additional Sources of Information

Supplementary assessment information can be obtained from previous teachers, school staff, and parents.

Teachers gather and consider helpful supplementary information provided by the students' prior teachers, school staff, and parents. Teachers routinely consult previous teachers to corroborate or reinforce current observations. Parents frequently volunteer information and respond to teacher queries. While useful, each of these supplementary sources of information has its limitations and should be treated with caution when making decisions.

APPROPRIATE ASSESSMENTS: VALID AND RELIABLE

Whether assessment information helps produce valid decisions depends on whether the assessment information is appropriate.

Regardless of its other characteristics, the most important characteristics in determining the appropriateness of assessment decisions are the reliability of assessment information and the validity of decisions based on that information.

For teachers to make informed decisions, the assessment information that is collected must be appropriate for the decision being made. Validity and reliability are two key concepts that help teachers determine whether assessment information is appropriate for informing a decision. We begin our examination of validity and reliability with an example.

Mr. Ferris has just finished a three-week math unit on computing long division problems with remainders. During the unit, he taught his students the computational steps involved in doing long division problems and the concept of a remainder. He gave and reviewed both homework problems and examples from the text, and he administered a few quizzes. Now, at the end of the unit, Mr. Ferris wants to gather assessment information to find out whether his students have learned to do computational problems involving long division with remainders so that he can assign a grade to each student.

To gather the information needed, Mr. Ferris decides to give a test containing items similar in content, format, and difficulty to those he has been teaching. From the millions of possible long division with remainder problems, Mr. Ferris selects 10 that are representative of his teaching. If Mr. Ferris picks 10 items that cover different content or are much harder or easier, or are presented in a different format from what he taught in class, the results of the test will *not* provide appropriate decision-making information.

Mr. Ferris avoids this problem by writing 10 items that are similar in content, difficulty, and format to the content taught and the types of mathematics problems practiced in his classroom. He assembles the items into a test, administers the test during one class period, and scores the tests on a scale of 0 to 100. Mr. Ferris then has the assessment information he needs to make a decision about each student's grade.

Manuela and Joe each score 100 on the test and receive an A grade for the unit. Stuart scores 50 and receives a D grade. The grades are based on Mr. Ferris's evaluation of the quality of their performance on the 10-item test. If Mr. Ferris is asked to interpret what Manuela's and Joe's A grades mean, he will likely say that "Manuela and Joe can do long division with remainder items very well." He will also likely say that Stuart's D is "indicative of his inability to do such items well."

In making these statements, Mr. Ferris illustrates the relationship between assessment information, the interpretation of that information, and the teacher's resulting decision. He says Manuela and Joe "can do long division with remainder items very well." He does not say "Manuela and Joe can do the 10 items I included on my test very well." He describes their performance in *general* terms rather than in terms of his specific 10-item test. Similarly, Stuart's performance is described in general rather than in test-specific terms. The logic that Mr. Ferris and all teachers use in making such inferences is that if a student can do well on the test items or performances that are actually assessed, the student is likely to do well on similar items and performances that are not tested. If students do poorly on the 10 test items, it is likely that they also will do poorly on similar, unasked items.

The essence of classroom assessment is to look at some of a student's behavior and to use that information to make a generalization or prediction about the student's behavior in similar situations or on similar tasks.

Mr. Ferris's 10-item test illustrates a characteristic that is common to virtually all classroom assessments, regardless of whether they are based on information that is collected through formal or informal procedures, student products, observations or oral responses, or standardized or nonstandardized assessments. The essence of classroom assessment is to look at a *sample* of a student's performance or behavior and use that sample to make a generalization or prediction about the student's performance on similar, unobserved tasks.

This process is not confined to assessments of students' learning. Teachers often form lasting impressions of their students' personalities or motivation based on a few brief observations made during the first week of school. They observe a small sample of the student's behavior and on the basis of this sample make inferences or decisions such as "he is unmotivated," "she is a troublemaker," and "they are hard workers."

These are informal generalizations about students based on a small sample of each student's school behavior.

What if the behavior sample the teacher collects is irrelevant or incomplete? What if the items on Mr. Ferris's test were not typical of his classroom instruction? What if the student has an "off day" or the teacher's impatience does not permit a student to show his or her "true" performance? If these things happen, then the decision made about the student is likely to be inaccurate, inappropriate, and probably unfair.

Let's now consider a related, more scientifically precise term than fairness.

Validity

Validity is concerned with whether the information being gathered is relevant to the decision that needs to be made.

The single most important characteristic of good assessment is its ability to help the teacher make appropriate decisions. This characteristic is called **validity.** The extent to which a decision is valid depends on the extent to which the assessment information is *sufficient* for making a given decision. Unless assessment information is appropriate for a decision and the information is interpreted accurately, valid decisions will not occur. When a teacher asks, as all teachers should, "Am I collecting the right information for the decision I want to make?" she is asking about the validity of her assessments (Linn, 1997). For any decision, some forms of evidence will lead to more valid decisions than others. For example, Mr. Ferris could make a more valid decision about his students' achievement by basing his decision on a test that contained items similar to those he had been teaching than if he asked students to write an essay about their feelings toward math. Similarly, a more valid decision about students' motivation or ability will occur by observing their classroom work over a period of time than basing such decisions on the performance of their older siblings or the neighborhood where they live. Use of these latter indicators is likely to result in less valid decision making than more direct classroom observations.

Validity (relevance to decision making) is just as applicable to informal teacher observations as it is to formally gathered product-based information.

Given that validity is the foundation on which sound assessment is based, we will revisit the concept of validity several times throughout this text. At this point it is sufficient to say three things about validity. First, validity is concerned with whether the information being gathered is relevant and appropriate to make the desired decision. Second, validity is the most important characteristic that an assessment decision can possess because, without it, the decision may be inappropriate or even harmful. Third, concerns about validity pertain to all classroom assessment, not just to those involving formal data- or information-gathering techniques. Each of the many decisions Ms. Lopez made during the school day was based on some type of assessment information. It is appropriate, therefore, to ask about the validity—that is, the appropriateness—of the assessment information and interpretations for each of Ms. Lopez's many daily decisions. Key Assessment Tools 1.1 identifies key concerns about the validity of assessment decisions.

Key Assessment Tools 1.1

KEY ASPECTS OF ASSESSMENT VALIDITY

1. Validity is concerned with this general question: "To what extent is this decision based on appropriate assessment information?"

2. Validity refers to the decisions that are made from assessment information, not the assessment approach itself. It is not appropriate to say that the assessment information is valid unless the decisions, purpose, and groups for which it is valid are identified. Assessment information that is valid for one decision or group of students is not necessarily valid for other decisions or groups.

3. Validity is a matter of degree; it does not exist on an all-or-nothing basis. Think of assessment validity in terms of categories: highly valid, moderately valid, and invalid.

4. Validity is always determined by a judgment made by the test user.

One other note of caution about validity should be mentioned at this point. Decisions that may affect a student's education in a major way should not be made on the basis of one observation or test result, even if the validity of a single assessment seems strong. It is always prudent to assess the student's behavior, ability, or performance on different occasions using several different means of information gathering in order to enhance the overall appropriateness of a major decision (Moss, 2003).

Reliability

Reliability refers to the stability or consistency of assessment information, that is, whether it is typical of a student's behavior.

A second important characteristic of appropriate decisions is that they are based on assessment information that has consistency, or **reliability.** Would the assessment information for this person or class be similar if it were gathered at some other time? If you weighed yourself on a scale, got off it, then weighed yourself again on the same scale, you would expect the two weights to be almost identical. If they weren't, you wouldn't trust the information provided by the scale. The information it provides you is not reliable. Similarly, if assessment information does not produce stable, consistent data, a teacher should exercise caution in using that information to make a decision about a student or the class.

To increase the reliability of assessment information, it is important to collect several pieces of information about the behavior or performance being assessed. Recall that Ms. Lopez observed Tabitha's class interruptions and Miguel's inattentive behavior over a period of time before deciding to take action. She did this to be sure that she was observing stable, consistent behavior from these students. Did they behave the same way at different times and under different circumstances? By observing them over a period of time, Ms. Lopez could have faith in the reliability of her observations.

> **Key Assessment Tools 1.2**
>
> ### KEY ASPECTS OF ASSESSMENT RELIABILITY
>
> 1. Reliability refers to the stability or consistency of assessment information and is concerned with this question: "How consistent or typical of the students' behavior is the assessment information I have gathered?"
> 2. Reliability is not concerned with the appropriateness of the assessment information collected, only with its consistency, stability, or typicality. Appropriateness of assessment information is a validity concern.
> 3. Reliability does not exist on an all-or-nothing basis, but in degrees: high, moderate, or low. Some types of assessment information are more reliable than others.
> 4. Reliability is a necessary but insufficient condition for validity. An assessment that provides inconsistent, atypical results cannot be relied on to provide information useful for decision making.

Similarly, Mr. Ferris included 10 long division with remainder questions on his test, not just one, so that he would obtain reliable information about his students' achievement. He can have more confidence about students' learning by assessing them on 10 items than on only one or two.

All assessment information contains some error or inconsistency; thus validity and reliability are both a matter of degree and do not exist on an all-or-nothing basis.

Since any single piece of assessment information provides only a limited sample of a student's behavior, no single assessment procedure or instrument can be expected to provide perfect, error-free information. All assessment information contains some unreliability or inconsistency because of such factors as ambiguous test items, interruptions during testing, differences in students' attention spans, clarity of assessment directions, students' luck in guessing items, changes in students' moods, mistakes in scoring (especially essay and observational assessments), and use of too small a sample of behavior to permit the student to show consistent, stable performance. Obviously, it is important to minimize the inconsistency. Key Assessment Tools 1.2 reviews key aspects of the reliability of assessment information.

Teachers must consider whether an assessment is valid as well as reliable.

One of the purposes of this text is to suggest methods that can help increase the reliability of information used for classroom assessment. If a teacher cannot rely on the stability and consistency of the information gathered during an assessment, he or she must be careful not to base important decisions on that information. Thus, along with validity, which asks if the assessment information being gathered is relevant to the decision to be made, the classroom teacher must also be concerned with reliability, which asks if the information obtained is consistent and stable.

Consider the following assertion regarding the relationship between validity and reliability: "Valid assessment must be reliable, but reliable assessment need not be valid." The first half of the statement is fairly straightforward. Valid decisions are not possible if the assessment data on which the decisions are based are not consistent. So, to make a valid decision, there must be reliable information.

As to the second part of the statement, imagine the following scenario. Suppose you ask a student in your class how many brothers and sisters he has. He says six, and you ask him again. He says six. You repeat the question several times, and each time the student indicates six brothers and sisters. You have measured the number of his brothers and sisters with consistency; the assessment information you have gathered from him is reliable. Suppose you then use this reliable information to make a decision about what reading group to place the student in: the more brothers and sisters, the higher the placement. Since the number of brothers and sisters has little relevance to the student's reading performance, a decision based on this information, no matter how reliable it is, will not be valid. In short, assessment information can be reliable, but decisions based on that information are not necessarily valid. In succeeding chapters, we will explore the relationship between validity and reliability in greater detail and offer suggestions for improving the reliability of assessment information and the validity of decisions.

ETHICAL ISSUES AND RESPONSIBILITIES

Thus far we have presented a general technical introduction to classroom assessment. However, assessment is more than just a technical activity; it is a human activity that influences and affects many people, including students, parents, teachers, coaches, college admissions counselors, and employers. Think about the different kinds and purposes of assessment described in this chapter, and then think about all the ways people can be affected by them. This will give you a sense of the human side of assessment.

Teachers' assessments have important long- and short-term consequences for students; thus teachers have an ethical responsibility to make decisions using the most valid and reliable information possible.

Appendix A lists some national standards for teacher competence in assessment. Teaching is a profession that has both a knowledge base and an ethical base. Like other professionals who have knowledge and expertise that their clients do not have and whose actions and judgments affect their clients in many ways, classroom teachers are responsible for conducting themselves in an ethical manner. This responsibility is particularly important in education, because students have no choice about whether they will attend school. Also, compared with their teachers, students tend to be less experienced and more impressionable. Among the ethical standards that cut across all dimensions of teaching are the need to treat each student as an individual, to avoid physical or emotional abuse of students, to respect diversity, to be intellectually honest with students, to avoid favoritism and harassment, to provide a balanced perspective on issues raised in instruction, and to provide the best instruction possible for all students.

In simple terms, each of these ethical standards refers to some aspect of a teacher's fairness in dealing with his or her students. Clearly, gathering and interpreting valid and reliable data for decision making are fundamental to the fairness of teachers' assessments. Other aspects of fairness include (1) informing students about teacher expectations and assessments before beginning teaching and assessment; (2) teaching students what they are to be tested on before summative assessment; (3) not making snap judgments and identifying students with emotional labels (e.g., uninterested, at-risk, slow learner) before you have spent time with them; (4) avoiding stereotyping students (e.g., "He's just a dumb jock," "Kids from that part of town are troublemakers," and "Students who dress that way have no interest in school"); (5) avoiding terms and examples that may be offensive to students of different gender, race, religion, culture, or nationality; (6) avoiding bias toward students with limited English or with different cultural experiences when providing instruction and constructing assessments (Holloway, 2003; Ben-Yosef, 2003). There are many dimensions to fairness in the classroom.

Fairness in Accommodating Special Needs

As part of their ethical responsibilities, teachers should be alert to indications of disabilities that some students may have—and be ready to participate in an Individual Education Program (IEP), as described in Chapter 3, to see that these students obtain needed help. Both law and general fairness to students with special needs require six things in this regard (McMillan, 2000):

1. Proper training for those administering tests of disabilities.
2. Assessment in the student's native language.
3. The identification of a student's specific needs, not just an overall judgment of ability.
4. Effective reflection of a student's ability or performance, in spite of any disability.
5. The use of multiple scores or assessments before an IEP decision is reached.
6. A multidisciplinary assessment team for assessing a suspected disability.

Ethical Issues and Assessment

In addition, there are ethical considerations specifically applicable to assessment. Classroom teachers are in a position to obtain a great deal of information about their students' academic, personal, social, and family backgrounds.

Beyond having access to such information, teachers use it to make decisions that can have important short- and long-term consequences for students. As an example, college entrance and future employment opportunities, not to mention student self-esteem, often hang in the balance of teachers' assessment decisions.

Clearly, there are responsibilities associated with the collection and use of assessment information. Moreover, once assessment information is collected, teachers have a responsibility to protect its privacy, recognize its decision-making limitations, and never use it to demean or ridicule a student. Table 1.3 presents a list of ethical standards for teachers developed by the National Education Association. Table 1.4 is a list related specifically to assessment. Note the range of ethical concerns and responsibilities that accompany teaching.

Teachers should always strive to obtain valid and reliable information before making important decisions that can influence students.

TABLE 1.3 ETHICAL STANDARDS FOR TEACHERS' RELATIONS WITH STUDENTS

Commitment to the Student

The educator strives to help each student realize his or her potential as a worthy and effective member of society. The educator therefore works to stimulate the spirit of inquiry, the acquisition of knowledge and understanding, and the thoughtful formulation of worthy goals.

In fulfillment of the obligation to the student, the educator:

1. Shall not unreasonably restrain the student from independent action in the pursuit of learning.
2. Shall not unreasonably deny the student access to varying points of view.
3. Shall not deliberately suppress or distort subject matter relevant to the student's progress.
4. Shall make reasonable effort to protect the student from conditions harmful to learning or to health and safety.
5. Shall not intentionally expose the student to embarrassment or disparagement.
6. Shall not on the basis of race, color, creed, sex, national origin, marital status, political or religious beliefs, family, social or cultural background, or sexual orientation, unfairly:
   a. Exclude any student from participation in any program
   b. Deny benefits to any student
   c. Grant any advantage to any student
7. Shall not use professional relationships with students for private advantage.
8. Shall not disclose information about students obtained in the course of professional service, unless disclosure serves a compelling professional purpose or is required by law.

SOURCE: *NEA Handbook*, 1992–1993. Reprinted with permission of the National Education Association.

TABLE 1.4   TEACHERS' ETHICAL RESPONSIBILITIES REGARDING ASSESSMENT

- Make fair and impartial decisions.
- Construct and administer fair and clear assessments.
- Motivate students to do their best.
- Make students familiar with the varied types of assessments.
- Provide opportunities for students to practice test approaches.
- Make reasonable accommodations for students with disabilities.

CHAPTER SUMMARY

CHAPTER REVIEW
Visit the Online Learning Center at **www.mhhe.com/ russell7e** to review the case study referenced in the chapter.

This chapter has indicated that classrooms are complex environments calling for teacher decision making in many areas. Within such an environment, teachers are not expected to be correct in every decision they make. That would be an unrealistic standard for anyone to attain, especially in fluid, decision-rich classroom settings where uncertainty abounds. However, teachers should be expected and are morally bound to provide defensible assessment evidence to support classroom decisions and actions. This is the least that can be expected in an environment where teacher actions have such vital consequences for students. Below are key concepts discussed in this chapter.

- Federal policies have increased the importance of assessment and now require every student in grades 3–8 and in at least one high school grade to be tested in mathematics and language arts.
- Every day in every classroom, teachers make decisions about their students, their instruction, and their classroom climate. Teachers collect and interpret various sources of evidence to help them make decisions about suitable courses of action.
- There are many purposes for classroom assessment: creating a classroom environment conducive to learning, planning and conducting instruction, placing students, providing feedback and incentives, diagnosing student problems, and grading academic learning and progress.
- All the purposes of assessment can be divided into three general phases: early or beginning assessment, which occurs early in the school year and is used by teachers to get to know their students; instructional assessment, which includes both planning and delivering instruction to students; and official assessments, such as grades, which teachers are expected to provide as part of their role in the school bureaucracy.
- Assessment is the general process of collecting, synthesizing, and interpreting information to aid teachers in their decision making. A test is a formal tool for gathering information. Measurement involves

describing performance numerically. Evaluation is making judgments about what is valuable or desirable.

- Many forms of assessment evidence are used by teachers, including student products, observations, oral questioning, interviews, comments from prior teachers, and school record folders.
- Standardized tests are intended to be administered, scored, and interpreted in the same way, no matter when or where they are given. These conditions are necessary because a primary purpose of standardized assessments is to make the same decisions about students across different classrooms. Nonstandardized assessments are typically developed by classroom teachers.
- The appropriateness of an assessment is determined by its validity and reliability. Validity, the most important characteristic of assessment, is concerned with the appropriateness of a decision based on the assessment information used to inform that decision. Reliability is concerned with the consistency of the assessment information collected.
- Although assessment is thought of as a technical activity, there are ethical concerns associated with the assessment process. Since teachers' decisions can influence students' self-perception and life opportunities, teachers must be aware of the many ethical responsibilities involved in assessment.

QUESTIONS FOR DISCUSSION

1. For what types of decisions might it be better to collect information through observations rather than from student products? For what types of decisions might student products be more appropriate?
2. Describe the relationship between early assessment, instructional assessment, and summative assessment. Is it ever useful to begin the instructional process by examining information from a summative assessment?
3. Given the importance of students' performance on state tests, is it appropriate to use old versions of state tests to create your tests for your own class? Is it a valid decision to tailor instruction to cover the content of a state test?
4. Do teachers' ethical responsibilities to their students change as students get older? If so, how? Are there some ethical responsibilities that remain constant across age levels?

ACTIVITIES

1. Interview a teacher about classroom decision making. Ask the teacher how he or she learns about students at the start of the school year: what characteristics are considered, on what basis decisions about students are made, and so forth.

2. Imagine you are a first-year teacher. School starts in three weeks. Discuss in small groups what you must do to prepare for its start. Select the three most important things to do and explain why each task is important.

REVIEW QUESTIONS

1. What are the three main types of classroom assessment? How do they differ in purpose, timing, and the types of information most likely to be used in carrying them out?
2. Explain the difference between standardized and nonstandardized assessments; supply and selection test items; and validity and reliability.
3. How would you explain the concept of validity to a fellow teacher? What examples would you use to make your point?
4. Why are validity and reliability important concerns in classroom assessment? Why is validity more important?
5. What are three ethical responsibilities a teacher has to her or his students? Give an example of how each responsibility might occur in a classroom.

REFERENCES

Ben-Yosef, E. (2003). Respecting students' cultural literacies. *Educational Leadership, 61* (2), 80–82.

Holloway, J. H. (2003). Managing culturally diverse classrooms. *Educational Leadership, 61* (1), 90–91.

Linn, R. L. (1997). Evaluating the validity of assessments: The consequences of use. *Educational Measurement: Issues and Practices, 16* (2), 14–16.

McMillan, J. H. (2000). *Essential assessment concepts for teachers and administrators.* Thousand Oaks, CA: Corwin Press.

Moss, P. A. (2003). Reconceptualizing validity for the classroom. *Educational Measurement: Issues and Practices, 22* (4), 13–25.

LEARNING ABOUT STUDENTS: EARLY ASSESSMENT

KEY TOPICS

- *Gathering Information about Students*

- *Sources of Learning about Students*

- *Forming Student Descriptions*

- *Concerns about Accuracy and Validity*

- *Identifying Special Needs*

- *Improving Early Assessments*

CHAPTER OBJECTIVES

After reading this chapter, you will be able to:

- Identify features of classrooms that make them social settings
- Explain the need for teacher early assessment
- Describe the sources of information about students available to teachers at the start of school
- Differentiate among cognitive, affective, and psychomotor behaviors
- Distinguish between formal and informal observations
- Identify weaknesses in the validity and reliability of early assessments and suggest ways to overcome them
- State potential effects of early assessments on students

THINKING ABOUT TEACHING

What can teachers do to have a smooth beginning of the school year? What are three important things for a teacher to do at the start of the school year?

The activities in the first few days of school set the stage for how well students will behave, attend, and learn during the school year. In the first days of school, teachers and students must get to know and understand one another.

The first days of the school year are important for both teacher and students. They set the tone and lay the foundation for the rest of the year. For both teacher and students, these days are the only opportunity to make an initial impression. It is in these early days that a group of diverse individuals begins to come together to form a class. Although most teachers and students have been through the beginning of school many times before, uncertainties always accompany the start of a new school year. Each group of students has its own special mix of backgrounds, abilities, interests, disabilities, needs, and personalities that make it unlike any other class the teacher has encountered.

In this chapter we explore questions that confront all teachers at the start of the school year: how to get to know new students, and what the teacher will need to know about them to create an environment that supports learning. To discover this information, teachers ask and try to answer questions such as the following about their students:

- Will they get along well and be cooperative with one another?
- Are they academically ready for my curriculum?
- What intellectual, emotional, and physical strengths and weaknesses do they have?
- Do some students have disabilities that require classroom accommodations?
- Are there particularly disruptive students in the class?

As a teacher, what other questions would you add to this list and why?

GATHERING INFORMATION ABOUT STUDENTS

In the early days of the school year, teachers try to learn about each individual student and the class as a whole and to organize a classroom society that is characterized by communication, respect, and learning (Garcia, 1994). It is very important to understand that a class is more than a group of students who happen to be in the same place at the same time.

Certain basic realities apply, like those summarized in Table 2.1. A class is a society, a social system, made up of people who communicate with one another, pursue common and individual goals, and follow rules of order. For example, all classrooms have rules that govern such matters as who can visit the bathroom and when, how tardiness or lost homework will be treated, and how papers are distributed and collected. There are also rules to govern the flow of communication in the classroom: "Don't talk when the teacher or another class member is talking"; "Raise your hand if you have a question"; "If you know the answer to a question, don't blurt it out"; "If you don't know the answer to a question, sit quietly and listen."

A classroom is more than a group of students who happen to be in the same place at the same time. It is a society of people who communicate with one another, pursue common goals, and follow rules of order.

Students learn quickly that the fastest way to anger a teacher is not by doing poorly on a homework assignment or a test, but by doing such things as talking out of turn, pushing in line, laughing at the teacher, or engaging in some other breach of classroom etiquette. Establishing a set of classroom rules and routines is one of the most important things a teacher can do to promote a positive social and learning environment. Without rules and routines, students may have difficulty anticipating how other students may behave, how long an activity is likely to last, what is likely to occur next, or when a "favorite" part of the day will come. The absence of rules and routines can create a sense of chaos, making instruction and learning more difficult. Of course, classrooms are more than just social settings; they are also instructional settings in which teachers plan and deliver instruction and assess students. And finally, classrooms are places where one member, the teacher, has responsibility for other members, the students, thus making it an ethical environment (McCaslin and Good, 1996). At the beginning of the school year, the teacher must begin to set up this complex social, academic, and ethical society.

Although all classrooms are simultaneously social, academic, and moral environments, the specific features of particular classrooms differ greatly from one another. For example, the academic and socioeconomic backgrounds of students, as well as their mix of personalities, learning styles, languages, needs, and interests, differ from classroom to classroom (Ladson-Billings, 1994; Delpit, 1995). From one year to the next, a teacher cannot count on having similar groups of students. Because of such differences, planning and delivering instruction are context-bound activities;

TABLE 2.1   THE BASIC REALITIES OF CLASSROOMS

1. The classroom is a social and cultural environment as well as an educational environment. The social and cultural dimensions influence greatly the educational dimension. Classrooms involve
   - persons interacting with persons
   - persons teaching persons
   - rules/order/communication/common goals

2. Each classroom culture differs in some ways from all others. There are few universals across all classrooms, except perhaps the teacher's moral responsibilities to students. Teachers must make sense of their classroom cultures and use this sense to understand who the students are, where they are, and what they need.

3. Because of the uniqueness of every classroom culture, teacher judgment is a critical ingredient of successful classrooms. Life in classrooms is a series of judgments or decisions about students, curriculum, instruction, and learning; no one can or should make these judgments for the classroom teacher.

4. The teacher is both a participant and an observer in the classroom, which makes it difficult for the teacher to recognize his or her own contributions to classroom problems.

5. It is not reasonable to expect the classroom teacher to be correct in every judgment or decision he or she makes, especially since there is little codified knowledge to guide teachers' judgments and actions. However, it is reasonable to expect that classroom teachers can provide good and defensible grounds for their decisions and actions.

that is, the ways that teachers plan and teach are dependent on the varied characteristics of their students. This means that the teacher must develop an intimate knowledge of the students' characteristics. Try to imagine planning and teaching a lesson for a group of students you know nothing about. What will interest the students? How long can they pay attention? What have they learned previously? What learning needs do they have? What accommodations must be met to help students with disabilities learn? Similarly, try to imagine how you would discipline students you did not know. What strategies might work with different students? Is a student acting out because she is bored, unable to follow the lesson, or testing the teacher? The extent to which a teacher can answer questions such as these determines the chances that he or she can create an environment, respond to students' issues, and modify instruction in ways that support student learning. To answer such questions, teachers learn about their students at the start of the year in a process we call "**early assessment.**"

All teachers must learn about their students, although teachers will gather different information depending on their goals for student development. At the elementary school level, curriculum goals include both academic and socialization outcomes. Elementary teachers were asked about the importance of socialization outcomes in their classrooms. Here are a few of their comments:

> Every spare minute I try to stress good citizenship and cooperation. If these issues arise during instruction, I stop the lesson and remind the students about good classroom behavior and cooperation. Even if a student just took someone's pencil, I would say, "Do you realize . . . ?" I think that good citizenship, civility, and cooperation are as important as learning subject matter. Some of them don't get it at home.

> I'm trying to make them good citizens in the classroom community and beyond, not only good learners. I make sure they know what is expected of them by the time they are out of the sixth grade, the difference between right and wrong.

In elementary schools, most students spend 5 to 6 hours a day in the same classroom with the same teacher and classmates. Often, much of the instruction is carried out in small groups, so that while one group is occupying the teacher's attention, other students must remain focused and productive without constant teacher supervision. In elementary classrooms, a teacher's initial assessments tend to embrace students' academic capabilities, their ability to work productively with other students, the amount of time they can remain focused on their own, and their general classroom behavior.

The goals of schooling at the high school level are predominantly academic and vocational. Students may already be grouped into tracks, and most have already been socialized in appropriate school behavior. Instead of seeing 20 to 25 students for 6 hours a day as in the elementary school, high school teachers often see 100 to 125 students in five different classes lasting about an hour each. While it is important for high school teachers to develop knowledge of their students' affective and personal characteristics, they often do not have as much time to interact with their students as compared with elementary school teachers. As a consequence, it is challenging for high school teachers to develop a more complete understanding of their students. Instead, high school teachers tend to focus on characteristics such as academic skills and knowledge, work habits, behavior, subject matter interest, and attitude. Still, to suggest that high school teachers are not concerned with emotional and interest outcomes is to overstate the matter. One high school business teacher notes: "I try to prepare my students for life. I want them to know how to keyboard and balance ledgers, but I am equally concerned that they are respectful, honest, good citizens, and so forth." All teachers are concerned with their students' cognitive and affective characteristics, although the relative emphasis on these characteristics differs by grade level.

TABLE 2.2   COMPARISON OF TWO CLASSROOM CONTEXTS

Classroom A	Classroom B
30 students	16 students
Students' abilities clustered at three disparate levels	Fairly homogeneous student abilities
Several students with speech impairments and physical disabilities	A few students who crave attention and a few who seem extremely shy
Range of socioeconomic backgrounds	Uniformly middle class
Parent pressures for multicultural learning	Parent pressures for high grades
Balanced gender mix	Predominantly boys
Separate art and music programs in another class	No separate art or music
Spacious, quiet room	Small room with noise from class next door
Nearly all students together for several years	Most students meeting one another for the first time
Individual student desks	Tables and chairs
Classroom aide available	No classroom aide

If early assessment is not done well, a disorganized, disruptive, unresponsive class is likely to develop, one in which communication and learning are inhibited. Each of us can recall a particular classroom in which the social system was characterized by anarchy, where personal impulse replaced social consideration, and where teaching and learning were constantly undermined by failure to establish etiquette.

Teaching is a context-bound activity involving many factors teachers cannot control, such as the resources available to them and the characteristics of their students.

While teachers do control many classroom features (e.g., rules and routines, methods of instruction, topics covered, and grading practices), there are some they do not control. Table 2.2 describes two teachers' classrooms. Imagine that these classrooms are at the same grade level. Notice that all of the characteristics listed in the table are those over which teachers normally have little control; of some the teacher may not even be aware until they suddenly pose a challenge; they are the factors that each teacher has to work with.

At the beginning of each year teachers must get to know their students so that they can organize them into a classroom learning community.

How might these various characteristics influence the way the two teachers guide student behaviors; organize activities for individuals, groups, or the class as a whole; or plan specific lessons? Which characteristics seem most advantageous to a teacher, and which seem disadvantageous? How might these factors influence approaches to teaching? Thinking about these questions should give you some sense of how approaches to teaching are always dependent on both the students and the classroom factors.

SOURCES OF INFORMATION
ABOUT STUDENTS

During the first days of a school year, teachers seek a wide variety of information about their students. This information relates to characteristics such as student' academic skills and knowledge, social behavior, self-discipline, beliefs and interests, family and social support system, and attitude toward school. Information about these and other characteristics comes from a variety of sources. Some of these sources of information result from direct observations of students in the classroom. Table 2.3 lists some common sources of classroom information available to teachers during the first days of school and the kinds of information these sources provide. Through typical classroom activities, such as discussion, homework, and writing assignments, teachers can quickly develop an initial impression about many important academic, social, and personal characteristics.

Teachers use a variety of information to size up their students, including personal observations, school records, comments from other teachers, and formal assessments.

Outside of the classroom teachers can find additional sources of information about students. Student records and past test scores can provide information about students' academic characteristics, behaviors, and special needs. School counselors and psychologists can provide insight into students' special needs and personal circumstances that may affect their school performance and behavior. Other teachers can also serve as an informal

TABLE 2.3   SOME COMMON EARLY ASSESSMENT SOURCES AND WHAT INFORMATION THEY MAY YIELD

What Students Say	What Students Do	What Students Write
Responses to questions	Early homework assignments	Early written homework assignments
Class discussion	In-class tasks	Early or prior journals
Interaction with others		Early or prior tests
Early oral reports		Prior portfolios
Potential Information	**Potential Information**	**Potential Information**
Attention span	Attention span	Organizational abilities
Oral fluency	Ability to complete work on time	Use of logic
Politeness	Ability to follow directions	Neatness
Vocabulary	Level of performance	Penmanship
Ease of participation	Ability to get along with others	Level of performance
Anxiety		
Ability to respond to prompts		
Tendencies to talk out of turn in class		

source of information. For one example, sit and listen in the teachers' room. Hear Ms. Robinson or Mr. Rutherford complain about Jim or Shaylah's continual inattentiveness or defiant behavior in class. Listen to Mr. Hobbs describe Marion's cooperation and insight. Hear Ms. Jeffry complain about Mike's interfering and demanding parents. One does not have to know Jim, Shaylah, Marion, or Mike personally to begin forming impressions of them as persons and students. Many students' reputations precede them into the classroom, and teachers who have never set eyes on them often already have heard a great deal about their strengths and weaknesses.

Several teachers relate how the information they collected helped them with the early assessment of their students at the start of the school year:

> School records are kept in the office and are available on all students. I could look at these before the school year started to get information about my students' abilities, prior school performance, home situation, and learning problems.

> In my school, classes are assigned by level. Before classes start I know whether a class is high or low level.

> Sometimes when I compare my class list with another teacher's, the other teacher may comment on a student, the sibling of the student, or the parents of the student. Susie's brother was a nice, quiet boy. Sam's sister was defiant and disruptive in class. Andy is the last of the eight Rooney children, thank goodness. Be careful, Mrs. Roberts is overly protective of Peter and very concerned about grades.

> By the end of the first week of school I will know whether each child is going to work, care about school, get along with the other students, be responsible enough to relay messages for me, and have a pleasant personality. I know these things by observing the children in class. Whether a student volunteers an answer or comments willingly or if he needs to be called on to give an answer tells me about the student's type of personality. I watch how they get along with one another. The look of interest on their faces tells me about how hard they will work.

At the start of school, teachers have their antennae up, constantly listening and watching for information about their students. Sometimes teachers purposefully collect information from a variety of these sources. At other times, a teacher's attention is drawn to things that seem, on the surface, to have little to do with the main task of the school: the way students dress, their posture and body language, student discussions in the hallways and cafeterias, and the peers they "hang around" with. Through both formal and informal sources of information, by the end of the first or second week of school, most teachers have sized up their students and classes and can provide fairly detailed descriptions of student characteristics.

Teachers rely heavily on informal observations when initially sizing up their students.

Two facts about this early information deserve attention. First, much of it comes from informal observations. As the word *could* in the first teacher's quotation hints, most teachers do not rely heavily on tests or formal assessments when initially determining student characteristics. If they seek formal information, and many do not, they often rely on the school record folders or give student pretests. Second, because this initial information is obtained largely by means of informal observations, it may not be representative of the students' typical or current academic performance, behavior, attitudes, or beliefs.

Two types of problems limit the validity and reliability of early assessments that are based on informal observations and communications. First, because of the limits of the human mind and memory, teachers may "lose," or forget, important pieces of information about a student or class. If memory is faulty or incomplete, the appropriateness or validity of the impression is lowered. A second problem concerns the amount of information teachers obtain to learn about a student or class. Since teachers can observe any given student only part of the time, it is inevitable that their observations will be incomplete. Personal communications are often brief and focused on either general observations or a single event that stands out in a colleague's mind, thus increasing the possibility that the information is insufficient to make reliable interpretations about student characteristics. Teachers need to recognize the problems that may result from selective memory and insufficient information.

FORMING STUDENT DESCRIPTIONS

On the basis of information they collect during the first days of class, teachers synthesize their early assessments into general descriptions of students, like the following:

Jemella (a second-grader) has had an exceptional beginning of school. She does her work very well and on time, raises her hand to answer questions, and seems to be enjoying school. This is not the case for many of the new second-graders.

Joslyn (a fifth-grader) walks into class each day with a worried and tired look on her face. Praising her work, or even the smallest positive action, will bring a smile to her face, though the impact is brief. She is inattentive, even during the exercises we do step-by-step as a class. She is shy, but sometimes will ask for help. But before she gives herself a chance, she will put her head down on her desk and close her eyes. I don't know why she lacks motivation so severely. Possibly it's a chemical imbalance or maybe problems at home. She will probably be this way all year.

Alfredo (an eighth-grader) is a smooth talker, a Casanova. He is a nice dresser, a nice kid with a head on his shoulders. Unfortunately he is very unmotivated, most likely because of his background. He's street smart, loves attention, and has a good sense of humor. He is able to "dish it out" but can also take it. Alfredo is loud in class but not to the point of disruption; he knows where to draw the limit. If only he had some determination, the kid could go a long way.

Larinda (an eleventh-grader) is athletic and good-natured. She flirts with the boys and sometimes with her teachers. She doesn't go beyond the bounds of good taste and is respectful in class. Her ability is average.

These are rich and detailed descriptions of students. Each includes many different student characteristics, relies heavily on informal information, and conveys a perception about many dimensions of student behavior and background. Notice that the teachers' descriptions include both academic and nonacademic factors. Notice also that they often make a prediction about how the student will perform during the school year. That teachers assess students is not in itself remarkable; people in any social system size one another up. What is important, however, is the speed at which teachers can form impressions about almost all the students in the class.

Early assessments produce a set of perceptions and expectations that influence the manner in which the teacher plans for, instructs, and interacts with the students throughout the school year (Good and Brophy, 1997). This is, after all, the purpose of early assessment: to help the teacher get to know the students so he or she can organize them into a classroom society and know how to interact with, motivate, and teach them.

To get a sense of the use and importance of early assessment, imagine that it is the middle of January and you have been called in to substitute for the regular eighth-grade teacher at Memorial Middle School. You have detailed plans for the subject matter you are to teach during the day. Just after the beginning bell rings and students are seated, a boy in the back of the room raises his hand and asks to go to his locker to get a book he has forgotten. Should you let him go? Can he be trusted to return after getting the book or will he wander the halls for an hour? What is the classroom teacher's policy on forgotten books? A few minutes later two girls get up and start to leave the room. "We always go to the library to see Ms. Flanders for extra help at this time on Wednesday. We'll be back in about twenty minutes." Do they? Will they? Shortly thereafter, two students start arguing over the last copy of a reference book. The argument grows louder and begins to disturb the class. How should you react? What strategy will pacify these particular students? The classroom teacher knows the answers to all these questions because she or he is a founding member of the classroom society. The teacher is the person who has developed familiarity with the students' characteristics and established the routines. As a substitute, you are an outsider, a stranger to this classroom society, and thus do not know its workings, personalities, rules, and routines. Early assessments provide the classroom teacher with the kinds of practical, nitty-gritty knowledge needed to establish rules, routines, and working relationships that help a classroom function productively.

These early assessments provide teachers with the kinds of practical, nitty-gritty information needed to make a classroom function effectively.

Table 2.4 reviews the main characteristics of early assessment.

Bear in mind that early assessments are an outgrowth of a natural tendency to observe and make judgments about people on the basis of what is seen and heard about them in everyday interactions. These assessments facilitate "knowing" or "labeling" others so that it is no longer necessary to interact with them as if they were strangers; they help bring

---

TABLE 2.4   CHARACTERISTICS OF EARLY ASSESSMENT

1. **Early assessment is done at the start of the school year.** Most teachers can describe the personal, social, and academic characteristics of each student and the class as a whole after the first two weeks of school.

2. **Early assessment is student-centered.** Students and their characteristics are the focus of assessment.

3. **Informal observation is used.** Much of the information about student behavior and performance is collected through spontaneous, informal observations.

4. **Observations are synthesized into perceptions.** Teachers put together their observations in idiosyncratic ways to form a generalized perception of students.

5. **Impressions are rarely written down.** Unlike test scores or grades, which are written down in grade books or report cards, the perceptions formed from early assessments are unwritten and selectively communicated.

6. **Observations are broad and diverse.** Teachers attend to a broad range of cognitive, affective, and psychomotor characteristics when they size up their students.

7. **Early impressions tend to become permanent.** Teachers are very confident about the accuracy of the assessments they do in the first days of school. Initial perceptions are very stable from the first week of school to the end of the school year.

---

order into social situations, including schools. They provide a frame of reference within which social interaction and meaningful instruction can take place.

CONCERNS ABOUT ACCURACY AND VALIDITY

Because early assessments create the foundation for many important judgments made throughout the school year, it is important to make these initial impressions as valid and reliable as possible. An assessment process that is based on quickly obtained, often incomplete evidence has the potential to produce incorrect, invalid, and unreliable decisions about students. While early assessment will always be shaped in part by information collected informally, the extent to which a teacher can collect information in a planned and systematic manner will increase the accuracy and validity of early assessments.

The General Problem

Because initial early assessments have important consequences for students, teachers have an ethical responsibility to make them as valid and reliable as possible.

Early assessments shape teachers' impressions of their students, their expectations for their students, the structure of classroom routines and learning activities. Given the important decisions made based on early assessments, there are four points about the effects of early assessment that teachers should keep in mind. First, teachers' initial impressions of their students tend to remain stable over time. Once a teacher forms an impression of a student, that impression is likely to stick, and teachers will act to maintain their student impressions, even in the face of contradictory evidence.

Second, classroom teachers are fairly accurate in their beginning-of-the-year predictions of students' academic performance as measured by test scores, although even the most accurate teacher is not correct about every student. However, teachers' accuracy when assessing students' personalities, interests, emotions, motivation, self-concepts, and social adjustment is lower. Overall, teachers' perceptions of these emotional characteristics are less accurate than their academic perceptions, at least at the start of the school year.

Teachers often communicate their assessments to students in unintended ways, and students may live up to these teacher perceptions.

Third, early assessments not only influence the way teachers perceive, treat, and make decisions about students, they are often transmitted to students. Teachers often unknowingly and unintentionally communicate the perceptions made based on early assessments. For example, offhand comments can tell individuals and the class a great deal about the teacher's perceptions: "Oh, Robert, can't you even remember what we just talked about?" "All right, Sarah, will you tell the rest of the class the answer it can't seem to come up with?" "Didn't Ruby read that paragraph with a lot of expression?" Perceptions are also conveyed indirectly, as when a teacher waits patiently for one student to think through a problem but allows another only a few seconds; expresses encouragement and assurance to one student but says "at least try" to another; or encourages one to "think" but another to "take a guess." Tone of voice, physical proximity, gestures, seating arrangements, and other signals all tell students how they are perceived in the classroom.

Fourth, teachers' perceptions and expectations may even create a **self-fulfilling prophecy,** in which the expectations for a student lead the teacher to interact with that student in a particular manner (Good and Brophy, 1997). The student, in turn, observes the way the teacher interacts with him or her and begins to behave in the way or at the level the teacher expects, whether or not the original expectation is correct.

Needless to say, it is the teacher's responsibility to avoid these situations by making early assessments as fair and accurate as possible for all students. Given the inaccurate perceptions that may result from the limited, and often informal, information on which early assessments depend, teachers must be aware that their initial perceptions may be inaccurate. Teachers must also be aware that their comments and actions can reveal their initial impressions and that such revelations can affect the behavior, attitude, and perceptions of their students. Because early assessments can be so influential in setting expectations, shaping student-teacher interactions, and affecting students' perform-ance and self-perceptions, it is important to examine more closely the dangers inherent in that process and the strategies teachers can use to improve their initial assessments.

The Problem in Terms of Validity and Reliability

As stated in Chapter 1, the two main criteria for good assessments are validity and reliability. Validity is concerned with the collection of *appropriate* evidence—that is, evidence that is related to the student char-acteristic under consideration: Does the evidence I have gathered tell me about the characteristic I wish to assess? Reliability pertains to collecting *enough* evidence to be relatively certain about the decision regarding the characteristic being assessed: Is there sufficient evidence to make a sta-ble decision about the student's performance, behavior, attitudes, or beliefs? Validity and reliability work hand in hand to ensure that the perceptions formed in assessment are appropriate and fair, leading to good decisions about students.

Threats to Validity

There are two main problems that occur during early assessment that diminish the validity of the information teachers gather: prejudgment and logical error. **Prejudgment** occurs when a teacher's prior knowledge, first impressions, or personal prejudices and beliefs interfere with the ability to make a fair and valid assessment of a student. All of us have personal prejudices or beliefs; we prefer some things to others and some people to others. We have beliefs, interests, ideas, and expectations that differenti-ate us from others. However, when these likes, dislikes, beliefs, and prej-udices interfere with our ability to make fair student assessments, there is a real problem.

Observer prejudgment can stem from prior knowledge, first impressions, or personal prejudices, and often interferes with fair and valid assessments.

Prejudging students results from three main sources. The first is *prior information,* information a teacher obtains before meeting a student. Infor-mation passed through the school grapevine or the performance of prior sib-lings often influences and prejudices a teacher's perceptions, even before the student enters the teacher's classroom: "Oh, you're Sarah's brother! I'm expecting you to do as well as she did when she was in my class."

The second is *initial impressions,* which tend to influence subsequent impressions. If the teacher's decision about a student's characteristic is based on how he is dressed on the first day of school or how she behaved in study hall last year, the teacher may unconsciously let this initial impression dictate subsequent observations and interpretations of the student's characteristics.

The third source of prejudging is teachers' *personal theories and beliefs* about particular kinds of students, which often lead to stereotyped perceptions. When teachers think "this student is from Oldtown, and kids from Oldtown are poor learners and discipline problems," or "girls do poorly in math," or "everyone knows that members of that group have no interest in school," or "he's just another dumb jock," they are expressing their personal theories or stereotypes of what they think certain people are like and how they behave. Being labeled with such stereotypes without a fair chance to show true characteristics can injure students and inhibit their learning.

Teachers should be careful not to interpret cultural differences as cultural deficits.

This is especially so with regard to teachers' racial, cultural, disability, and language prejudices or stereotypes. The variety of languages, cultures, races, and disabilities present in American classrooms is increasing quickly. When making early assessments, teachers who are not familiar with students' cultures and languages often interpret what are really cultural *differences* as cultural *deficits* (Ladson-Billings, 1994; Delpit, 1995). Similarly, teachers' stereotypes or personal beliefs can produce invalid early assessments for students who are different from the teacher. For example, many Americans, including many teachers, believe that the majority of children of color are poor, live in large cities, come from single-parent homes, and live on public assistance. How might a teacher who erroneously believes these misconceptions perceive a student of color on the first day of school? How might impressions based on these misconceptions influence the way in which the teacher interacts with the student? The dangers of prejudgment are real and consequential. Teachers must strive to recognize their personal beliefs and stereotypes and judge each individual student on the basis of who he or she actually is and how he or she actually performs in class. Each student is entitled to be judged on his or her own merits, not on the basis of stereotypes and personal beliefs.

Many teachers recognize that prejudgments and stereotyping can invalidate early assessments, as the following statements indicate.

> I don't like to hear anything about a student's behavior from past teachers. Every teacher is different, just like every student is different. A student may have a negative experience with one teacher, but a positive experience with another teacher. I prefer to make my own decision about every child.

> I remember the time I stereotyped three of my female students as "Valley" girls—not too bright and mainly superficial—on the first day of class. This assessment came about due to their physical appearance and their shallow contributions in discussion. Yet when it came time for formal assessment, these three individuals ranked the highest in the class.

olc

CHAPTER CASE STUDY

Visit the text Online Learning Center to read the case of Marsha Warren, an experienced third-grade teacher who is overwhelmed by the problems created by her heterogeneous class.

www.mhhe.com/ russell7e

Logical error occurs when teachers select the wrong indicators to assess desired student characteristics, thereby invalidating their judgments. It is tempting to read a great deal into a single observation, especially at the start of the year when teachers want to quickly characterize each student in order to organize their classes. It would be convenient, for example, to make a whole series of inferences about motivation, attention span, interest in the subject, self-concept, and leadership from a student's eager hand raising. Maybe all the interpretations will prove to be correct, but it is dangerous not to recognize the difference between what is directly observed and interpretations made from an observation. When observation of one characteristic (hand raising) is used to make inferences about other, unobserved characteristics (motivation, interest), the potential for logical errors and invalid assessment is great.

A third-grade teacher described Matthew's first day in school in this way: "I could tell that Matthew was going to have trouble working in groups. He did not say a word throughout an entire activity when he was asked to work with three other students. He just sat there, letting his group members make all the decisions and do all of the work."

Is poor group working skills the only interpretation of Matthew's behavior? What are some others? If Matthew had been grouped with a different set of students, would he have behaved the same way? If Matthew had not had an argument with one of his group mates during recess, might he have behaved differently during the small-group activity?

To state the issue in another way, the labels teachers use to describe their students represent their interpretations of observed behaviors. Teachers do not directly observe characteristics such as motivation, intelligence, leadership, self-confidence, aggressiveness, anxiety, shyness, intolerance, and the like. Rather, teachers observe a student behaving in some way, interpret what the behavior signifies, and give the behavior a name. For example, a teacher may see one student push another student. Based on this behavior, the teacher may conclude that the student is physically aggressive and a bully. In reality, though, the student may have been breaking up an argument between two students rather than instigating a fight. While pushing another student to stop an argument may not be an acceptable strategy, concluding that a student is a bully based on such an action results in a logical error.

In most cases, it is the name given to the behavior that attaches to the student, not the specific behavior that prompted the name. Teachers remember that a student is a bully, self-confident, aggressive, aloof, motivated, or shy, but they rarely remember the specific observations that led them to label the student in that way. Because teachers' labels "stick" to students, it is important that the observations leading to a label be valid indicators of that label.

Teachers should be careful not to mislabel students based on observations that do not justify the label.

Threats to Reliability

*Teachers should be
careful not to form a
permanent perception of
students based on one or
two observations that
may not be typical
behavior.*

While validity is concerned with collecting information that is appropriate for determining a student's characteristics, reliability is concerned with collecting enough information to be sure that it represents typical student behavior. For example, was the teacher's observation of Matthew's performance in the small-group activity sufficient to conclude that he has difficulty engaging in group work? Probably not. Why? Whether formal or informal, teachers' assessments are based on samples of their students' behavior. These samples are used to determine students' more general behavior patterns. Thus, an important issue in teacher assessment is how well the observed samples provide consistent information about the behavior of interest. When information is not reliable, teachers will form different decisions depending on which information is used to form those decisions. Reliable information enables teachers to form consistent and stable decisions about student characteristics.

The nature of early assessment creates special reliability problems. As noted earlier, the spontaneity of many teacher-student interactions limit what teachers are able to see and what students are willing to show. Also, the time available to observe students often is brief, since attention must be distributed among many students and classroom activities, especially at the beginning of the school year. In short, the few initial samples of behavior that are observed under these circumstances may not provide reliable indicators of students' typical behavior.

Many teachers recognize this problem, as evidenced by the following statements:

> First impressions are so important. They can either make or break a child. It all depends on how much opportunity a particular teacher gives to a student to prove him- or herself before passing a judgment.

> The first three days are very difficult. The students will not even present their normal classroom behaviors to you in the first three days. They are somewhat intimidated and uncomfortable; they don't know you. Even kids who are badly behaved in the first three days, they're just feeling you out, they're testing, trying to see how far they can get.

> Carol breaks up with her boyfriend a week before the beginning of school, leaving her depressed and unmotivated. Does her English teacher know the reason for Carol's behavior? Is her assessment of Carol after one day of school correct?

The implication of these comments is that teachers must be sure they observe sufficient samples of students' behavior before they solidify their initial perceptions and use them to make decisions. There are times, such as the start of the school year, when students' behavior may not be indicative of their typical behavior. Typical behavior cannot be determined by observing a student just once, especially at a time when the student may feel uncomfortable in new surroundings. Key Assessment Tools 2.1 summarizes the threats to validity and reliability.

> **Key Assessment Tools 2.1**
>
> ## THREATS TO THE VALIDITY AND RELIABILITY OF EARLY ASSESSMENTS
>
> **Validity Threats**
> 1. Observer prejudgments that prevent teachers from making an objective assessment of students
>   a. Prior information from school grapevine, siblings, or nonclassroom experiences
>   b. First impressions that influence subsequent impressions
>   c. Personal theories or attitudes that influence subsequent observation (e.g., girls can't do math, or athletes have no interest in serious academic pursuits)
> 2. Logical errors that cause teachers to judge students based on the wrong characteristics (e.g., observe attention and judge learning; observe clothes and judge ability).
>
> **Reliability Threats**
> 1. Inadequate behavior, sampling in which too few observations prevent learning about students' typical behavior and characteristics
>   a. Basing decisions about a student on a single piece of information
>   b. Observing behaviors in one setting (e.g., the playground) and assuming behavior will be the same in another setting (e.g., the classroom)

IDENTIFYING SPECIAL NEEDS

In recent years there has been increasing emphasis on integrating students with special learning needs into regular classrooms. "Pull out" programs that educate students with special needs in classrooms separate from the majority of students are diminishing. Instead, there is growing emphasis on the inclusion of students with special needs in the same classroom as their peers (Ferguson, 1995). Increased inclusion has placed greater responsibility and challenge on the classroom teacher, who is often charged with educating students with varied special needs (Hoy and Gregg, 1994; Roach, 1995).

At the start of the school year, classroom teachers need to become familiar with the special needs that may have been previously identified for each of their students. In addition, it is the teacher's responsibility to assist in identifying additional needs of individual students. Issues related to identifying and developing plans to meet the special needs of students have been codified by federal law. In this section we will briefly examine the laws that define how students with disabilities must be diagnosed and the Individual Education Plans (IEP) that are developed for students who have been identified with special needs.

Since the 1970s, the importance of classroom teachers working with other specialists in a school to meet the special needs of each individual student has grown rapidly. In this text, we provide a brief introduction to some of the complex and important issues related to identifying and meeting the special needs of students. Given the many excellent resources that exist to assist teachers in designing instruction that meets the diverse needs of their students, readers are encouraged to consult these additional resources to learn more about the variety of special needs students may have, strategies for identifying these needs, and methods for meeting these needs. Some of these resources are listed in Appendix E.

Legal Issues

Figure 2.1 summarizes recent federal legislation related to teaching children with disabilities. The enactment of the Education for All Handicapped Children Act of 1975 mandated that free public education be provided for *all* school-age children, including those with disabilities, many of whom had been excluded from a free public education. This act also prescribed assessment procedures and practices for students identified as having special needs. The Individuals with Disabilities Education Act of 1990 (IDEA) extended the rights of students with disabilities by requiring a free and appropriate education for preschool students with disabilities. This act called for the placement of students with disabilities in the least restrictive environment, requiring that, to the maximum degree possible, students with disabilities should be educated in classrooms with students who do not have disabilities. Section 504 of the Vocational Rehabilitation Act of 1973 reinforced and expanded protection of students with disabilities by broadening the definition of what constitutes a disability. These acts have substantially increased classroom teachers' responsibilities for identifying, instructing, and assessing students with disabilities (*Phi Delta Kappan,* 1995). Figure 2.2 describes the major provisions of IDEA. More wide-ranging discussion of legal issues in educating such students can be found in Ordover and Boundy (1991), Rothstein (2000), and Overton (2000).

The law requires school systems and teachers to identify and assess all children who have disabilities or are at risk of having their learning impaired because of a cognitive, affective, or psychomotor disability. The number of conditions that qualify as disabilities is large, ranging from physical disabilities and hearing or visual impairments to emotional disorders, learning disorders, and speech impairments. Although the manner of identifying such students varies greatly, the classroom teacher is a primary source, especially in the preschool, elementary, and middle school grades. These teachers spend a great deal of time each day with a small group of students and thus are in an advantageous position to observe and identify students' strengths, weaknesses, needs, and potential disabilities. One of the teacher's assessment responsibilities is to identify students suspected of having a special learning need or disability.

School systems must identify and assess students with learning disabilities. The classroom teacher is a primary resource in this process.

When a teacher identifies a student who may have a special need that affects his or her learning, the law requires formal assessment of the student. The assessment helps determine whether the student does have special needs, what the needs are, and how they may best be addressed in instruction. Referrals for such student assessments can come from teachers,

FIGURE 2.1 *History of the Federal Laws for the Education of Learners Who Are Exceptional*

SOURCE: Vaughn, S., Bos, C., and Schumm, J. (2003). *Teaching Exceptional, Diverse, and At-Risk Students in the General Education Classroom,* 3rd ed. Boston, Allyn & Bacon.

1973 Vocational Rehabilitation Act (VRA) (Public Law 93–112, Section 504)
- Defines "handicapped person"
- Defines "appropriate education"
- Prohibits discrimination against students with disabilities in federally funded programs

1974 Educational Amendments Act (Public Law 93–380)
- Grants federal funds to states for programming for exceptional learners
- Provides the first federal funding of state programs for students who are gifted and talented
- Grants students and families the right of due process in special education placement

1975 Education for All Handicapped Children Act (EAHCA) (Public Law 94–142, Part B)
- Requires states to provide a free and appropriate public education for children with disabilities (ages 5 to 18)
- Requires individualized education plans (IEPs)
- First defined "least restrictive environment"

1986 Education of the Handicapped Act Amendments (Public Law 99–457)
- Requires states to extend free and appropriate education to children with disabilities (ages 3 to 5)
- Establishes early intervention programs for infants and toddlers with disabilities (ages birth to 2 years)

1990 Americans with Disabilities Act (ADA) (Public Law 101–336)
- Prohibits discrimination against people with disabilities in the private sector
- Protects equal opportunity to employment and public services, accommodations, transportation, and telecommunications

- Defines "disability" to include people with AIDS

1990 Individuals with Disabilities Education Act (IDEA) (Public Law 101–476)
- Renames and replaces P. L. EAHCA
- Establishes "people first" language for referring to people with disabilities
- Extends special education services to include social work and rehabilitation services
- Extends provisions for due process and confidentiality for students and parents
- Adds two new categories of disability: autism and traumatic brain injury
- Requires states to provide bilingual education programs for students with disabilities
- Requires states to educate students with disabilities for transition to employment, and to provide transition services

1997 Individuals with Disabilities Education Act (IDEA) (Public Law 105–17)
- Requires that all students with disabilities must continue to receive services, even if they have been expelled from school
- Allows states to extend their use of the developmental delay category for students through age 9
- Requires schools to assume greater responsibility for ensuring that students with disabilities have access to the general education curriculum
- Allows special education staff who are working in the mainstream to assist general education students when needed
- Requires a general education teacher to be a member of the IEP team
- Requires students with disabilities to take part in state- and districtwide assessments

FIGURE 2.2
Major Provisions of the Individuals with Disabilities Education Act

SOURCE: Adapted from Individuals with Disabilities Education Act, P. L. 101–476.

Free and Appropriate Public Education

All children are entitled to a free and appropriate public education, regardless of the nature or severity of their disability.

Nondiscriminatory Assessment

Requires planning to ensure that tests, evaluation materials, and procedures for evaluating and placing children with disabilities will be selected and administered so as not to be culturally or racially discriminatory.

Development of an Individual Education Plan (IEP)

Requires the development of a written IEP for each child with a disability that will include a statement of current levels of educational achievement, annual and short-term goals, specific educational services to be provided, dates of initiation and duration of services, and criteria for evaluating the degree to which the objectives are achieved.

Due Process

Requires an opportunity to present complaints with respect to any matter relating to the identification, evaluation, or educational placement of a child. Specific due process procedures include: (a) written notification to parents before evaluation, (b) written notification when initiating or refusing to initiate a change in educational placement, (c) an opportunity to obtain an independent evaluation of the child, and (d) an opportunity for an impartial due process hearing.

Privacy and Records

Requires that educational and psychological records pertaining to a child remain confidential except to those individuals who are directly involved in a child's education and who have a specific reason for reviewing the records. Further, the law provides an opportunity for the parents or guardian of a child with a disability to examine all relevant records with respect to the identification, evaluation, and educational placement of the child.

Least Restrictive Environment

Requires to the maximum extent appropriate that children with disabilities be educated with children who are not disabled in as normal an environment as possible.

Related Services

Requires that support services (e.g., psychological, audiology, occupational theory, music therapy) be available to assist the child with a disability to benefit from special education.

parents, counselors, physicians, and others. The composition of the assessment team that reviews a referred student varies, but it is usually made up of some or all of the following individuals: one or more special education teachers, the student's classroom teacher(s), specialists in areas of the student's perceived needs, parents, child advocates, counselors, and a social worker. The assessment conference must be carried out according to the following procedures and guidelines:

- A parent must have written notice, in nontechnical language and in the parent's native language, that a school system proposes to conduct an assessment. Prior notice is needed for a "preplacement" assessment to determine whether a child needs special education, as well as subsequent assessments.
- Parental consent must be obtained before students are assessed.
- Assessments must not be racially or culturally discriminatory.
- Assessments must be conducted in the student's native language.
- No single test or procedure can be the basis for deciding that the student has a disability and requires help through instructional accommodations. Instead, multiple sources of evidence must be collected and confirm a need.
- Assessments must be conducted by a multidisciplinary team, including at least one teacher knowledgeable about the student's area of disability; the assessment must address all areas related to the student's disability, including health, vision, hearing, emotional status, and so forth.
- The assessments used must have proven validity applicable to the decision to be made.
- Formal tests and assessments of the student must be administered by trained individuals.
- A written report must be presented after the assessment process is complete.

Although these procedures say little about the role of the classroom teacher, it is often the teacher who identifies a student's disability. Common areas of disability such as oral expression, listening comprehension, written expression, reading fluency, reading comprehension, and attention deficit are best identified by the classroom teacher.

While it is the teacher's responsibility to be watchful for potential special needs throughout the school year, early assessments provide an important opportunity at the start of a school year for a classroom teacher to identify special needs that may have been overlooked in previous years or have recently developed. If a potential need is detected and a formal assessment is conducted, the teacher will provide important information about a student's classroom performance and behavior at the assessment conference.

If a student is identified as having a disability, the results of the assessment conference will be used to develop appropriate educational objectives, instructional approaches, and assessment methods for the student. Here again, the classroom teacher's recommendations are important in deciding how and what the student will be taught and assessed. Because the emphasis in assessment and instruction is on the individual student, not the identified disability, each assessed student is treated as an individual, and the most suitable educational arrangement for that student is the primary focus. Two students with the same disability may have different objectives, instruction, and assessment strategies.

The specific educational plan developed for a student, called an **Individual Education Plan (IEP),** must include information about the student's present level of educational performance, annual goals and short-term objectives, prescribed educational services, degree of inclusion in regular education programs, and assessment criteria for determining achievement of the goals and objectives. An example of a complete IEP form is shown in Appendix C. In essence, the IEP defines a student's special needs and the ways that the teacher must modify objectives, instructional strategies, and assessment methods to best suit the student's needs and learning style. Key Assessment Tools 2.2 lists the required parts

---

Key Assessment Tools 2.2

REQUIRED CONTENTS OF AN INDIVIDUAL EDUCATION PLAN

1. A statement of the child's present levels of educational performance, including academic achievement, social adaptations, prevocational and vocational skills, psychomotor skills, and self-help skills.

2. A statement of annual goals which describes the educational performance to be achieved by the end of the school year under the child's individualized education program.

3. A statement of short-term instructional objectives, which must be measurable intermediate steps between the present level of educational performance and the annual goals.

4. A statement of specific educational services needed by the child (determined without regard to the availability of services), including a description of

   a. all special education and related services which are needed to meet the unique needs of the child, including the type of physical education program in which the child will participate, and

   b. any special instructional media and materials which are needed

5. The date when those services will begin and length of time the services will be given.

6. A description of the extent to which the child will participate in regular education programs.

7. A justification of the type of educational placement that the child will have.

8. A list of the individuals who are responsible for implementation of the Individual Education Plan.

9. Objective criteria, evaluation procedures, and schedules of determining, on at least an annual basis, whether the short-term instructional objectives are being achieved.

SOURCE: *Federal Register.* 41(252). p. 5692.

of an IEP. Examination of these parts shows how a student's IEP influences the planning, instruction, and assessment of the student. Once the IEP is developed and agreed on, it may not be unilaterally changed by school personnel or the classroom teacher.

Decisions about students' disabilities and accommodations focus on placing students in the least restrictive environment, which enables them to be educated in the most normal environment their disabilities allow. The overriding purpose of referral, IEP development, and placement in the least restrictive environment is to ensure that students receive an education appropriate for their needs.

IMPROVING EARLY ASSESSMENTS

Following are some strategies that can be used to improve early assessments. Since teachers will never be fully accurate with their early assessments, it is their responsibility to do everything possible to minimize errors and to revise judgments when initial impressions prove to be wrong.

How effective you can be in early assessment will always depend in part on having an orderly and supportive classroom and school environment in which to observe your students and gather other data about them. In that spirit, Tables 2.5 and 2.6 can be helpful.

1. *Be aware of early assessment and its effects on students.* Early assessment is such a natural part of the start of the school year that many teachers are unaware that they are doing it. They do not recognize the dangers of forming incorrect impressions of students. As a first step, then, it is important for teachers to be aware of this type of assessment and to be sensitive to the consequences of making incorrect decisions based on incomplete or invalid observations.

2. *Treat initial impressions as hypotheses to be confirmed or corrected by subsequent observations and information.* First impressions should be considered tentative hypotheses that need to be confirmed or disproved by subsequent observation and information. Teachers should refrain from judging and labeling students on the basis of hearsay, a single brief observation, or a student's race, culture, gender, or language. They should also gather their own evidence about students, develop tentative hypotheses, and confirm initial hypotheses with subsequent observations and information. They should be prepared to change an incorrect first impression. One way to make your observations more thorough, and less likely to be unconsciously selective, is to pick one or two student characteristics per day and structure classroom activities to collect information about those characteristics from all students in the class.

Teachers should treat initial impressions as hypotheses to be confirmed or corrected by later information.

3. *Use direct indicators to gather information about student characteristics.* To learn about students, teachers must interpret the observations they gather. Making decisions about some characteristics based on

When making assessments, teachers should try to use information that requires minimum interpretation.

TABLE 2.5 A DISCIPLINE "DAILY DOZEN" FOR TEACHERS

1. *Be consistent.* When you reprimand an action one day and ignore it the next, children don't know what to expect. As a result, they'll try it again to see if they can "get away with it." They are also quick to see and resent the basic unfairness of inconsistency.

2. *Don't make idle threats.* If you decide that punishment is necessary, carry it out, or your words will mean nothing.

3. *Look for the reasons behind misbehavior.* It often stems from the lack of interest by your students in the curriculum or the teaching approach.

4. *Be sure that they know the rules.* If you expect your students to behave in a certain way, tell them so, and explain the reason. A class discussion of these rules can be enlightening both to you and your class. You may discover that some of your rules have no real purpose.

5. *Check your own feelings about individual students.* Do you "play favorites"? It's hard to like sullen or rebellious students, and easy to like the quiet conformists. But your dislike of the rebel incites more rebellion.

6. *Watch your tongue.* "The teacher's tongue, sharper than a two-edged sword, sometimes stabs children, leaving wounds that never heal," said R. L. Frye, supervisor of secondary education, Louisiana State Department of Education. A tongue lashing may end the disturbance—but at what cost?

7. *Don't make study a punishment.* The teacher who keeps students after school to study arithmetic or spelling, as a penalty for misbehavior, is saying: "Study is an unpleasant thing. There is no joy or satisfaction in it. It's so painful that I use it as a punishment." This hardly creates a thirst for learning in youngsters.

8. *Let them know that you like them.* Look for things to praise, especially in students who are discipline problems. Accept them as worthwhile in spite of their misbehavior. Disapprove the act but not the individual.

9. *Don't try to do the impossible.* Some students have emotional problems only a better-trained person can solve. When a youngster is a consistent troublemaker and all your efforts to help him fail, the time has come to refer him to the ACT team or vice principal. There are limits to what a teacher can do in child study, diagnosis, and treatment.

10. *Control your temper.* Flying off the handle merely shows students that they've gotten through to you. When you "lose your cool" you lose your ability to solve the discipline problem sanely, rationally, and thoughtfully.

11. *Don't be afraid to apologize if you've treated a student unjustly.* You will gain, not lose, the respect of the class for admitting your error.

12. *Recognize that what you see as delinquent behavior may be normal behavior in a child's cultural background.* It may take time, patience, and tact to break the pattern.

> **TABLE 2.6   SUGGESTIONS FOR THE BEGINNING OF SCHOOL FOR NEW TEACHERS**
>
> **1.** Create classroom plans for the first few days. Plan at least twice as much as you think you will need.
>
> **2.** Find someone who "knows the ropes," likely an experienced teacher, who can serve as a mentor.
>
> **3.** Watch your conversation in the faculty room.
>
> **4.** Learn to use the school copying machine, scanner, computers, and so on.
>
> **5.** Never, ever leave your class alone. Find someone to cover.

observations requires less interpretation than others. The closer the behavior observed is to the student characteristic a teacher wishes to describe, the more valid the resulting information is and the more confident the teacher can be about the student's true characteristic. For example, actually listening to a student read aloud provides more direct and valid evidence about the student's oral reading skills than the reading grades the student received from a prior teacher or the student's reported interest in reading.

In early assessments, teacher-student encounters are often brief, and it is tempting for the teacher to focus on superficial, indirect characteristics such as dress, facial expression, helpfulness, mood, or general appearance. Teachers then read into these superficial observations complex traits and personality factors such as motivation, self-concept, trustworthiness, self-control, and interest. Such indirect generalizations are likely to have low validity. More valid decisions will result when evidence gathering focuses on direct observation of behaviors and skills.

4. Supplement informal observations with more formal, structured activities. There is no rule that demands that only informal observations be used to assess students. Good teachers recognize this limitation and supplement their informal early observations with more structured activities. For example, they:

Because informal observations involve spontaneous behavior that may not be repeated, teachers should supplement their informal observations with more structured activities.

- Administer textbook review or diagnostic pretests to assess students' entering levels.
- Require students to keep a journal during the first week of school or write an essay on What I Did Last Summer to assess students' experiences, writing skills, and thought processes.
- Carry out group discussions or group projects to assess how students interact and work in groups.
- Assign students to work in small groups, purposefully forming each group to observe which students seem to work well together, which students tend to be leaders, and which students seem to be disengaged during group work.
- Let students read aloud to determine reading facility.

- Play classroom games based on spelling words, math facts, geographical knowledge, or current events to assess general knowledge, interest, and competitiveness.
- Use games related to listening skills to assess students' abilities to follow directions and process auditory information.
- Give students review tests and pretests.

Formal assessments that require students to perform the same behavior permit comparison among students.

Some school systems collect samples of students' work into what are called **portfolios.** These portfolios often accompany the students as they progress from grade to grade and provide a new teacher with concrete examples of a student's work. Having actual samples of a student's work from previous years is quite different from and more informative than the hearsay evidence teachers accumulate through the school grapevine. (Portfolios and other formal methods of assessing student performance are described more fully later, beginning in Chapter 6.) Formal assessments provide information about students' interests, styles, and academic performance that is not always obtainable from informal observations. Formal assessments also often require all students to perform the same behavior and thereby permit teachers to develop a more accurate understanding of how these behaviors vary among their students.

Reliable assessments usually require multiple observations in order to identify typical student behavior.

5. *Observe long enough to be fairly certain of the student's typical behavior.* Reliable information is that which represents the *typical* behavior of a student. To obtain reliable data, the teacher must look for *patterns* of behavior, not single, one-time behaviors. The greater the consequences that an assessment is likely to have for students, the more the teacher should strive to gather reliable information. A good rule of thumb to follow is see it *at least* twice, thus making sure the behavior being observed is not atypical. The more times a behavior is observed, the more confident a teacher can be about his or her assessment of the student characteristic.

Whenever possible, teachers should base their decisions on different kinds of information that support one another.

6. *Determine whether different kinds of information confirm one another.* Teachers can have more confidence in their student perceptions if they are based on two or more kinds of supporting evidence. For example, are test scores supported by classroom performance? Are classroom observations of a student's needs consistent with those identified by last year's teacher and the student's parents? Do classroom behavior patterns persist in the lunchroom and on the playground?

These questions suggest the use of multiple sources of information to corroborate the teacher's perception of a student. The extent to which different sources of information lead a teacher to the same decision generally increases the validity of that decision. However, note that it is better if the present teacher forms his or her own initial hypothesis about a student's behavior *before* obtaining corroborative information from other sources. By doing this, the teacher avoids letting his or her initial perceptions be prejudiced by the perceptions of others.

CHAPTER SUMMARY

- In the first few days of school, teachers must learn about their students and organize them into a classroom society characterized by communication, respect, and learning. Making decisions that help create a classroom environment that supports learning is one goal of early assessment.
- Information for student descriptions comes from a variety of sources, including classroom discussions and observations, student comments, pretests, body language, student dress, school records, the school grapevine, and comments by other teachers, among others.
- Informal assessments are a natural part of social interactions. In classrooms they lead teachers to form and often communicate expectations to students. Moreover, teachers' first impressions of students tend to remain stable, although they are not always accurate. As a consequence, teachers must think carefully when considering information and making decisions about students at the start of the school year.
- Two main problems affect the validity of assessments: prejudgment and logical error. Prejudgments occur when a teacher's prior knowledge, first impression, or personal beliefs interfere with his or her ability to make a fair and objective assessment of a student. This is of special concern when teachers know little about the racial, cultural, handicapping, and language characteristics of their students. Teachers who are not familiar with students' varied cultures and languages often interpret what are really cultural differences as cultural deficits when they judge students who are different from themselves. Logical error occurs when teachers use the wrong kind of information to judge student characteristics, as, for example, when they judge interest by where a student sits in a class.
- Reliability is a special problem in early assessment because the process takes place so quickly and is based on a few fleeting observations; thus, it is difficult to collect enough information to serve as a basis for consistent decisions about a student's performance or behavior. However, reliability is important in early assessments, and teachers should not make decisions about students based on only a few observations.
- Six suggestions for improving early assessments are (1) be aware of early assessments and their potential effects on students; (2) treat initial impressions as hypotheses to be confirmed or altered based on subsequent observation and information; (3) use direct indicators to gather information about student characteristics; (4) supplement informal observations with more formal, structured activities; (5) observe students long enough to be fairly certain of the student's typical behavior; and (6) determine whether different kinds of information confirm one another.

olc

CHAPTER REVIEW

Visit the Online Learning Center at **www.mhhe.com/ russell7e** to review the case study referenced in the chapter.

QUESTIONS FOR DISCUSSION

1. How does the fact that a classroom is a social setting influence planning, teaching, grading, managing, and interacting with students?
2. What are the advantages and disadvantages of examining a student's school (cumulative) record folder before the start of class? Under what circumstances would you examine a student's record folder?
3. How much must teachers really know about a student's home and family background? What home and background information is absolutely essential for teachers to know? Why? What information does a teacher have no right to know about a student's home or background?
4. Why do teachers rely so heavily on informal observation when sizing up students? Should teachers use such observations to label students?

ACTIVITIES

1. Table 2.2 shows the resources available in two different classrooms. In small groups, compare the two classrooms. How do the resources in each classroom influence planning and instructing students? Give specific examples.
2. Interview a classroom teacher. Find out the answers to questions like the following: What information does the teacher have about students before the first day of class? What are the sources of that information? How much does the teacher rely on the comments of other teachers when getting to know a new class? If the teacher could know only two specific characteristics of each student at the end of the first day of class, what would these be? Why? What information is most useful for managing students in the classroom? Add three questions of your own to this list. Why did you select those three questions?

REVIEW QUESTIONS

1. What factors make a classroom a social setting or society? How do these factors influence a teacher's assessment responsibilities?
2. What is early assessment? How is it done? How does it differ from other types of classroom assessments? What are three dangers that can reduce the validity and reliability of early assessment? What are three strategies a teacher can use to improve early assessments?
3. What are the main problems of validity and reliability in early assessment and assessments for planning and delivering instruction?
4. Why are early assessments important? What do they help teachers accomplish?
5. What are some differences between formal and informal observation?
6. What might be early signs of a reading disability?

REFERENCES

Delpit, L. (1995). *Other people's children: Cultural conflict in the classroom.* New York: The New Press.

Ferguson, D. L. (1995). The real challenge of inclusion. *Phi Delta Kappan, 77,* 281–287.

Garcia, E. (1994). *Understanding and meeting the challenge of student cultural diversity.* Boston: Houghton Mifflin.

Good, T. L., and Brophy, J. E. (1997). *Looking in classrooms.* New York: Longman.

Hoy, C., and Gregg, N. (1994). *Assessment: The special educator's role.* Pacific Grove, CA: Brooks/Cole.

Ladson-Billings, G. (1994). *The dreamkeepers.* San Franciso: Jossey-Bass.

McCaslin, M., and Good, T. (1996). *Listening to students.* New York: Harper-Collins.

Ordover, E. L., and Boundy, K. B. (1991). *Educational rights of children with disabilities.* Cambridge, MA: Center for Law and Education.

Overton, T. (2000). *Assessment in special education: An applied approach,* 3rd ed. New York: Merrill.

***Phi Delta Kappan* (1995).** Race, testing and I.Q., *77*(4), 265–328.

Roach, V. (1995). Supporting inclusion. *Phi Delta Kappan, 77,* 295–299.

Rothstein, L. F. (2000). *Special education law,* 3rd ed. New York: Longman.

CHAPTER 3

LESSON PLANNING AND ASSESSMENT OBJECTIVES

After reading this chapter, you will be able to:

- Define *curriculum, instruction, achievement, ability, educational objective,* and other basic terms
- Describe the main considerations in planning lessons
- Write a lesson plan that communicates purpose, process, and assessment strategy
- State educational objectives, differentiate well-stated from poorly stated objectives, and distinguish between and write higher-level and lower-level educational objectives
- Cite common errors in planning instruction
- Compare features of assessment used for planning and delivering instruction
- Suggest ways to improve the validity and reliability of assessment during instruction
- Discuss accommodations for students with disabilities

THINKING ABOUT TEACHING

What is the role of planning in teaching? What kind of planning do teachers do?

The purpose of schools is to educate students, but what does it mean to educate? To **educate** means to help students change in important and desirable ways. When teachers have helped students to read, identify parts of speech in a sentence, use the scientific method, or write a cohesive paragraph, they have helped students become educated. Viewing education as a process of helping students change leads to a fundamental question all teachers have to ask themselves: What do I want my students to know or be able to do following instruction that they did not know or do at the start of instruction? Education is the process of fostering these important and desired student changes.

Education is the process of helping to change students' knowledge and behavior in desired ways.

It is important to point out, however, that there is debate about the extent to which education should be conceived solely as a process of preplanned student behavior change. Some educators believe that unless students are engaged in the creation of their own educational programs, educators can become preoccupied with narrow outcomes. These educators suggest that it is important for teachers to build on a student's prior experience and to seek multiple, not necessarily predefined, outcomes from instruction. Despite the extent to which students' interests and educational desires help define learning outcomes, the primary function of education is helping students to change in desired ways.

A **curriculum** describes the skills, performances, knowledge, and attitudes students are expected to learn in school. The curriculum contains statements of desired student learning and descriptions of the materials that will be used to help students attain this learning. The methods and processes actually used to change students' behavior are called **instruction.** Lectures, discussions, worksheets, cooperative projects, and homework are but a few of the instructional techniques used to help students learn.

Achievement refers to school-based learning, while ability and aptitude refer to broader learning acquired mostly through nonschool sources such as parents and peer groups.

Students undergo many changes during their school years, and many sources besides the school contribute to these changes: maturation, peer groups, family, reading, and TV, among others. The term **achievement** is used to describe school-based learning, while terms like **ability** and **aptitude** are used to describe broader learning that stems from nonschool sources. Since the focus of schooling is to help students develop particular behaviors, habits, understandings, and processes, almost all of the formal tests that students take in school are intended to assess their achievement. The Friday spelling test, the unit test on chemical equations, the math test on the Pythagorean theorem, the delivery of an oral speech, the autobiography, and midterm and final examinations all should focus on assessing student achievement—that is, what they have learned of the things to which they were exposed in school.

The central concept in this chapter is that planning and assessment should be driven by a clear knowledge of desired objectives about what students will learn and master. Some have called this planning backwards, inasmuch as it starts by defining the intended results and then developing a plan for reaching those results (Wiggins and McTighe, 1998). Indeed they are correct; beginning by defining desired learning outcomes facilitates good instructional planning.

THE INSTRUCTIONAL PROCESS

The instructional process involves three interdependent steps: planning, delivering, and assessing.

The instructional process comprises three basic steps. The first is *planning instruction,* which includes identifying desired student learning outcomes, selecting materials to help students reach these outcomes, and organizing learning experiences into a coherent sequence that fosters student development. The second step involves *delivering instruction* to students, that is, helping them to change. The third step involves determining whether students have learned or achieved the desired outcomes, or *assessing student outcomes.* Notice that to carry out the instructional process the three steps should be aligned with one another. That is, the planned instruction should be logically related to the desired learning outcomes, the delivered instruction should focus on helping students achieve the learning outcomes, and the assessments should enable teachers to decide how well students have progressed toward achieving the learning outcomes.

Figure 3.1 shows these three steps and the relationships between them. Notice that the diagram is presented as a triangle rather than as a straight line. This indicates that the three steps are interrelated in a more

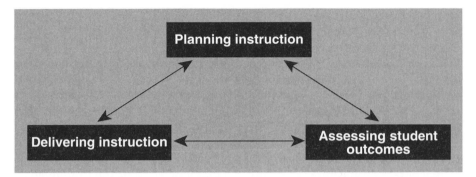

FIGURE 3.1
*Steps in the
Instructional Process*

complicated way than a simple one-two-three sequence. For example, in planning instruction, the teacher considers the characteristics of students and the resources and materials available to help attain desired changes. Similarly, the information gained at the time of student assessment is useful in assessing the effectiveness of the learning experiences in which students engage and the suitability of intended student outcomes. Thus, the three steps are interdependent pieces in the instructional process that can be aligned in different orders.

All three steps in the instructional process involve teacher decision making and assessment. Obviously, assessing student outcomes involves the collection and synthesis of formal information about how well students are learning or have learned. But the other two steps in the instructional process also depend on a teacher's assessment activities. For example, a teacher's planning decisions incorporate information about student readiness, appropriateness of instructional methods given students' characteristics, available instructional resources, materials, student culture, language, and other important characteristics obtained from early assessments. Similarly, during instruction the teacher is constantly "reading" the class to obtain information to help make decisions about lesson pace, reinforcement, interest, and comprehension. Thus, the entire instructional process depends on decisions that rely on assessment evidence of various kinds collected prior to, during, and following instruction.

All three steps in the instructional process involve assessment and teacher decision making.

The processes of planning and providing instruction are important activities for classroom teachers. Not only do they occupy a substantial amount of their time, but teachers define their teaching rewards in terms of their students' instructional successes. Teachers like to work with students, make a difference in their lives, and feel rewarded when they know that their instruction has helped a student develop new understanding, skills, or behaviors.

Teachers define their own success and rewards in terms of their students' learning.

INSTRUCTIONAL PLANNING

The true rewards of teaching are identified in terms of the impact that the teachers' instruction and mentoring has on students. Pride in teaching does not come from collecting lunch money, planning field trips, meeting the morning bus, and the many other semi-administrative tasks teachers perform. It comes from teachers' knowledge that they have helped students to do, think, or perform some things they otherwise would have been unable to do, think, or perform.

Teachers plan in order to modify the curriculum to fit the unique characteristics of their students and resources. To plan, teachers reflect on and integrate information about their students, the subject matter to be taught, the curriculum they are following, their own teaching experience, the resources available for instruction, the classroom environment, and other factors. Their reflection and integration of these factors leads to an instructional lesson plan. The plan helps teachers allocate instructional time, select appropriate activities, link individual lessons to the overall unit or curriculum, sequence activities in which students engage, set the pace of instruction, select the homework to be assigned, and identify techniques to assess student learning. Planning helps teachers in five basic ways:

1. Helping teachers feel empowered and giving them a sense of understanding and ownership over the teaching they plan.
2. Establishing a sense of purpose and subject matter focus.
3. Affording the chance to review and become familiar with the subject matter before actually beginning to teach it.
4. Ensuring that there are strategies in place to engage students in the topic of instruction and a framework to follow during instruction.
5. Linking daily lessons to broader goals, units, or curriculum topics.

Planning instruction is a context-dependent activity that includes consideration of students, teacher, and instructional materials.

Classrooms are complex environments that are informal rather than formal, ad hoc rather than linear, and ambiguous rather than certain. In such a world, some form of planning and organization is needed. A lesson that fails to take into account the needs and prior knowledge of the students or that poorly matches desired outcomes to instructional activities is doomed to failure. Similarly, a lesson that does not take into account the context in which it will be taught can also lead to difficulty.

Teachers have a great deal of control over many classroom features associated with lesson planning. For example, most teachers have control over the physical arrangement of the classroom, the rules and routines students are expected to follow, the interactions with students, the kind of instruction planned and the nature of its delivery, and the methods used to assess and grade students. However, there are important features

TABLE 3.1   COMPARISON OF TWO CLASSROOM CONTEXTS

Classroom A	Classroom B
22 students	34 students
Range of student abilities	Mainly low-ability students
Strong student self-control	Poor student self-control
Good prerequisite skills	Range of prerequisite skills
Intense parental interest	Moderate parental interest
10-year-old textbooks	New textbooks
Mandated district curriculum	Teacher-selected instructional topics
Poor school library	Excellent school library
Small classroom size	Large classroom size
Individual student desks	Students sit at four-person tables
Little colleague support	Strong colleague support

that teachers do not control. For example, most teachers have little control over the number and characteristics of the students in their classes, the size of their classroom, the quality of their instructional resources, and the state and district curriculum guidelines. In planning, teachers must arrange the factors they do control in response to the factors they do not.

Table 3.1 allows us an exercise similar to the one we did in Chapter 2, comparing two teachers' classroom situations. Once again, imagine that these classrooms are at the same grade level but in different schools. Suppose the teachers are each planning a lesson on the same topic. How might these different classroom characteristics influence the ways these two teachers plan instruction? What features are especially influential in developing teaching plans? Which characteristics would be advantageous to a teacher, and which ones might be disadvantageous? Do you think the teachers would construct identical instructional plans? In what ways might they differ? The following discussion examines in more detail how student and teacher characteristics, as well as instructional resources, can affect instructional planning.

Student Characteristics

Initial and extremely important considerations when planning instruction are the present status and needs of the students. What are they developmentally ready to learn? What topics have they mastered thus far in the subject area? What are their learning styles? What materials are available to help engage students in their learning? How well do they work in groups? What disabilities do they have and how are they accommodated?

What is the range of students' culture and language in a given classroom? The answers to these questions provide needed and valuable information about what and how to teach. Note that teachers obtain much of the information to answer these questions from their early assessments.

Planning in elementary school classrooms generally is more complex than planning in high school classrooms because the range of student characteristics within a class is often broader in lower grades. In addition, most elementary school teachers are responsible for planning instruction in many subjects, not just one or two as is typical at the high school level. However, although middle and high school teachers often teach multiple sections of the same course, the same lesson may not be effective for all of their classrooms. When planning instruction, both elementary and upper school teachers must take into account student readiness, behavior, and learning styles. The ebb and flow of classroom activities from small-group instruction to seatwork to large-group instruction and back again make consideration of student characteristics such as independence, work habits, and attention span very important. When the teacher is working with one reading or math group, seatwork for students not in that group must be aligned with their learning needs and allow them to work independently and quietly. Since teachers work with many different groups of students, sometimes within the same classroom and sometimes across multiple sections of a course, plans for each group differ according to the ability, prior achievement, needs, and socialization levels in the group. Planning is a complex and time-consuming task for teachers.

Planning is a complex and time-consuming task for teachers.

At the start of the school year, most teachers begin instruction by reviewing subject matter concepts and skills normally mastered in the prior grade or course. The information gained in such a review provides the most direct evidence about students' readiness and needs. It is especially important to assess readiness and needs in those subjects that are sequentially organized, such as mathematics, foreign languages, and reading. The structure of these subjects is such that concepts and ideas build on one another. For example, in order to do long division problems correctly, a fourth- or fifth-grader must be able to use the processes of addition, subtraction, regrouping, and multiplication. Thus, it would make little sense for a fifth-grade teacher whose students did not yet understand regrouping and multiplication to teach long division, even though it might be the normal focus of fifth-grade mathematics instruction.

In other subjects, such as social studies and English, the content is not as sequential and interdependent as in math, reading, and foreign languages. The "expanding horizons" focus of elementary school social studies texts, for example, moves from homes and neighborhoods to communities to regions of America to U.S. history to world history. For the most part, each year's text and content is distinct from that of prior or succeeding years. In this case, the teacher has more discretion in planning what to stress.

It is obvious that student characteristics such as disability, readiness, independence, and self-control should be taken into account in planning instructional activities. To ignore these factors would be irrational. However, it is very important to recognize that much of the needed information comes to teachers from their initial early assessments. Consequently, it is crucial that teachers strive to make their initial assessments as valid and reliable as possible.

Teacher Characteristics

Most beginning teachers do not take their own characteristics into account when planning instruction. However, subject matter knowledge, personality, and time and physical limitations are important factors in planning and delivering instruction. It is impossible for teachers to know everything about all the topics they teach. Nor can they be expected to keep abreast of all advances in subject matter knowledge or pedagogy. Consequently, the topics teachers choose to cover, the accuracy and up-to-dateness of their topical coverage, and their teaching methods all are influenced by their own knowledge limitations. Moreover, teachers' personalities often lead them to favor certain instructional techniques over others. While individual preferences are to be expected among teachers, it is important to understand that when carried to the extreme, they can result in an overly narrow repertoire of teaching methods. This has the potential to limit learning opportunities for those students who could learn better from other instructional techniques. Finally, since teaching is a rigorous, fatiguing activity, teachers should consider their own physical limitations when planning instruction. This caution is especially appropriate for beginning teachers, whose enthusiasm and lack of experience often lead them to overestimate what they can accomplish during a classroom period. A common complaint heard from college students during their first full-time classroom practicum is how mentally and physically draining a day in the classroom can be and how quickly time seems to pass when interacting with students.

When planning instruction, teachers should take their own characteristics and knowledge into account along with their students' characteristics and the time and resources available.

Instructional Resources

The instructional resources available to a teacher influence not only the nature of instruction but also the learning outcomes that are possible. The term *resources* is used here in its broadest sense to include available supplies, equipment, space, aides or volunteers, texts, and time. Each of these resources influences the nature of instruction and therefore the student achievements that can be pursued.

A second-grade teacher may wish to have his students construct felt picture book covers, but be unable to do so because the school cannot afford to provide the felt. A biology teacher may wish his or her class to learn about the internal organs of a frog by having each student perform a frog dissection. However, if the school has no biology laboratory and no dissecting equipment, the teacher must forgo this objective. In these and other ways, material resources matter.

Classroom aides or volunteers who read to students, work with small groups, or serve as "computer assistants" can free the classroom teacher to plan and pursue enrichment activities that might not have been possible otherwise. Resources of all kinds are important to consider when planning instruction.

Another resource that greatly influences what is planned, taught, and learned in classrooms is the textbook. More than any other single resource, the textbook determines instructional plans in many classrooms. A large part of students' learning time and a large part of the teacher's instructional time are focused on textbook use. The teacher's edition of most textbooks contains many resources to help teachers plan, deliver, and assess instruction. In addition, on the Internet teachers can find many lesson plans that have been developed and used by other teachers. While both the textbook and lesson plans developed by others can provide time-saving models, teachers should not abdicate their planning, teaching, and assessment decision-making responsibilities to the textbook or other teachers. To do so reduces the classroom teacher from a professional decision maker to a technician carrying out the instructional programs and plans of others. It is incumbent on all teachers to assess the status and needs of *their* students, the curriculum requirements of *their* state or community, and the resources available in *their* classrooms when planning instruction for their students. In the end, decisions about what to emphasize rest with the individual classroom teacher, who knows his or her students better than anyone else and who is in the best position to plan and carry out instruction that is suited to their needs.

To slavishly follow the lessons in a textbook is to abdicate instructional decision making.

A final important, though often overlooked, resource that greatly influences teacher planning is time. Because there is never enough time to teach students all the important skills and concepts in a subject area, teachers must carefully match their instructional time to their intended instructional outcomes. Each teacher's decisions about what content to stress or omit is based in part on the instructional time available. When a teacher skips a concept, unit, or chapter in a textbook, the teacher is saying, "All other things being equal, I prefer to spend my limited instructional time focusing on other topics and skills that I believe are more important."

While teachers make decisions about the allocation of instructional time daily, it is often in the last few weeks of the school year that these decisions become most apparent. The end of the school year always seems to arrive before all the planned topics can be taught. At this point, explicit decisions about how to allocate scarce time are made: "We must cover subtraction of fractions before the end of the year, but we can omit rate, time, and distance word problems." "If I don't finish parts of speech this year, next year's teacher will be upset. I'll take the time from the poetry unit to work on parts of speech." Time is a limited resource that

> **TABLE 3.2   AREAS TO CONSIDER WHEN PLANNING INSTRUCTION**
>
> | **Student Characteristics** | **Teacher Characteristics** | **Instructional Resources** |
> | --- | --- | --- |
> | Prior knowledge | Content knowledge | State curriculum standards |
> | Prerequisite skills and knowledge | Instructional method preferences | Time |
> | Work habits, socialization | Assessment preferences | Textbook materials |
> | Special learning needs | Physical limitations | Technology |
> | Learning styles | | Collegial and administrative support |
> | Cultural/language differences | | Other resources (space, aides, equipment) |
> | Disabilities | | |

has important consequences for planning instruction. Table 3.2 summarizes student, teacher, and instructional resources that should be considered while planning instruction.

THREE LEVELS OF TEACHING OBJECTIVES

In our everyday activities, objectives help us focus on what's important; they remind us of what we want to accomplish. Objectives in teaching describe the kinds of content, skills and behaviors teachers hope their students will develop through instruction.

Other names for objectives are learning targets, educational objectives, instructional objectives, behavioral objectives, student outcomes, and curriculum objectives, among others. If teachers don't identify their objectives, instruction and assessment will be purposeless.

Objectives are particularly crucial in teaching because teaching is an intentional and normative act. Teaching is intentional because teachers teach for a purpose; they want students to learn something as a result of teaching. Teaching is also normative because what teachers teach is viewed by them as being worthwhile for their students to learn.

Because teaching is both intentional and normative, it always is based on objectives. Normative teaching is concerned with selecting objectives that are worthwhile for students to learn. Intentional teaching is concerned with issues of how teachers will teach their objectives—what learning environments they will create and what methods they will use to help students learn the intended objectives. Although teachers' objectives may sometimes be implicit and fuzzy, it is best that objectives be explicit, clear, and measurable.

Objectives are important in developing lesson plans. Teachers cannot help students meet their objectives if they do not know what their objectives are.

There are three general levels of objectives: global, educational, and instructional, ranging from most broad to least broad.

Objectives can range from very general to very specific. Compare the following two objectives: "The student can add three one-digit numbers," and "The student will become mathematically literate." Clearly the former is more specific than the latter. Notice how different instructional time, learning activities, and range of assessments would be needed for the two objectives.

Depending on their specificity, objectives can be classified into one of three levels: global, educational, and instructional (Krathwohl and Payne, 1971). Note that regardless of the type or specificity, an objective should focus always on *student* learning and performance rather than on teacher actions or classroom activities.

Global objectives, often called "goals," are broad, complex student learning outcomes that require substantial time and instruction to accomplish. They are very general, encompassing a large number of more specific objectives. Examples include the following:

- The student will become a lifelong learner.
- The student will become mathematically literate.
- Students will learn to use their minds well, so that they may be prepared for responsible citizenship, further learning, and productive employment in our nation's economy.

Because they are broadly inclusive, global objectives are rarely used in classroom assessment unless they are broken down into more narrow objectives. Global objectives mainly provide a rallying cry that reflects what is important in education policy. The breadth encompassed in global objectives makes them difficult for teachers to use in planning classroom instruction. Narrower objectives must be identified to meet classroom needs.

A number of guidelines can improve planning instruction: knowing students' needs and strengths; being sure that the textbook includes all the important topics to be taught, including both lower-level and higher-level objectives; planning activities that fit students' needs and readiness; aligning objectives, instruction, and assessment; and being aware of one's own limits.

Educational objectives represent a middle level of abstraction. Here are several examples:

- The student can interpret different types of social data.
- The student can correctly solve addition problems containing two digits.
- The student distinguishes between facts and hypotheses.
- The student can read Spanish poetry aloud.

Educational objectives are more specific than global objectives. They are sufficiently narrow to help teachers plan and focus teaching, and sufficiently broad to indicate the richness of the objective and to suggest a range of possible student outcomes associated with the objective.

Instructional objectives are the most specific type of objective. Examples of instructional objectives include the following:

- The student can correctly punctuate sentences.
- Given five problems requiring the student to find the lowest common denominator of a fraction, the student can solve at least four of the problems.
- The student can list the names of the first five U.S. presidents.

TABLE 3.3   COMPARING THE THREE LEVELS OF TEACHING OBJECTIVES

Level of Objective	Global	Educational	Instructional
Scope	Broad	Intermediate	Narrow
Time to Accomplish	One or more years	Weeks or months	Hours or days
Function	Provide vision	Develop curriculum, plan instruction, define suitable assessments	Plan teaching activities, learning experiences, and assessment exercises
Examples of Breadth	The student will acquire competency of worldwide geography	The student will gain knowledge of devices and symbols in maps and charts	Given a map or chart, the student will correctly define 6 of the 8 representational devices and symbols on it
	The student will be aware of the roles of civics and government in the United States	The student will interpret various types of social data	The student can interpret bar graphs describing population density
	The student will know how to repair a variety of home problems	The student will use appropriate procedures to find solutions to electrical problems in the home	Given a home repair problem dealing with a malfunctioning lamp, the student will repair it

Instructional objectives focus teaching on relatively narrow topics of learning in a content area. These concrete objectives are used in planning daily lessons.

Table 3.3 illustrates the difference in degree of breadth among the three types of objectives and compares their purposes, scopes, and time frames. The distinctions among these three levels of objectives are far more than semantic. The level at which an objective is stated influences its use in planning, instructing, and assessing. For example, the perspectives of teachers planning instruction and assessment for a global objective such as "The student will become mathematically literate" are quite different from those of teachers planning instruction and assessment for an instructional objective such as "The student will write common fractions in their lowest terms." Thus, the level at which an objective is stated—global, educational, or instructional—has an impact on the manner in which processes such as planning, instructing, and assessing will be structured and carried out.

THREE DOMAINS OF OBJECTIVES

Classroom assessments cover cognitive, affective, and psychomotor behaviors.

By this point it should be clear that objectives are logically and closely tied to instruction and assessment. In addition to differing in terms of level, classroom objectives (and their related instruction and assessments) differ in terms of three general types of human behavior: the cognitive, affective, and psychomotor domains.

The Cognitive Domain

Cognitive assessments involve intellectual activities such as memorizing, interpreting, applying, problem solving, reasoning, analyzing, and thinking critically.

The most commonly taught and assessed educational objectives are those in the cognitive domain. The **cognitive domain** includes intellectual activities such as memorizing, interpreting, applying, problem solving, reasoning, analyzing, and thinking critically. Virtually all the tests that students take in school are intended to measure one or more of these cognitive activities. Teachers' instruction is usually focused on helping students attain cognitive mastery of some content or subject area. A weekly spelling test, a unit test in history, a worksheet on proper use of *lie* and *lay,* an essay on supply and demand, and an oral recitation of a poem all require cognitive behaviors. The Scholastic Assessment Test (SAT), the ACT, the written part of a state driver's test, an ability test, and standardized achievement tests such as the Iowa Test of Basic Skills and the Stanford, Metropolitan, Special Review Assessment (SRA), and California Achievement tests also are intended to assess students' cognitive behaviors.

In Chapter 1, Ms. Lopez was relying primarily on cognitive information about her students when she made the following decisions: assigned grades, moved Tamika from the middle to the high reading group, planned instruction, identified students for remedial work in basic skills, graded students' American government projects, and consulted last year's standardized test scores to find out whether she needed to review the rules of capitalization for the class. In each case, Ms. Lopez was assessing her students' thinking, reasoning, memory, or general intellectual behaviors.

Bloom's Taxonomy

The many cognitive processes have been organized into six general categories. This organization is presented in the *Taxonomy of Educational Objectives: Book 1, Cognitive Domain* (Bloom et al., 1956). Commonly referred to as Bloom's Taxonomy, or the Cognitive Taxonomy, it is widely used by teachers to describe and state cognitive objectives (see Appendix B). Bloom's cognitive taxonomy is organized into six levels, with each successive level representing a more complex type of cognitive process. Starting with the simplest and moving to the most complex, the six cognitive taxonomic processes are knowledge, comprehension, application,

TABLE 3.4   TYPES OF COGNITIVE PROCESS IDENTIFIED IN BLOOM'S TAXONOMY

Taxonomy Level	Related Verbs	General Description
1. Knowledge	Remember, recall, identify, recognize	Memorizing facts
2. Comprehension	Translate, rephrase, restate, interpret, describe, explain	Explaining in one's own words
3. Application	Apply, execute, solve, implement	Solving new problems
4. Analysis	Break down, categorize, distinguish, compare	Breaking into parts and identifying relationships
5. Synthesis	Integrate, organize, relate, combine, construct, design	Combining elements into a whole
6. Evaluation	Judge, assess, value, appraise	Judging quality or worth

analysis, synthesis, and evaluation (see Table 3.4). Although the word "knowledge" or "know" is often used when describing the skills students have developed (e.g., Steven knows how to write a persuasive essay, Megan knows how to read with expression, etc.), in Bloom's Taxonomy "knowledge" refers only to memorizing, recognizing, and recalling information. The table provides some action verbs indicative of each cognitive process of Bloom's Taxonomy along with a general description of each process. Below are sample objectives derived from Bloom's Taxonomy with the taxonomic category shown in parentheses:

- The students can name the first three presidents of the United States. (knowledge; recall)
- The students can identify punctuation marks in a sentence. (knowledge; recognize)
- The students can translate French sentences into English. (comprehension; state in your own words)
- The students can punctuate correctly in a writing task. (application; solve a problem)
- The students can add previously unseen proper fractions. (application; solve a new problem)
- The students can distinguish facts from opinions in eight newspaper editorials. (analysis; categorize)
- The students can categorize paintings by their historical periods. (analysis; identify relationships)
- The students can integrate information from the science experiment into a lab report. (synthesis; organize into a whole)
- The students can judge the quality of varied persuasive essays. (evaluation; judge quality)

TABLE 3.5   REVISED COGNITIVE PROCESSES AND DEPTHS OF KNOWLEDGE

Depth of Knowledge	Revised Cognitive Process					
	Remembering	Understanding	Applying	Analyzing	Evaluating	Creating
Factual	Listing	Summarizing	Classifying	Ordering	Ranking	Combining
Conceptual	Describing	Interpreting	Experimenting	Explaining	Assessing	Planning
Procedural	Tabulating	Predicting	Calculating	Differentiating	Concluding	Composing
Meta-cognitive	Determining appropriate use	Executing	Constructing	Achieving	Acting	Actualizing

Source: Anderson et al. (2001).

More recently, a former student of Bloom developed a revised version of the cognitive taxonomy (Anderson, 2001). The revised taxonomy differs in two important ways. First, it focuses on actions rather than skills. The six skills comprised in the revised taxonomy are remembering, understanding, applying, analyzing, evaluating, and creating.

Second, the taxonomy was expanded from one dimension to two, enabling educators to focus on both cognitive actions and depth of knowledge. The levels of knowledge include factual knowledge, conceptual knowledge, procedural knowledge, and meta-cognitive knowledge. Table 3.5 displays the revised cognitive actions, the depths of knowledge, and actions students might take to demonstrate depth of knowledge for cognitive action. Others have developed different versions of the cognitive taxonomy. As an example, the NorthWest Regional Labs offered a condensed version of Bloom's taxonomy that included recall, analysis, comparison, inference, and evaluation. A third revision, known as the Marzano Model, includes eight categories of cognitive skills: focusing, information gathering, remembering, organizing, analyzing, generating, integrating, and evaluating (Marzano, Pickering, and McTighe, 1993).

Lower-level cognitive behaviors involve rote memorization and recall; cognitive behaviors that involve more than rote memorization or recall are termed higher-level cognitive behaviors.

Although cognitive taxonomies can differ in the particular levels or categories they include, their most important function is to remind teachers of the distinction between higher- and lower-level thinking behaviors. In general, any cognitive behavior that involves more than rote memorization or recall is considered to be a **higher-level cognitive behavior.** Thus, the knowledge level of Bloom's Taxonomy represents **lower-level cognitive behavior,** since the focus is on memorization and recall. All succeeding levels in these taxonomies represent higher-level behaviors that call for students to carry out thinking and reasoning processes more complex than memorization. There is a growing emphasis in classroom instruction and assessment to focus on teaching students higher-order thinking skills that go beyond rote memorization.

The Affective Domain

A second behavior domain is the affective domain. The **affective domain** involves feelings, attitudes, interests, preferences, values, and emotions. Emotional stability, motivation, trustworthiness, self-control, and personality are all examples of affective characteristics. Although affective behaviors are rarely assessed formally in schools and classrooms, teachers constantly assess affective behaviors informally, especially when sizing up students. Teachers need to know who can be trusted to work unsupervised and who cannot, who can maintain self-control when the teacher has to leave the classroom and who cannot, who needs to be encouraged to speak in class and who does not, who is interested in science but not in social studies, and who needs to be prodded to start class work and who does not. Most classroom teachers can describe their students' affective characteristics based on their informal observations and interactions with the students.

Affective assessments involve feelings, attitudes, interests, preferences, values, and emotions.

Ms. Lopez was relying mainly on her assessment of students' affective behaviors when she selected Rosa, not Sarah, to deliver a note to the school principal; when she changed the class seating plan to separate Jamar and Ramon, who were unable to remain focused on the learning activities when seated together; when she switched instruction from discussion to seatwork to help avoid distractions; and when she selected students to work together on a cooperative assignment.

Teachers rarely make formal affective assessments but are constantly making them informally.

There is no single, widely accepted taxonomy of affective behaviors, although the taxonomy prepared by Krathwohl and associates (Krathwohl, Bloom, and Masia, 1964) is the most commonly referred to and used. In general, affective taxonomies are all based on the degree of a person's involvement in an activity or idea. The lower levels of affective taxonomies contain low-involvement behaviors such as paying attention, while the higher levels contain high-involvement behavior characterized by strong interest, commitment, and valuing.

The Psychomotor Domain

A third behavior domain is the psychomotor domain. The **psychomotor domain** includes physical and manipulative activities. Holding a pencil, using a mouse, keyboarding, setting up laboratory equipment, building a bookcase, playing a musical instrument, shooting a basketball, buttoning a jacket, and brushing teeth are examples of activities that involve psychomotor behaviors. Although psychomotor behaviors are present and important at all levels of schooling, they are especially stressed in the preschool and elementary grades, where tasks like holding a pencil, opening a locker, and buttoning or zipping clothing are important to master. Similarly, with certain special needs students, a major part of education involves "self-help" skills such as getting dressed, attending to personal hygiene, and preparing food, all of which are psychomotor accomplishments.

Psychomotor assessments involve physical and manipulative behaviors.

Psychomotor assessments are particularly important with very young or some special needs students.

There are a number of psychomotor behavior domain taxonomies (Hannah and Michaels, 1977; Harrow, 1972). As with the affective domain, however, no single taxonomy has become widely accepted and used by the majority of teachers and schools. The organization of psychomotor taxonomies typically ranges from a student showing a readiness to perform a psychomotor task, to the student using trial and error to learn a task, to the student actually carrying out the task on his or her own.

Ms. Lopez was concerned with her students' psychomotor behavior when she moved Claudia to the front of the room so that she could see the chalkboard better, sent Antonio to the school nurse because he felt ill, and referred Aaron to the Special Education Department because he continued to exhibit poor gross motor skills. In each case, Ms. Lopez's decision was based on assessment evidence that pertained to some aspect of a student's physical or motor behavior.

As noted previously, early assessments encompass the cognitive, affective, and psychomotor domains because teachers are interested in knowing about their students' intellectual, attitudinal, and physical characteristics. Notice, however, that different assessment approaches characterize the different behavior domains. For example, the cognitive domain is most likely to be assessed using paper-and-pencil tests or various kinds of oral questioning. Behaviors in the affective domain are most likely to be assessed by observation or questionnaires—for example, which subject do you prefer, English or chemistry? Which do you believe provides more valid information about a student's development throughout the year: classroom grades, a portfolio containing a student's best work, or performance on an end-of-year test? Psychomotor behaviors are generally assessed by observing students carrying out the desired physical activity.

STATING AND CONSTRUCTING OBJECTIVES

There are many ways to state objectives, but not all of them convey clearly what students are to learn from instruction. Ensuring clarity requires being aware of what makes an objective statement complete.

Essential Elements of the Statement

Consider the following three objectives:

1. Students will learn to use their minds well, so that they may be prepared for responsible citizenship, further learning, and productive employment in our nation's economy.

2. The student can read Spanish-language poetry.

3. The student can correctly punctuate sentences.

Although they represent a global, educational, and instructional objective, respectively, these objectives have common characteristics. First, all are stated in terms of what the student is to learn from instruction. Objectives describe *student learning,* not teacher learning or the activities the teacher or students engage in during instruction. Although activities are an important aspect of lesson planning and must be described, *instructional activities are not objectives.* Second, each objective specifies the content or skill that a student is expected to develop and describes how students are expected to use or apply that content or skill. The content in the three objectives above is, respectively, "citizenship," "Spanish-language poetry," and "sentences." How students are expected to apply that content is embodied in the terms "develop," "read," and "punctuate."

Another way to think about an objective's content and process is in terms of nouns and verbs. The content is the noun, and the process or skill is the verb. Thus, at a minimum, an objective is stated in terms of the content (noun) and process (verb) the student is expected to learn. Third, notice that the verbs in the objectives we have examined (e.g., summarize, add, remember, categorize, explain) do *not* match Bloom's generic taxonomy names (e.g., knowledge, comprehension, analysis). Instead, the objectives are described using narrower, more specific verbs. These more specific and observable cognitive verbs are preferred over the generic taxonomy names because they more clearly indicate the particular process (verb) the students will be expected to carry out. Table 3.6 provides a

TABLE 3.6   EXAMPLES OF TERMS USED TO WRITE EDUCATIONAL OBJECTIVES FOR EACH CATEGORY OF BLOOM'S TAXONOMY

Knowledge	Comprehension	Application	Analysis	Synthesis	Evaluation
count	classify	compute	break down	arrange	appraise
define	compare	construct	diagram	combine	conclude
identify	contrast	demonstrate	differentiate	compile	criticize
label	convert	illustrate	discriminate	create	critique
list	discuss	solve	outline	design	grade
match	distinguish		separate	formulate	judge
name	estimate		subdivide	generalize	recommend
quote	explain			generate	support
recite	generalize			group	
repeat	give examples			integrate	
reproduce	infer			organize	
select	interpret			relate	
state	paraphrase			summarize	
	rewrite				
	summarize				
	translate				

TABLE 3.7   SAMPLE STATEMENTS OF POOR EDUCATIONAL OBJECTIVES

1. The Civil War
2. American government
3. The laws of motion
4. Analyze
5. Understand
6. Appreciate
7. Worthy use of leisure time
8. Pursue lifelong learning
9. Become a good citizen

number of these more *precise verbs* to use in stating clear objectives for each category of Bloom's Taxonomy.

It is important to be precise when defining instructional objectives. Precise instructional objectives help teachers determine the appropriateness of a potential instructional activity given the objectives of the lesson. Precision also helps teachers develop assessment activities that are aligned with the intended outcomes of instruction.

Developing Complete and Precise Statements

olc
CHAPTER CASE STUDY
Visit the text Online Learning Center to read the case of Therese Carmen, a first-grade teacher in her second year of teaching. Therese is presented with a new districtwide science curriculum that she finds unteachable.
www.mhhe.com/ russell7e

Examine the sample objectives in Table 3.7 and consider their usefulness in helping a teacher plan and guide instruction and assessment. Remember, the intent of an objective is to clearly identify what students are expected to learn in order to (1) communicate to others the purpose of instruction, (2) help teachers select appropriate instructional methods and materials, and (3) help plan assessments that will allow teachers to decide whether students have learned desired content and skills that are the focus of instruction.

In Table 3.7, objectives 1, 2, and 3 all have the same deficiency. Each describes a body of content that will be covered in instruction, but each omits information about what the students will be expected to do with that content. Will they be expected to identify causes of the war, match generals to battles, cite strengths and weaknesses of the two sides, or explain in their own words why Gettysburg was the turning point of the war? What should students know or understand about American government and the laws of motion? Without including information about what students are to know or do about the Civil War, American government, or the laws of motion, it is hard to select appropriate instructional materials, activities, and assessment techniques. For example, it will make a difference in instruction and assessment if students have to match generals to battles (teach recall and assess with a matching item) or explain in their own words why Gettysburg was the turning point of the war (teach interpretation and assess with an open-ended question).

Objectives 4, 5, and 6—analyze, understand, and appreciate—provide no reference to content matter. These statements prompt the question: Analyze, understand, and appreciate what? Just as a content description by itself lacks clarity because it does not include a desired student performance, so too does a behavior by itself lack clarity if there is no reference to a targeted body of content.

There is an additional problem in objectives 4, 5, and 6. Words like *analyze, understand,* and *appreciate* are themselves nonspecific. They can be interpreted in many different ways and hence do not clearly convey what students will learn. For example, one teacher might interpret the objective "understanding the basic features of a society" to mean that students will be able to explain the features in their own words. Another teacher might interpret the same objective to mean that students will give a real-life example of the social features studied. A third teacher might want students to distinguish between correct and incorrect applications of features. Although each teacher taught "understanding the basic features of a society," each would teach and assess completely different outcomes. Such misunderstandings can be avoided if teachers describe their educational objectives in terms of the actual behaviors or skills they expect their students to perform after instruction. For example, students can explain features in their own words, give real-life examples of the features, or distinguish correct from incorrect applications of the features. This level of specificity distinguishes clearly the different interpretations of *understand.*

Objectives 7, 8, and 9 are too general and complicated to be achieved by students in a single subject area or grade level. They are, as noted previously, goals. Not only do these outcomes take years to develop, but their generality provides the classroom teacher with little guidance regarding the activities and materials that could be used to attain them. Broad goals such as these must be narrowed by the classroom teacher before they can be used to instruct and assess students.

In stating instructional objectives, it is better to clearly describe the behavior the student will perform than to use more general, ambiguous terms that are open to many different interpretations. Thus, it is better to say *explains* the importance of conserving natural resources than to say *realizes* the importance of conserving natural resources; better to say *translates* Spanish sentences into English than to say *understands* Spanish sentences; better to say *can differentiate* subjects and predicates than to say *knows* about subjects and predicates; better to say *states* three differences between good and bad art than to say *appreciates* art. In each example, the first statement describes a student behavior that can be observed, instructed, and assessed, while the second uses less clear, unobservable, and ambiguous terms. Being precise about what students are expected to

Well-written instructional objectives should clearly specify what students are to learn and how they are to demonstrate that learning.

learn and aligning these expectations with the focus of instruction and assessment are necessary for making valid decisions about the effectiveness of instruction and the extent to which students reach the instructional objectives.

Some Examples of Well-Stated Objectives

The basic requirements for well-stated instructional objectives are that they (1) describe a student behavior that should result from instruction; (2) state the behavior in terms that can be observed and assessed; and (3) indicate the content on which the behavior will be performed. A simple model for preparing instructional objectives is "the students can" (observable behavior) (content). Here are examples of well-stated instructional objectives:

- The students can list three causes of the Civil War.
- The students can solve word problems requiring the sum of two numbers.
- The students can write a correctly formatted and punctuated business letter.
- The students can translate a French paragraph into English.
- The students can count to 20 aloud.
- The students can list three differences between the climates of Canada and Mexico.
- The students can write balanced chemical equations.
- The students can state the main idea of short stories.
- The students can explain the water cycle in their own words.

Notice how these objectives specify the outcome of the intended student learning. Based on the intended outcome, the teacher can then identify suitable instructional activities and materials that will help students attain the objective. In addition, these objectives clarify the skills and knowledge that should be the focus of assessment during and following instruction.

Other information can be added to elaborate an objective. For example, some teachers wish to include information in their objectives about the conditions of student performance and about how well the student must perform the objective in order to master it. Such extended objectives would be written as follows:

- Given 10 word problems requiring the sum of two numbers, the students can solve at least 8 correctly.
- Given a diagram of the water cycle, the students can explain in their own words what the water cycle is with fewer than two errors.
- Given a French paragraph of less than 20 lines and a dictionary, the students can translate the paragraph into English in 5 minutes with fewer than six errors.

Extended objectives provide more details about the conditions under which the behavior must be performed and the level of performance the student must show. Extended objectives take more time to prepare than their simpler counterparts and are sometimes difficult to state prior to the start of instruction. However, extended objectives aid in the development of assessment activities since the conditions and level of performance are clearly defined. Despite this advantage, the simpler model suffices in most instructional situations. Key Assessment Tools 3.1 is a brief reminder of criteria for successful objectives.

Extended objectives provide additional details about the conditions under which students must demonstrate their learning and the level of performance they must show.

Key Assessment Tools 3.1

CRITERIA FOR SUCCESSFUL OBJECTIVES

1. The objectives have clear answers.
2. The objectives represent important aspects of a lesson or chapter.
3. The objectives center on a verb that specifies student performance.
4. The objectives can be fulfilled in a reasonable amount of time.

Questions Often Asked about Instructional Objectives

1. Is it necessary to write down objectives? Beginning teachers and students in a teaching practicum usually are required to write lesson objectives. Even if you are an experienced teacher, listing your objectives reminds you to focus on what students are expected to get out of instruction, not just what your teaching activities will be. Annual assessment of existing objectives is an important part of any teacher's classroom assessment responsibilities, because each year students and curriculum change.

2. What are higher-level objectives? Cognitive behaviors can be divided into lower-level ones, such as memorizing and recalling information, and higher-level ones, which require more complex thinking behaviors. Higher-level behaviors, or higher-order thinking skills, include activities such as analyzing information, applying information and rules to solve new problems, comparing and contrasting objects or ideas, and synthesizing disparate pieces of information into a single, organized idea. In the following examples, the lower-level objective calls only for memorization and recall, while the higher-level objective calls for a more complex behavior.

Higher-level objectives include cognitive activities such as analysis, application, synthesis, and evaluation. These take longer to learn and evaluate than lower-level objectives, which involve rote memorization.

Lower level: The student can write a definition of each vocabulary word.
Higher level: The student can write sentences using each vocabulary word correctly.

Lower level: The student can match quotes from a short story to the characters who said them.

Higher level: The student can contrast the motives of the protagonist and the antagonist in a short story.

Lower level: The student can write the formula for the Pythagorean theorem.

Higher level: The student can use the Pythagorean theorem to solve word problems involving the length of ladders needed by the fire department.

All teachers should be aware of the difference between lower- and higher-level thinking skills and should strive to incorporate some higher-level objectives in their plans and instruction.

3. *How many objectives should I state in a subject area?* The answer to this question depends in part on the time frame being considered and the specificity of the objectives: the longer the period of instruction and the more specific the objectives, the more objectives that can be stated with expectation for students to attain. In general, there may be many instructional objectives and fewer educational objectives. Also, higher-level objectives usually take longer to teach and learn, so fewer of them can be taught in a given instructional period; it takes longer to teach students to interpret graphs than to memorize a formula. Teachers who have hundreds of objectives for the year's instruction either are expecting too much of themselves and their students or are stating their objectives too narrowly. On the other hand, teachers who have only five objectives for the school year are either underestimating their students or stating their objectives too broadly.

Because instructional objectives are written before instruction begins, teachers must be ready to deviate from them when necessary.

4. *Are there any cautions I should keep in mind regarding objectives?* Objectives are usually stated before instruction actually begins and are meant to guide both instruction and assessment. However, objectives are not meant to be followed slavishly when circumstances suggest the need for adjustments. Because objectives are written before instruction starts and because it is difficult to anticipate the flow of classroom activities during instruction, teachers must exercise discretion regarding how closely they will follow the objectives they stated prior to the start of actual instruction.

LESSON PLANS

Key Assessment Tools 3.2 shows the components of a lesson plan. Once relevant information about the students, the teacher, and the instructional resources is identified, this information must be synthesized into a set of instructional plans. When planning, teachers try to visualize themselves teaching, mentally viewing and rehearsing the learning activities they contemplate using in the classroom. In a sense, a lesson plan serves as the screenplay for what will occur in the classroom and includes elements

> ## Key Assessment Tools 3.2
> ### COMPONENTS OF A LESSON PLAN
>
> **Educational objectives**—also called "targets" by some: Description of the things students are to learn from instruction: what students should be able to do after instruction (e.g., the students can write a summary of a story, the students can differentiate adverbs from adjectives in a given passage).
>
> **Materials:** Description of the resources, materials, and apparatus needed to carry out the lesson (e.g., overhead projector, clay, map of the United States, Bunsen burners, video on the civil rights movement).
>
> **Teaching activities and strategies:** Description of the things that will take place during instruction; often includes factors such as determining student readiness, identifying how the lesson will start, reviewing prior lessons, providing advanced organizers, identifying specific instructional techniques to be used (e.g., discussion, lecture, silent reading, demonstrations, seatwork, game, cooperative activities) specifying the sequence of techniques, providing students practice, and ending the lesson.
>
> **Assessment:** Description of how student learning from the lesson will be assessed (e.g., homework assignment, oral questions, essay).

such as the objectives for the lesson, the materials needed, the planned activities, and methods for assessing student progress during the lesson as well as their achievement following the lesson. This mental dress rehearsal provides an opportunity for teachers to anticipate problems that may arise during a lesson and to incorporate strategies that will help provide direction to instruction.

Many Instructional Approaches

There are many different instructional approaches that teachers can and do use when helping students learn, such as Madeline Hunter's lesson design cycle model (Hunter, 1982), cooperative learning models (Slavin, 2003), and, more recently, the work of Howard Gardner on multiple intelligences (Gardner, 1995). Gardner's approach divides intellectual or thinking abilities into seven distinct kinds of intelligence:

1. Linguistic (using words).
2. Logical/mathematical (using reasoning).
3. Spatial (using images and pictures).
4. Musical (using rhythms).
5. Interpersonal (using interpersonal interactions).
6. Intrapersonal (using meditation or planning).
7. Body/kinesthetic (using physical activities).

Different methods of instruction lead to different forms of instruction and assessment. Teachers must be able to teach students in more than one way.

Employing Gardner's approach to multiple intelligences—or any other approach to learning—influences the objectives of instruction and the activities employed to help students attain those objectives. For example, Gardner would argue that his approach demands that teachers teach a broader range of outcomes using a broader range of styles that engage students in different multiple intelligences. While simultaneously helping students develop each of the seven multiple intelligences may be very difficult, Gardner's theory reminds teachers that there is more than one way for all students to learn and be assessed. How might instruction and assessment based on a cooperative learning approach differ from instruction and assessment in a multiple-intelligences approach? Different methods often lead to different instructional strategies and different outcomes (Wiggins and McTighe, 1998).

Planning Formative and Summative Assessment Activities

When planning assessment activities for a lesson or series of lessons, there is a tendency to focus on summative assessment rather than on formative assessment. Summative assessment activities, such as taking a quiz or test, completing homework or worksheets, or producing an essay or project, are often included in the assessment section of a lesson plan. When the skills and knowledge required to perform well on these activities are aligned with the objectives of the lesson and the instruction experienced by students, these summative assessment activities provide useful information about what students know and are able to do following instruction. While it is important for teachers to examine student achievement following instruction, it is equally important, if not more so, that they collect and use information about student learning while instruction is occurring. This formative assessment information allows teachers to modify instructional activities and alter the pace of instruction to better meet students' needs.

During instruction, formative assessment strategies include activities such as directly questioning students during full class discussions, questioning students individually during small-group or individual learning activities, circling among students to observe them working on an activity, asking students to share preliminary work with the teacher or the whole class, observing whether students are on-task, and reviewing homework, products developed during class time, or reports generated by computer-based educational software to identify problems or misconceptions that students may be developing. Each of these activities allows teachers to generate a snapshot of student learning. Depending on what the snapshot reveals about an individual student, a group of students, or the whole class, the teacher may opt to proceed with the lesson as planned or modify the lesson to address a need that has emerged.

Although many of these formative assessment activities occur naturally in the classroom, it is important for teachers to consider how information will be collected about student learning as it develops so that formative assessment activities are purposefully built into a lesson. Planning for formative assessment activities also provides a teacher with an opportunity to anticipate the types of problems and misconceptions that may emerge during the lesson and to develop formative assessment activities that are sensitive to these problems and misconceptions. When creating a lesson plan, teachers should develop and articulate strategies and activities for both formative and summative assessment decisions.

Writing a Plan

A common misconception, especially on the part of pre-service teachers, is that there is only one way to develop a daily lesson plan. But there is no single way (i.e., one "correct" format) to write a lesson plan. The format of a lesson plan is largely determined by the purpose of the lesson. In some instances, it may be more appropriate to focus on your behavior as well as that of the students; other times, you may decide that the focus of the lesson should be entirely on what the students will be doing. The detailed format of a lesson plan is not something that can be determined by someone who is not familiar with your classroom and teaching style. You must find a format that works for you and your style of planning and teaching.

There is no one correct method of writing a lesson plan.

Even though they are detailed, lesson plans are not written in stone and do allow for flexibility. Lesson plans can appear rigid if they are developed, and ultimately followed, as if they were scripts. Remember that lesson plans are guides; their purpose is to *direct* your instruction, not *dictate* your instruction. They are meant to provide direction, while at the same time allowing you to act as a professional, making appropriate decisions and adjustments as you proceed through a lesson.

The key is always that the lesson plan is written in conscious awareness of the instructional objective(s).

TEXTBOOK OBJECTIVES AND ASSESSMENTS

Modern textbooks and their accompanying teacher aids provide a great deal of information to help teachers plan, deliver, and assess their instruction. The richest and most used source of information is the teacher's edition of the textbook. Figure 3.2 illustrates the range of resources found in the teacher's editions of most textbooks. While not every textbook or instructional package provides every one of the resources listed in the figure, at the very least, one can count on finding objectives, teaching suggestions, instructional activities, and assessment instruments. If you have

FIGURE 3.2
*Common
Instructional
Resources in
Teacher's
Editions of
Textbooks*

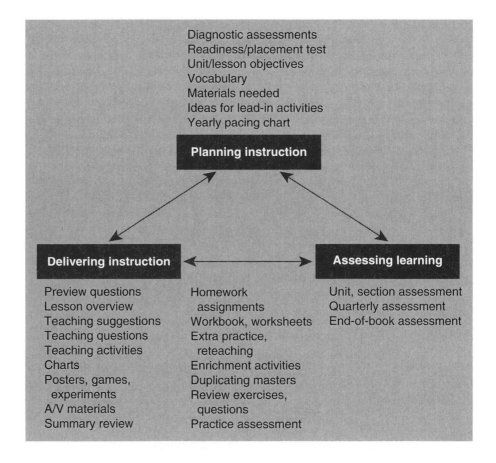

Diagnostic assessments
Readiness/placement test
Unit/lesson objectives
Vocabulary
Materials needed
Ideas for lead-in activities
Yearly pacing chart

Planning instruction

Delivering instruction   **Assessing learning**

Preview questions	Homework	Unit, section assessment
Lesson overview	assignments	Quarterly assessment
Teaching suggestions	Workbook, worksheets	End-of-book assessment
Teaching questions	Extra practice,	
Teaching activities	reteaching	
Charts	Enrichment activities	
Posters, games,	Duplicating masters	
experiments	Review exercises,	
A/V materials	questions	
Summary review	Practice assessment	

never seen a teacher's edition of a textbook or the resources that accompany it, visit the curriculum library of a local school to examine some. Review a number of teacher's editions, and compare the objectives and resources provided for the teacher's planning, teaching, and assessment. Pay special attention to the introductory sections of the teacher's edition, which describe the resources and materials provided.

Evaluating Textbook Objectives and Lesson Plans

Textbook objectives and questions can be useful to teachers in planning instruction, but they are not a substitute for the teacher's own careful planning of objectives, instruction, and assessment.

The objectives and other resources that accompany textbooks can be very useful to the classroom teacher—so useful that a teacher might be tempted to rely exclusively on them. To do so, however, is to abdicate one's decision-making responsibilities, which require a teacher to carefully assess the adequacy of the textbook objectives and other materials relative to student needs and resources available in the classroom. In addition, critics of textbooks assert that many textbooks are too long and at

the same time superficial and poorly organized. Strictly following a
textbook to determine the objectives of instruction may lead to lessons
that attempt to cover too much information in a very short period of time
and that do not connect well to other lessons. Some critics also argue that
basing instructional objectives solely on a textbook tends to steer students toward accepting one authority and one point of view (Daniels and
Zemelman, 2004).

Regardless of the merits of an individual textbook, textbook authors
cannot take the status, needs, readiness, and resources of all teachers and
classes into account when stating objectives. Instead they offer objectives
and materials that they think most teachers would agree with and accept.
It is the responsibility of all classroom teachers to assess the suitability
of the textbook objectives and materials for their own particular situations. Blindly following the suggestions in the teacher's textbook can
undermine the teacher's responsibility to determine objectives and
instructional activities that are well matched to the needs of students.

Textbook authors target the majority; teachers must assess the texts themselves to determine whether they meet their students' needs.

Teachers should screen textbook objectives using three criteria: (1)
Are the objectives and text materials clearly stated? (2) Are they suitable for students in this particular classroom? (3) Do they exhaust the
kinds of objectives and activities these students should be exposed to?
If the text material appears useful after these criteria have been applied,
a teacher may use the text to help focus instruction and assess student
learning.

The first criterion examines the way objectives and lesson plans are
stated. Do they contain a clear description of the process and content
knowledge that students will learn and the instructional activities that
support learning? Most, though not all, textbook objectives do provide a
clear description of the desired process and content. In the event that the
author's objectives are vague and ambiguous, the teacher must define
these terms, recognizing that his or her definition may differ from the
author's and thus may not be reflected in the instructional suggestions
and materials that accompany the text.

The second criterion examines appropriateness for the particular students in a teacher's class. When teachers develop their own objectives
and plans, they take into account the status, needs, and readiness of
the students. Not to do so is to risk irrelevant instruction. Textbook
authors, however, can only state a single set of objectives and plans for
all the classes and students who will use the book. Often, these objectives and plans are more suitable for some classes than for others. Consequently, teachers must ask, "Do my students have the prerequisites
needed to master the textbook objectives? Can they be taught these
objectives in a reasonable amount of time? Will the lesson activities
interest them? Do the lesson activities pertain to all the important
objectives in the unit?"

The final criterion examines completeness. Do the textbook objectives exhaust the important outcomes students should learn? Lesson

TABLE 3.8   ADVANTAGES AND DISADVANTAGES OF TEXTBOOK OBJECTIVES
AND LESSON PLANS

Advantages	Disadvantages
Convenient, readily available objectives and plans	Designed for teachers and students in general, not necessarily for a given teacher or class
Can save valuable time in planning	
Provide an integrated set of objectives, plans, activities, and assessments	Heavy emphasis on lower-level objectives and activities
	Lesson activities tend to be didactic and teacher-led
Contain many ancillary materials for planning, instructing, and assessing	If accepted uncritically, can lead to inappropriate instruction for students

plans in textbooks tend to emphasize structured, didactic methods in which the teacher either tells students things or elicits brief replies to teacher questions. Lessons using such objectives are easier to devise and present than more complex ones in which students engage in cooperative or hands-on activities. Relatively few textbook objectives call for synthesis or analysis of ideas, themes, or topics. Although teachers commonly omit topics from a text when teaching, they rarely introduce new topics that are not in the text. If teachers wish to include or emphasize higher-level objectives in their instruction, they may be forced to break this pattern and introduce additional objectives that round out student learning. Table 3.8 summarizes the advantages and disadvantages of textbook objectives and lesson plans. Key Assessment Tools 3.3 presents factors to consider when examining textbook objectives and lesson plans.

Evaluating Textbook Assessment Instruments

Textbooks furnish ready-made instruments for assessing the objectives stressed in the textbook. The tests and quizzes provided by textbooks can save classroom teachers much time. However, before using these tests, teachers should consider the criteria that allow a teacher to use a textbook or teacher-made test with confidence. The basic concern is whether the items on the test align with the instructional objectives of the actual lessons and the instruction experienced by students.

Regardless of whether a teacher is constructing his or her own test or judging the adequacy of a textbook test, the same basic validity issue

---

Key Assessment Tools 3.3

BASIC FACTORS TO CONSIDER WHEN EXAMINING TEXTBOOK OBJECTIVES AND LESSON PLANS

Textbook Objectives

1. **Clarity:** Are objectives clearly stated, especially the process and knowledge?

2. **Comprehensiveness:** Do the objectives include most learner outcomes for this topic?

3. **Level:** Do the objectives include both higher- and lower-level thinking behaviors?

4. **Prerequisites:** Do students have the prerequisite skills needed to master the objectives?

5. **Time:** Can students reasonably be expected to master the objectives in the time available for instruction?

Lesson Plans

1. **Pertinence:** Do plans help foster the stated objectives?

2. **Level:** Do plans include activities for fostering both higher- and lower-level objectives?

3. **Realism:** Are plans realistic given student ability, learning style, reading level, attention span, and so on?

4. **Resources:** Are the resources and materials needed to implement plans and activities available?

5. **Follow-up:** Are follow-up materials (e.g., worksheets, enrichment exercises, and reviews) related to the objectives, and do they reinforce lesson plans and activities?

---

must be considered: Are the items on the test aligned with the instruction provided to students? The more a teacher alters and reshapes the textbook curriculum, the less valid its accompanying tests become. As one teacher put it, "The textbook tests look good and can be time-savers, but they often don't test exactly what I've been doing in the classroom. Every time I change what I do from what the text suggests I do, and every time I leave out a lesson or section of the text from my instruction, I have to look at the text test carefully to make sure it's fair for my students." As a teacher plans and provides instruction, it is essential to align instructional and assessment activities with the objectives so that valid decisions about student learning can occur during and following instruction.

To summarize, both textbook and teacher-made tests should (1) assess the objectives and instruction provided, and (2) include

> **TABLE 3.9 COMMON PROBLEMS IN DEVELOPING OR SELECTING TESTS TO ASSESS STUDENT ACHIEVEMENT**
>
> 1. Failing to consider objectives and instructional emphases when planning a test.
> 2. Failing to assess all of the important objectives and instructional topics.
> 3. Failing to select item types that permit students to demonstrate the desired behavior.
> 4. Adopting a test without reviewing it for its relevance to the instruction provided.
> 5. Including topics or objectives not taught to students.
> 6. Including too few items to assess the consistency of student performance.
> 7. Using tests to punish students for inattentiveness or acting out.

sufficient questions to measure all or most of those objectives. That way, the test provides a valid sample of student learning. Table 3.9 summarizes the problems teachers encounter in addressing these two important aspects.

STATE CONTENT STANDARDS

State-mandated standards are used to assess students, teachers, and schools in a particular state. The standards are intended to guide statewide learning and assessments.

Statewide standards for instruction have been around for many years, but in the past decade, the focus and emphasis of statewide assessment has changed greatly. Nearly every state has now adopted state curriculum frameworks or content standards. In addition, nearly all states have implemented an assessment program designed to measure student achievement of these curricular standards (Quality Counts, 2002). By 2008, almost half of the states (24) required students to pass a state test that measures the achievement of these standards in order to graduate.

Content standards are at the heart of statewide educational reform. In order to help students achieve these standards, it is important for teachers to incorporate the standards into their instructional objectives. When developing lesson plans, teachers should examine the state content standards and consider how they can be broken down into specific instructional objectives. Once the state content standards have been translated into a teacher's own instructional objectives, the teacher can then identify instructional activities and assessment methods that will help students attain the state standards.

Statewide standards can be expressed in a wide variety of forms. Table 3.10 presents common terms employed by states when presenting

---

TABLE 3.10   SOME HIGH-STAKES TERMINOLOGY*

Standard: A generic statement of what a student should know and be able to do in a subject area.

Benchmark: A specific statement of what a student should know at a specific time.

Indicator: A specific statement of knowledge or skills that a student demonstrates in order to meet the benchmark.

Framework: The governing document for a subject area, to be used for developing curriculum in that area.

Curriculum framework: A state's contents, standards, and benchmarks for a subject area.

*These terms and definitions are now widely, though not universally, accepted and used.

---

their content standards. Figure 3.3 shows excerpts of a Tennessee standard on developing knowledge, skills, and attitude to enhance personal growth. Note the levels of focus and detail associated with the standard: (1) the statement of the standard, (2) the learning expectations—what students will learn, (3) the performance indicators—evidence of meeting the standard, and (4) sample performance tasks. The tasks help students and teachers to know how to focus on the standard.

Table 3.11 lists the six Colorado standards for reading and writing, and Figure 3.4 shows excerpts that elaborate on two of them in terms of expectations, rationale, and how each standard applies at three different levels of schooling.

Figure 3.5 from West Virginia shows a glimpse of a different statewide approach to standards. It gives an overview and objectives for a specific course.

The point of these examples is to show the variety of ways that states define standards. For your own edification, try to find and examine the standards that are in effect in the state in which you plan to teach.

The growing importance of state standards, as well as decisions based on students' performance on tests designed to measure achievement of the standards, places additional pressure on teachers to carefully plan their instruction. Although many textbooks and instructional materials are being modified to cover standards that are common across many states, most commercially produced resources do not adequately cover all of the standards within a state. For this reason, it is important for teachers to regularly compare the instructional objectives contained in the textbook with their state content standards. When there is not a direct match, it is important to develop instructional objectives that are aligned with the content standards and to incorporate these into lesson plans.

FIGURE 3.3
A Tennessee Standard for Personal Growth

Standard

1.0 The student will develop knowledge, skills and attitudes to enhance personal growth.

Learning Expectations

The student will:

1. Demonstrate a sense of purpose and direction and make decisions based on positive goals and values (believes self can make a significant difference; nothing is left to chance or luck).

2. Demonstrate positive attitudes toward self and others (self-respect, self-confidence and self-esteem; feels worthwhile, confident, and competent).

3. Develop capacity for resiliency in relationships. . . .

4. Demonstrate self-management. . . .

5. Choose ethical courses of action (integrity and honesty).

6. Develop openness to new experiences and roles.

Performance Indicators: Evidence Standard Is Met

The student is able to:

1. Select, research, and organize a project after identifying and exploring a variety of options.

2. Demonstrate growth through reflection (e.g., journals, attitudinal surveys, . . .).

3. Use problem-solving techniques to interact with others.

4. Set a personal goal and create benchmarks to reach that goal.

5. . . . (and so forth)

Sample Performance Task

The student will:

1. Identify a problem within the school or community and implement an action plan. . . . .

2. Create a "This Is Your Life" video for a student from a different cultural background.

3. Create a reflection portfolio including an end-of-semester self-assessment.

4. Write about times when he or she has experienced conflict and role-play to resolve the conflict.

5. . . . . (and so forth)

TABLE 3.11 COLORADO MODEL CONTENT STANDARDS FOR READING AND WRITING

1. Students read and understand a variety of materials.

2. Students write and speak for a variety of purposes and audiences.

3. Students write and speak using conventional grammar, usage, sentence structure, punctuation, capitalization, and spelling.

4. Students apply thinking skills to their reading, writing, speaking, listening, and viewing.

5. Students read to locate, select, and make use of relevant information from a variety of media, reference, and technological sources.

6. Students read and recognize literature as a record of human experience.

SOURCE: http://www.cde.state.co.us/download/pdf/reading.pdf (Colorado Content Standards adopted 7-13-95).

FIGURE 3.4
Elaborations of Colorado Standards 1 and 3

SOURCE: http://www.cde.state.co.us /download/pdf/reading.pdf (Colorado Contents Standards adopted 7-13-95)

STANDARD 1

Students read and understand a variety of materials.

To meet this standard, students will:

- Use comprehension skills such as previewing, predicting, inferring, comparing and contrasting, rereading and self-monitoring, summarizing, etc.

- Make connections between their reading and what they already know, and identify what they need to know about a topic before reading about it.

- Adjust reading strategies for different purposes such as reading carefully idea by idea; skimming and scanning, etc.

- Use word recognition skills and resources such as phonics, context clues, picture clues, etc.

- Use information from their reading to increase vocabulary and enhance language usage.

Rationale: The goal for students at all levels is that they know and can use strategies—various ways of unlocking the meaning of words and larger blocks of text—to become successful readers. The strategies are applied in increasingly difficult reading material at each grade level. At all levels, students should be challenged to read literature and other materials that stimulate their interests and intellectual abilities. Reading from a wide variety of texts, both assigned and student selected, provides experience in gaining information and pleasure from diverse forms and perspectives.

Grades K–4. In grades K–4, what the students know and are able to do includes using a full range of strategies to comprehend materials such as directions, nonfiction material, rhymes and poems, and stories.

(continued)

FIGURE 3.4
Elaborations of
Colorado Standards
1 and 3 (continued)

Grades 5–8. As students in grades 5–8 extend their knowledge, what they know and are able to do includes using a full range of strategies to comprehend technical writing, newspapers, magazines, poetry, short stories. Students extend their thinking and understanding.

Grades 9–12. As students in grades 9–12 extend their knowledge, what they know and are able to do includes using a full range of strategies to comprehend essays, speeches, autobiographies.

For students extending their English/language arts education beyond the standards, what they know and are able to do may include using a full range of strategies to comprehend literary criticism and literary analysis, professional and technical journals.

STANDARD 3

Students write and speak using conventional grammar, usage, sentence structure, punctuation, capitalization, and spelling.

To meet this standard, students will:

- Know and use correct grammar in speaking and writing.
- Apply correct usage in speaking and writing.
- Use correct sentence structure in writing.
- Demonstrate correct punctuation, capitalization, and spelling.

Rationale: Students need to know and be able to use standard English. Proficiency in this standard plays an important role in how the writer or speaker is understood and perceived. All skills in this standard are reinforced and practiced at all grade levels and should be monitored by both the teacher and student to develop lifelong learning skills.

Grades K–4. In grades K–4, what the students know and are able to do includes knowing and using subject/verb agreement; knowing and using correct modifiers; knowing and using correct capitalization.

Grades 5–8. As students in grades 5–8 extend their knowledge, what they know and are able to do includes:

- Identifying the parts of speech such as nouns, pronouns, verbs, adverbs.
- Using correct pronoun case, regular and irregular noun and verb forms, and subject-verb agreement involving comparisons in writing and speaking.
- Using modifiers, homonyms, and homophones.
- Using simple, compound, complex, and compound/complex sentences.

Grades 9–12. As students in grades 9–12 extend their knowledge, what they know and are able to do includes:

- Using pronoun references correctly in writing and speaking.
- Using phrases and clauses for purposes of modification and parallel structure in writing and speaking.
- Using internal capitalization and punctuation of secondary quotations in writing.
- Using manuscript forms specified in various style manuals for writing.

FIGURE 3.5 *West Virginia Standard for Algebra I*

SOURCE: West Virginia Department of Education Policy 2520.2. Effective Jul 1, 2003.
http://wvde.state.wv.us/csos/

Algebra I Objectives

Algebra I is a course that provides the gateway to all higher mathematics courses. This course uses a conceptual approach to mathematics and does not focus on algorithmic methods. Algebraic representations will be used to generalize, and the algebraic method will be viewed as a problem-solving tool. In planning for instruction, consideration should be given to the student's readiness for abstract concepts. Manipulatives, such as algeblocks, should be used to bridge the gap from the concrete to the abstract. Available technology such as calculators, computers, and graphing utilities are to be used as tools to enhance learning.

Students will:

- demonstrate understanding of patterns, relations, and functions;
- represent and analyze mathematical situations and structures using algebraic symbols;
- use mathematical models. . . .

Algebra I Objectives

Students will:

A1.2.1   simplify and evaluate algebraic expressions using grouping symbols, order of operations and properties of real numbers with justification of steps.

A1.2.2   solve multi-step linear equations in one variable and apply skills toward solving practical problems. . . .

A1.2.3   . . . .

Performance Descriptors

- **Distinguished** The student demonstrates exceptional and exemplary performance. . . .
- **Above Mastery** The student demonstrates competent and proficient performance. . . .
- **Mastery** The student demonstrates fundamental course or grade level knowledge . . .
- **Partial Mastery** The student demonstrates basic but inconsistent performance. . . .
- **Novice** The student demonstrates substantial need for the development of fundamental knowledge. . . .

PLANNING, SPECIAL NEEDS, AND ACCOMMODATIONS

Meeting students' special needs is a very important issue that must be addressed during a teacher's instructional planning. As discussed in Chapter 2, an Individual Education Plan (IEP) is developed for students who have previously been identified with a special need. When planning instruction, teachers should use the IEP for students in their class to identify specific accommodations that may be needed to assist a student in meeting the instructional objectives. In classrooms that contain an instructional aide, the teacher should work closely with the aide while planning a lesson so that the teacher and aide can work in a coordinated manner during the lesson to help students meet the instructional objectives. While a full discussion of the variety of accommodations provided to students during instruction is beyond the scope of this book, some of the more common accommodations include giving students more time to complete tasks, providing students with physical tools or manipulatives with which they can work, and creating materials that make the text more accessible (e.g., large-print text, electronic files that can be read by software such as the Kurzweil Reader, books on tape or Braille). In some cases, the instructional objectives may also need to be modified for some students within a classroom. Accommodations such as these are specified in a student's IEP.

Increasingly, students with disabilities are placed in general education classrooms. Because teachers must accommodate many students with disabilities in the classroom, they should be aware of the legal issues related to these students and some of the common accommodations used in classrooms.

When planning assessment activities for a lesson, teachers must also be aware of specific accommodations required by students. In most cases, students should be provided with the same accommodations during assessment activities that they receive during instruction. This means that if a student is able to have text read aloud by an aide while working on classroom activities, the student can also have text on a test or quiz read aloud by an aide. Similarly, if the student is to be provided with manipulatives, a keyboard, Braille or enlarged text copies of written materials, extended time, or any other accommodation while working on instructional activities, these same materials, timing, and setting accommodations should also be provided when students work on assessment activities. Providing adequate accommodations requires forethought and is an important component of instructional planning. For those who would like to learn more about instructional accommodations, Appendix E identifies additional resources that focus specifically on accommodations.

IMPROVING THE LINK BETWEEN PLANNING AND ASSESSMENT

In planning instruction, there are a few common guidelines that teachers can follow to strengthen the effectiveness of their planning.

1. *Perform complete early assessments of students' needs and characteristics.* Because the purpose of instruction is to help students do things they were unable to do before instruction, planning responsive lessons requires that the needs and characteristics of students be taken into consideration. Knowledge of students' readiness, abilities, special needs, and attention spans helps the classroom teacher determine how long lessons should be, whether they should involve whole-class or small-group activities, and whether they should be teacher-led or student-directed. The more valid and reliable early assessments are, the more appropriate the lesson plans are likely to be.

2. *Use early assessment information when planning.* A teacher may have done an exceptional job with the early assessment of students, but if the teacher does not use that information when planning lessons, it is useless. Planning involves fitting instruction to student needs and characteristics, and it is the teacher's responsibility to plan accordingly.

3. *Do not rely entirely and uncritically on textbooks and their accompanying aids when planning.* The teacher's edition of textbooks can provide much of the information needed to plan, carry out, and assess instruction, but usually not all. It is important to consider the degree to which textbook plans and assessments match student characteristics and needs. Teacher's guides should be assessed, adapted, and supplemented to provide the best possible instruction to each teacher's class.

4. *Include a combination of lower-level and higher-level objectives.* The instructional activities offered in most teachers' editions are heavily weighted toward whole-class practices such as recitation, teacher presentation, and seatwork. Such practices normally emphasize lower-level objectives. It is important, therefore, that lesson plans and activities (whether textbook or teacher-made) include *both* lower- and higher-level objectives.

5. *Include a wide range of instructional activities and strategies to fit your students' instructional needs.* Teachers who use the same strategy (e.g., lecture, seatwork, or board work) every day with little change or variety create two problems. First, they risk boring students and reducing their motivation to attend to the repetitive activity. Second, by limiting their teaching repertoire to a single or very few strategies, they may not be reaching students whose learning styles are best suited to some other method (e.g., small-group instruction, learning games, or hands-on materials). It is important to include varied teaching strategies and activities in lesson plans.

6. *Align teaching strategies and assessment activities with the educational objectives.* Objectives describe the desired results of instruction. Teaching strategies and activities represent the means to achieve those results. Assessment activities provide information that helps the teacher to decide how well students are progressing or have attained the objectives. To reach the desired ends, the means must be relevant and appropriate. Without student ends clearly in mind, it is difficult to judge the adequacy of an instructional plan or the appropriateness of an assessment. Developing a lesson plan begins by defining objectives and then aligning instruction and assessment with those objectives. Figure 3.6 shows the relationship between statements of ends (objectives) and statements of means (teaching activities).

7. *Recognize one's own knowledge and pedagogical limitations and preferences.* Teachers assess many things when planning instruction, but they often neglect an assessment of themselves. Content knowledge limitations may lead a teacher to omit an important topic, teach it in a

FIGURE 3.6
Examples of
Instructional
Means and Ends

> **Means:** Read a short story silently.
> **End:**   Students can summarize a short story in their own words.
>
> **Means:** Show a film about computers.
> **End:**   Students can differentiate between computer hardware and software.
>
> **Means:** Discuss the organization of the periodic table.
> **End:**   Students can place an element in its periodic group when given a
>   description of the element's properties.

perfunctory or superficial manner, or provide students with incorrect information. Likewise, preferences for one or two teaching methods may deprive students of exposure to other methods or activities that would enhance their learning. When a teacher's knowledge limitations and pedagogical preferences outweigh student considerations in determining what is or is not done in classrooms, serious questions must be raised about the adequacy of the teacher's instructional plans.

8. *Include assessment strategies in instructional plans.* The object of planning and conducting instruction is to help students learn new content and behaviors. Consequently, lesson plans should include some formal measure or measures to determine whether students have learned the desired objectives and to identify areas of misunderstanding or confusion. While informal assessments about student enthusiasm and participation can be useful, they are not substitutes for more formal assessments such as follow-up seatwork, homework, quizzes, or oral questioning. Key Assessment Tools 3.4 summarizes the guidelines to follow in planning lessons.

Key Assessment Tools 3.4
GUIDELINES IN PLANNING INSTRUCTION

- Perform complete early assessments of students' needs and characteristics.
- Use early assessment information when planning.
- Do not rely entirely and uncritically on textbooks and their accompanying aids when planning.
- Include a combination of lower-level and higher-level objectives.
- Include a wide range of instructional activities and strategies to fit your students' instructional needs.
- Match educational objectives with teaching strategies, activities, and planned assessments.
- Recognize one's own knowledge and pedagogical limitations and preferences.
- Include assessment strategies in instructional plans.

CHAPTER SUMMARY

- Education is the process of helping students to acquire new skills and behaviors. A curriculum is the statement of the things students are expected to learn in school or in a course. Instruction includes the methods used to help students acquire the desired skills and behaviors. Changes in students brought about through formal instruction are called achievements.

- The instructional process comprises three steps: identifying desirable ways for students to learn, selecting materials and providing experiences to help students learn, and assessing whether students have learned. All three of these steps require teacher decision making and therefore involve assessment.

- Planning instruction involves teachers understanding and modifying the curriculum and instruction to fit the needs and characteristics of their students. Planning helps teachers approach instruction with greater confidence, review and become familiar with the subject matter before teaching, select ways to get the lessons started, and integrate lessons into units.

- Planning is dependent on the context in which instruction takes place and must take into account both the classroom characteristics teachers control (e.g., arrangement of the classroom, methods of instruction, or strategies for assessment) and those they do not (e.g., student characteristics, classroom size, or instructional resources).

- Four basic elements that teachers should include in their lesson plans are educational objectives, materials needed, teaching strategies and activities, and assessment procedures. Lesson plans should be written down in advance of instruction.

- Objectives are statements that describe what students are expected to learn from instruction and a process by which they will demonstrate that learning. Objectives have three general levels of abstraction— global, educational, and instructional—that range from broad to moderate to narrow. Classroom teaching relies primarily on educational and instructional objectives.

- Objectives fall into three domains: cognitive, affective, and psychomotor. Bloom's Taxonomy describes important cognitive processes: knowledge, comprehension, application, analysis, synthesis, and evaluation.

- Higher-level educational objectives require students to do more than just memorize facts and rules. Higher-level objectives involve behaviors that require application, analysis, synthesis, or evaluation of content and ideas.

- Although educational objectives are useful in planning instruction, the fact that they are stated before instruction begins means that they may need to be amended once instruction is under way. It is appropriate to make such adjustments based on student readiness.

olc

CHAPTER REVIEW
Visit the Online Learning Center at **www.mhhe.com/ russell7e** to review the case study referenced in the chapter.

- Lesson planning can be improved by avoiding the following mistakes: not knowing students' learning needs and characteristics; ignoring student needs and characteristics in planning; relying uncritically on the textbook and its accompanying aids; emphasizing only lower-level educational objectives in plans; using a narrow range of instructional strategies and activities; failing to align objectives and teaching activities; overlooking one's own weaknesses in content and teaching strategy; and omitting formative and summative assessment activities from plans.
- An important part of planning instruction is to take into account student needs and their accommodations.
- Students who are identified as having special needs may be given an Individual Education Plan (IEP) that defines the services and accommodations that they should receive. How these needs will be met must be considered when a teacher plans instruction.

QUESTIONS FOR DISCUSSION

1. What student characteristics are most important to take into account when planning instruction? How realistic is it to expect a teacher to plan instruction that takes into account the important needs of all the students?
2. Which subject areas are most difficult to plan for? Why?
3. What would be the characteristics of a class that would be easy to plan for? What would be the characteristics of a difficult-to-plan-for group?
4. Why do you think that many teachers describe stating objectives as "backward planning"? Is "backward planning" useful? Why?
5. What differentiates a well-stated objective from one that is poorly stated?
6. What are some strategies teachers can use to ensure that their instruction addresses state content standards? How might teachers use textbooks and standards when planning instruction?
7. What are important guidelines for planning instruction?

ACTIVITIES

1. Ask a teacher to show and discuss with you a lesson plan that he or she has used. Report on the teacher's objectives and how the plan took various resources and conditions into account, as well as how closely the plan was actually followed when the lesson was taught.
2. Develop a lesson plan in a topic of your choice. Include the four components of lesson plans discussed in the chapter.
3. In a small group, choose an imaginary student with a certain disability in a certain grade. To each student in the group, assign the

role of teacher, parent, a school administrator, and possibly a special resources member of the school staff. Go over the IEP form in Appendix C together, each taking your respective role. Fill out as much of the form as you can. (You may want to consult the accommodations information in Chapter 4 as well.)

REVIEW QUESTIONS

1. Explain the differences among education, achievement, instruction, and curriculum.
2. What three steps form the educational process?
3. What are the differences between Bloom's six cognitive processes and the three types of content knowledge?
4. What defines a good objective?
5. What are common errors made in planning instruction, and how can they be overcome?
6. How do objectives influence decisions about instruction and assessment?

REFERENCES

Anderson, L. W., et al. (2001). *A taxonomy for learning, teaching, and assessing: A revision of Bloom's taxonomy of educational objectives.* New York: Longman.

Bloom, B. S., et al. (1956). *Taxonomy of educational objectives: Handbook I: Cognitive domain.* New York: McKay.

Daniels, H., and Zemelman, S. (2004). *Subjects matter: Every teacher's guide to content-area reading.* Portsmouth, NH: Heinemann.

Gardner, H. (1995). Reflections of multiple intelligences: Myths and messages. *Phi Delta Kappan.* 77(3), 200–207.

Hannah, L. S., and Michaels, J. U. (1977). *A comprehensive framework for instructional objectives: A guide to systematic planning and evaluation.* Reading, MA: Addison-Wesley.

Harrow, A. H. (1972). *A taxonomy of the psychomotor domain.* New York: McKay.

Hunter, M. (1982). *Mastery learning.* El Segundo, CA: TIP Publications.

Krathwohl, D. R., Bloom, B. S., and Masia, B. B. (1964). *Taxonomy of educational objectives: Handbook II: Affective domain.* New York: Longman.

Krathwohl, D. R., and Payne, D. A. (1971). Defining and assessing educational objectives. In R. L. Thorndike, *Educational measurement* (pp. 17–41). Washington, DC, American Council on Education.

Marzano, R. C., Pickering, D., and McTighe, J. (1993). *Assessing student outcomes: Performance assessment using the dimension of learning model.* Alexandria, VA: Association for Supervision and Curriculum Development.

Quality Counts (2002). Building blocks for success. *Education Week* 21 (17).

Slavin, R. (2003). *Educational psychology: Theory and practice,* 7th ed. Boston: Allyn and Bacon.

Wiggins, G., and McTighe, J. (1998). *Understanding by design.* Alexandria, VA: Association for Supervision and Curriculum Development.

CHAPTER 4

FORMATIVE ASSESSMENT

KEY TOPICS

- *Assessment Tasks during Instruction*

- *Validity and Reliability in Instructional Assessment*

- *Formal Formative Assessment Activities*

- *Questioning: Purposes and Strategies*

- *Accommodations during Instruction*

After reading this chapter, you will be able to:

- Distinguish between planning and instructional assessment
- Describe what teachers do in the course of instructional assessment
- Explain the use of level of tolerance and practical knowledge
- Identify problems that influence validity and reliability in instructional assessment
- Write or ask higher-level and lower-level questions and convergent and divergent questions
- Cite strategies for effective questioning
- Accommodate students with disabilities during instruction and instructional assessment

THINKING ABOUT TEACHING

What are the most important activities a teacher should prepare for while planning for instruction?

T he assessment activities that teachers carry out when planning instruction are very different from those carried out when delivering instruction (see Table 4.1). Planning assessments are developed during quiet time, when the teacher can reflect on what students seem to know and be able to do and then identify appropriate objectives, content topics, and assessment activities. Formative assessments take place while

Instructional assessment refers to assessments made during instructions that indicate how well the lesson is going.

TABLE 4.1   CHARACTERISTICS OF PLANNING AND INSTRUCTIONAL ASSESSMENTS

Planning Assessment	Formative Assessment
1. Occurs before or after instruction	1. Occurs during instruction
2. Is carried out away from class	2. Is carried out in front of the class
3. Allows for reflective decisions	3. Requires instantaneous decisions
4. Focuses on identifying objectives, content, and activities	4. Focuses on collecting information to gauge current understanding
5. Is based on many kinds of formal and informal evidence	5. Provides feedback to the student about how to improve work or deepen their understanding
	6. Based on both formal questions and activities and informal student cues and responses

interacting with students and are focused on making quick and specific decisions about what to do next in order to help students learn. Formative assessment can take many forms, but they all rely on information collected through either structured formal activities or informal observations made during the process of instruction. Formal information is collected through preplanned questions and activities that are presented during instruction to help a teacher gauge students' current understanding. Informal information is used to modify instruction based on less direct evidence of student understanding and engagement such as attention, facial expressions, posture, eagerness to participate in classroom discussions, and questions raised by students.

Despite these differences, planning and delivering instruction are integrally related. Successful delivery of instruction depends on effective planning. During the planning stage, identifying concepts, skills, or activities that may cause students to become confused, frustrated, or bored allows teachers to develop brief assessment activities that gauge students' current state of understanding or engagement. By planning for such formative assessments prior to instruction, alternate strategies, activities, or approaches to explaining concepts can be prepared prior to instruction. Similarly, reflecting on the successful and less successful components of previous lessons enables teachers to avoid strategies and activities that do not work well with a group of students. By anticipating challenges in an upcoming lesson and reflecting on past lessons, teachers may reduce the need to adapt a lesson while delivering instruction.

Good planning reduces uncertainty. Rather than preventing a teacher from taking advantage of unexpected teaching opportunities, it frees the teacher to watch for such moments and adapt instruction.

Although good planning reduces uncertainty during instruction, it rarely eliminates it. The teaching process must, to some extent, be free-flowing and adaptable, allowing for interruptions, digressions, and unexpected happenings. What the teacher does influences what the students do, which in turn influences what the teacher does, and so on throughout the instructional process. To understand the formal and informal process of assessment during instruction, it is necessary to look beyond the teacher's written lesson plans to examine the classroom as a learning society. This chapter discusses both informal and formal formative assessment activities, and explores how teachers think of instructional assessment, how they carry it out, and how they can ensure the quality of their ongoing assessment. The chapter also discusses the use of questioning, feedback, and students self-assessment to support students' learning. Finally, it describes accommodations appropriate for students with disabilities during instruction and in-class assessments.

INFORMAL ASSESSMENT TASKS DURING INSTRUCTION

Effective instruction includes accurate assessment of student progress and adaptation to their changing needs.

Once instruction begins, teachers carry on two tasks: (1) they initiate the instructional activities that they have planned, and (2) they assess the progress and success of these instructional activities in order to modify them if necessary. For many reasons, things do not always go as planned.

Interruptions, misjudgments about student readiness and attention, shifts in student interest, and unexpected events (e.g., fire drills, assemblies, and squawk box interruptions) all can alter planned instructional activities. As a result, the teacher must constantly sense the mood and learning of the class to make decisions about what to do next. Once the teacher initiates instruction, he or she engages in an ongoing process of assessing its progress and determining how students are reacting to it.

Note that when planning instruction, the focus is on student characteristics, readiness, subject matter objectives, and learning activities. Once instruction actually begins, the focus shifts to more action-oriented concerns, especially how students are developing skills and knowledge. During instruction, teachers collect informal assessment data to help monitor factors such as the following:

- Interest level of individual students and the class as a whole
- Apparent or potential behavior problems
- Appropriateness of the instructional technique or activity being used
- Which student to call on next
- Students who may become off-task
- Adequacy of students' answers
- Pace of instruction
- Confusion or misconceptions students may be developing
- Smoothness of transitions from one concept to another and from one activity to the next
- Suitability of examples used to explain concepts
- Degree of comprehension on the part of individual students and the class as a whole
- Desirability of starting or ending a particular activity

Such monitoring, of course, is a complicated task, since instruction, assessment, and decision making are taking place almost simultaneously. For example, during class discussion,

> a teacher must listen to student answers, watch other students for signs of comprehension or confusion, formulate the next question, and scan the class for possible misbehavior. At the same time, the teacher must attend to the pace of the discussion, the sequence of selecting students to answer, the relevance and quality of the answers, and the logical development of the content. When the class is divided into small groups, the number of simultaneous events increases, and the teacher must monitor and regulate several different activities at once. (Doyle, 1986)

Certainly, many decisions are required during instruction, and these decisions, in turn, are informed by assessments that teachers make as part of the instructional process.

Figure 4.1 illustrates this process of ongoing assessment. Once *teaching* begins, the teacher continually *assesses* its progress by observing students' reactions and asking them questions. On the basis of these reactions and responses, the teacher makes a *decision* about how instruction is going. If the teacher decides that the lesson is progressing satisfactorily, he or she

FIGURE 4.1
Steps in
Instructional
Assessment

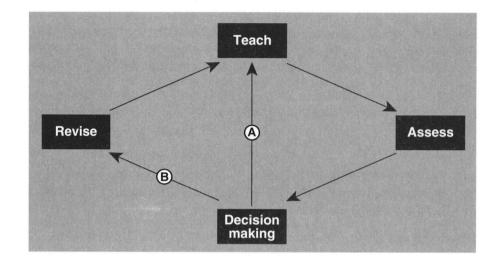

continues teaching as planned (path A). If the teacher senses a problem, such as lack of student understanding or interest, the planned instructional activity should be *revised* to alleviate the problem, with another teaching activity or strategy initiated (path B). This cycle is repeated many times in the course of a single lesson.

Informal Assessment Indicators during Instruction

Informal indicators include cues from the students, such as attention, facial expressions, and questions asked by students.

Given the pace and complexity of instructional activities and the need to keep instruction flowing smoothly, it is no surprise that teachers rely on informal indications to monitor their instruction. To determine what types of indicators teachers use to monitor and judge the success of their instruction, they were asked how they knew when their instruction was successful. Their responses included the following:

It is easy to tell when things are not running as planned. Children get impatient; facial expressions become contorted; their body language, voice level, and eyes tell the story of their reaction to instruction.

If my class is daydreaming—looking blankly out the window and unresponsive—that tells me something. At times like these I have to decide what to do, since I don't want the students to think that by acting uninterested they always can make me change my plans.

The assessment information that teachers gather during instruction comes mostly from informal observation of their students.

Some examples of a good lesson are when the students are eager to be called on, raise their hands, give enthusiastic answers, look straight at me, scream out answers, show excitement in their eyes. During a bad lesson, the kids have their heads on the desk, look around the room, play with little objects at their desks, talk to their neighbor, or go to the bathroom in droves.

Responding to a variety of immediate classroom needs allows teachers little time to reflect on what they are doing or the motives for their actions. Nonetheless, most teachers feel that they have a good sense of their instructional success, which implies that they do assess many environmental cues.

When monitoring the success of a lesson during instruction, it is important not to confuse high levels of interest and participation with effectiveness. At times, students may be very eager to participate in a discussion or to engage in an activity. This eagerness and interest can make a teacher feel good about a lesson. But, if the focus of the discussion or the learning that results from the activity do not contribute to helping students achieve the instructional objectives for that lesson, the lesson will not be effective. As we explore below, it is important to consider the validity of the interpretations teachers make during instruction about the effectiveness of an instructional activity based on informal cues and observations.

In summary, the direction, flow, and pace of instruction are dictated by the chemistry of the classroom at any given time. The teacher's assessment task during instruction is to monitor the progress and success of the instruction. In most classrooms, monitoring boils down to assessing the appropriateness of the instructional procedures and the students' reaction to them. Most decisions that teachers make during instruction are prompted by (1) unusual student behavior that requires a response or reaction from the teacher and (2) typical issues that arise during instruction, such as responding to a student's question, deciding whom to call on next, and deciding whether to move on to the next topic. The assessment information that teachers gather when they monitor their instruction comes mostly from informal observations of the students. These cues, plus the teacher's knowledge of the class, support the quick assessments and decisions that teachers make during classroom instruction. Assessments of atypical behavior help to maintain whatever level of tolerance the teacher intends to allow. Above all, ongoing assessment is rooted in a teacher's practical knowledge of the class.

olc

CHAPTER CASE STUDY

Visit the text Online Learning Center to read the case of Karen Lee, a first-year Spanish teacher. Karen takes over a high school Spanish III class midyear and faces an unruly group of students. One student in particular seems determined to make her miserable.

www.mhhe.com/ russell7e

Teachers' Thinking during Instruction

A large proportion of teachers' thinking during instruction concerns the adequacy of their instruction. Teachers describe their thinking in these ways:

I was thinking about the need for another example of this concept.

I was trying to get him to see the relationship between the Treaty of Versailles and Hitler's rise to power without actually telling him.

I was thinking about a worksheet that would reinforce the idea. I decided that it was necessary to review yesterday's lesson.

Teachers' thoughts are particularly concerned with the *effect* of instruction on students—that is, the degree to which students are interested in

Teachers tend to look more for signs of student engagement than of student learning.

and profiting from instruction. When teachers infer that students are struggling with a concept, they make deliberate decisions about their next actions. These decisions are captured in the following teacher comments:

> I realized that they didn't understand the concept of borrowing at all. I thought, at least everyone is concentrating on the topic. I figured I'd better call on Larry, just to make sure he was with us.

> I asked Mike to explain the material because I thought he would know it and could explain it in a way many students could understand.

Assessing Abnormal and Normal Behavior

Instructional assessment includes noticing abnormal behavior in order to maintain the right level of tolerance.

Over time, through observations and experience, teachers establish **levels of tolerance** that indicate what is normal student or class behavior. These tolerance levels vary from class to class and teacher to teacher. In some classrooms, for example, "normal" tolerance of noise when students are working individually is very low; students are not permitted to interact, converse, or speak out. In other classrooms, "normal" tolerance permits more noise, student movement around the room, and conversation. Tolerance levels are also established for individual students. When we hear a teacher say things like "John acted out much more than usual today; he must be upset about something," "Anush is mad at her parents again because she had that sulky expression and didn't say a word in class," or "Eugenio turned in a sloppy, unfinished homework assignment today—something's wrong," we are witnessing teacher decision making based on student behaviors that are "out of tolerance" based on normal student behavior.

Part of the process of "reading" the class during instruction involves knowing when the class or some students are exhibiting out-of-tolerance behaviors that call for a response from the teacher. Thus, a large proportion of teachers' decisions during instruction result from monitoring signs that tell the teacher whether the students' behavior is in or out of tolerance.

But teachers' decisions during instruction are not based solely on perceptions of unusual student behavior. Many involve normal classroom routines. For example, many teacher decisions are the result of a student's question ("If Pedro doesn't understand, I'd better review this topic for the whole class") or the teacher's need to choose a student to respond during instruction ("Holly hasn't raised her hand to answer for three days; I'll call on her"). Likewise, when there is a transition point in the lesson from one activity to another, when the teacher anticipates a problem teaching a concept, when there is insufficient time to complete planned activities, or when there is a shortage of materials, the teacher must make a decision about the course and nature of subsequent instructional activities.

VALIDITY AND RELIABILITY IN INSTRUCTIONAL ASSESSMENT

Because teachers have little time to reflect on what is observed or to collect additional information during instruction, they must make decisions and act on the basis of incomplete and uncertain evidence. Even so, good teachers are able to collect and evaluate informal information in order to make appropriate instructional assessment decisions. Nonetheless, it is important to consider issues related to the quality of informal observations and information collected during instructional assessment.

Problems That Affect Validity of Informal Assessments

During instruction, teachers depend on informal observations to collect information about students' current interest levels and understanding. Based on this informal information, teachers make inferences about the effectiveness of the instructional strategies they are employing at that time and make decisions about how to modify these strategies or whether to transition to a different instructional activity. For instructional assessments, validity relates to the accuracy of the inferences teachers make based on informal observations about students' interest levels, their current understanding, the pace of instruction, and the appropriateness of the subsequent decisions teachers make about their instruction. An important validity question is this: Are the inferences teachers make based on these informal observations accurate and do they lead to appropriate decisions about instructional success? Two potential threats to validity are (1) lack of objectivity by teachers when judging their own instruction and (2) incompleteness of the evidence used to make decisions about instruction and student learning.

Objectivity of the Teacher as an Observer

Being a participant in the instructional process can make it difficult for the teacher to be an objective, detached observer who can make unbiased judgments about his or her own instruction. Teachers have a stake in the success of instruction and derive their primary rewards from it; they have a strong personal and professional investment in the instructional process. Every time teachers make a favorable judgment about instruction or student learning, they are also rewarding themselves. Because teachers rely heavily on their observations to assess instruction, they may see only what they want to see—that is, only those things that will give them reinforcement. If so, the evidence they use to assess their instruction is potentially

Because teachers want to feel good about their instruction, there is the danger that they will look only for positive student reactions.

Teachers sometimes ask easy, low-level questions in order to get correct answers that make them feel good about their instruction.

invalid. Evidence of invalid assessments of instruction is not hard to find. For example, the types of questions teachers ask can influence their sense of personal effectiveness. Simple, factual questions are likely to produce a greater number of correct student responses than open-ended, complex ones. Concentration on lower-level rote skills and information, rather than on higher-level skills and processes, can ensure more student participation and mastery. Teacher comments, such as "This topic is too hard for my students, so I'll skip over it," may be a realistic appraisal of student readiness, or they may simply be a way for teachers to avoid instructional disappointments. In short, the desire to achieve teaching satisfaction may bias teachers' observations and produce invalid conclusions about the success of instruction, with harmful consequences for students.

Incompleteness of Informal Indicators

The informal indicators that teachers use to monitor instruction are those that are most readily available, most quickly surveyed, and least intrusive: reactions from students such as facial expressions, posture, participation, questions, and attention. Using such informal indicators, teachers "read" a student or the class and judge the success of the current instructional activity. But the real criterion of teachers' instructional success is *student learning.* Although the *process* of instruction—its flow and pace, and student reactions—is important and should be assessed, it does not provide direct evidence of student learning. It deals only with intermediate events that may or may not lead to a more important outcome—namely, learning.

Instructional assessment should focus on student learning as well as student involvement.

Being attentive and involved in instruction is desirable, but does not necessarily mean that learning is taking place. Thus, valid assessment of instruction should include appropriate information about both student involvement and student learning. If it focuses only on student interest and facial expressions, judgments about the ultimate goal—how well students are learning—may be invalid.

Instructional assessment that involves feedback from a broad range of students is more reliable than assessments based on the reactions of one or two students.

When collecting information through informal observations about the whole class or a group of students within the class, it is important to sample broadly from the classroom. Often, because of seating arrangements or an unconscious preference for certain students, teachers tend to use an overly narrow sample of students when assessing the success of instruction. This inadequate sampling, of course, reduces the validity of their assessment.

Problems That Affect Instructional Reliability

Reliability is concerned with the stability or consistency of the assessment data that are collected. One of the features of teaching is the fast-changing nature of instruction. If the message a teacher gets from his

> **Key Assessment Tools 4.1**
>
> ### VALIDITY AND RELIABILITY PROBLEMS OF INSTRUCTIONAL ASSESSMENT
>
> **Validity Problems**
> 1. Lack of objectivity by the classroom teacher
> 2. Overreliance on objectives and assessments that provide the teacher with maximum reinforcement but narrow instruction for pupils
> 3. Focus on instructional process indicators (e.g., facial expressions, posture, or participation) without consideration of instructional outcome indicators (e.g., student learning)
>
> **Reliability Problems**
> 1. Inadequate collection of corroborative evidence
> 2. Focus on a limited number of students to obtain information about the instructional process and student learning

or her observations changes each time new evidence is gathered, the teacher cannot rely on that evidence to help in decision making. Since teachers obtain most of their information about the success of instruction by observing their students, the more frequently they observe student behaviors and informally monitor students' understanding, the more reliable the information about student attention, learning, or instructional pace will be. Of course, given the fluidity of classroom events and the quick pace with which circumstances may change within a classroom, it is not always possible to collect multiple observations before making an inference and forming a decision. Nonetheless, the extent to which multiple observations of multiple students are made affects the reliability of the information teachers use to inform their instructional decisions.

Key Assessment Tools 4.1 summarizes validity and reliability problems in instructional assessment.

FORMAL FORMATIVE ASSESSMENT ACTIVITIES

In basketball there are players who are said to have a shooting "touch." Beyond the mechanics of knowing how to shoot a basketball, the player has an intangible ability to put the ball into the basket with unusual success. Likewise, an actor's ability to "read" the audience and react to it goes beyond the technical aspects of acting; it involves a special sensitivity to the audience. Just as the basketball player needs "touch" and the actor must be able to "read" an audience, successful instructional assessment depends on a teacher's "feel" for the instructional process. This "feel" is dependent in large measure on the teacher's early assessments and practical knowledge of the students' typical behavior. It permits the

Good teachers can sense the success or failure of their instruction just as a skillful actor can sense the reaction of an audience.

teacher to anticipate instructional problems, select the correct instructional procedure from the many options available, and use a few valid indicators to determine how instruction is going.

Assessments during instruction depend in some measure on an intangible, unarticulated process. To try to describe the instructional assessment process by spelling out a detailed list of rules and procedures would be to corrupt the natural flow of classroom events and likely destroy the process altogether. Teachers will always have to rely in part on their "feel" for the classroom situation when gathering assessment information and making decisions during instruction. However, this does not mean that the process cannot be made more valid and reliable, so that decision making is improved and student learning enhanced.

Great teachers will always be those who develop a feel for how things are going in the classroom, moment by moment.

Improving assessment during instruction does not require the teacher to become an automaton who blindly follows a set of prescribed rules. It is, after all, the feel of teachers for their students and classroom situations that makes it impossible for machines to replace teachers. Nonetheless, research shows that taking a more systematic approach to formative assessment and incorporating formal formative assessment activities into instruction has positive effects on student learning. (Black and Wiliam, 1998)

Teachers should supplement their informal assessments of instruction with formal feedback such as homework, worksheets, and lesson reviews.

Formal formative assessment activities involve thoughtful planning prior to instruction and purposeful actions during instruction. Formal formative assessments provide teachers with specific information about students' current understanding and often allow feedback to students to help refine their thinking or skills. Formal formative evidence can be collected through a variety of techniques including preplanned questions, formal activities, self-assessment by students, and feedback provided by peers or the instructor. Formal activities include short problems, homework designed to elicit student understanding or misconceptions, quizzes, essays, and formal observations of laboratory or other hands-on activities. In all cases, what separates formal from informal assessment data is the purposeful, preplanned collection of information about student learning. Notice that formal formative assessment focuses closely on student learning, while informal assessment often focuses on students attitudes, engagement, or other affective characteritics.

Research has shown that three forms of formal formative assessment are particularly effective for helping students learn (Black, Harrison, Lee, Marshall, and Wiliam, 2004): purposeful questioning, teacher feedback, and self- and peer assessment.

Effective Questioning

Teachers ask many questions of their students during the course of instruction, with some teachers asking as many as 300 to 400 questions a day (Morgan and Saxton, 1991; Christensen, 1991). Questions are generally asked for one of two purposes: (1) to maintain student attention or

(2) to collect information about students' current understanding. Questions asked to maintain attention are often short ones framed during teaching that require factual responses by a single student. In contrast, questions designed to assess students' current understanding are often more open-ended and focus on conceptual understanding. In addition, responses by multiple students are often solicited, and the responses form the basis for the teacher's judgment about students' understanding and serve as a springboard for further discussion. Since it is difficult to form effective open-ended questions during the act of teaching, questions designed to assess students' current understanding often are developed during the planning phase of instruction and modified during instruction.

A critical component of effective questoning is wait time. Most teachers wait only a few seconds after asking a question before soliciting an answer. While short wait times may be appropriate for factual quesitons, students often need significantly more time to reflect on and develop a response to an open-ended question. Short wait times convey a message to students that answers should be readily available and do not require careful thought: Their job is to spot the right answer rather than to describe their own understanding or thoughts. Although it can seem like an eternity, for open-ended questions, students may require 20 to 30 seconds before being able to provide thoughtful responses.

When using questions to assess students' current understanding, it is also important to obtain answers from multiple students. Not only does this increase the amount of information available to make an instructional decision, it also provides students an opportunity to compare and contrast their thinking with that of their peers. Further, multiple answers provide the teacher with more examples that can be used to foster classroom discussion and to build student understanding.

When asking questions, it is important not to call only on students who have their hands raised. Instead, consider directing a related or clarifying question to a student whose hand is not raised and then asking for an additional response from a student who was quick to raise his or her hand. This technique can be useful for generating different perspectives on an issue and may lead to surprising insight from students who are less eager to share their thinking. Paying attention only to the few students who always share their thinking or who are first to raise their hands might cause the teacher to lose touch with the class as a whole.

Feedback to Students

Feedback to students occurs in many ways. Teachers provide feedback during instruction through their facial expressions, comments, and reactions to questions students ask and responses they provide. A raise of the eyebrow suggests that the student's answer is either unexpected or off the mark. A frown indicates disapproval. A nod reassures the student that he or she is on a track that is agreeable to the teacher. These informal forms of feedback can impact students' feelings about their own learning and their willingness to share their thinking in the future.

More formal feedback often takes the form of grade, scores, and written comments teachers provide in response to student work. Research on formative assessment shows that this more formal feedback can have a powerful effect on student learning. Regarding grades and scores, this research indicates that such feedback is viewed as more important by students than the lengthy comments a teacher may provide. Rather than carefully reading comments, students accept grades and scores at face value, and are often willing to move onto the next assignment. In contrast, when assignments are returned without a grade or score, students pay closer attention to comments and are more willing to revise and improve their work.

When providing written comments, it is important to inform students about both positive aspects of their work and elements that can be improved. A useful technique is to begin by describing at least two positive aspects of the work and then focus on only one element for improvement. Research on feedback suggests that students, particularly those in earlier grades, have difficulty focusing on and improving more than one element of their work at a time.

To help focus comments on one element of student work, it is also helpful to identify beforehand the main instructional goal addressed by the assignment. This is particularly important for writing assignments. Analyzing written work provides opportunities to comment on many aspects of writing, including spelling, capitalization, sentence structure, and grammar, as well as higher-level characteristics such as providing supporting evidence and developing ideas or arguments. While each of these elements are important, deciding the main purpose of the assignment ahead of time helps focus comments on a single topic.

When possible, comments should also present students with encouragement to provide more information or questions to think about rather than instructing them how to improve their work. For writing assignments, comments may ask students to provide more evidence to support their argument, to describe a situation in greater detail, or to explain why they took a position. Rather than being instructive, effective comments should spur student thinking.

Peer and Self-Assessment

Thoughtful questions and comments are two powerful tools that help develop student learning. Teachers, however, rarely have time to pose questions to all students. The amount of time teachers have to provide feedback on students' work is also limited. Peer and and self-assessment, however, can increase the amount of feedback students receive. Peer assessment also provides valuable opportunities for students to learn about their own ideas and the quality of their work by carefully examining work samples produced by their peers.

To assist students in conducting self- and peer assessments, it is important for the teacher to make expectations and criteria for evaluating a performance clear to students. When possible, concrete examples of high-quality work, as well as work that is in need of further development, are also effective in making abstract criteria more concrete.

Just as teacher comments should focus on one or two characteristics of student work, students should also be guided to focus on only one or two issues when assessing their own work or the work of their peers. To the extent possible, students should be encouraged not to make summative judgments about their peers' work, but instead to identify effective elements, point out points of confusion, ask for additional examples or evidence, or ask questions about why decisions were made.

Beyond using questions to extract assessment information and keep students engaged in the class, teachers should ask questions that can serve as models for the types of questions students need to ask of themselves as they self-assess their own work (Chappuis and Stiggins, 2002). Developing students' ability to self-assess their own work can provide them with the tools to identify strengths and weaknesses in their work and to identify areas in need of improvement. Self-assessment can also empower students to determine whether they have fulfilled the requirements of an assignment. To help students develop effective self-assessment questioning strategies, teachers should model questions that focus on student process and work ("Have I stated a point of view?" "Have I included supporting facts and details?" "Have I used adjectives to provide descriptions of characters"), rather than on approval or disapproval ("Did I do a good job?"). Key Assessment Tools 4.2 suggests some ways to encourage students in this direction.

Purposes and Types of Questioning

As we have seen, questioning is a very important element of formative assessment. During instruction, teachers ask questions for many reasons:

1. *To promote attention.* Questioning is a way to keep students' attention during a lesson and to engage them in the process of learning.

2. *To promote deeper processing.* Questioning lets students verbalize their thoughts and ideas, thereby promoting the thinking and reasoning that lead to deeper processing of information.

3. *To promote learning from peers.* Questioning allows students to hear their peers' interpretations and explanations of ideas, processes, and issues. Often, other students explain things in ways that are more in tune with the minds of their peers.

4. *To provide reinforcement.* Questioning is used by teachers to reinforce important points and ideas. The questions teachers ask cue students regarding what and how they should be learning.

Teachers ask questions in order to reinforce important points, to diagnose problems, to keep students' attention, and to promote deeper processing of information.

Key Assessment Tools 4.2

ENCOURAGING STUDENT QUESTIONING SKILLS AND SELF-ASSESSMENT OF LEARNING

1. Model and encourage the use of three basic self-assessment questions:
   Where am I going?
   Where am I now?
   How do I close the gap?

2. Show students samples of anonymous work, and teach them how to ask and answer questions about the attributes of good performance.

3. Involve students in constructing lists of questions or criteria to serve as a scoring guide for a specific assignment. Start with just one question and gradually increase the number.

4. Have students create their own sets of questions for practice tests; discuss the merits of the questions.

5. Have students communicate with others about their progress toward a goal.

6. Display learning objectives in the classroom, and ask students to rephrase them.

Source: Adapted from Chappuis and Stiggins (2002).

5. *To provide pace and control.* Questions that require brief, correct responses keep students engaged in learning and require them to pay continuous attention.

6. *To provide diagnostic information.* Questions provide the teacher with information about student and class learning. Teachers' questions can supplement their informal observations of student learning in the least disruptive way. Also, for group or cooperative learning activities, questioning of group members after completion of their task is a useful way to assess the success of the group.

Not all of these reasons for asking questions support formative assessment. Asking questions to provide promote attention, to encourage deeper processing, or to control pace serve instructional rather than formative assessment purposes. In contrast, asking questions to serve diagnostic purposes or to allow students to compare their thinking with that of their peers supports formative assessment. It is a mistake to assume that simply asking any type of question means that a teacher is engaged in formative assessment.

Questions differ also in other respects. Questions can be classified as lower- or higher-level. Alternatively, some people refer to these categories as convergent or divergent questions. Lower-level or convergent questions have a single correct answer and require recall or memorization, which are the two lowest levels of thinking in Bloom's Taxonomy. Lower-level questions generally begin with words such as "who," "when," "what," and "how many": "When did the American Civil War take place?" "What is the definition of *taxonomy*?" "Where is the city of Beijing located?" "How much is 9 times 8?" Such questions focus on factual information that the student is expected to remember and produce when questioned.

Higher-level or divergent questions may have many appropriate answers and require students to perform processes more complicated than pure memorization, such as understanding conceptual knowledge and applying procedural knowledge. Higher-level or divergent questions also require students to apply, analyze, and synthesize the factual knowledge they have attained in order to help them solve new problems. Higher-level or divergent questions typically start with words such as "explain," "predict," "relate," "distinguish," "solve," "contrast," "judge," or "produce": "Explain in your own words what the main idea of the story was." "Predict what will happen to the price of oil if the supply increases but the demand remains the same." "Distinguish between statements of fact and statements of opinion in the passage we have just read." "Give three examples of how the self-fulfilling prophecy might work in a school." Questions such as these pose tasks that require students to think and to go beyond factual recall.

Note that if the answers to these questions had been specifically taught to students during instruction, they would not be higher-level questions because students could answer them from memory, rather than having to construct an answer for themselves. It is also important to recognize that since higher-level or divergent questions require students to apply factual knowledge they have already attained, both convergent and divergent questions are important to use during instruction (Wiggins and McTighe, 1998). Christensen (1991) has developed a typology of questions that shows the breadth of information that can be obtained from varying types of questions:

Convergent questions are those that have a single correct answer, whereas divergent questions may have several appropriate answers.

- Open-ended questions — What is your reaction to this poem?
- Diagnostic questions — What is the nature of the problem in this short story?
- Information questions — What was the last state to be admitted to the United States?
- Challenge questions — What evidence is there to support your conclusion?
- Action questions — How can we go about solving the problem of high school dropouts?
- Sequence questions — Given limited resources, what are the two most important steps to take?
- Prediction questions — What do you think would happen if the government shut down for three months?
- Extension questions — What are the implications of your conclusion that grades should be abolished in schools?
- Generalization questions — Based on your study of classroom assessment, how would you sum up the general concept of validity?

TABLE 4.2   EXAMPLES OF QUESTIONS FOR THE LEVELS OF BLOOM'S COGNITIVE TAXONOMY

Knowledge (remembering)	What is the definition of a noun? How many planets are in our solar system? In what year did the Boston Tea Party occur?
Comprehension (understanding)	Summarize the story in your own words. Explain what $E = MC^2$ means. Paraphrase the author's intent.
Application (using information to solve new problems)	What is a real-world example of that principle? Predict what would happen if the steps in the process were reversed. How could the Pythagorean theorem be used to measure the height of a tree?
Analysis (reasoning, breaking apart)	Which of these statements are facts and which are opinions? How did the main character change after her scary nightmare? Explain the unstated assumption that underlies this argument.
Synthesis (constructing, integrating)	What do all these pictures have in common? Describe a generalization that follows from these data. State a conclusion supported by these facts.
Evaluation (judging)	What was the most important moment in the story and why? What is your opinion of the school policy for grades and extracurricular participation?

Table 4.2 provides examples of questions at different levels of Bloom's Taxonomy. While the taxonomy provides a useful model, it is less important to ask questions at specific taxonomic levels than it is to match questions with the teacher's learning objectives.

Although most teachers want their students to attain both lower- and higher-level outcomes from instruction, they tend to focus instruction and classroom questions on lower-level questions. Only about 10 to 20 percent of teachers' classroom questions are higher-level. Students are not frequently asked to explain ideas in their own words, apply knowledge in unfamiliar situations, analyze components of an idea or story, synthesize different pieces of information into a general statement or conclusion, or judge the pros and cons of particular courses of action. This emphasis on lower-level questions also can be found in some teacher's edition textbooks, statewide standards, and state tests.

Questioning Strategies

The following strategies can be used to increase the effectiveness of oral questioning.

1. *Ask questions that are related to the objectives of instruction.* Teachers' questions communicate what topics are important and the how these topics should be learned, so there should be consistency among objectives, instruction, and questioning. This consistency is especially important when higher-level objectives are stressed. It is useful to prepare a few higher-level questions before instruction begins and then incorporate them into the lesson plan.

2. *Avoid global, overly general questions.* Do not ask, "Does everyone understand this?" because many students will be too embarrassed to admit they do not, and others will think they understand what has been taught when in reality they do not. Ask questions that probe students' comprehension of what is being taught. Similarly, avoid questions that can be answered with a simple yes or no unless the students are also expected to explain their answers.

3. *Involve the entire class in the questioning process.* Do not call on the same students time after time. Occasionally call on nonvolunteers in order to keep everyone attentive. Arrange students into a circle or a U, and ask questions in a variety of ways in order to adapt them to students' varying ability levels. Finally, support the response efforts of weak students and encourage everyone who tries.

4. *Be aware of patterns in the way questions are distributed among students.* Some teachers call on high-achieving students more frequently than low achievers, on girls more than boys, or on those in the front rows more than those in the back. Other teachers do the opposite. Be sensitive to such questioning patterns, and strive to give all students an equal opportunity to respond.

5. *Allow sufficient "wait time" after asking a question.* Students need time to process their thoughts, especially in response to a higher-level question. Remember, silence after a question is good because it means the students are thinking. Three to 5 seconds is a suitable wait time for lower-level questions, while a minimum of 10 to 30 seconds may be needed for higher-level questions. Giving students time to think also leads to improved answers.

6. *State questions clearly and directly to avoid confusion.* Avoid vague questions or prompts like "What about the story?" or "Talk to me about this experiment." If students are to think in desired ways, the teacher must be able to state questions in ways that focus and produce that type of thinking. Clarity focuses thinking and improves the quality of answers. Again, preparing key questions before teaching a lesson is a useful practice.

7. *Probe student responses with follow-up questions.* Probes such as "Why?" "Explain how you arrived at that conclusion," and "Can you give me another example?" indicate to students that the "whys" or logic behind a response are as important as the response itself. Such probing will encourage them to articulate their reasoning.

8. *Remember that instructional questioning is a social process that occurs in a public setting.* Consequently, all students should be treated with encouragement and respect. Incorrect, incomplete, or even unreasonable answers should not evoke demeaning, sarcastic, or angry teacher responses. Be honest with students; do not try to bluff them when they pose a question that you cannot answer. Find the answer and report it to students the next day.

9. *Allow private questioning time for students who are shy or have difficulty engaging in the questioning process.* If possible, allow private questioning time for these students, perhaps during seatwork or study time. Then, as they become more confident in their private responses, gradually work them into public discussions, first with small groups and then with the whole class.

10. *Recognize that good questioning also involves good listening and responding.* In addition to framing good questions, it is important to be both a good listener and a good responder to students' answers. Good listening means identifying the meaning and implications of students' responses. Good responding means following up on students' answers with comments that will benefit the students.

11. *Avoid questions that require only a yes or no response.*

12. *Avoid always asking students the same types of questions.* Ask for facts. But also ask students to apply, evaluate, or synthesize these facts into arguments, reasons, or judgments.

ACCOMMODATIONS DURING INSTRUCTION

An effective instructor must anticipate student needs and accommodate them when planning and delivering instruction.

An important aspect of planning and delivering instruction is accommodating student needs and disabilities. Clearly, student needs and disabilities span a broad range, from students with severe cognitive, affective, or psychomotor disabilities to students with mild attention problems (Cegelka and Berdine, 1995; Cartwright, Cartwright, and Ward, 1995). While it is not possible here to address all available accommodation strategies for instruction, we will review a sample of useful strategies to illustrate the breadth of options. For an excellent in-depth survey of strategies to accommodate varied student needs and disabilities, see Price and Nelson (2003, Chapter 6).

Common Disabilities and Accommodations

For a hearing-impaired student, the teacher can:

- Use written rather than oral directions
- Face the student when speaking
- Speak slowly and distinctly
- Use sign language

For a vision-impaired student, the teacher can:

- Use large print
- Provide recorded materials
- Let other students read out loud
- Seat the student near the chalkboard

For a student with poor comprehension, the teacher can:

- State directions orally and in writing
- Increase time for assignments
- Sequence directions
- Shorten directions

For a student with a lack of attention, the teacher can:

- Repeat major points
- Change the tone of voice
- Call the student's name before questioning
- Ask frequent questions
- Have the student write down directions

For a student who lacks respect, the teacher can:

- Inform the student that such behavior is unacceptable
- Make the consequences of future disrespect clear
- Try to determine the basis for the student's disrespect
- Have an individual conference or a conference with a mediator such as the student's advisor
- Model respect to the student

Table 4.3 provides additional suggestions. Many other strategies apply to students with specific disabilities. For example, for students who have difficulty maintaining attention, provide a seat near an adult or quiet peers; seat them away from high-traffic areas of the classroom; provide more breaks or task changes; and use more active participation activities. For students who have trouble beginning a task, provide a cue card of

TABLE 4.3   INTERVENTIONS

Problem	Solution
Listening	Provide visual displays (e.g., flowcharts, pictorials; wheels); prereading questions/terms at end of chapter; assigned reading; keyword note.
Distractibility	Minimize visual distractors in the environment; don't have interesting activities going on in one corner of the room while expecting the student to do his or her seatwork; provide a "quiet corner" for anyone who wishes a distraction.
Attention span	Have student work in short units of time with controlled activity breaks (i.e., reading break or magazine break); activities need to be interspersed throughout instruction.
Short-term memory	Offer review systems in a flashcard style so frequent practice can be done independently; material may need to be reviewed frequently.
Task completion	Present work in short units (i.e., five problems on paper cut into quarters rather than on one sheet); time frames should be short, with clear deadlines and checkpoints to measure progress; have a model available so product can be examined if directions can't be retained.
Impulsivity	Have as few distractions as possible.
Inattention to detail	Show the student how to do the work; have a checklist for what he [or she] needs to do, and have a reward system tied to the completion of all the steps.
Test taking	Emphasize detail through color coding or isolation. Have the student review critical details and main ideas in a flashcard system to support attention and practice specific retrieval.

SOURCE: Rooney (1995). Teaching students with attention disorders. *Intervention in School and Clinic, 30*(4), 221–225. Copyright 1995 by PRO-ED, Inc. Reprinted by permission.

steps on the desk that the student can check off as steps are completed; go to the students quickly at the start of the task and help them get started (indicate that you will return to check progress); and provide a peer helper. For students who have difficulty organizing, list assignments and materials needed on the board or a transparency; have students use notebooks with pocket dividers; color-code materials needed for various subjects; and provide time to gather books and materials at the start and end of school (Nissman, 2000; Price and Nelson, 2003).

These accommodations represent only a few of the ways lessons can be planned to help students get the most out of instruction. Based on the knowledge gained from early assessment and the teaching of initial lessons, teachers should begin to identify needs and to plan and implement accommodations that will help students learn. In this way, teachers can improve the validity of their instruction and assessments.

CHAPTER SUMMARY

- During instruction, teachers must accomplish two tasks simultaneously. They must deliver instruction to students, and they must constantly assess the progress and success of that instruction.
- Formative assessments are often more spontaneous and informal than planning assessments.
- Formal formative assessment requires thoughtful planning and focuses on collecting information in a systematic manner about specific learning objectives or misconceptions that students may develop.
- Informal formative assessment focuses on indirect indicators of engagement or understanding, such as body language, facial expressions, inattentiveness, and student questions.
- Studies of teachers' thoughts during instruction indicate that most attention is given to how learners are attending to and profiting from instruction, followed by teachers' own thoughts about their instructional actions. Teachers also assess to maintain class order at their level of tolerance.
- Because of its spontaneous nature, informal formative assessment must overcome some validity problems, including a lack of objectivity by the teacher regarding the success of instruction and the tendency to judge instructional success by facial expressions and participation rather than by actual student learning.
- Reliability problems during formative assessment center on the teacher's difficulty in observing students given the fast pace of instruction and the tendency to observe or call on only certain students in the class, thus limiting perception of the interest and understanding of the class as a whole.
- Formative assessments can be improved by observing a broader sample of students, supplementing informal assessment information with more formal information, and using appropriate questioning techniques during instruction.
- Questioning is the most useful strategy a teacher can employ to assess the progress of instruction. It gives the teacher information about student learning, lets students articulate their own thoughts, reinforces important concepts and behaviors, and influences the pace of instruction.
- Good questioning techniques include asking both higher- and lower-level questions, keeping questions related to the objectives of instruction, involving the whole class in the process, allowing sufficient "wait time" for students to think about their responses, probing responses with follow-up questions, and never demeaning or embarrassing a student for a wrong or unreasonable answer.
- Numerous types of accommodation can be made during instruction and ongoing assessment for students with disabilities.

olc

CHAPTER REVIEW

Visit the Online Learning Center at **www.mhhe.com/ russell7e** to review the case study referenced in the chapter.

QUESTIONS FOR DISCUSSION

1. What challenges do you see during instruction in the need to both monitor your students' learning and maintain the right level of tolerance? What is likely to be difficult for you about doing both more or less at the same time?
2. In what situations should a teacher change instruction in response to student interest and attentiveness, and in what situations should a teacher not change instruction?
3. Under what circumstances would you call on a shy student who never raises a hand for oral questions?

ACTIVITIES

1. Over the next 24 hours, try to notice what questions you tend to ask or not ask of those around you. In writing, summarize how well your current question-asking skills are likely to serve you in the classroom. What might you do to improve them?
2. Interview a teacher about how he or she knows when a lesson is going well or poorly. Ask the teacher to recall a recent lesson, and ask what his or her main thoughts were during the lesson.

REVIEW QUESTIONS

1. How is assessment for planning instruction different from assessment during instruction?
2. What are a teacher's main assessment tasks during instruction?
3. How does the concept of "level of tolerance" apply to instructional assessment?
4. What are the main kinds of evidence teachers collect to assess instruction, and what are the problems with these kinds of evidence?
5. What are three ways to improve assessment during instruction?
6. What are the validity and reliability issues in assessing during instruction?
7. What are the purposes of oral questioning?
8. What strategies of oral questioning can a teacher use to make assessment during instruction more valid and reliable?
9. What accommodations can be made for students with disabilities during instruction?

REFERENCES

Black, P. and Wiliam, D. (1998a). Assessment and classroom learning. *Assessment in Education, 7–74.*

Black, P., Harrison, C., Lee, C., Marshall, B., and Wiliam, D. (2004). Working Inside the Black Box: Assessment for Learning in the Classroom. *Phi Delta Kappan, 86, 9–21.*

Cartwright, P. G., Cartwright, C. A., and Ward, M. (1995). *Educating special learners,* 4th ed. Belmont, CA: Wadsworth.

Cegelka, P. T., and Berdine, W. H. (1995). *Effective instruction for students with learning difficulties.* Needham Heights, MA: Allyn and Bacon.

Chappuis, S., and Stiggins, R. J. (2002). Classroom assessment for learning. *Educational Leadership, 60*(1), 40–43.

Christensen, C. R. (1991). The discussion teacher in action: Questioning, listening, and response. In C. R. Christensen, D. A. Garvin, and A. Sweet, *Education for judgment.* Boston: Harvard Business School Press.

Doyle, W. (1986). Classroom organization and management. In M. C. Wittrock, *Handbook of research on teaching* (pp. 392–431). New York: Macmillan.

Morgan, N., and Saxton, J. (1991). *Teaching, questioning, and learning.* New York: Routledge.

Nissman, B. (2000). *Teacher-tested classroom management strategies.* Upper Saddle River, NJ: Merrill.

Price, K. M., and Nelson, K. L. (2003). *Daily planning for today's classroom: A guide to writing lesson and activity plans,* 2nd ed. Belmont, CA: Wadsworth.

Wiggins, G., and McTighe, J. (1998). *Understanding by design.* Alexandria, VA: Association for Supervision and Curriculum Development.

CHAPTER 5

SUMMATIVE ASSESSMENTS

KEY TOPICS

- *Formative and Summative Assessments*

- *The Logic of Summative Assessments*

- *Planning a Summative Assessment*

- *Preparing Students for Official Assessments*

After reading this chapter, you will be able to:

- Contrast summative assessment with initial and instructional assessment
- Differentiate between formative and summative assessment
- Explain when a summative assessment is an official assessment
- Explain the difference between good teaching and effective teaching
- Describe the decisions needed to develop and plan an official assessment
- State activities that help prepare students for official assessments

THINKING ABOUT TEACHING

In what ways can teachers use the results of assessments to improve student learning? Cite three or more ways.

In previous chapters, we have seen that assessment plays an important role in classrooms and that teachers use assessment to help them do the following:

- Get to know students early in the school year
- Establish the classroom as a learning community with rules and order
- Select appropriate educational objectives for students
- Develop lesson plans
- Select and critique instructional materials and activities
- Monitor the instructional process and student learning during instruction

Thus far, we have focused on assessments that occur prior to and during instruction. This chapter focuses on summative assessment that takes place after learning has occurred. All teachers assess their students' achievements with more than one approach, and the official tests that they give also vary. For example, one test might attempt to measure how much students remember while another focuses on higher-level thinking. But all good tests have much in common. This chapter lays a basis for preparing yourself and your students for effective summative assessment.

FORMATIVE AND SUMMATIVE ASSESSMENTS

Much of the evidence that supports teachers' decisions during instruction comes from formative assessments. Rarely saved in formal records, this information is used to guide teachers' interactions with students while working

Formative assessments are used to alter or improve instruction while it is still going on.

with students in the classroom. These observations and perceptions help teachers make moment-to-moment decisions about specific student problems, control of the class, what to do next in a lesson, and how students are reacting to instruction. Formative assessments are used primarily to "form" or alter ongoing classroom processes or activities. They provide information when it is still possible to influence or "form" the everyday processes that are at the heart of teaching.

Although formative assessments are critical to teachers' decision making, they should be supplemented by more formal assessments of learning. Such formal assessments usually come at the end of a classroom process or activity and aim to provide a summary of what students are able to do as a result of instruction. Called **summative assessments,** these procedures include end-of-chapter tests, projects, term papers, and final examinations. Table 5.1 contrasts formative and summative assessments.

Summative assessments are used to evaluate the outcomes of the instruction and take the form of tests, projects, term papers, and final exams.

In addition to providing information teachers can use to make decisions about how much a student knows or has learned as a result of instruction, summative assessments can also be used to make an **official assessment.** Official assessments help teachers make decisions that the school bureaucracy requires of them: grading and grouping students; recommending whether students should be promoted or placed in an honors section; and referring students to special education services if they have special needs. The most common forms of these assessments are midterm or final tests and report card grades.

Official assessments are needed by the school bureaucracy for purposes such as student testing, grading, and placement.

Unlike other assessments based largely on informal observations, official assessments are formal, appearing in report cards, school record folders, and standardized test reports, as well as in reading group or ability level designations. Further, most official assessment decisions involve individual students rather than groups or classes. Because they have important public consequences for students and must often be defended

TABLE 5.1	COMPARISON OF FORMATIVE AND SUMMATIVE ASSESSMENTS	
	Formative	**Summative**
Purpose	To monitor and guide a process while it is still in progress	To judge the success of a process at its completion
Time of assessment	During the process	At the end of the process
Type of assessment technique	Informal observation, quizzes, homework, questions, and worksheets	Formal tests, projects, and term papers
Use of assessment information	Improve and change a process while it is still going on	Judge the overall success of a process; grade, place, promote

by teachers, official assessments are generally based on systematically gathered summative evidence. In the classroom, official assessments almost always focus on students' cognitive performance, usually how well students have learned what has been taught.

Official, summative assessments and their resulting decisions are usually administered at the end of a unit of instruction or the end of a grading period. As a consequence, they occur much less frequently than formative assessments.

Teachers have mixed emotions about official assessments, and especially about tests, as the following comments show.

> I hate giving them. I find the testing situation to be one where tests become public expressions of what I already knew about the kid and what the kid already knew about the subject matter. In other words, I knew who would get A's and who would get F's because I taught the class. I knew who knew it and who didn't, so when kids take a test it is a public transmission to say "Yes, you know it" or "No, you don't know it."

> I need to use tests in algebra for grading my students and having objective information I can show parents when they complain about their child's grade. With so much emphasis on grades, I'm sure my students work mostly for a test grade and not for their enjoyment or understanding of the subject matter.

> The pressure to perform is too great for anyone, let alone a seven-year-old who's still trying to figure out what in the world he needs education for. Because the school system requires it, I test my students once a week in math and vocabulary and about once every two weeks in science, social studies, and religion. The only advantage I see in testing is that it gives the teacher a number on which to base the student's academic progress.

> Each test gives me some feedback on what I'm doing right and what I'm not, as well as what the class is learning best. I like to give a large number of tests to get this feedback and because I feel that the larger the number of test grades, the better indication I have of a student's learning.

> My tests are helpful in that they offer concrete evidence to show parents if the student is deficient in an area. I'll tell a parent that Johnny can't add and they'll sometimes respond, "I know he can add when he wants to." Then I show them a classroom test which shows Johnny's deficiency. One drawback to the tests, especially in the early grades, is that a child sometimes will become upset during testing, either because the child is having difficulty with the test or because the child wants to be doing something more enjoyable.

> The statewide standards are supposed to focus and guide my instruction and assessment. In some respects they are useful because they specify exactly what students are to learn, but it is also true that many of my students are not well prepared enough to begin instruction where the standards decree they should. This causes problems with planning my instruction.

Clearly, teachers differ in their views of official assessments, but no matter how they feel about them, teachers must use them at least some of the time in their classrooms.

Official assessments can have important consequences for students and should be taken quite seriously by teachers.

Despite their sometimes lukewarm endorsement by teachers, it would be a grave mistake to underestimate the importance of official assessments. Official assessments have important consequences for students and should be taken quite seriously by teachers, especially so-called high-stakes assessments, such as statewide tests of basic skills that may be required for graduation. The grading, placement, promotion, and other decisions that result from official assessments can influence students' lives both in and out of school. They are the public record of a student's school accomplishments and are often the sole evidence a parent has of how his or her child is doing in school. Students, their parents, and the public at large consider them to be very important and take them very seriously. The following teacher comments illustrate the degree of importance parents and students attach to official assessments.

> Every year at open house I can count on at least one parent asking how much test scores count in the final grade and another asking me if I allow children to make up a poor test grade in some way. Test scores are like the currency of the classroom for many of them.

> The kids are forever asking "Do we have to know this?" "Is this going to be on the test?" and "Will this be a big part of the test?" They define what's valuable and important in terms of what's going to be on the test.

For students, teachers, and administrators, official assessments are, in some respects, the "coin of the realm" for assessments.

THE LOGIC OF SUMMATIVE ASSESSMENTS

Good teaching refers to what teachers do during instruction, while effective teaching refers to the outcomes of instruction.

There is an important difference between good teaching and effective teaching. Good teaching refers to a *process* of instruction while *effective* teaching refers to the *outcomes* of instruction (Did students learn?). Among other things, a good teacher is one who provides a review at the start of a new lesson, states reasonable objectives, maintains an appropriate level of lesson difficulty, engages students in the learning process, emphasizes important points during instruction, gives students practice doing what they are expected to learn, and maintains a classroom environment that is conducive to learning. Good teaching focuses on the processes and procedures that a teacher uses while preparing for and delivering instruction.

But effective teaching goes one step beyond the process of teaching. Effective teaching focuses on whether students actually learn from instruction. An effective teacher is one whose students learn what they have been taught. Summative assessments seek to obtain evidence about teaching effectiveness, so they should be linked to the objectives, activities, and instruction provided students. It is impossible to evaluate students' achievement if the things assessed do not match the things students were taught.

Reflecting on your own experiences as a student, you may remember a test or quiz that contained "trick" questions. Or you may remember a test that contained questions that made you laugh or were intended to be fun. The primary aim in assessing student achievement is to *provide students a fair opportunity to demonstrate what they have learned from the instruction provided.* The primary aim is not to trick students into doing poorly, entertain them, or ensure that most of them get A's. It is not to determine the total knowledge students have accumulated as a result of their learning experiences, both in and out of school. It is simply to let students show what they have learned from the things they have been taught in their classroom.

The primary aim of assessing achievement is to provide students an opportunity to demonstrate what they have learned from the instruction provided.

PLANNING A SUMMATIVE ASSESSMENT

At the time of formal achievement testing, usually at the completion of instruction for a unit or chapter, the teacher must decide the following:

1. What should I test?
2. What type of assessment items or tasks should be given?
3. How long should the test take?
4. Should a teacher-made test or textbook assessment be used?

To explore how these questions inform the process of developing a summative assessment, we will examine closely the decisions Mr. Wysocki made as he created a unit test. Mr. Wysocki is a seventh-grade English teacher who is teaching his class about descriptive paragraphs. Based on earlier assessments, the students' previous English curriculum, the textbook, and other instructional resources available to him, Mr. Wysocki decides that the unit will focus on the following objectives, to which we have added labels from Bloom's Taxonomy:

1. The student can name the three stages of the writing process (i.e., prewriting, writing, and editing). (knowledge)
2. The student can explain in his or her own words the purposes of the three stages of the writing process. (comprehension)
3. The student can select the topic sentences in given descriptive paragraphs. (application)
4. The student can write a topic sentence for a given descriptive writing topic. (analysis)
5. The student can write a descriptive paragraph with a topic sentence, descriptive detail, and a concluding statement. (synthesis)

To organize his objectives, Mr. Wysocki develops a table of specifications that identifies the cognitive processes students are to demonstrate, the

olc
CHAPTER
CASE STUDY

Visit the text Online Learning Center to read the case of Diane News, an elementary school teacher who must choose only four students for the school district's gifted and talented program. How does she make the choice?

www.mhhe.com/ russell7e

TABLE 5.2   TABLE OF SPECIFICATIONS

Content Dimension	Process Dimension					
	Knowledge	Comprehension	Application	Analysis	Synthesis	Evaluation
Stages of writing	X (L)	X (M)				
Topic sentences			X (M)	X (L)		
Writing essay					X (H)	

L = Low   M = Middle   H = High

content on which they are to demonstrate these processes, and the amount of emphasis each objective receives in instruction (low, middle, or high). Table 5.2 shows Mr. Wysocki's specifications.

Using a Table of Specifications

The table of specifications has two dimensions: content and process. The content dimension includes the main topics of instruction and assessment. The process dimension, which you will recognize as the six categories of Bloom's Taxonomy, lists the cognitive processes related to each content topic. In Mr. Wysocki's table, for example, the intersection of knowledge (process dimension) and stages of writing (content dimension), represented by the X, refers to the objective: *The student can name the three stages of the writing process* (i.e., prewriting, writing, and editing); that is, the student will remember the names of the three writing stages. The L after the X refers to the amount of time allotted to this objective. Since it is a simple memorization task, a low (L) amount of time is spent teaching it. The intersection of comprehension (process dimension) and stages of writing (content dimension) refers to the objective: *The student can explain in his or her own words the purposes of the three stages of the writing process.* Notice that stages of writing relate to two different objectives, because Mr. Wysocki is concerned with two processes: remembering and explaining. Notice also that Mr. Wysocki places more emphasis on the students' own explanation of the three stages (M) than on remembering the stages (L). He also could have stated the planned number of test items to be used with each intersection of content and process instead of using L, M, and H.

Mr. Wysocki's third and fourth objectives indicate that he wants his students to both select and write their own topic sentences. Selecting calls for an analysis that differentiates topic sentences from other types of sentences. Writing a topic sentence calls for application of a procedure. Writing an essay, the final objective, calls for a correct synthesis of the three stages of descriptive writing. The writing objective is the most important and complex outcome, so more time is allotted to it than to the other four objectives.

Once his objectives are identified and organized, Mr. Wysocki develops lesson plans for them. In selecting activities, he considers the ability levels of his students, their attention spans, suggestions made in the textbook, and additional resources available to supplement and reinforce the textbook. He also plans activities that will give students practice in each objective. One of the benefits of a table of specifications is that it emphasizes the different processes that intersect with the content. Thus, the table reminds Mr. Wysocki that he needs both remembering and explaining activities to attain his first two objectives.

With the objectives and the planned activities identified, Mr. Wysocki commences instruction. First, he introduces students to the three steps in the writing process: (1) prewriting (identifying the intended audience, purpose, and initial ideas), (2) writing, and (3) editing what has been written. He tells students they are expected to memorize the names of the three stages. Next, he assigns students topics and has them describe how they will go through the three steps. He has them give reasons that each step is necessary for good writing. He then introduces them to the concept of a paragraph, and they read descriptive paragraphs to find a common structure. He notes that a paragraph is made up of a topic sentence, detail sentences, and a concluding sentence. Then he has the students identify the topic sentences in several paragraphs. Later, he has them write their own topic sentences. The instruction should be linked to the objectives. Different instructional techniques are linked to different types of objectives. Lower-level objectives focus on memorizing factual information, and higher-level objectives require application and synthesis.

Instruction seems to go along fairly well except that students have a hard time finding the common structure in paragraphs. Mr. Wysocki has to give additional explanation to the class. Even after instruction, his end-of-lesson assessments indicate that many students have the mistaken idea that the topic sentence always comes first in a paragraph, so he devises a worksheet in which many of the topic sentences are not at the beginning of the paragraph. Finally, Mr. Wysocki has students write descriptive paragraphs. First, he has them write on the same topics so they can compare topic sentences and the amount of detail in one another's paragraphs. He thinks this strategy is useful because students can learn from one another's efforts. Homework assignments are returned to students with suggestions for improvement, and students are required to edit and rewrite their paragraphs. Later, students are allowed to construct descriptive paragraphs on topics of their choice.

Not all teachers would have instructed their students in this fashion; different teachers have different students, resources, and styles. But Mr. Wysocki did what he judged was best for his particular class. He instituted instructional procedures that gave students practice on the behaviors they were expected to learn, provided feedback on student performance during instruction, and revised his plans based on his observations during instruction. He demonstrated the characteristics of a good teacher.

Mr. Wysocki felt that he had a fair sense of how well the class had mastered the objectives. Although he knew something about the achievement of each student, he was not sure about each one's achievement of all five objectives. He felt that a formal, end-of-unit assessment would provide information about each student's mastery of all he had taught. By conducting a formal summative assessment, he would not have to rely on incomplete, informal perceptions when grading his students. To develop the assessment, however, he had to make some decisions about the nature of the test he would administer.

Decisions in Planning a Test

The most useful strategy to assess the progress of instruction is oral questioning, which serves a number of purposes from both instructional and assessment perspectives. Unfortunately, most classroom questions tend to be lower level and convergent.

A fair and valid test covers information and skills similar to those covered during instruction.

When deciding what he should include in his formal summative assessment and what form the assessment task should take, Mr. Wysocki answered four important questions teachers ask as they develop summative assessments.

1. *What should I test?* The first important decision when preparing to assess student achievement is to identify the information, processes, and skills that will be tested. A valid achievement test is one that provides students a fair opportunity to show what they have learned from instruction. Therefore, in deciding what to test, it was necessary for Mr. Wysocki to focus attention on both his objectives and the actual instruction that took place. Usually the two are very similar, but sometimes it is necessary to add or omit an objective once teaching begins. In the final analysis, the things that are actually presented during instruction are the most important to assess.

Mr. Wysocki knew, then, that he had to gather information about how well students could memorize and explain in their own words the three stages of the writing process, select topic sentences in a paragraph, write suitable topic sentences, and compose a descriptive paragraph with a topic sentence, descriptive detail, and summarizing statement. But what about other important skills such as taking notes on a topic or knowing the difference between a descriptive and an expository paragraph? These are also useful, so should they be on Mr. Wysocki's test?

The answer to this question is no! There will always be more objectives to teach than there is time to teach them. There will always be useful topics and skills that have to be omitted from tests because of lack of time. This is why thoughtfully planning instruction in terms of students' needs and resources is so important. Including untaught skills on an achievement test diminishes its validity, making it less than a true and fair assessment of what students have learned from classroom instruction. By confining his test questions to what he actually taught, Mr. Wysocki could say to himself, "I decided what the important objectives were for students, I provided instruction on those objectives, I gave students practice performing the objectives, and I gave a test that asked students to do things similar to those I taught. The results of the test should fairly reflect how much the students have achieved in this unit and permit me to grade fairly."

2. *What type of assessment items or tasks should be given?* This question is answered by reference back to the learning objectives. Each objective contains a target process or behavior that students have been taught. For example, three of Mr. Wysocki's objectives referred respectively to comprehending (explain in one's own words), applying (write a topic sentence), and synthesizing (integrate and write an essay). These three processes are best assessed by **supply questions,** questions that require the student to produce (supply) an answer or product. Another one of his objectives referred to analyzing (selecting a topic sentence). This type of behavior can be assessed efficiently by **selection questions,** questions that present the student with a set of choices from which the student selects one or more. Yet another of Mr. Wysocki's objectives referred to remembering (name the three stages of the writing process). This behavior can be assessed by either a supply question (list or orally state the three stages) or a selection question (pick out the three stages from a set of choices). Thus, the format used to assess learning is largely predetermined by the statement of the objective.

The type of assessment procedure chosen depends on the nature of the objective being assessed.

Many teachers feel that only essay tests are good. Others use multiple-choice items as much as possible, and still others believe that tests should contain a variety of question types. Here is how several teachers responded when asked about the kinds of questions they use in their tests:

> I always give the kids essay tests because that's the only way I can see how well they think.

> Multiple-choice items are easy and fast to score, so I use them most of the time to test students' achievement.

> I make sure that every test I make up has some multiple-choice questions, some fill-in questions, and at least one essay question. I believe that variety in the kinds of questions keeps students interested and gives all students a chance to show what they know in the way that's best for them.

Each of these teachers states a reason for following a particular classroom testing strategy. The reasons are neither wrong nor inappropriate, but they are secondary to the main purpose of official achievement testing, which is *to permit students to show how well they have learned the behaviors or processes they were taught.* Thus, no single type of assessment item is applicable all the time. What makes a particular procedure useful is whether it matches the objectives and instruction provided.

3. *How long should the test take?* Since time for testing is limited, choices must be made in deciding the length of a test. Usually, practical matters such as the age of the students or the length of a class period are most influential. Since the stamina and attention spans of young students are less

The age of the students, the subject being tested, and the length of the class period all affect the length of a test.

than those of older ones, a useful strategy to follow with elementary school students is to test them fairly often using short tests that assess only a few objectives. Because of their typical attention spans, 15- to 30-minute tests, depending on the grade and group, are suggested for elementary students.

Curricula for some school subjects such as history, social studies, and English are composed of relatively discrete, self-contained units. In other subjects such as mathematics, foreign language, and science, knowledge must be built up in a hierarchical sequence. Whereas topics in history may stand on their own, topics in mathematics or Spanish usually cannot be understood unless prior math and Spanish lessons have been mastered. Consequently, when teaching in a hierarchical subject area, it is useful to give more frequent tests to keep students on task in their studying and to make sure they grasp the early ideas that provide the foundation for subsequent, more complex ideas. Testing in middle, junior, and high schools is usually restricted by the length of the class period. Most teachers at these levels plan their tests to last almost one complete class period.

Mr. Wysocki's class periods are 50 minutes long. He wanted a test that would take about 40 minutes for most students to complete. A 40-minute test would allow time for distribution and collection of the tests, as well as a few minutes for those students who always want "one more minute" before handing in their test.

The number of test questions per objective depends on the instructional time spent on each objective and its importance.

In deciding how many questions to ask for each objective, Mr. Wysocki tried to balance two factors: (1) the instructional time spent on each objective and (2) its importance. Some objectives are usually more important than others. These objectives tend to be the more general ones that call for the integration of several narrower objectives. Even though a great deal of instructional time was spent on writing and identifying topic sentences, Mr. Wysocki values this skill less for its own sake than for its contribution to the more general objective of constructing a descriptive paragraph. Thus, the number of test questions dealing with writing and identifying topic sentences was not proportional to the instructional time he spent on it. It is not necessary to include an equal number of questions for each objective, but all objectives should be assessed by some items. On the basis of these factors and the instruction he had provided, Mr. Wysocki felt that a test with the following format would be fair to students and would provide a valid and reliable assessment of their learning:

- The students can *name* the three stages of writing. Use one supply question: list the three names.
- The students can *explain* in their own words the three stages of the writing process (i.e., prewriting, writing, and editing). Use a short essay question.
- The students can *select* the topic sentence in a given descriptive paragraph. Use three multiple-choice questions, each consisting of a paragraph and a list of possible topic sentences from which each student has to select the correct one.

- The students can *write* a topic sentence for a given descriptive topic. Use three short-answer questions that give the students a topic area and require them to write a topic sentence for each area.
- The students can *write* a descriptive paragraph using a topic sentence, descriptive detail, and a concluding statement. Use an essay question in which each student writes a descriptive paragraph on a topic of his or her choice. The paragraph cannot be on a topic the student used previously during instruction or practice.

Mr. Wysocki thought that writing topic sentences was an important enough skill to state it as a separate objective. Because he had spent considerable time teaching the objective, he decided to test it separately. When teachers focus their tests solely on their general, integrative objectives, students may answer questions incorrectly because they cannot successfully integrate the separate skills they have learned. Teachers may conclude that students do not understand or have not learned specific skills because they cannot answer such questions successfully, even though the students may have learned all the more specific skills they were taught.

4. Should a teacher-made test or a textbook test be used? Teachers are inevitably confronted with the question of whether to use the textbook test or to construct their own. The very availability of textbook tests can be seductive. Teachers may think: "After all, the test comes with the textbook, seems to measure what is in the chapter I'm teaching, looks attractive, and is readily available, so why shouldn't I use it?" Mr. Wysocki asked himself the same question.

Notice that the decision about using a textbook test or constructing one cannot be answered until *after* the teacher has reflected on what was taught and has identified the topics and behaviors to be tested. The usefulness of any achievement test (high stakes or low stakes) cannot be judged without reference to the planned objectives and actual instruction.

Textbook tests furnish a ready-made instrument for assessing the objectives stressed in the textbook and can save classroom teachers much time. Test formats vary across textbook publishers in terms of length, layout, and question type. Look through the teacher's editions of some textbooks to see the range of tests available.

Before using these tests, teachers should consider the criteria that permit a teacher to use a textbook or teacher-made test with confidence. The basic concern is whether the items on the test match the instruction provided to students.

Regardless of whether a teacher is constructing his or her own test or judging the adequacy of a textbook test, he or she must consider the same basic validity issue: Do the items on the test match the instruction provided to students? The more a teacher alters and reshapes the textbook curriculum, the less valid its accompanying tests become. As one teacher put it, "The textbook tests look good and can be time-savers, but they often

The main consideration in judging the adequacy of a textbook test is the match between its questions and what students were actually taught in class.

don't test exactly what I've been doing in the classroom. Every time I change what I do from what the text suggests I do, and every time I leave out a lesson or section of the text from my instruction, I have to look at the text test carefully to make sure it's fair for my students."

Teachers can and should combine textbook materials with their own constructed items to create assessment items.

Remember that it is possible to combine textbook items and teacher-constructed items into an assessment. Often the textbook test has some appropriate assessment items that can be used in conjunction with the items the teacher has constructed. This approach is used by many teachers. The key issue, however, is the relevance of the assessment items to the instruction provided to the students. Key Assessment Tools 5.1 focuses on judging a textbook test.

To summarize, both textbook and teacher-made tests should (1) clearly relate to the objectives of instruction, (2) include enough questions to assess all or most of the objectives, and (3) use assessment methods suited to the backgrounds and prior experiences of the students (Joint Advisory Committee, 2002). Tests that meet these criteria will provide a valid indication of student learning. Key Assessment Tools 5.2 provides a summary of common problems teachers encounter in judging achievement tests.

Key Assessment Tools 5.1

KEY POINTS TO CONSIDER IN JUDGING TEXTBOOK TESTS

1. The decision to use a textbook test or premade standard achievement test must come *after* a teacher identifies the objectives that he or she has taught and now wants to assess.

2. Textbook and standard tests are designed for the typical classroom, but since few classrooms are typical, most teachers deviate somewhat from the text in order to accommodate their students' needs.

3. The more classroom instruction deviates from the textbook, the less valid the textbook tests are likely to be.

4. The main consideration in judging the adequacy of a textbook or standard achievement test is the match between its test questions and what students were taught in their classes:

   a. Are questions similar to the teacher's objectives and instructional emphases?

   b. Do questions require students to perform the behaviors they were taught?

   c. Do questions cover all or most of the important objectives taught?

   d. Are the language level and terminology appropriate for students?

   e. Does the number of items for each objective provide a sufficient sample of student performance?

Key Assessment Tools 5.2

COMMON PROBLEMS IN DEVELOPING OR SELECTING TESTS TO ASSESS STUDENT ACHIEVEMENT

1. Failing to consider objectives and instructional emphases when planning a test.
2. Failing to assess all of the important objectives and instructional topics.
3. Failing to select item types that permit students to demonstrate the desired behavior.
4. Adopting a test without reviewing it for relevance to the instruction provided.
5. Including topics or objectives not taught to students.
6. Including too few items to assess the consistency of student performance.
7. Using tests to punish students for inattentiveness or acting out.

PREPARING STUDENTS FOR OFFICIAL ASSESSMENTS

The rest of this chapter discusses how to prepare students for testing. Many of these practices may appear to be commonsensical things that all teachers would normally do. However, such is not the case. It is remarkable how often these commonsense practices are ignored or overlooked. Failure to carry out these activities can jeopardize the validity of the inferences and decisions a teacher makes based on student test performance.

Issues of Test Preparation

We use tests and other assessments to help make decisions about students' learning in some content area. A student's performance on a test or assessment is meant to represent the student's mastery of a broader body of knowledge and skills than just the specific questions included on the test or performance task. Remember from Chapter 1 that when Ms. Lopez described Manuela's and Chad's scores of 100 on her long division with remainder test, she said, "Manuela and Chad can do long division with remainder items very well." She did not say, "Manuela and Chad can do the 10 specific long division with remainder items that were on my test." Tests and other assessments gather a sample of a student's behavior and use that sample to generalize how the student is likely to perform if confronted with similar tasks or items. For example, the performance of

Fair and valid assessment involves preparing appropriate objectives, providing good instruction on these objectives, and determining how these objectives are assessed.

a student who scores 90 percent on a test of poetry analysis, chemical equation balancing, or capitalization rules is interpreted as indicating that the student has mastered about 90 percent of the general content domain he or she was taught. The specific tasks or test items are selected to represent the larger group of similar tasks and items.

Objectives, instruction, and the test items *should* all be aligned with one another. After all, the purpose of an achievement test is to determine how well students have learned what they were taught. By definition, an achievement test must be related to instruction, and instruction is, in a real sense, preparation for the test. The important question, however, is this: When does the relationship among objectives, instruction, and the test become so close that it is inappropriate or unethical?

An achievement test should give information about how well a student can answer questions similar but not identical to those taught in class.

There is an important ethical difference between teaching to the test and teaching the test itself. Teaching to the test involves teaching students the general skills, knowledge, and processes that they need to master in order to answer the questions on a test. This is an appropriate and valid practice. It is what good teaching and testing are all about. But teaching the test itself—that is, teaching students the answers to specific questions that will likely appear on the test—is neither appropriate nor ethical. It produces a distorted, invalid picture of student achievement. Such a test will give information about how well students can remember the specific items they were taught, but it will not tell how well they can do on questions that are similar, but not identical, to the ones they have been taught. Teachers have an educational and ethical responsibility not to corrupt the validity of students' achievement test performance by limiting their instruction to the types of skills and knowledge that they believe will be on the test or by teaching students how to succeed on specific test items. Instead of using the content of a test to guide instruction, a teacher's instruction should be guided by the content and skills contained in the learning objectives or in the state standards.

There is an important difference between teaching to the test and teaching the test itself.

When working with a predetermined curriculum, it is appropriate for teachers to place additional emphasis on the objectives that will be tested, so long as they do not prepare the students for the specific test items that will be used to measure these objectives. However, it is improper for teachers to consciously exclude important objectives from their instruction solely because those objectives are not on the test provided by a text or other outside sources. Instead of linking assessment to the curriculum objectives, such teachers have let the test objectives define their curriculum.

Mel Levine, MD, professor of pediatrics at the University of North Carolina Medical School in Chapel Hill, suggests a "do no harm" approach to testing practices that states some important and useful strategies. See Key Assessment Tools 5.3.

The following sections describe other actions that teachers should carry out to prepare their students for achievement tests. As you read these sections, bear in mind the preceding list of inappropriate practices. Also bear in mind that concern about test preparation is not confined to paper-and-pencil tests, but also includes other assessment strategies and tasks.

Key Assessment Tools 5.3

"DO NO HARM" TESTING PRACTICES

1. Testing can help elevate education standards, but not if it creates larger numbers of students who are written off as unsuccessful. When a student does poorly, determine which link in the learning chain is uncoupled. Always have constructive, nonpunitive contingency plans for students who perform poorly on a test. Testing should not be an end in itself, but rather a call to action.

2. Not all students can demonstrate their strengths in the same manner. Allow different students to demonstrate their learning differently, using the means of their choice (portfolios, expert papers, oral presentations, and projects, as well as multiple-choice tests).

3. Never use testing as justification for retaining a student in a grade. Retention is ineffective and seriously damaging to students. How can you retain a child while claiming you are not leaving anyone behind?

4. Some students who excel on tests might develop a false sense of security and confidence, failing to realize that adult careers tap many abilities that no test can elicit. Take care to nurture vital capacities that are not testable.

5. Avoid the hazard of teachers' teaching to the tests because your work or school is being judged solely on the basis of examination scores. Teachers should never have their students rehearse or explicitly prepare for tests. Testing should be unannounced. Good results on such tests should be the product of the regular, undisturbed curriculum.

Source: Levine. 2003.

Provide Good Instruction

The single most important thing a teacher can do to prepare students for formal classroom achievement tests is to provide them with good instruction. Earlier it was noted that good teaching includes activities such as providing a review at the start of a new lesson, setting an appropriate difficulty level for instruction, emphasizing important points during instruction, giving students practice on the objectives they are expected to learn, and maintaining an orderly classroom learning environment. These practices will prepare students for testing better than anything else a teacher might do. A primary ethical responsibility of teaching, therefore, is to provide the best instruction possible, without corrupting the achievement test in the ways described above. In the absence of good instruction, all aspects of assessment are greatly diminished.

Good instruction is the most important preparation for formal achievement testing.

Review before Testing

Teaching a unit or chapter means introducing students to many different objectives, some early and others at the end of instruction. Because the topics students remember best are the ones most recently taught, it is good practice to provide students with a review prior to formal testing. The review can take many forms: a question-and-answer session, a written or oral summary of main ideas, or administration of a review test. Review serves many purposes: to refresh students on objectives taught early in the unit, to provide one last chance to practice important behaviors and skills, and to afford an opportunity to ask questions about things that are unclear. Often, the review exercise itself provokes questions that help students grasp partially understood ideas.

Test reviews often provoke questions that help students grasp partially understood ideas.

The review should cover the main ideas and skills that were taught. Many teachers fail to conduct a review because they feel the review might "tip off" students to the kinds of things that will be on the test. This is faulty reasoning. A review is the final instructional act for the chapter or unit. It gives students an opportunity to practice skills and clarify misunderstandings about the content. If the review focuses mainly on peripheral topics and behaviors in an attempt to "protect" the areas to be tested, students will not be afforded a final practice on the important outcomes. They will not have their questions answered and, after experiencing a few irrelevant review sessions, will cease taking them seriously.

The purpose of a review, especially a review for a test, is to prepare students for the test. In essence, the review is the teacher's way of saying, "These are examples of the ideas, topics, and skills that I expect you to have learned. Go over this review and see how well you have learned them. Practice one last time before I ask you to demonstrate your learning on the test that counts toward your grade. If you have questions or difficulties, we'll go over them before the test. After that, you're on your own." The review exercises or questions should be similar, but not identical, to the exercises or questions that will make up the final test. Most textbooks contain chapters or unit reviews to use prior to testing. Go to your curriculum center or library or to a local school and examine the chapter tests and reviews in a variety of textbooks.

A classroom achievement test should not trick students, make them answer questions on topics they haven't been taught, or create a high-anxiety test situation. It should give students a fair chance to show what they have learned. A pertinent review prior to the test will help them do this.

Ensure Familiarity with Question Formats

If a classroom test contains questions that use an unfamiliar format, students should be given practice with that format prior to testing. The need for such practice is especially important in the elementary and middle grades where students first encounter matching, multiple-choice, true-false, short-answer, and essay questions. Students must learn what is expected of them for each type of question and understand how to record their answer. One opportune time to familiarize students with question formats is during the review exercises prior to the chapter or unit test. Pretest practice with new types of question and response formats can reduce anxiety and permit a more valid assessment of student learning. In addition to familiarizing students with new types of question and response formats, there is a general set of test-taking guidelines that can help students do their best on tests. These guidelines will not enable students to overcome the handicaps of poor teaching and lack of study, but they can help focus students during testing. Table 5.3 lists some advice that you may want to give students before a test (Ebel and Frisbie, 1991).

Another set of skills, called **testwise skills,** help students identify errors on the part of the question writer that provide clues to the correct answer. For example, when responding to multiple-choice questions, the testwise student applies the following probabilities:

- If the words "some" or "often" or similar vague words are used in one of the options, it is likely to be the correct option.
- The option that is longest or most precisely stated is likely to be the correct one.
- Any choice that has grammatical or spelling errors is not likely to be the correct one.
- Choices that do not attach smoothly to the stem of the question are not likely to be correct.

Teachers should be aware of common test errors so they can guard against them when they construct or select test items. To increase the validity of the inferences and decisions made based on test performance, ensure that students who answer test questions correctly do so because they have

If students are not familiar with the types of questions used on a test, the test does not produce a valid assessment of what they have learned.

TABLE 5.3   COMMON TEST-TAKING STRATEGY ADVICE FOR STUDENTS

- Read test directions carefully.
- Find out how questions will be scored. Will all questions count equally? Will points be taken off for deficiencies in spelling, grammar, or neatness?
- Pace yourself to ensure that you can complete the test.
- Plan and organize essay questions before writing.
- Attempt to answer all questions. Guessing is not penalized, so guess when you don't know the answer.
- When using a separate answer sheet, check often to make certain that you are marking your responses in the correct space.
- Be in good physical and mental condition at the time of testing by avoiding late-night cram sessions.

mastered the content or skill taught and not because they have strong test-wise skills.

There are many other testwise strategies that students use to overcome a lack of content knowledge. With regard to one's own classroom tests, it is best to make students aware of such general test-taking skills and then concentrate on writing fair, appropriate test questions that do not contain errors that can be "psyched out." Chapter 7 provides a more detailed description of testwise strategies and describes how to write or select test questions that have few of the faults that testwise students thrive on.

Scheduling the Test

It has already been recommended that teachers provide students the opportunity to review, study, and reflect on the instruction before being tested. However, there are other considerations about the times when students are most likely to show their best performance. For example, if a teacher were to test students the day of the school's championship football game, the period after an assembly or lunch, or the first day after a long school vacation, it is likely that students' performance on the test would underrepresent their achievement of the instructional objectives. Likewise, a teacher should not schedule a test on a day that he or she will be away just so the substitute teacher will have something to keep the students busy. The substitute may not be able to answer students' questions about either the test or the meaning of particular questions. Furthermore, if it is an elementary classroom, the presence of a stranger in the classroom may make the students uncomfortable and unable to do their best.

In the elementary school there is more flexibility in scheduling tests than in the middle school or high school, where 50-minute periods and departmentalized instruction mean that students must be in certain places at certain times. The algebra teacher who has a class immediately after lunch has no choice but to test students then. While no teacher has complete control over scheduling tests, it is useful to bear in mind that students are able to perform better on tests at certain times than at others.

Giving Students Information about the Test

In order to reduce test anxiety, teachers should formally inform students when a text will be given, what areas will be covered, what kinds of questions it will contain, how long it will take, and how much it will count.

It is good practice to formally inform students when the test will be given, what areas will be covered, what types of questions it will contain, how much it counts, and how long it will take. These factors undoubtedly influence your own test preparation. By providing this information, the teacher can help reduce some of the anxiety that inevitably accompanies the announcement of a test. When information is provided, an upcoming test becomes an incentive for students to study.

The hardest achievement test for students to prepare for is the first one they take in a class. Even if a teacher provides detailed information about topics to be covered, types of items, number of questions, and the like, students always have some uncertainty about the test. It is not until they take a teacher's first test that they get a sense of how that teacher tests and whether the review given by the teacher can be trusted as a basis for test preparation. Once students know the teacher's style, they have a sense of what to expect on subsequent tests and whether the teacher's pretest information is useful.

Of course, unless a teacher has thought about the nature of the test to be given, it is impossible to provide the pretest information students need to prepare for the test. The specifics of test content, types of questions, and test length should be considered well before the test is given. Hastily planned tests too often focus mainly on memorization skills and fail to cover a representative sample of the instruction provided to students. Thus, to inform students about test characteristics, a teacher cannot put off planning the test until the last minute.

Hastily planned tests too often focus on memory items and fail to cover a representative sample of the instruction provided.

CHAPTER SUMMARY

- Summative assessments allow teachers to make decisions about the extent to which students have achieved the objectives that were the focus of instruction.
- Unlike early and instructional assessments, summative assessments are based on formal, systematically gathered, end-of-instruction evidence.
- The main types of summative assessment instruments are teacher-made tests, textbook tests, and standardized high-stakes tests.
- Summative assessments become official assessments when they are used to help teachers make decisions that the school bureaucracy requires of them, such as assigning grades, recommending students for promotion, placing students in groups, and referring students to special education services.
- Official assessments are taken very seriously by students, parents, school administrators, and the public at large because they have lasting consequences for students.
- Good summative assessments have three features: (1) students are expected to perform what the teacher has stated in the objectives and instruction; (2) the questions provide a representative sample of the things students were taught; and (3) the questions, directions, and scoring procedures are clear and appropriate. Incorporating these three features in summative assessments help provide valid and reliable information for decision making.
- Because the aim of summative assessments is to provide students a fair opportunity to show what they have learned from instruction, it is very important that assessments reflect what students have been taught. This is the most basic requirement for summative assessments.
- The methods used to gather information about student learning depend on the objectives and instruction provided. Methods that

olc

CHAPTER REVIEW

Visit the Online Learning Center at **www.mhhe.com/ russell7e** to review the case study referenced in the chapter.

permit the students to show the behaviors taught are essential for valid assessment. Use multiple-choice, matching, or true-false questions when students are taught to "choose" or "select" answers; short-answer or essay questions when students are taught to "explain," "construct," or "defend" answers; and actual performances when students are taught to "demonstrate" or "show."

- A table of specifications can be used to ensure that test items reflect specific objectives.
- Test length is determined by the age and attention span of the students and the type of test questions used.
- The decision whether to construct one's own test or use a textbook test depends on how closely instruction followed the lead of the textbook. The more a teacher supplements or omits material from the textbook, the less likely the textbook test will be a valid indication of students' learning.
- Preparing students for summative assessments requires careful thought and planning on the part of the teacher. First and foremost, teachers should provide the best instruction possible prior to assessment. Good instruction should be followed by a review that gives students a chance to ask questions and practice important behaviors and skills that will be tested. Use of textbook review tests is one way to prepare students. Students, especially those in early elementary grades, should be given practice with unfamiliar test item formats before testing. Students should be informed in advance of the time, nature, coverage, and format of the test.
- The test should be scheduled, when possible, at a time that will permit students to do their best work.
- In preparing students for testing, the teacher should *not* focus instruction only on items or item formats used on the test, use classroom examples taken directly from the test, or give students practice taking the actual test. These practices corrupt the validity of inferences and decisions based on test results. Instruction should be focused on the general skills and knowledge teachers want students to learn in a subject area, not on the specific test questions that will be asked about those areas.

QUESTIONS FOR DISCUSSION

1. What are some things that a teacher can do to help prepare students for classroom testing? What are some dangers of test preparation that should be avoided?
2. If higher-level thinking requires students to work with material and concepts they have not been taught specifically, what are some ways to prepare students to take tests that include higher-level items?
3. What are the hallmarks of *effective* teaching?

4. How do official assessments differ from early assessments and instructional assessments?

5. What are the criteria for judging how good a classroom achievement test is? Aside from what is on the test, what other information would you need to judge a test's validity and reliability?

ACTIVITY

Select a chapter from a teacher's edition of a textbook. Read the chapter and examine the aids and resources provided for planning, delivering, and assessing instruction. Compare the objectives of the chapter to the suggestions for instruction provided by the textbook author. Will the suggested instructional experiences help students attain the objectives? Is there a match between objectives and instructional experiences? Examine the end-of-chapter test. Is it a good test in terms of the chapter's objectives and the instructional suggestions? Do the types of test items used match the objectives? What is the proportion of higher- and lower-level items in the test?

REVIEW QUESTIONS

1. What is the fundamental purpose of assessing students' achievement? What decisions must a teacher make when preparing to assess student achievement?

2. How should the validity of an achievement test be determined?

3. List some ethical and unethical ways to prepare students for achievement testing. Why are the unethical ways you identified unethical?

4. What factors should be considered in determining whether to use a textbook test or construct your own?

5. In what way are the methods used to gather information about student learning dependent on the teacher's objectives and the instruction provided?

6. What are the characteristics of a good official assessment?

REFERENCES

Ebel, R. L., and Frisbie, D. A. (1991). *Essentials of educational measurement,* 5th ed. Englewood Cliffs, NJ: Prentice-Hall.

Joint Advisory Committee, Centre for Research in Applied Measurement and Evaluation (2002). *Principles for fair student assessment practices for education in Canada.* Edmonton: University of Alberta. http//www.2Learn.ca/Projects/Together/fair.html.

Levine, M. (2003). Celebrating diverse minds. *Educational Leadership,* (61) 2, 12–18.

CHAPTER 6

DESIGNING, ADMINISTERING, AND SCORING ACHIEVEMENT TESTS

KEY TOPICS

- *Selection and Supply Test Items*

- *Higher-Level Questions*

- *Guidelines for Writing and Critiquing Test Items*

- *Assembling Tests*

- *Issues of Cheating*

- *Scoring Paper-and-Pencil Tests*

- *Analyzing Item Validity*

- *Discussing Test Results with Students*

After reading this chapter, you will be able to:

- Define basic item-writing terms such as *selection item, supply item, item stem,* and *specific determiner*
- Distinguish between higher-level and lower-level test items
- Assemble tests
- Administer tests
- Identify methods of cheating and ways to prevent cheating
- Score paper-and-pencil tests
- Analyze item validity
- Discuss test results with students

THINKING ABOUT TEACHING

Can you write a multiple-choice, true-false, short-answer, and essay question appropriate for the grade and subject you wish to teach?

A t most grade levels, achievement tests are the most commonly used procedure for gathering formal evidence about student learning. These tests may be developed by teachers, textbook publishers, statewide test constructors, or standardized test publishers. We have seen that a good assessment plan has several key components: identifying important instructional objectives, selecting question formats that match these objectives, deciding whether to construct one's own test or use one from the textbook, providing good instruction, and providing a review of and information about the test. The beneficial effects of these important preparatory steps can be undone, however, if the actual test questions do not provide valid measures of knowledge and skills, or if they are subjectively scored. Such problems do not give students a fair chance to show what they have learned and, consequently, do not provide information that enables valid decision making. No matter whether they are concerned with teacher-made, textbook, statewide, or standardized tests, teachers should use items that are appropriate for the knowledge and skills they are assessing, score answers objectively, prevent cheating, and provide feedback to students that helps support their learning.

This chapter examines and contrasts different types of test questions and provides guidelines for assembling items into tests. Issues of scoring student responses objectively, preventing cheating, and sharing results with students are also discussed. The guidelines and practices explored in this chapter will help teachers design and administer tests that allow them to make valid inferences about their students' learning.

SELECTION AND SUPPLY TEST ITEMS

Multiple-choice, true-false, and matching questions are examples of selection items. Supply items are those in which the student constructs his or her own answer.

The two most common types of test questions are selection items and supply items. As their names suggest, **selection items** require the student to select the correct answer from among a number of choices. **Supply items** require the student to supply or construct his or her own answer.

Selection Items

Within the general category of selection items are multiple-choice, true-false, and matching questions.

Multiple-Choice Item

A multiple-choice item consists of a **stem,** which presents the problem or question to the student, and a set of **options,** or choices, from which the student selects an answer. The multiple-choice format is widely used in achievement tests of all types, primarily to assess learning outcomes at the factual knowledge and comprehension levels. However, this format can also be used to assess higher-level thinking involving application, analysis, and synthesis. (Item 3 from the following example is a multiple-choice item that assesses higher-level thinking.) Multiple-choice items are popular because they are easy to score and several items can be completed by students in a relatively short time. The main limitations of the multiple-choice format are that it does not allow students to construct, organize, and present their own answers, and it is susceptible to guessing.

A multiple-choice item consists of a stem that presents the problem or question, followed by a set of options from which the student selects an answer.

Here are four examples of multiple-choice items:

1. You use me to cover rips and tears. I am made of cloth. What am I?
   A. perch **B.** scratch **C.** patch **D.** knot

2. What is the smallest state in the United States?
   A. Massachusetts
   B. South Carolina
   C. Rhode Island
   D. Illinois

3. Read the following passage:
   (1) For what men say is that, if I am really just and am not also thought just, profit there is none, but the pain and the loss on the (3) other

hand is unmistakable. But if, though unjust, I acquire the reputation
of justice, a heavenly life is promised to me. Since then
(5) appearance tyrannizes over truth and is lord of happiness,
to appearance I must devote myself. I will describe around me a
(7) picture and shadow of virtue to be the vestibule and exterior of
my house; behind I will trail the subtle and crafty fox.

Which one of the following states the major premise of the passage?
A. For what men say (line 1)
B. if I am really just (line 1)
C. profit there is none, but the pain and the loss (line 2)
D. appearance tyrannizes over truth and is lord of happiness (lines 5–6)
E. a picture and shadow of virtue to be the vestibule and exterior of
my house (lines 7–8)

True-False Items

The true-false format requires students to classify a statement into one of
two categories: true or false; yes or no; correct or incorrect; fact or opinion. True-false items are used mainly to assess factual knowledge and
comprehension behaviors, although they also can be used to assess higher-
level thinking (Frisbie, 1992). Like multiple-choice items, true-false items
are easy to score and can efficiently present students with several items
that broadly sample the domain of interest. The main limitation of true-
false questions is their susceptibility to guessing.

The main limitation of true-false questions is their susceptibility to guessing.

The following are typical true-false items:

1. $5 + 4 = 8$ T   F

2. In the equation $E = mc^2$, when m increases, E also increases.   T   F

3. Read the statement below, and circle T if true and F if false. If the
statement is false, rewrite it to make it true by *changing only the
underlined part of the statement.*

    The level of the cognitive taxonomy that describes recall and   T   F
memory behaviors is called <u>the synthesis</u> level.

Although primarily used to assess knowledge and comprehension, both multiple-choice and true-false items can be used to assess higher-level thinking.

Matching Items

Matching items consist of a column of **premises,** a column of **responses,**
and directions for matching the two. The matching exercise is similar to
a set of multiple-choice items, except that in a matching question, the
same set of options or responses is used for all the premises. In addition
to being easy to score, matching items decrease the amount of reading
students must perform in order to display knowledge of several terms,
people, or facts. The chief disadvantage of this type of exercise is that it
is limited mainly to assessing lower-level behaviors. The following is an
example of a matching exercise:

Matching items consist of a column of premises, a column of responses, and directions for matching the two. They assess mainly lower-level thinking.

On the line to the left of each invention in column A, write the *letter* of the person in column B who invented it. Each name in column B may be used only once or not at all.

Column A
_____ (1) telephone
_____ (2) cotton gin
_____ (3) assembly line
_____ (4) polio vaccine

Column B
A. Eli Whitney
B. Henry Ford
C. Jonas Salk
D. Henry McCormick
E. Alexander Graham Bell

Multiple-choice questions generally do not effectively test higher-level thinking, but multiple-choice interpretive questions can do so. We will discuss them later in the section on higher-level questions.

Supply Items

Supply items consist of completion (also called fill-in-the-blank) items, short-answer items, essay questions, or questions requiring the student to create things such as diagrams or concept maps.

Short-Answer and Completion Items

Short-answer items use a direct question to present a problem; completion items use an incomplete sentence. Both tend to assess mainly factual knowledge and comprehension.

Short-answer and completion items are very similar. Each presents the student with a question to answer. The short-answer format states the problem as a direct question (e.g., "What is the name of the first president of the United States?"), while the completion format may state the problem as an incomplete sentence (e.g., "The name of the first president of the United States is _____") or a picture, map, or diagram that requires labeling. In each case, the student must supply his or her own answer. Typically, the student is asked to reply with a word, phrase, number, or sentence, rather than with a more extended response. Short-answer questions are fairly easy to construct and diminish the likelihood that students will guess answers. However, they tend to assess mainly factual knowledge or comprehension.

The following are examples of completion and short-answer items:

1. Scientists who specialize in the study of plants are called _____.

2. In a single sentence, state one way that inflation lowers consumers' purchasing power.

Next to each state write the name of its capital city.
3. Michigan _____
4. Massachusetts _____
5. South Carolina _____

Essay Items

Essay questions give students the greatest opportunity to supply and construct their own responses, making them the most useful for assessing higher-level thinking processes such as analyzing, synthesizing, and evaluating (this topic is discussed below). The essay question is also the primary means by which teachers assess students' ability to organize, express, and defend ideas. The main limitations of essays are that they are time-consuming to answer and score, and they place a premium on writing ability.

Essay questions are mostly useful for assessing higher-level thinking skills but are time-consuming to answer and score; in addition, they favor the student who has writing ability.

Here are some examples of essay questions:

1. How did the Dred Scott decision contribute to the onset of the Civil War? Give your answer in complete, correct sentences. Write at least five sentences.

2. "In order for revolutionary governments to build and maintain their power, they must control the educational system." Discuss this statement using your knowledge of the American, French, and Russian revolutions. Do you agree with the statement as it applies to the revolutionary governments in the three countries? Include specific examples to support your conclusion. Your answer will be judged on the basis of the similarities and differences you identify in the three revolutions and the extent to which your conclusion is supported by specific examples. You will have 40 minutes to complete your essay.

3. Describe in your own words how an eclipse of the sun happens.

4. Why are some parts of the world covered by forests, some parts by water, some parts by grasses, and some parts by sand? Discuss some of the things that make a place a forest, an ocean, a grassland, or a desert.

Comparing Selection and Supply Items

Supply questions are much more useful than selection questions in assessing students' ability to organize thoughts, present logical arguments, defend positions, and integrate ideas. Selection questions, on the other hand, are more useful when assessing application and problem-solving skills. Given these differences, it is not surprising that knowing the kind of item that will be on a test can influence the way students prepare for the test. Supply items encourage global, integrative study, while selection items encourage a more detailed focus on specific facts, definitions, people, and events.

Supply questions are most useful for assessing students' ability to organize and present their thoughts, defend positions, and integrate ideas.

In general, supply items require less time to construct than selection items. However, supply items generally take longer for students to complete; thus, fewer supply questions can be asked of students within a given period of time. Supply items are also generally more time-consuming to score and occasionally require more subjective decisions on the part of the person reading student responses. Table 6.1 summarizes the differences.

Selection items are most useful when application and problem-solving skills are assessed.

TABLE 6.1   COMPARISON OF SELECTION AND SUPPLY TEST ITEMS

	Selections Items	**Supply Items**
Types of Items	Multiple-choice, true-false, matching, interpretive exercise	Short-answer, essay, completion
Behaviors Assessed	Factual knowledge and comprehension; thinking and reasoning behaviors such as application and analysis when using interpretive exercises	Factual knowledge and comprehension; thinking and reasoning behaviors such as organizing ideas, defending positions, and integrating points
Major Advantages	1. Items can be answered quickly, so a broad sample of instructional topics can be surveyed on a test. 2. Items are easy and objective to score. 3. The test constructor has complete control over the stem and options, so the effect of writing ability is controlled.	1. Preparation of items is relatively easy; only a few questions are needed. 2. Afford students a chance to construct their own answers; the only way to test behaviors such as organizing and express-ing information. 3. Lessen the chance that students can guess the correct answer to items.
Major Disadvantages	1. Time-consuming to construct. 2. Many items must be constructed. 3. Guessing is a problem.	1. Time-consuming to score. 2. Covers small sample of instructional topics. 3. Bluffing is a problem.

HIGHER-LEVEL QUESTIONS

There is a growing emphasis on teaching and assessing students' higher-level thinking. As the following quotes show, teachers recognize the importance of students' learning how to understand and apply their knowledge. They know that knowledge takes on added meaning when it can be used in real-life situations.

Facts are important for students to learn in all subjects, but if students do not learn how to understand and use the facts to help them solve new problems, they haven't really learned the most important part of instruction.

The kids need to go beyond facts and rote learning. You can't survive in society unless you can understand, think, reason, and apply what you know.

What is more exciting for a student and her teacher than that moment when the student's eyes light up with recognition that she can solve a new problem? Something that was confusing all of a sudden became clear and a whole new skill is born. That kind of excitement doesn't come very often when instruction is focused on rote, memorization-oriented behaviors.

Many people believe that the only way to test higher-level thinking skills is with essay items. That is not the case. Any test question that demands more from a student than memorization is a higher-level item. Thus, any item that requires the student to solve a problem, interpret a chart, explain something in his or her own words, or identify the relationship between two phenomena qualifies as an item that tests higher-level thinking. Similarly, any assessment that requires students to demonstrate their ability to carry out an activity (e.g., give a talk, construct a mobile, or read an unfamiliar foreign language passage aloud) also allows them to demonstrate higher-level thinking.

Higher-level test item ask students to demonstrate higher-level thinking skills and are not limited to essay items.

Interpretive Exercises

The interpretive exercise is a common form of multiple-choice item that can assess higher-level thinking. An interpretive exercise gives students some information or data and then asks a series of selection-type questions based on that information. Item 3 on page 146 is an example of an interpretive exercise. Figure 6.1 on page 152 contains two more examples. Generally, multiple-choice items that ask for interpretations of graphs, charts, reading passages, pictures, or tables (e.g., "What is the best title for this story?" or "According to the chart, which year had the largest decline?") are classified as interpretive exercises. These exercises can assess higher-level behaviors such as recognizing the relevance of information, identifying warranted and unwarranted generalizations, recognizing assumptions, interpreting experimental findings, and explaining pictorial materials.

To answer the questions posed, students have to interpret, comprehend, analyze, apply, or synthesize the information presented. Interpretive exercises assess higher-level skills because they contain all the information needed to answer the questions posed. Thus, if a student answers incorrectly, it is because he or she cannot do the thinking or reasoning required by the question, not because the student failed to memorize background information.

When testing students' interpretive skills, it is often a good practice to provide them with the necessary information and then ask questions that require them to use that information. As we see in the examples below, when the necessary information is not provided, a teacher may have a difficult time determining why a student did not succeed on an item.

Interpretive exercises assess higher-level skills by requiring students to interpret or apply given information.

FIGURE 6.1   *Examples of Interpretive Exercises*

SOURCE: Educational Testing Service, *Making the Classroom Test: A Guide for Teachers*, p. 6. Copyright © 1973 by Educational Testing Service (Princeton, NJ). Used by permission of the publisher.

Example 1

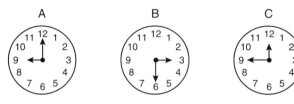

A   B   C   D

Use Oral Questions

What clock shows the time that school starts?	(A) B C D	
What clock shows the time closest to lunch time?	A B (C) D	
What clock shows half past the hour?	A (B) C D	

Example 2

1. The cartoon illustrates which of the following characteristics of the political party system in the United States?
   - (A) Strong party discipline is often lacking.
   - B The parties are responsive to the will of the voters.
   - C The parties are often more concerned with politics than welfare.
   - D Bipartisanship often exists in name only.

2. The situation shown in the cartoon is *least* likely to occur at which of the following times?
   - A During the first session of a new Congress
   - B During a political party convention
   - C During a primary election campaign
   - (D) During a presidential election campaign

Compare what a teacher might conclude based on these two versions of the same question.

Version 1

In one or two sentences, describe what Henry Wadsworth Longfellow is telling the reader in the first two verses of his poem "A Psalm of Life," which we read in class but did not discuss.

Version 2

In one or two sentences describe what Henry Wadsworth Longfellow is telling the reader in these lines from his poem "A Psalm of Life."

Tell me not, in mournful numbers,
   Life is but an empty dream!—
For the soul is dead that slumbers,
   And things are not what they seem.
Life is real! Life is earnest!
   And the grave is not its goal;
Dust thou art, to dust returnest,
   Was not spoken of the soul.

If a student does poorly on the first version, the teacher does not know whether the student failed to remember the poem or, despite remembering the poem, could not interpret what Longfellow was trying to say. In the second version, memory is made irrelevant by providing the needed lines of the poem.

Like the essay question, the interpretive exercise is a useful way to assess higher-level thinking. However, unlike essay questions, interpretive exercises cannot show how students organize their ideas when solving a problem or how well they can produce their own answers to questions. Other disadvantages of interpretive exercises are the difficulty of constructing them and the heavy reliance they often place on reading ability. Students who read quickly and with good comprehension have an obvious advantage over students who do not. This advantage is particularly evident when the test involves reading and interpreting many passages in a limited amount of time.

An interpretive exercise, the exercise should meet five general guidelines before it is used to assess student achievement:

1. Relevance. The exercise should be related to the instruction provided students. If it is not, it should not be used.

2. Similarity. The material presented in the exercise should be new to the students, but similar to material presented during instruction.

3. Brevity. There should be sufficient information for students to answer the questions, but the exercises should not become tests of reading speed and accuracy.

4. Answers not provided. The correct answers should not be found directly in the material presented. Interpretation, application, analysis, and comprehension should be required to determine correct answers.

5. *Multiple questions.* Each interpretive exercise should include more than one question to make the most efficient use of time.

Table 6.2 summarizes the pros and cons of the different types of test items.

TABLE 6.2   ADVANTAGES AND DISADVANTAGES OF TYPES OF TEST ITEMS

Test Type	Advantages	Disadvantages
Multiple-choice items	1. Large number of items can be given in a short period. 2. Higher- and lower-level objectives can be assessed. 3. Scoring is usually quick and objective. 4. Less influenced by guessing.	1. Takes substantial time to construct items. 2. Not useful when "show your work" is required. 3. Often hard to find suitable options. 4. Reading ability can influence student performance.
True-false items	1. A large number of items can be given in a short time. 2. Scoring is usually quick and objective.	1. Guessing correct answer is a problem. 2. Difficult to find statements that are clearly true or false. 3. Items tend to stress recall.
Matching items	1. An efficient way to obtain a great deal of information. 2. Easy to construct. 3. Scoring is usually quick and objective.	1. Focus is mainly on lower-level outcomes. 2. Homogeneous topics are required.
Short-answer items	1. Guessing is reduced; student must construct an answer. 2. Easy-to-write items. 3. Broad range of knowledge can be assessed.	1. Scoring can be time-consuming. 2. Not useful for complex or extended outcomes.
Essay items	1. Directly assess complex higher-level outcomes. 2. Take less time to construct than other item types. 3. Assess integrative, holistic outcomes.	1. Difficult and time-consuming to score. 2. Provide a deep but small sample of students' performance. 3. Bluffing and the quality of writing can influence scores.
Interpretive exercise items	1. Assess integrative and interpretive outcomes. 2. Assess higher-level outcomes. 3. Scoring is usually quick and objective.	1. Heavily dependent on students' reading ability. 2. Difficult to construct items.

GUIDELINES FOR WRITING AND CRITIQUING TEST ITEMS

Cover Important Objectives

No matter what types of items a teacher decides to include on a test, it is important that each item focus on important instructional objectives and not trivial knowledge and skills. Simply because a ready-made test is available from a textbook is no reason for a teacher to assume that the test adequately assesses his or her instruction on the chapter or unit. Each classroom teacher has a responsibility to determine the suitability of a textbook test for assessing his or her instructional emphases. Studies that examined the nature of the test items written by classroom teachers have found that the vast majority assessed memory-level behaviors (Marso and Pigge, 1989, 1991). From elementary school to the university, items that stress recall and memory are used much more extensively than items that assess higher-level thinking and reasoning, mainly because short-answer or multiple-choice questions are easier to write. In far too many instances, the richness of instruction is undermined by the use of test items that trivialize the breadth and depth of the concepts and skills taught.

Test items should reflect important topics and skills emphasized during instruction, should be stated briefly, and should be presented clearly.

Each example that follows states the objective taught, the test item used to assess it, and an alternative item that would have provided a more suitable assessment of the objective. Note that the poor items trivialized higher-level objectives by assessing them with a memory item.

1. **Objective:** Given a description of a literary form, the students can classify the form as fable, mystery, folktale, or fantasy.

   Poor item: What kind of stories did Aesop tell?

   A. fables   B. mysteries   C. folktales   D. fantasies

   Better item: A story tells about the year A.D. 2020 and the adventures of a young Martian named Zik, who traveled to other worlds to capture strange creatures for the zoo at Martian City. This story is best classified as a _____.

   A. fable   B. mystery   C. folktale   D. fantasy

2. **Objective:** The students can describe similarities and differences in chemical compounds and elements _____.

   Poor item: Chlorine and bromine are both members of a chemical group called the _____.

   Better item: Chlorine and bromine are both halogens. What similarities do they possess that make them halogens? What are two differences in their chemical properties?

3. **Objective:** The students can explain how life was changed for the Sioux Indians when they moved from the forests to the grasslands.

   Poor item: What animal did the Sioux hunt on the grasslands?

   Better item: What are three changes in the life of the Sioux that happened when they moved from the forests to the grasslands?

Test items that do not reflect the important topics of instruction are not valid indicators of student achievement.

There are two main reasons for ensuring that the questions in an achievement test align with the important topics and skills that were emphasized during instruction. First, if there is not a good alignment between instruction and the test questions, performance on the test will be a poor indicator of actual learning. Students may have learned what was taught but be unable to demonstrate their achievement because the test did not contain questions that tapped that learning. Using scores from a test whose content is not aligned with learning objectives will lead to invalid inferences and decisions about how well students have achieved the learning objectives.

Second, tests that do not align with instruction have little positive influence on motivating and focusing student study. If students find little relationship between instruction and test content, they will undervalue instruction. You can remember instances when you prepared well for a test based on the teacher's instruction and review only to find that the test contained many questions that focused either on isolated details or on material that was not discussed in class. Recall how you felt when you tried to prepare for the next test given by that teacher.

The problem of mismatch between tests and instruction can be overcome to a large degree by reviewing the learning objectives to be tested prior to developing the test and continually referring back to those objectives while creating test questions. By using the learning objectives to frame the content of the test, problems of misalignment can be decreased greatly.

Review Items before Testing

It is helpful to have a colleague or friend critique test items before the test is administered to students.

The best advice that can be given to improve most classroom tests is to review them before reproducing and administering them to students. After writing or selecting the items for a chapter or unit test, it is recommended that a teacher wait one day and then reread the items. While reading the items, consider whether any of the above rules are violated. Also attempt to match each item to an instructional objective. If an item violates a rule or cannot be linked to an instructional objective, then it needs to be modified or deleted. The teacher should also ask a colleague, spouse, or friend to review the items critically.

Most of the links in the chain of achievement testing—the importance of providing students with good instruction, the decisions that must be made in planning achievement tests, the instructional review that should precede testing, and the construction or selection of test items that give students a fair chance to demonstrate their learning—have been examined.

Two additional links that influence the adequacy of achievement tests are (1) assembling and administering the test and (2) scoring the test. These topics will be covered in Chapter 8. Key Assessment Tools 6.1 summarizes advice regarding different types of items.

Key Assessment Tools 6.1

WRITING TEST ITEMS

Multiple-choice items
1. Put each test item on a different line.
2. Place the student tasks in the item stem.
3. Put repeated terms in the item stem.
4. Construct at least three alternative choices.
5. Put options in logical order, if possible.
6. Avoid grammatical clues to the answer.
7. Be sure that items match students' reading level.
8. Eliminate unneeded words.
9. If "no" is used, underline it.
10. Reread the item to identify spelling and other errors.
11. The item stem should clearly state the question to be answered.

True-false items
1. Make items clearly true or false.
2. Be sure that the item is important in the assessment.
3. Avoid specific determiners.
4. Make the true and false items about the same length.
5. Do not use items in a repetitive pattern.
6. Do not use textbook sentences.

Short-answer items
1. Make sure the item relates to the assessment being taught.
2. Provide a clear focus for the intended answer.
3. Make answers possible in short responses; construct item so that student answers are short.

(Continued)

Key Assessment Tools 6.1 (*Continued*)

WRITING TEST ITEMS

4. Ask students to reply in only one or two responses.

5. Be sure item assesses the intended responses.

6. Put space for the item at the end of the item.

7. Avoid giving grammatical clues.

Matching answer items

1. Be sure the exercise reflects the objective being tested.

2. Compare homogeneous topics.

3. Make sure the directions are clear.

4. Put the longer options in the left-hand column.

5. Number one set of items; mark the other set with letters.

6. Do not ask for more than 10 responses in the assessment. If more responses are desired, begin a new matching test.

7. Provide one or two additional options on one column to avoid the final option being the correct answer by default.

Essay questions

1. Use several short essays rather than one long one.

2. Be sure that the reading level is appropriate for students.

3. Be sure the essay reflects your objectives.

4. Base the essay on a fresh example, if examples are used.

5. Provide a clear focus on the desired outcome of the essay.

6. Do not use essays that require a great deal of memory.

7. Aid students by focusing them with terms such as "state and defend the topic," "apply the principle to," "develop a valid conclusion," and so on. These kinds of instructions focus students and also help to focus the grading.

8. Provide students with clear directions about the expected length of essay responses and the amount of time for completion.

9. Provide students with clear scoring criteria—for example, will spelling count?

ASSEMBLING TESTS

Once test items have been written or selected and reviewed, they must be arranged into a test. In assembling a test, similar types of items should be grouped together and kept separate from other item types. All of the short-answer questions should be together and separate from the multiple-choice, matching, completion, and essay questions. Grouping test items by type avoids students having to shift from one response mode to another as they move from item to item. It also means that a single set of directions can be used for all of the items in that test section, helping students cover more items in a given time. Finally, grouping test items makes scoring easier.

Another important consideration in assembling the test is the order in which the item types are presented to students. In most tests, selection items come first and supply items come last. Within the supply section, short-answer or completion questions should be placed before essay questions. Supply items are placed at the end of the test so that students will not devote a disproportionate amount of time to this part of the test.

When arranging items on a test, remember these commonsense practices:

1. Designate a space for the student's name and/or ID number.

2. Do not split a multiple-choice or matching item across two pages of the test. This can cause unintended errors when students flip from one page to the next to read the second half of a matching question or the last two options of a multiple-choice question.

3. Number test items, especially if students must record answers on a separate answer sheet or in a special place on the test.

4. Space items for easy reading, and be sure to leave enough space for students to complete supply items. Remember that young students often have large writing. Do not place items close together.

Each section of a test should have directions that focus students on what to do, how to respond, and where to place their answers. Lack of clear directions is one of the most common faults in teacher-prepared tests and often reduces test validity. Here are some sample directions:

- Items 1–15 are multiple-choice items. Read each item carefully and write the *letter* of your answer on the line in front of the question number.
- Use words from the boxes to complete the sentences. Use each word only once.
- Answer each question by writing the correct answer in the space below the question. No answer should be longer than one sentence.
- For items 10–15, circle T or F (true or false).
- Use the chart to help you answer questions 27–33. Write your answers in the space provided after each question.

Directions such as these at the start of a test section focus students by telling them where and how to respond to the questions. To emphasize a point made earlier, it is especially important that each essay question spell out clearly for students the scope and characteristics of the desired answer. For older students, it is also helpful to indicate the number of points that will be given to each test section so they can make decisions about how to allocate their time.

Key Assessment Tools 6.2 summarizes guidelines for assembling tests.

> **Key Assessment Tools 6.2**
>
> ## GUIDELINES FOR ASSEMBLING A TEST
>
> This list combines some suggestions from the discussion with several other good ideas.
>
> 1. Organize the test by item type: selection before supply, essay last.
> 2. Allow sufficient space for written responses, especially for young children's essay items.
> 3. Do not split multiple-choice or matching items across two pages.
> 4. Separate stem from options in multiple-choice questions.
> 5. Number test items.
> 6. Provide clear directions for each section of the test; for older students, indicate the value of each section or question.
> 7. Provide enough questions to ensure reliability.
> 8. Proofread the test before copying, and make extra copies.

ISSUES OF CHEATING

Teachers should be alert to the possibility of cheating on tests, projects, quizzes, and assignments. Unfortunately, cheating is a common occurrence, both in school and in life. Students cheat for many reasons: external pressure from teachers or parents; failure to prepare and study for tests; internal pressure from being in an intensively competitive major or course that gives a limited number of high grades; danger of losing a scholarship; and, unfortunately, the belief that "everybody else does it." No matter how and why it is done, cheating is an unacceptable classroom behavior. Cheating is analogous to lying. When students cheat and turn in work or a test under the pretense that they did the work themselves, that is lying and should be recognized as such.

Types of Cheating on Tests

How do students cheat on tests? Cizek (1999) has written a useful and comprehensive book that explores cheating in depth. He identifies and gives examples of a very large number of ways that students cheat. The following examples adapted from Cizek's work represent a small sample of common ways students cheat. He provides many additional and esoteric methods.

1. Looking at another student's paper during a test.
2. Dropping one's paper so that other students can cheat off it.
3. Dropping one's paper and having another student pick it up, cheat from it, and then drop it again so the original dropper can reclaim it.
4. Passing an eraser between two students who write test information on the eraser.
5. Developing codes such as tapping the floor three times to indicate that a multiple-choice item should be answered "C".
6. Looking at other students' papers while walking up to the teacher to ask a question about the test.
7. Using crib notes or small pieces of paper to cheat.
8. Wearing a T-shirt with useful test information written on it.
9. Changing answers when teachers allow students to grade each other's papers.

Plagiarizing

Plagiarism is defined as presenting someone else's work as one's own, without attribution. There are four types:

1. Presenting someone else's whole paper as one's own.
2. Deliberately copying from someone else without indicating quotations and without acknowledging the source.
3. Copying in essence, disguised by changing words or using synonyms.
4. Assuming the copied information is "common knowledge".

With access to the Internet and tools that make it easy for students to copy and paste the work of others into their own papers, concern about plagiarizing has increased. While it is unclear whether plagiarism is occurring more frequently today than it was before the Internet was widely accessible, it certainly has become easier to plagiarize.

Why do students plagiarize? As noted previously, for a variety of reasons, including these:

• Out of ignorance that it's wrong
• Because passing is important to graduation
• Because students think they won't be caught
• Because teachers don't bother to check for plagiarism
• Because of parental pressure for good grades

- Because of last-minute panic
- Because "everybody does it"

Clearly, several of these causes are at least partially under a teacher's control.

Deterring Cheating

olc

CHAPTER CASE STUDY

Visit the text Online Learning Center to read the case of Scott Donovan, a high school English teacher who discovers that four of his students plagiarized parts of an assignment.

www.mhhe.com/ russell7e

Teachers should monitor test taking in order to deter cheating and to enhance test validity. A number of methods can be used to deter cheating, some relatively easy to apply and others more complicated. Two approaches that help eliminate or lessen cheating are (1) providing students with good instructions and information about the test and (2) observing students during testing. Prior to testing, students' books and other materials should be out of sight under their desks or elsewhere. Students' seats should be spread out in the classroom as much as possible. Some teachers do not permit students to wear baseball caps during testing because when the visors are tilted below the eyes, the teacher cannot see where the students' eyes are directed. During testing, the teacher should quietly move about the classroom and observe students as they take the test. While observation rarely "catches" a student cheating, the presence of the teacher moving about the classroom is a deterrent to cheating.

Although the Internet may make it easier for students to plagiarize, it can also make it easier for teachers to detect. As described in greater detail in Chapter 11, several Web-based tools are available to help teachers detect plagiarism. Perhaps the most freely available tool, however, is Google. By simply typing or pasting a suspicious block of text into the Google search engine, a teacher can often immediately find the source of that text if it was plagiarized verbatim.

Table 6.3 shows a variety of strategies to deter plagiarism and other forms of cheating and the degree to which university students report that the strategies are successful. The Online Learning Center for this chapter provides more ideas.

Many schools and school systems develop honor codes or cheating rules that all students are to respect. Such codes or rules spell out in detail what is and is not cheating. Table 6.4 excerpts a cheating policy from a middle school in California.

It is the teacher's responsibility to discourage cheating with seating arrangements, careful proctoring, and other activities. Teachers should discourage cheating and penalize students caught doing it, because it is an unethical activity and because it provides invalid information about a student's achievement. It is, however, important to have strong evidence to support charges of cheating, because students have due process rights if accused.

TABLE 6.3   STUDENT PERCEPTIONS OF THE EFFECTIVENESS OF CHEATING-PREVENTION STRATEGIES

Rank	Strategy	% Rating Strategy as "Effective" or "Very Effective"
1.	Scrambled test forms	81.6
2.	Small classes	69.8
3.	Using several proctors during examinations	68.4
4.	Using two or more test forms	66.6
5.	Providing study guides	54.8
6.	Making old examinations available for review	52.4
7.	Assigning seats for examinations	26.9
8.	Checking footnotes in student papers	26.4
9.	Giving more in-class tests and fewer take-home tests	23.7

SOURCE: From R. C. Hollinger and L. Lanza-Kaduce, 1996, "Academic Dishonesty and the Perceived Effectiveness of Countermeasures: An Empirical Survey of Cheating at a Major Public University," *NASPA Journal, 33*(4), p. 301. Copyright © 1996. Reprinted with permission of NASPA, Student Affairs Administrators in Higher Learning.

TABLE 6.4   EXCERPTS FROM THE CHEATING POLICY OF HUNTINGTON MIDDLE SCHOOL

You are cheating if you:
* Copy, fax, or duplicate assignments that will each be turned in as an "original."
* Exchange assignments by printout, disk transfer, or modem, then submit as "original."
* Write formulas, codes, or key words on your person or objects for use in a test.
* Use hidden reference sheets during a test.
* Use programmed material in watches or calculators, when prohibited.
* Exchange answers with others (either give or receive answers).
* Take someone else's assignment and submit it as your own.
* Submit material (written or designed by someone else) without giving the author/artist name and/or source (e.g., plagiarizing, or submitting work created by family, friends, or tutors).
* Take credit for group work, when little contribution was made.
* Do not follow additional specific guidelines on cheating as established by department, class, or a certain teacher.

Students caught cheating on any assignment (homework, tests, projects) will be referred to our Assistant Principal. The schoolwide citizenship grade will be lowered at least one grade and the parents will be called. Subsequent offenses may result in a "D" or "F" in citizenship, suspension, removal from elected positions and honorary organizations, the inability to participate in school activities, and similar consequences.

SOURCE: From Huntington Middle School Cheating Policy, by Huntington Middle School, San Marino (CA) Public Schools. Reprinted with permission of Gary McGuigan, Principal, Huntington Middle School.

Table 6.5 lists some clues for identifying plagiarized work.

TABLE 6.5 CLUES FOR IDENTIFYING PLAGIARIZED WORK

1. Writing style, language, vocabulary, tone, grammar, and so forth are above or below what the student usually produces. It doesn't sound like the student.

2. Spelling or idioms used are not found in the student's native language—for example, using British spellings or phrasing in an American paper and vice versa.

3. Pronouns do not agree with the gender of the writer.

4. An essay is printed out from the student's Web browser.

5. A Web address or other anomalous text appears at the top or bottom of the page.

6. There are references to graphs, charts, or accompanying material that aren't there.

7. Quotations in the paper do not have citations.

8. Citations in the bibliography or works cited list cannot be verified.

9. All citations are to materials that are older than five years.

10. References are made to historical persons or events in the current sense.

11. A student cannot summarize the main points of the paper or answer questions about specific sections of the paper.

SOURCE: Adapted from Peggy Bates and Margaret Fain, *Cheating 101: Paper mills and you—Internet subject specific paper mills.* http://www.coastal.edu/library/mills5.htm. Revised September 17, 2003.

SCORING PAPER-AND-PENCIL TESTS

The process of scoring a test involves **measurement**—that is, assigning a number to represent a student's performance. In the case of achievement tests, performance on the test items is translated into a score that is used to make decisions about the student.

The complexity of scoring tests varies with their type. Selection-type items are easiest to score, short-answer and completion items are next easiest, and essays are the most difficult. The reason for this is obvious if one thinks about what a teacher has to do to score each item type. How much time and judgment is involved in scoring each? What precisely does the teacher have to look at to determine whether an item is correct or incorrect? Which type of item requires the most concentration to score? The answers to these questions illustrate the range of ease and difficulty encountered when scoring various item types.

Scoring Selection Items

Students respond to selection items by writing, circling, or marking the letter of their response. Scoring selection items is essentially a clerical task in which the teacher compares an answer **key** containing the correct answers with the answers the student has given. The number of matches indicates the student's score on the test. Before using an answer key, it is a good idea to check to make sure that the key is correct. Similarly, if the test is machine-scored, it is good practice for the teacher to hand-score a few answer sheets to verify that the machine scoring is accurate.

Scoring selection test items is relatively **objective**—that is, independent scorers will usually arrive at the same or very similar scores for a given student's test. Conversely, **subjective** scoring means that independent scorers would not necessarily arrive at the same or similar scores for a given student's test. In a subjective test, a student's performance depends as much on *who* scores the test as on the student's answers. Selection items produce objective scores because there usually is one clearly correct answer to each item, and that answer is identified by a single letter. However, as students' responses become lengthier and more complex—as they do with short-answer, completion, and essay items—the judgment of what is a correct or incorrect answer often blurs, and scoring becomes more subjective. It has long been known that even when the same person scores the same essay test twice, there is no guarantee that the scores will be the same or similar (Starch and Elliott, 1912, 1913). This is a problem because, if we are to have confidence in test scores, it is important that the scores be objective. Fortunately, there are several ways to make the scoring of essays less subjective, as we will see later.

Selection items can be scored objectively because they are usually brief and have only one correct answer.

Subjective test scores are those for which independent scorers have difficulty arriving at the same or similar scores.

Scoring Short-Answer and Completion Items

As long as short-answer and completion items are clearly written, focus students on their task, and call for a short response such as a word, phrase, date, or number, scoring is not difficult and can be quite objective. However, as items require lengthier responses, subjectivity of scoring will increase because more and more interpretations of what students know or meant to say will have to be made.

Three guidelines can help teachers overcome problems of scoring supply items:

1. Prepare an answer key before scoring, so that you know what you are looking for in student responses when scoring.
2. Determine how factors such as spelling, grammar, and punctuation, which are usually ancillary to the main focus of the response, will be handled in scoring. Should points be taken off for such factors? Decide before scoring and inform students before testing.

3. If student responses are technically correct but not initially considered in the scoring guideline, give credit to each unexpected but correct response.

By being clear about the expected answer for each question and determining what will and what will not count prior to administereing a test, scoring of completion and short-answer items will be less subjective.

Scoring Essay Items

Essay questions represent the ultimate in scoring complexity because they permit each student to construct a unique and lengthy response to the question posed. This means that there is no single definitive answer key that can be applied uniformly to all responses. Moreover, the answer to an essay question is presented in a form that contains many distracting factors that contribute to subjective scoring. These factors may include the following:

- Handwriting
- Writing style, including sentence structure and flow
- Spelling and grammar
- Neatness
- Fatigue
- Identity of the student
- Location of one's test paper in the pile of test papers

Each of these factors can influence a teacher's reaction to an essay answer, although none of them has anything to do with the actual content of the student's response. For example, a student whose penmanship is so poor that it forces the teacher to decipher what each scribbled word means may frustrate the teacher and divert attention from the content of the answer. The essay likely will get a lower score than that of another student who provides the same answer in more legible handwriting. The reverse may occur when some essays are typed and others are handwritten. Typed responses often make spelling, punctuation, and capitalization errors more obvious, which can lead some readers to award lower scores. Meanwhile, handwritten essays may be more difficult to read, which can lead some readers to skim the essay for the presence or absence of important facts or arguments. When such facts and arguments are detected, the reader may automatically award a high score even though the fact or argument is misrepresented (Russell and Tao, 2004a, 2004b). A student who uses interesting words in a variety of sentence structures to produce an answer that flows smoothly from point to point likely will get a better score than a student who states the same points in a string of simple declarative sentences.

Scoring essays is a time-consuming and difficult task, so student scores may be influenced by how alert the teacher is when the essays are read. The first few essays that are read seem new and fresh, and students who wrote them tend to get good scores. However, after the teacher has read the same response 15 or more times, familiarity and fatigue set in, and responses similar to the initial ones often get lower scores.

Knowledge of who wrote the essay can also influence the scoring process. In almost all essay questions, there is at least one point when the teacher must interpret what a student was trying to say. Knowledge of who wrote the answer can influence the teacher's interpretation. One way to avoid biased scoring is to identify papers by number or have students put their names on the last page of a test.

Holistic versus Analytic Scoring

Teachers typically use two approaches to scoring essay questions: holistic scoring and analytic scoring. **Holistic scoring** reflects a teacher's *overall impression* of the essay as a whole and results in a *single score or grade.* **Analytic scoring,** on the other hand, views the essay as being made up of many components and so provides *separate scores* for each component. An essay that is scored analytically might result in separate scores for accuracy, organization, supporting arguments, and grammar and spelling. Analytic scoring provides detailed feedback that students can use to improve different aspects of their essays. However, attempting to score more than three or four separate features often makes scoring confusing and time-consuming. Whether a teacher uses holistic or analytic scoring should depend on the purpose of the assessment. In cases when a broad judgment about a student's achievement or performance is being made, holistic scoring is usually appropriate. When the purpose of assessment is to identify strengths and weaknesses in students' work or to assess multiple objectives that are integrated in the essay, then analytic scoring is most appropriate. Regardless of whether teachers employ holistic or analytic scoring, they should give helpful and encouraging suggestions on students' drafts and tests.

Steps to Ensure Objectivity

When assessing student work using either holistic or analytic scoring, certain steps should be followed to ensure that students' essays are scored objectively. Although the following suggestions are time-consuming, they are necessary if scores are to be valid for decision making. In addition, scoring guides are very helpful (see Chapter 9).

1. *Define what constitutes a good answer before administering an essay question.* The less focused an essay question is, the broader the range of student responses will be, and the more difficult it will be to apply uniform scoring criteria. Including information about the student's specific task, the scope of the essay, and the scoring criteria in the essay directions helps teachers define the criteria they will apply when scoring student responses before the essay question is administered to students.

2. *Decide and tell students how handwriting, punctuation, spelling, and organization will be scored.* Students should know in advance what factors will count in scoring the essay.

3. *If possible, score students anonymously.* This will help keep the scoring objective by eliminating the influence of perceptions of the student's effort, ability, interest, and past performance. Each student should be scored on the basis of present, not past, performance.

4. *In tests with multiple essay items, score all students' answers to the first question before moving to the second question.* Scoring responses to more than one question at a time is challenging for two reasons. First, it is difficult to shift content orientation and criteria for each question. Second, scoring all the answers to a single essay question at one time helps protect against the "carryover" effect, the tendency to let one's reaction to a student's initial essay influence one's perception of succeeding essays written by that same student.

5. *Read essay answers a second time after initial scoring.* The best way to check for objectivity in essay scoring is to have a second individual read and score students' papers using the same criteria the teacher used to score them. Since this is usually impractical, except when making very important decisions (e.g., awarding a scholarship or selecting for an honor society), an acceptable procedure is for the teacher to reread and, if necessary, rescore a sample of the essays before finalizing the scores.

Essay questions permit the assessment of many thought processes that can be assessed in no other way. A teacher should use essay questions if they are the best way to assess what has been taught, but time should be set aside to score them objectively so that their results can be used with confidence. Key Assessment Tools 6.3 provides guidelines to follow when scoring tests.

Key Assessment Tools 6.3
GUIDELINES FOR SCORING A TEST

This list combines suggestions from the discussion with some other good ideas.

1. Base test scores on topics that were taught and items that are clearly written.

2. Make sure the same rules are used to score all students.

3. Be alert for the following distractors that may affect the objectivity of essay scores: writing style, grammar and spelling, neatness, scorer fatigue, prior performance, and carryover effects.

4. Define what constitutes a good answer before administering an essay question.

5. Score all answers to the first essay question before moving on to score the succeeding questions.

6. Read essay question answers a second time after initial scoring.

7. Carry out a posttest review to locate faulty test items and, when necessary, to make scoring adjustments.

ANALYZING ITEM VALIDITY

The steps described in the preceding section are intended to produce test scores that can be used with confidence to make valid decisions about student achievement. Although these steps will eliminate most of the common problems found in classroom achievement tests, a teacher never really knows how well test items will work until after they have been administered to students. It is all but impossible to anticipate how students will react to a given item. Thus, a review of student performance after testing in order to identify faulty items is an important final step before using test results to make decisions. There are two reasons for performing such posttest reviews: (1) to identify and make scoring adjustments for any items that students' answers show were misunderstood or ambiguous, and (2) to identify ways to improve items for use on future tests.

The Need for After-Test Reviewing: Two Examples

The following examples illustrate the need for posttest reviewing. A social studies teacher who taught a unit on the Low Countries (e.g., Belgium, Luxembourg, and Holland) asked the following short-answer question:

What are the Low Countries?

She expected that her students would respond with the names of the Low Countries even though the item did not ask explicitly for the names. While many students did supply the names, many others responded that the Low Countries were "a group of countries in Europe that are largely below sea level." How should the teacher treat the responses of this latter group of students?

A health teacher wrote the following multiple-choice question:

The main value of a daily exercise program is to:
A. eat less
B. develop musculature
C. raise intelligence
D. keep physically fit

Choice B was keyed as the correct answer, but many students selected D as their answer. What should the teacher do about the students who selected option D?

Notice that these problems did not become apparent until *after* the teacher looked over the student responses and found unexpected or odd response patterns for a few items: almost everyone missing a particular

In scoring unexpected responses, teachers must decide if wrong answers are the result of faulty test items or a lack of student learning.

item, some students giving strange or unexpected answers to an item, and all of the high-scoring students doing poorly on an item. As these scoring patterns emerge, teachers should inspect student responses to determine whether the problem was related to test construction or student learning. It is important to emphasize that test scores should not automatically be raised simply because many students got an item wrong. In each case, the teacher must make a judgment regarding the source of the problem and the way it will be rectified, if at all.

Selective Reviewing of Multiple-Choice Items

Problems in selection items, especially multiple-choice ones, are harder to detect because students select rather than construct their own responses, which gives little insight into their thinking. To identify problems with multiple-choice items, teachers must view response patterns on the various options provided. While it is desirable to review all items in a multiple-choice test, limitations in time make it more realistic to review those items that half or more of the students answered incorrectly. This is where most, if not all, of the faulty items are likely to be found.

There are many ways to examine patterns for multiple-choice items. A number of statistical indices can be calculated to describe each test item (Kubiszyn and Borich, 2003). The **difficulty index** of an item describes the proportion of students who answered it correctly. For example, an item of .70 difficulty (70 percent of the class answered correctly) is easier than one of .40 difficulty (40 percent of the class answered correctly). The **discrimination index** describes how an individual item fares with students who scored high and low on the overall test. An item with positive discrimination is one that is more frequently answered correctly by students who score high on the test as a whole than by students who score low. The discrimination index can range in value from +1.0 to −1.0. A positive value is always desired, and values between .3 and .8 are generally desirable. An item that has a negative value or a value less than .2 warrants close examination to see if it has been miskeyed or if there are other problems with it.

Because most classroom teachers lack the time and resources to perform the numerical analyses required to calculate difficulty and discrimination indices, they must rely on simple methods to understand and improve those items that a large proportion of the class answered incorrectly. The following are examples of item response patterns teachers can use to answer the question "What's the problem, if any, with this item?" Each of these patterns indicates a different possible reason that large numbers of students might answer incorrectly. In each case, an asterisk indicates the keyed answer.

This first response pattern is typical of multiple-choice items that have two correct or defensible answers, similar to the health item shown previously. Two choices, A and C, were rarely selected. The majority of students split themselves almost evenly between options B and D. Only the students who marked B, the keyed response, received credit on the item when it was initially scored.

Options	A	*B	C	D
Number of students choosing option	2	8	2	8

When the teacher saw that most students missed this item, he looked at option D, decided that it was also a correct choice, and decided to give full credit to those who selected D. For a classroom test, the final decision about whether the item or the students are at fault rests with the teacher.

The next pattern is one where most students select an option other than the keyed one. In the example below, most students chose C rather than D, the keyed option. Many times this pattern is simply the result of miskeying on the part of the teacher. In this case, the teacher wrote D next to this item when she meant to write C. While miskeying is not always the explanation for such a response pattern, it is a good starting point. If the item was not miskeyed, closer inspection of option C should provide a clue as to why it was chosen so often. If a reason for students selecting option C cannot be identified, students should be consulted to explain their answers.

Options	A	B	C	*D
Number of students choosing option	2	1	15	2

Finally, consider the following pattern in which all options are selected by about the same number of students. Such a pattern may be an indication that students are simply guessing, that they probably have no idea which option is correct. Faulty wording or untaught material are likely explanations for such a response pattern. If the content of an item has not been taught or the wording is the source of an unexpected answer pattern, the teacher should seriously consider not counting the item for students' test scores.

Options	*A	B	C	D
Number of students choosing option	5	6	4	5

After-test reviews using the above strategies can help teachers better understand how well their items are working and why students responded as they did. Asking students what they were thinking when they answered an item can also produce useful information. While the decision about how to score an item ultimately rests with the classroom teacher, information of the kind described in this section is helpful in making that decision. An after-test review will enhance the accuracy of the test scores and the validity of decisions made based on them.

DISCUSSING TEST RESULTS WITH STUDENTS

Students want information about their test performance. Teachers can provide this information through comments written on papers, tests, or projects that indicate to students what they did well and how they might improve. It also is helpful to review the results of tests with students. This is especially useful when the students have their marked tests in front of them during the review. The teacher should pay special attention to items that a large proportion of the class got wrong in order to clear up misconceptions and to indicate the nature of the desired answer. For older students, it also is helpful to explain how the tests were scored and graded. Finally, opportunities should be provided for shy students to discuss the test in private with the teacher.

CHAPTER SUMMARY

CHAPTER REVIEW

Visit the Online Learning Center at **www.mhhe.com/ russell7e** to review the case study referenced in the chapter.

- The central focus of achievement testing is to obtain a fair and representative indication of what students have learned from teachers' instruction.
- Achievement tests are usually composed of two types of test items: selection (multiple-choice, true-false, and matching) and supply (short-answer, completion, and essay). Each item type can test both higher- and lower-level thinking.
- Selection items can be answered quickly, can cover a broad sample of instructional topics, and can be scored objectively. However, they are time-consuming to construct and leave open the possibility of guessing.
- Supply items can be prepared easily, afford students the opportunity to construct their own answers, and are rarely subject to guessing. However, they are difficult and time-consuming to score, and tend to cover a limited range of instructional topics.
- Teachers should try to include higher-level questions in their instruction and assessments. The interpretive item is a useful way to incorporate higher-level skills into achievement tests.
- Test questions should cover important topics and behaviors that were the focus of instruction.
- Most of the items in teacher-prepared and textbook tests are at the recall or memory level because such items are easier to write than higher-level questions. However, if tests are to provide information that can be used to make valid decisions, they should reflect all the content and processes taught at both lower and higher levels. Tests that do not represent instruction can provide a poor indication of student learning and may have a negative effect on students' motivation to study.

- Each section of the test should have directions that tell students what to do, how to respond, and where to place their answers. Older students may also be helped by knowing how much each item is worth.
- Cheating is unacceptable and dishonest; it is also common. It is a teacher's responsibility to establish conditions that reduce cheating.
- Teachers can deter cheating by scrambling test forms, arranging student seating, circulating within the classroom during testing, providing study guides, using more essay items, forbidding students from sharing materials, and enforcing cheating rules and penalties, among other strategies.
- Measurement is a form of scoring in which numbers are assigned to describe students' performance.
- An objective test item is one that independent scorers would score the same or similarly. A subjective item is one that independent scorers would not score the same. Factors that contribute to subjectivity include handwriting, style, grammar and spelling, and the teacher's perception of the student.
- Selection items are easy to score objectively. Supply items become increasingly subjective as students are given more freedom to construct their own answers. Essay items are the most subjective kind of item to score.
- The two common methods of scoring essay tests are holistic scoring, which produces a single overall score, and analytic scoring, which produces a number of scores corresponding to particular features of the essay (e.g., organization and style).
- To make essay scores objective, a teacher should decide what factors constitute a good answer before giving the test, provide those factors in the test item, read all responses to a single essay question before reading responses to other questions, and reread essays a second time to corroborate initial scores.
- After a test is scored, the teacher should review items that show unusual answers or response patterns to determine if the items are faulty. If faulty items are judged to be responsible, a scoring adjustment may be in order.
- It is good practice to conduct an after-test review with students in order to (1) help identify any misconceptions, (2) locate faulty test items and make necessary scoring adjustments, and (3) build up a permanent test item file.

QUESTIONS FOR DISCUSSION

1. What are some objectives that are best assessed by supply items? What are some objectives that are best assessed by selection items?
2. How are early assessment, lesson plans, and instruction related to tests of student learning?

3. What harm could result if a teacher's tests produced invalid information about student learning?
4. What are some ways that scoring essay questions can be made more objective? What are some consequences of subjective essay scoring?
5. How should a teacher respond to cheating? Should all forms of cheating be treated in the same way? What cautions should a teacher keep in mind before accusing a student of cheating?

ACTIVITIES

1. Rewrite the following essay question to make it more focused for students. Then state a set of criteria you would use to judge the quality of your students' answers.

   Compare the Democratic and Republican parties.

2. Talk to two teachers about how they deal with and prevent cheating on tests.
3. In a small group, talk with other students about types of cheating they have noticed and what can be done to reduce it.

REVIEW QUESTIONS

1. What are the differences between selection and supply items? What are the advantages and disadvantages of each? What are common faults in each type?
2. What are the differences between higher- and lower-level test items?
3. What is an interpretive exercise, and why is it a useful method for assessing higher-level thinking?
4. How do tests of factual knowledge differ from tests of conceptual knowledge?
5. What are some differences between scoring selection and supply items?
6. What is the difference between objective and subjective scoring? What factors make it difficult to score essay questions objectively? What steps can a teacher take to make essay scoring more objective?
7. What guidelines should be followed in arranging the items in a test?
8. What are some strategies that can be used to limit cheating on tests?
9. How do holistic and analytic scoring differ? When should each be used?

REFERENCES

Cizek, G. J. (1999). Cheating on tests: How to do it Detect it and Prevent it. New Jersey: Lawrence Erlbaum Associates.

Frisbie, D. A. (1992). The multiple true-false item format: A status review. *Educational Measurement: Issues and Practice, 11* (4), 21–26.

Kubiszyn, T., and Borich, G. (2003). Educational Testing and Measurement: Classroom Application and Practice (7th ed.). Hoboken, NJ: John Wiley & Sons, Inc.

Marso, R. N., and Pigge, F. L. (1989). Elementary classroom teachers' testing needs and proficiencies: Multiple assessments and inservice training priorities. *Educational Review, 13,* 1–17.

Marso, R. N., and Pigge, F. L. (1991). The analysis of teacher-made tests: Testing practices, cognitive demands and item construction errors. *Contemporary Educational Psychology, 16,* 179–286.

Michael Russell and Wei Tao (2004). Effects of handwriting and computer-print on composition scores: a follow-up to powers, fowles, farnum, and ramsey. Practical Assessment, Research and Evaluation, 9(1). Retrieved February 28, 2011 from http://PAREonline.net/getvn.asp?v=9&n=1

Russell, Michael and Wei Tao (2004). The influence of computer-print on rater scores. Practical Assessment, Research and Evaluation, 9(10). Retrieved February 28, 2011 from http://PAREonline.net/getvn.asp?v=9&n=10

Starch, D., and Elliot, E. C. (1912). Reliability of the grading of high school work in English. *School Review, 21,* 442–457.

Starch, D., and Elliot, E. C. (1913). Reliability of grading work in mathematics. *School Review, 22,* 254–259.

CHAPTER 7

UNIVERSAL DESIGN
FOR ASSESSMENT

KEY TOPICS

- *How Test Items Work*

- *Accessibility*

- *Universal Design and Assessment*

- *Guidelines for Writing and Critiquing Test Items*

- *Administering Tests*

- *Universal Design and Test Accommodations*

CHAPTER OBJECTIVES

After reading this chapter, you will be able to:

- Describe how an item is designed to measure a targeted skill or knowledge
- Identify intended and unintended constructs
- Write high-quality test items
- Create appropriate conditions for administering tests
- Apply principles of universal design to provide more accurate measures of student achievement
- Describe how a test item is designed to measure a targeted skill or knowledge
- Create accommodations that reduce barriers to student performance

THINKING ABOUT TEACHING

What is a test? What purpose does a test serve?

Tests are the most common tool used to measure student achievement. In the classroom, teachers are often most interested in measuring important cognitive skills and knowledge that are the target of instruction. Cognitive skills and knowledge, however, cannot be observed directly. Tests are used to provide indirect observations of specific skills and knowledge.

In Chapter 6, we saw that an indirect observation is provided by each item that appears on a test. The quality of information provided by such observations is strongly influenced by the quality of the items used to produce those observations. In this chapter, we examine in greater detail how test items function and explore strategies for creating high-quality test items. Recognizing that each student is a unique individual, with his or her own strengths and needs, we also learn how principles of universal design can be applied to improve the accuracy of testing for all students. Finally, we consider how the special needs that some students have can be further supported by providing test accommodations.

HOW TEST ITEMS WORK

We have all seen and answered thousands of test items as students. But have you ever thought about how test items are supposed to work? Test items are designed to provide a context in which the test taker must apply a targeted skill or knowledge in order to produce a response. More technically, the targeted skill or knowledge is referred to as a *construct*. Based on the test taker's performance on a specific sample of items or tasks, inferences are made about the extent to which he or she is able to apply the targeted construct across all possible items and tasks that measure that skill and knowledge. In this way, a student's score on a test actually is an estimate of how well the student would perform on the total population of items and tasks that require the application of the tested construct.

Since a construct cannot be directly observed, items and tasks are designed to stimulate or activate the construct of interest. To provide an observable record of the construct, an item or task also requires a student to produce an observable product or response. For a multiple-choice test, the observable product is the option selected by the student. For an open-response item, the observable product is the response the student records on paper using a pencil or on computer using a keyboard, mouse, or any other device. For an oral exam, the observable product is the verbal response provided by the student. While the focus of a student's interaction with an item or task is often on the answer or product, that product is useful only if it accurately reflects the construct of interest.

Measuring a Targeted Construct

Test items must measure students' ability to perform or demonstrate specific skills and knowledge, based on the target of instruction.

Each test item must be designed to measure a specific construct. The constructs that are of most interest when assessing student achievement are the skills and knowledge that are the target of instruction. Examples of constructs include the ability to perform addition, the ability to decode text, knowledge of historical facts related to the American Revolution, and writing ability. Rather than attempting to measure all constructs of interest, a classroom test focuses on a targeted subset of constructs that are of immediate interest to the teacher. When creating test items, it is important to keep in mind the targeted construct.

To accurately measure the targeted construct, a test item must successfully perform three functions. First, the item must present information that will activate the targeted construct. Information designed to stimulate the targeted construct is contained in the item's prompt or stem. In order for an item to provide a measure of the targeted construct, the information presented in the prompt must be understood by the student and appropriately set the context in which the student can apply the construct of interest.

Second, the test item must provide an opportunity for each student to apply the targeted construct while responding to the prompt. To stimulate the application of the targeted construct, many items present information with which the student interacts. Examples of information with which a student may interact while applying the targeted construct include a reading passage that accompanies a reading comprehension item, a set of numbers with which the student performs addition, a table that contains information the student is asked to interpret, and a periodic table that the student uses to form a chemical equation. To provide an

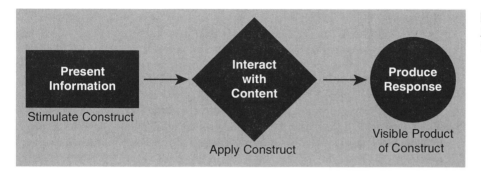

FIGURE 7.1
Model of How a
Test Item Functions

accurate measure of the construct, an item must be designed to allow all students an opportunity to apply the targeted construct as they interact with content presented in the item.

Third, the test item must provide each student an opportunity to produce an observable response that is the product of his or her application of the targeted construct. The extent to which the student response reflects the outcome of the construct influences the accuracy of the indirect observation.

Figure 7.1 shows the three functions that all test items must perform.

ACCESSIBILITY

There are two ways to think about accessibility. First, from the student's perspective, accessibility focuses on the ease with which the student is able to access the information contained in a test item. Barriers to student access may include inability to clearly see information presented in the item, inability to decode text, and lack of familiarity with vocabulary contained in the item. From the student's perspective, information that cannot be accurately viewed or understood presents a barrier to his or her ability to demonstrate knowledge or skill.

A second way to think about accessibility is from the perspective of the test creator. Each test item is designed to measure a targeted construct. The accuracy of the measure depends on the extent to which each item is able to access the targeted construct and produce an observable product of that construct. As shown in Figure 7.1, an item's ability to access a construct is influenced by three factors: (1) the extent to which information presented in the item stimulates the targeted construct, (2) the extent to which the item allows the student to apply the targeted construct, and (3) the extent to which the product produced by the student accurately reflects the application of the targeted construct. From the test creator's perspective, accessibility focuses on the extent to which each of these three steps factors is realized in the measurement process.

The better students understand what they are asked to do on a test, the more likely they are to demonstrate their knowledge and skills.

How an Item Accesses a Construct

In order to access the targeted construct, the item must accurately establish the context for the test taker, allow uninhibited application of the construct, and enable accurate production of a response. The extent to which an item is able to accomplish these three tasks is influenced by a variety of factors. These factors can be sorted into three broad categories, each of which relates to a step in the measurement process, namely (1) presentation, (2) interaction, and (3) response. A fourth category, representational form, is also relevant in some cases.

Presentation focuses on the ways in which item content is presented to students. The presentation of content can be adapted in several ways, including changing the font size of text-based content, altering the contrast of text and images, increasing white space, and reducing the amount of content presented on the page.

Interaction focuses on the ways in which students engage with item content. Examples of interactions include assisting students with pacing, highlighting important content, and scaffolding by separating steps in solving a problem.

Response focuses on the methods students use to provide responses to instructional activities or assessment tasks. Examples of response modes include producing text orally or using speech-to-text software; pointing to answers or using a touch screen instead of circling, clicking, or bubbling; and using assistive communication devices to produce responses.

The final aspect of accessibility focuses on representational forms. As Mislevy and his colleagues (2010) explain, alternate representations change the form in which item content is presented to students. Unlike presentation, which focuses the way in which the same content is displayed for the test taker, representational forms present students with different versions of the item content. Reading content aloud, presenting text-based content in sign language or Braille, providing tactile representations of graphical images, and translating items to a different language are all forms of alternate representations.

Making Decisions about Accessibility

Decisions about presentations, interactions, response modes, and representational forms must be made in the context of the construct that is measured by an item. An important consideration when trying to measure a construct is not only the skills and knowledge one is trying to measure—the *intended construct*—but also other skills and abilities that one is not trying to measure—the *unintended construct*. For example, if one is interested in a student's ability to do mathematical problem solving, one may measure this by presenting a word problem. To solve this problem, the student must use both mathematical problem-solving skills and reading skills to understand

and interpret what the question is asking. For a word problem, the mathematical problem-solving skills are the intended construct and the reading skills are the unintended construct. Examples of other unintended constructs include decoding skills when teaching or assessing science knowledge, visual perception when teaching or testing graphing ability, and fine motor skills when teaching or testing ability to communicate in writing.

It is important to recognize that the extent to which a construct is intended or unintended depends on the type of information the test is designed to produce. However, just because a construct may be viewed as unintended when measuring the intended construct does not mean that the unintended construct is unvalued, unimportant to develop, or unworthy of assessment. For example, understanding the extent to which a student has developed decoding skills is important, but when one is interested in assessing scientific knowledge, these skills are secondary to the scientific knowledge that is the target of the assessment. In other instructional and assessment contexts, decoding skills may in fact be the target of instruction (e.g., during English language arts) or of assessment (e.g. on a reading test), and may represent the intended construct. Identifying a construct as intended or unintended depends on the current focus of instruction and the purpose of the test.

UNIVERSAL DESIGN AND ASSESSMENT

The concept of universal design originated in the field of architecture and aims to make structures accessible to as many people as possible. Rather than retrofitting a stairway with an elevator, ramp, or stair lift after a structure has been built, universal design aims to seamlessly build ways for people with ambulatory challenges to easily access all areas of a structure. As an example, the New England Aquarium contains a three-story water tank in which a variety of fish swim. Rather than having several different viewing levels that are accessed by staircases, the water tank is embraced by a ramp that gradually spirals up around it. The glass tank inside the ramp allows people with a variety of ambulatory needs to move up or down the levels of the tank with relative ease. Interestingly, many visitors without ambulatory needs who visit the aquarium might also say that the spiral ramp enhances their experience by allowing them greater exposure to the fish inside the tank as they move up and down through the levels. The concept of universal design has extended from the field of architecture to many other arenas including product design, media, and recreation. Rather than creating a single solution, universal design has come to embrace the concept of allowing users to select from among multiple alternatives.

In the field of education, universal design for learning (UDL) applies these same design principles by considering the variety of accessibility

Rather than creating a single solution, universal design has come to embrace the concept of designing flexible approaches that can be adapted based on individuals' needs.

and learning needs of students when developing instructional materials. The three principles of UDL are as follows:

1. Provide alternative formats for presenting information (multiple or transformable accessible media).
2. Provide alternative means for action and expression (writing, drawing, speaking, switching, using graphic organizers, etc.).
3. Provide alternative means for engagement (background knowledge, options, challenge and support, etc.).

When applied to achievement tests, universal design has important implications for the development of test content, the presentation of items, and the conditions under which a test is administered. It is important to note that the goal of universal design is not to create a single solution that is accessible for all students (Rose and Meyer, 2000). Instead, a universally designed assessment will anticipate the variety of accessibility needs of potential students and build in methods that allow all students to access, engage with, and respond to test content.

There are two important steps in developing a universally designed assessment. First, test content must be developed in a way that anticipates the different needs of students and the representational forms that meet those needs without violating the tested construct. Second, the way in which items are presented must meet the access needs of all students. When successfully executed, a universally designed assessment shifts the adaption of content and test interactions from post hoc changes required when providing test accommodations to a priori design decisions and development of alternate representations during the item and test development stage. Given the potential benefits of applying universal design principles to student assessment, some researchers have argued that these principles should be applied as items are developed and tests are being assembled, and when administering a test to students.

GUIDELINES FOR WRITING AND CRITIQUING TEST ITEMS

Test items should reflect important topics and skills emphasized during instruction, should be stated briefly, and should be presented clearly.

Tests are composed of questions or **items.** Each question must set a clear problem for the student to think about. Each question must also be complete in itself and independent of other questions. Further, because students will mentally debate the nuances of each word to be sure they are not misinterpreting the intent of the item, it is crucial that questions be stated in clear, precise language. Whether writing test items or selecting those prepared by others, there are three general guidelines that can help you improve the quality of the test. Each item should (1) cover important objectives, (2) be stated clearly and simply, and (3) contain no misleading statements, confusing formatting, or excess verbiage. This section discusses and illustrates these guidelines.

Write Clearly and Simply: Seven Rules

If test questions use ambiguous words or sentence structure, include inappropriate vocabulary, or contain clues to the correct answers, the test will not be a valid indicator of student achievement. The most important skill in writing or selecting good test items is the ability to express oneself clearly and succinctly. Test items should be (1) briefly stated so students do not spend a disproportionate amount of time reading, (2) clearly expressed so students understand their task, and (3) capable of standing alone since each item provides a separate measurement. Following are seven rules for writing sound test items. Each is illustrated by some confusing test items prepared by teachers who knew the content they wanted to test but who were unable to clearly state their intent. A better version of each item is also shown for comparison.

Rule 1: Avoid ambiguous and confusing wording and sentence structure

Students must understand test questions. If the wording or sentence structure is confusing and prevents students from figuring out what they are being asked, students cannot demonstrate their learning. Consider the following test items:

1. All but one of the following is not an element. Which one is not?
   A. carbon   B. salt   C. sugar   D. plastic

2. Maine is not the only state that does not have a border with a
   neighboring state.   T F

In these examples, the wording and sentence construction are awkward and confusing. The student has to sort through multiple negatives to figure out what is being asked. It is better, therefore, to phrase questions briefly, directly, and in the positive voice, as shown in these edited versions:

1. Which one of these is an element?
   A. carbon   B. salt   C. sugar   D. plastic

2. Maine borders another state.   T F

Other questions, such as items 3 and 4, are more than just confusing; they are virtually incomprehensible:

3. What is the relative length of the shortest distance between Chicago and
   Detroit and Sacramento?

4. The _____ produced by the _____ is used by the green _____ to change
   _____ and _____ into _____. This process is known as _____.

Test items should be brief, clearly written, and free of ambiguous words so that comprehension is not an issue.

What is a reasonable answer to each? Taken individually, the words in item 3 are not overly difficult, but their sequencing makes their intent unclear. Item 4 is so riddled with blank spaces that a student would have to be a mind reader to figure out what is being asked. No student should be confronted by such a question. Students will answer items like items 3 and 4 incorrectly regardless of how well they have mastered the information and skills taught them. The following changes overcome the problems in these two examples:

3. Which is closer to Sacramento: Chicago or Detroit?

4. The process in which green plants use the sun's energy to turn water and carbon dioxide into food is called _____.

If a student answers the revised items incorrectly, it is reasonable to infer that he or she does not know the desired answer. Remember, the purpose of a test item is not to guarantee correct answers, but to give students an opportunity to show how much they know about the things they were taught. To do this, test items must be readily comprehended.

Another factor that prevents students from being able to focus quickly and clearly on the question being posed is the use of ambiguous words or phrases. Read items 5, 6, and 7, and try to identify a problem in each that could cause students difficulty in deciding how to answer.

5. Shakespeare was the world's greatest playwright.   T   F

6. The most important city in the Southeast is:
   A. Atlanta   B. Miami   C. New Orleans   D. Tuscaloosa

7. Write an essay in which you consider the future of atomic energy.

Each example contains an ambiguous term that could be puzzling to students and make their choice of an answer difficult. The true-false example contains the undefined word *greatest*. Did the teacher mean that Shakespeare wrote more plays than any other playwright? That more of his plays are still being performed than those of any other playwright? That his plays are required reading in more American classrooms than those of any other playwright? Until students know what the teacher means by *greatest*, they will have difficulty responding. Item 6 has the same fault. What does the phrase *most important* mean? Each of these cities is important in many ways. Words like *greatest, most important,* and *best,* and similar ambiguous words should be replaced by more specific language, regardless of the type of test item used. Note the rewritten versions of items 5 and 6:

5. William Shakespeare's plays are required reading in more
   American classrooms than those of any other playwright.   T   F

6. The main transportation center for train and airplane traffic in the Southeast is:
   A. Atlanta   B. Miami   C. New Orleans   D. Tuscaloosa

In item 7, the teacher wants the students to consider the future of atomic energy. Does the teacher mean compare and contrast atomic energy to fossil fuel? Discuss the relative merits of fission versus fusion as a means of generating energy? Explain the positive and negative consequences of increased use of atomic energy? The intent is not clear. The item needs to be more specific for the students to respond in the way the teacher desires, as shown in this revised version:

> 7. Describe the advantages and disadvantages of increased use of atomic energy in the automobile manufacturing process.

In most cases, the teachers who wrote the preceding examples knew what they wanted to ask students but were unable to write items that clearly conveyed their intent. Teachers must say precisely what they mean, not assume or hope that their students will interpret their test items in the ways intended.

Rule 2: Use appropriate vocabulary

The difficulty level of test questions can be influenced dramatically by vocabulary. If students cannot understand the vocabulary used in test questions, their test scores will reflect their vocabulary deficiencies rather than how much they have learned from instruction. Based on early assessments, every teacher should take into account the vocabulary level of his or her students when writing or selecting the items for achievement tests.

Note the difference in the following two ways of writing a true-false question to assess students' understanding of capillary action, a principle that explains how liquids rise in narrow passages:

> The postulation of capillary effectuation promotes elucidation of how pliant substances ascend in incommodious veins.   T   F

> The principle of capillary action helps explain how liquids rise in small passages.   T   F

Clearly, vocabulary level can affect the ability of students to understand what is being asked in a test question.

Rule 3: Keep questions short and to the point

Items should quickly focus students on the question being asked. Examine these examples:

> 8. Switzerland
>   A. is located in Asia.
>   B. produces large quantities of gold.
>   C. has no direct access to the ocean.
>   D. is a flat, arid plain.
>
> 9. Billy's mother wanted to bake an apple pie for his aunt and uncle, who were coming for a visit. Billy had not seen them for many months. When Billy's mother saw that she had no apples in the house, she sent Billy to

Questions should be short, specific, and written at students' vocabulary level.

the store to buy some. Her recipe called for eight apples to make a pie. If apples at the store cost 30 cents for two, how much money will Billy need to buy eight apples?

A. $.30   **B.** $.90   **C.** $1.20   **D.** $2.40

In item 8, the stem does not clearly set a problem for the student; that is, after students read the item stem *Switzerland*, they still have no idea what question is being asked. Only after reading the stem *and* all the options does the point of the item begin to become clear. The item could be more directly stated as follows:

8. Which of the following statements about the geography of Switzerland is true?
   A. It is located in Asia.
   B. It is a flat, arid plain.
   C. It has no direct access to the ocean.
   D. It has a tropical climate.

Item 9 is intended to determine whether the student can correctly calculate the cost of some apples. The information about the aunt and uncle's visit, how long it had been since Billy last saw them, or the lack of apples in the house is not important, can be distracting, and takes time away from the relevant information in the item. A better way to state the item is shown here:

9. To make an apple pie, Billy's mother needed 8 apples. If apples cost 30 cents for 2, how much will 8 apples cost?
   A. $.30   **B.** $.90   **C.** $1.20   **D.** $2.40

In short-answer or completion items, the blanks should come at the end of the sentence so students know what kind of a response is required. Compare these two examples, and notice how placing the blank at the end helps convey what the item is about:

_____ and _____ are the names of two rivers that meet in Pittsburgh.
The names of two rivers that meet in Pittsburgh are _____ and _____.

Matching items can also be written to help students focus more quickly on the questions being asked. Look over item 10 and suggest a change that would focus students more clearly on the questions they have to answer:

10. Draw a line to match the president in Column A with his accomplishment in Column B.

Column A
G. Washington
T. Jefferson
U. Grant
F. Roosevelt

Column B
signed the Emancipation Proclamation
president during the New Deal
first president of the United States
head of Northern troops in the Civil War
main author of the Declaration of Independence

Most matching items can be improved by placing the column with the lengthier descriptions on the left and the column with the shorter descriptions on the right, as shown here:

10. Draw a line to match the president in Column B with his accomplishment in Column A. One accomplishment will not be used.

Column A	Column B
Signed the Emancipation Proclamation	G. Washington
President during the New Deal	T. Jefferson
First president of the United States	U. Grant
Head of Northern troops in the Civil War	F. Roosevelt
Main author of the Declaration of Independence	

Rule 4: Write items that have one correct answer

With the exception of essay questions, most paper-and-pencil test items are designed to have students select or supply one best answer. With this goal in mind, read items 11 and 12, and see how many correct answers you can provide for each item:

11. Who was George Washington?

12. Ernest Hemingway wrote _____.

Each of these items has more than one correct answer. George Washington was the first president of the United States, but he also was a member of the Continental Congress, commander of the Continental Army, a Virginian, a surveyor, a slave owner, and a man with false teeth. Faced with such an item, students might ask themselves, "Which of the many things I know about George Washington should I answer?" Similarly, Ernest Hemingway wrote short stories and letters, he wrote in Spain and in Florida, he wrote in pencil, and he wrote famous novels such as *The Old Man and the Sea*. Items 11 and 12 can be restated so that students know precisely what is being asked. Notice how each question asks for something specific—a name or a country—thus indicating to students the nature of the expected answer.

11. What is the name of the first president of the United States? _____.

12. The name of the author of *The Old Man and the Sea* is _____.

Items with more than one correct answer occur much more often in short-answer and completion items than in selection items. Unless short-answer or completion items are stated specifically and narrowly, the teacher can expect many different responses. The dilemma for the teacher then becomes whether to give credit for answers that are technically correct but not the desired one.

Rule 5: Give information about the nature of the desired answer

With the exception of essays, most test items should have only one correct answer.

While the failure to properly focus students is common to all types of test items, it is most often seen in essay items. Despite students' freedom to structure their own responses, essay questions should still require students to demonstrate mastery of key ideas, principles, or concepts that were taught. An essay, like any other type of test item, should be constructed to find out how well students have achieved the instructional objectives.

Here are a few typical essay questions written by classroom teachers:

13. Compare and contrast the North and the South in the Civil War. Support your views.

14. Describe what happened to art during the Renaissance.

15. Why should you study science?

In each of these questions, the students' task is not clearly defined. When students encounter global questions such as these, they may have little idea of what the teacher is looking for and may end up incorrectly guessing the teacher's intent. This practice produces test results that do not reflect students' achievement.

A well-focused essay item includes scoring criteria and specific information about the students' task.

To determine whether students have learned what was taught, essay questions should be narrowed to focus students on the areas of interest. Students should be informed about the nature and scope of the expected answer. While essay questions should provide the students freedom to select, organize, state, and defend positions, they should not give students total freedom to write whatever they want. To develop a well-focused essay question, the teacher must give considerable thought to the purpose and scope of the question before actually writing it.

Essay questions should focus students' answers on the major points covered by instruction.

Items 13, 14, and 15 have been rewritten to more precisely reflect the teacher's intent. Notice how the vague and ambiguous directions (support your views; describe) are made clearer to students in the revised questions:

13. What forces led to the outbreak of the Civil War? Indicate in your discussion economic conditions, foreign policies, and social conditions in the North and the South before the war. Which two factors were most influential in the start of the Civil War? Give two reasons to support your choice of each factor. Your answer will be graded based on your discussion of the differences between the North and the South at the start of the war and the strength of the arguments you advance to support your choice of the two factors most influential in the start of the war. (30 minutes)

14. Compare art during the Renaissance with art prior to the movement in terms of the portrayal of the human figure, use of color, and emphasis on religious themes. Your essay will be judged in terms of the distinctions you identify between the two periods and the explanations you provide to account for the differences.

15. Give two reasons a third-grade student should study science. What are some things that studying science teaches us? What are some jobs that use science? Write your answer in at least five complete sentences.

Certainly, these are not the only ways that these essay items could have been rewritten, but these revisions demonstrate the need for focus in essay questions. When students approach these revised items, they have a clear sense of what is expected of them; they no longer have to guess what the scope and direction of their answers should be. Note also that it would much more difficult for students to bluff answers to the revised items than to the initial, broadly stated items. The revised items call for answers specifically related to the instructional objectives, and therefore test what was taught and make scoring easier. To write such items, however, the teacher must have a clear sense of what he or she is trying to assess before forming the essay questions.

To summarize, regardless of the particular type of test item used, students should be given a clear idea of what their task is. In the case of multiple-choice items, this may mean elaborating a stem in order to clarify the options. In matching items, it may involve putting the longer options in the left column. In short-answer or completion items, it may mean placing the blank at the end of the statement or specifying precisely the nature of the desired answer. In essay questions, it may mean elaborating to include information about the scope, direction, and scoring criteria for a desired answer. In all cases, the intent is to allow the student to respond validly and efficiently to the items.

For all types of test items, students should have a clear sense of what is expected of them.

Test item writers should take care not to provide grammatical clues, implausible option clues, or specific determiner clues.

Rule 6: Do not provide clues to the correct answer

The item-writing rules discussed thus far have all been aimed at problems that inhibited students from demonstrating their achievement. However, the opposite problem arises when test items contain clues that help students answer questions correctly even though they have not learned the content being tested. Many types of clues may appear in items: grammatical clues, implausible option clues, and specific determiner clues. Try to identify the clues in items 16 and 17:

16. A figure that has eight sides is called an:
    A. pentagon   B. quadrilateral   C. octagon   D. ogive

17. Compared with autos of the 1960s, autos in the 1980s:
    A. more horsepower.
    B. to use more fuel.
    C. contained more safety features.
    D. was less often constructed in foreign countries.

These examples contain grammatical clues. In item 16, using the article *a* or *an* at the end of the question or stem indicates to students what letter will begin the next word. The *an* before the colon tells students that the next word must begin with a vowel, so the options "pentagon" and "quadrilateral" cannot be correct. There are two ways to correct this problem: (1) Replace the single article with the combined *a(n)*, or (2) get rid of the article altogether by writing the question in plural form:

16. Figures that have eight sides are called:
    A. pentagons   B. quadrilaterals   C. octagons   D. ogives

In item 17, only option C grammatically fits the stem. Regardless of students' knowledge, they can select the correct answer because of the grammatical clue. The corrected item might read:

17. Compared with autos of the 1960s, autos in the 1980s:
    A. had more horsepower.
    B. used more fuel.
    C. contained more safety features.
    D. were always constructed in foreign countries.

Now try to find the clues in items 18 and 19:

18. Which of the following best describes an electron?
    A. negative particle
    B. neutral particle
    C. positive particle
    D. a voting machine

19. Match the correct phrase in Column A with the term in Column B. Write the *letter* of the term in column B on the line in front of the correct phrase in column A.

Column A	Column B
_____ 1. type of flower	A. cobra
_____ 2. poisonous snake	B. fission
_____ 3. how amoebae reproduce	C. green
_____ 4. color of chlorophyll	D. hydrogen
_____ 5. chemical element	E. rose

Item 18 contains a clue that is less obvious than those in items 16 and 17, but one that is quite common in multiple-choice items. One of the options is inappropriate or implausible and therefore can be immediately dismissed by the students. Option D, a voting machine, would be dismissed as an unlikely answer by all but the most careless readers. As much as possible, options in test questions should be realistic and reasonable. A useful rule of thumb is to have at least three incorrect (but reasonable) options, or **distractors,** in each multiple-choice item.

A distractor is a reasonable but incorrect option in a multiple-choice item.

The more choices students have, the less likely it is that they can guess the correct answer. Understanding this, teachers sometimes write three or four good options for an item, and then add a fourth or fifth, such as "none of the above" or "all of the above." It is usually better to avoid such general options.

Item 19 is a very easy question; the topics are so different from one another that many of the options in Column B are implausible matches to the statements in Column A. This set of matching items does not test one homogeneous subject area.

A matching item should test the students' knowledge of a single homogeneous topic.

Consider the following matching item, which tests students' knowledge of a single, homogeneous topic. Note the difficulty in answering this item compared with the previous version of item 19:

19. Match the names of the animals in Column A to their correct classification in Column B. Write the *letter* of the correct classification on the line in front of each animal name. The choices in Column B may be used more than once.

Column A
_____ 1. alligator
_____ 2. condor
_____ 3. frog
_____ 4. porpoise
_____ 5. snake
_____ 6. salamander

Column B
A. amphibian
B. bird
C. fish
D. mammal
E. reptile

The revised item is a better test of students' knowledge in two ways. First, it does not include the obvious matches and mismatches that occur when many unrelated topics are contained in the same matching item. Instead, the revised version focuses on a single topic: classification of animals into groups. Second, the revised item has an unequal number of entries in Columns A and B. Having unequal entries in the two columns of a matching-item question prevent students from getting the last match correct by the process of elimination.

Look for the clues in items 20 and 21:

20. Some people think the moon is made of green cheese.   T   F

21. One should never phrase a test item in the negative.   T   F

These items contain clues that are called **specific determiners.** In true-false questions, words such as *always, never, all,* and *none* tend to appear in statements that are false, and testwise students tend to answer accordingly. Conversely, words like *some, sometimes,* and *may* tend to appear in statements that are true. Thus, in item 20, it is reasonable to assume that *some* people think the moon is made of green cheese, so T should be marked. On the other hand, item 21 must be marked F if there is even a single situation in which a test item can reasonably be stated in the negative.

Rule 7: Don't overcomplicate test items

Occasionally, teachers and textbooks overcomplicate test items. Consider the following item, which was given to sixth-graders to test their mastery of applying the procedure to calculate simple interest:

John borrowed $117.55 from Bob at an interest rate of 9.73 percent a
  year.
How much simple interest must John pay Bob at the end of
  15 months?

The numbers in this example are difficult and almost ensure that many sixth-grade students will make computational errors. Unless the teacher was specifically testing computational accuracy, the following example would better assess the students' ability to apply the procedure:

John borrowed $150 from Bob at an interest rate of 9 percent a year.
How much simple interest must John pay Bob at the end of 1 year?

The latter item assesses students' mastery of simple interest without complicating the computation so much that errors are likely to occur.

ADMINISTERING TESTS

Once high-quality items are developed to form a test, the test should be administered under conditions that provide all students with an opportunity to accurately demonstrate what they know and can do. The aim of test administration is to establish both a physical and a psychological setting that permits students to demonstrate their best performance. The setting should also make it easy for students to keep track of the time.

Physical Setting

One way to minimize interruptions is to post a sign on the door indicating that testing is occurring.

Students should have a quiet, comfortable environment in which to take the test. Interruptions should be minimized; some teachers post a sign on the door indicating that testing is in progress. During testing there is little one can do about interruptions like fire drills or announcements from the school office. When such interruptions occur, the teacher must make a judgment about whether it is fair for students to continue with testing. Obviously a 1-minute interruption from the main office is less disruptive than a 20-minute fire drill, during which students may talk to one another about the test. If an interruption is judged sufficiently disruptive to diminish students' ability to provide a fair and representative indication of their achievement, testing should be terminated and repeated at another time.

Often interruptions occur when students ask questions during testing. A good way to minimize many of these questions is to proofread items and directions prior to administering the test. Occasionally, typographical errors or unclear items are not detected until testing has begun. Usually, a student raises his or her hand or approaches the teacher to ask a question or point out a problem. When such situations arise, an announcement should be made to the whole class informing them of the problem (e.g., "Please correct item 17 in the following way," or "Option B in item 29 should be changed to . . ."). In the end, the decision of whether and how to answer student questions rests with the individual teacher. Answering questions during testing is appropriate as long as the teacher is consistent in responding to all students who ask questions.

Psychological Setting

Establishing a productive psychological setting that reduces student anxiety and sets a proper atmosphere for testing is as important as providing a comfortable physical environment. Giving students good instruction, advance notice of the test, a day or two to prepare for it, and a good chapter or unit review will help diminish students' test anxiety. Even so, it is probably impossible to completely allay all test anxiety.

Test anxiety is diminished by giving students advance notice of the test, an opportunity to prepare for it, and a pretest review.

No teacher should precede test administration with a comment like "This is the most important test you will take this term. Your grade and your future in this course will be determined primarily by how you do on this test." A statement like this will raise students' anxiety levels appreciably and hamper their ability to show what they have learned. Conversely, test administration should not be prefaced with remarks such as "Everybody knows that tests don't mean much; I just give tests because I have to" or "Don't worry about it—it counts very little in your final grade." Describing and treating a test as if it were a trivial interruption in the school day will diminish its ability to motivate students to study and will interfere with their test performances.

The line between overemphasizing and underemphasizing the importance of a test is hard to draw. Students should take tests seriously, and they should be encouraged to do their best. The appropriate middle ground between over- and underemphasizing the importance of tests will vary with the age and characteristics of students. The more students know about the test, the more likely their anxiety will be lowered. Good instruction, a thorough review, and prior knowledge of which types of items will be on the test help students relax at test time. Of course, fair, valid test items and no "surprises" such as unannounced tests, unfamiliar item types, and untaught topics also will help allay test anxiety. Each teacher must find the middle ground for his or her class, knowing that whatever is done, there will be some students who will be very anxious about their performance and some who will not care.

Key Assessment Tools 7.1 summarizes important concerns in test administration.

> **Key Assessment Tools 7.1**
>
> ## GUIDELINES FOR ADMINISTERING A TEST
>
> 1. Provide a quiet, comfortable setting.
> 2. Try to anticipate and avoid questions during the test by supplying clear directions.
> 3. Provide a good psychological setting, as well as advance notice, review, and encouragement for students to do their best.
> 4. Discourage cheating through seating arrangements, your own circulation about the room, and enforcement of rules and penalties.
> 5. Help students keep track of time.

Keeping Track of Time

During testing it often helps students if the teacher keeps track of the remaining time with announcements such as "There are 20 minutes left until the test is over." Such reminders can initially be made at 15-minute intervals, then changed to 5-minute intervals near the end of the test. Such reminders are most useful at the middle and high school levels during final exams, which usually take longer than a single class period to administer. In self-contained elementary school classrooms, where testing and instruction are ruled less by the bell, the teacher has discretion regarding when and how to start and end testing.

UNIVERSAL DESIGN AND TEST ACCOMMODATIONS

As we learned in Chapter 2, the Individuals with Disabilities Education Act of 1990 (IDEA) requires that students with special needs receive appropriate educational services. Given the importance of assessment throughout the instructional process, IDEA has several implications for formative and summative assessment. Traditionally, these implications have focused on providing students who have special needs with accommodations during testing. A test accommodation occurs when one or more aspects of a test are changed in order to provide a student with greater access to the content of the test or to increase his or her ability to record responses to test items. The type of accommodation provided to an individual student depends on the student's specific needs. A student with low vision may require text printed in large font or in Braille. A student with attention deficit disorder may require additional time when taking a test, with the test administered in a setting with limited distractions. A student with reading issues may require that math, social studies, and science tests be read aloud. A student with needs related to fine motor skills may require that written responses be composed on the computer or by a scribe.

While the range of accommodations is expansive, the purpose of all accommodations is the same: to reduce barriers that may interfere with students demonstrating their achievement of the knowledge and skills being tested. Thinking back to our discussion of test validity, the aim of all accommodations is to remove the influence of constructs and skills that are not being tested in order to allow students to demonstrate the constructs and skills that are being tested. For a mathematics test that contains word problems, the test developer is interested not in whether students can read the questions, but in whether they can do the mathematics to solve the problem described in the written question. For students who are dyslexic, have poor vision, or have difficulty reading, providing an accommodation that enables them to access the written text eliminates the influence of reading skills on their ability to demonstrate their mathematics skills.

While accommodations during testing do enable many students to more accurately demonstrate their achievement of the knowledge and skills being tested, recently, many advocates for students with special needs have argued that barriers should be removed when a test is being designed. Rather than making changes to the test after it has been produced in order to provide an accommodation for a given student, these advocates suggest that the test be designed to meet a wide range of needs.

The principles of universal design are intended to remove barriers to effective assessment by creating tests that can be used by students regardless of their specific educational needs.

In testing, principles of universal design can be applied to increase access for students with a variety of needs without having to make changes to the test on the day it is being administered. For example, rather than having students record answers on a separate answer sheet, which can present challenges for students who find it dificult to manage multiple sheets of paper, have poor vision, or have attention deficits, answers could be recorded directly on the same sheet as the test questions. Similarly, rather than using a small font in order to fit as many questions as possible on a page, a larger font with more spacing between questions will provide greater access to students with poor vision or other visual perception needs. In addition, using simple sentence structures and common vocabulary in word problems may make mathematics test items more accessible for students who speak English as a second language or who read at a lower reading level.

Just as the spiral ramp proves beneficial for all visitors to the New England Aquarium, many of these test design features often prove useful for students who do not have a specific learning need. As an example, larger font and increased spacing may allow all students to make notes or to work on problems directly in their test booklet without having to transfer information to scratch paper. Having all students record answers in their test booklets may save time that otherwise would be spent moving between the test booklet and answer sheet or checking to be sure answers are being recorded in the proper place. Using simplified language may help many students who are unfamiliar with a given word to focus on the problem itself rather than trying to figure out what the word means.

Although applying principles of universal design can help reduce the need to make specific accommodations during testing, it may still be necessary to make specific changes to the test or test conditions for a student on the day of testing. Specific accommodations required for a given student will be guided by his or her Individual Education Plan (IEP). Below, several common accommodations are organized into four general categories that focus on the presentation format, the response format, test timing, and the test setting. Keep these potential accommodations in mind when designing a test and when administering tests to students with IEPs.

Modifying the Presentation Format
- Read directions for each test section, slowly and clearly.
- Provide verbal or oral directions as needed.
- Present directions as a sequence of steps for the student to follow.
- Have the student repeat directions to ensure understanding.
- Read test questions aloud.
- Spread items over the page; put each sentence on a single line.
- Present the test in Braille, large print, sign language, native language, or bilingually.
- Revise or simplify the language level.

Modifying the Response Format
- Allow dictionaries, texts, or calculators.
- Allow responses in Braille, large print, sign language, or native language, or on tape.
- Provide verbal prompts to items.
- Provide a scribe to write student answers.
- Provide examples of expected test responses.
- Give students an outline for essay items.
- Include definitions or formulas for the student; allow the use of notes.
- Double-check the student's understanding of the items and desired responses.
- Make the test similar to what was taught during instruction.

Modifying Test Timing
- Avoid timed tests.
- Provide extra time.
- Test over a period of short testing sessions.
- Give extra breaks during testing.
- Allow unlimited time.

Modifying the Test Setting

- Test in a separate and quiet location.
- Seat the student away from distractions.
- Test one-on-one: one student, one test administrator.

The above categories include many of the most common accommodations used in classrooms. Many other accommodations can be applied to provide valid assessment of students with disabilities, but this list provides a useful beginning for our exploration into this area. The student's IEP will guide the teacher in preparing students for testing.

One additional issue requires attention. The above accommodations are generally those that all students in a classroom will notice during a test. While it is usually clear that students with disabilities are being treated differently from nondisabled students, teachers should try not to bring undue attention to students with disabilities during testing. For example, teachers can confer privately with students with disabilities when setting up needed accommodations. They can make the modified test similar in appearance to the regular test. They can try to be unobtrusive when helping students with disabilities during testing and try to monitor all students in the same way. The aim of such practices is to be sensitive to embarrassment for students with disabilities during testing and to avoid it as much as possible.

Instructors should be sensitive to students' perceptions of one another and should make modified assessments and procedures as unobtrusive as possible, so as not to call attention to a student's different needs.

CHAPTER SUMMARY

- Seven rules guide the writing of test items: (1) Avoid wording and sentence structure that is ambiguous and confusing; (2) use vocabulary appropriate for the students tested; (3) keep test items short and to the point; (4) write items that have one correct answer; (5) give students information about the characteristics of the desired answer; (6) avoid providing clues to test answers; and (7) don't overcomplicate test items.
- In assembling items into a test, group the same item types together, with selection items placed at the start of the test and supply items at the end. Short-answer items should be placed before essay items.
- A proper physical climate for testing is one in which students are comfortable and interruptions are minimized.
- A proper psychological climate is more difficult to attain because some students are always more anxious about testing than others. Providing advance warning of a test, reviewing important objectives, and encouraging students to do their best without exerting undue pressure will help set a suitable psychological climate in which students can perform their best. Make it easy for students to keep track of the time.

- A student's IEP may specify that accommodations be provided during testing.
- Applying principles of universal design can help make tests accessible for more students and reduce the need to provide some accommodations on the day of testing.

QUESTIONS FOR DISCUSSION

1. Why is it important to consider accessibility when developing test items?
2. When is it appropriate to change a test item to overcome an access barrier, and when is it inappropriate to do so?
3. What is universal design, and how does it apply to test development?
4. How do you know when a construct is intended or unintended?
5. How can a teacher reduce students' test anxiety while maintaining their motivation to do well on a test?
6. When might it be inappropriate to provide a test accommodation?

ACTIVITIES

1. Each of the following eight test items has at least one fault. Read each item, identify the fault(s) in it, and rewrite the item to correct the fault(s). When you have finished rewriting the items, organize them into a test to be given to students. Include directions for items and group items of a similar type together.

   1. Robert Fulton, who was born in Scotland and came to the U.S. in 1843, is best known for his invention of the steamboat that he called the *Tom Thumb*. T F
   2. Minor differences among organisms of the same kind are known as:
      A. heredity
      B. variations
      C. adaptation
      D. natural selection
   3. The recall of factual information can best be assessed with a _____ item.
      A. matching
      B. objective
      C. essay
      D. short-answer
   4. Although the experimental research completed, particularly that by Hansmocker, must be considered too equivocal and the assumptions viewed as too restrictive, most testing experts would recommend that the easiest method of significantly improving paper-and-pencil achievement test reliability would be to:
      A. increase the size of the group
      B. increase the weighting of items

    C. increase the number of items
    D. increase the amount of testing time
5. F. Scott Fitzgerald wrote _____.
6. Boston is the most important city in the Northeast.   T   F
7. An electric transformer can be used:
    A. for storing up electricity
    B. to increase the voltage of alternating current (correct answer)
    C. it converts electrical energy into direct current
    D. alternating current is changed to direct current
8. The Confederate states were admitted back into the Union shortly
    after the Civil War.   T   F

2. Below are five objectives. For each objective, write one test item of
the type specified in parentheses to assess the objective.

   1. The student can match the symbols of chemical elements to their
     names. (matching)
   2. The student can identify the nouns in a sentence that contains
     more than one noun. (multiple-choice)
   3. The student can indicate whether a statement about the U.S.
     Constitution is true or false. (true-false)
   4. The student can state the name of the Speaker of the House of
     Representatives. (short-answer)
   5. The student can write the correct definition of an adverb. (short-
     answer)

REVIEW QUESTIONS

1. What is the fundamental purpose of assessing students' achievement?
What decisions must a teacher make when preparing to assess
student achievement?
2. How is the validity of an achievement test determined?
3. What are examples of clues to be avoided in multiple-choice, true-
false, completion, and matching items?
4. What is the relationship among educational objectives, instruction,
and achievement testing?

REFERENCES

Mislevy, R. J., Behrens, J. T., Bennett, R. E., Demark, S. F., Frezzo,
D. C., Levy, R., Robinson, D. H., Rutstein, D. W., Shute, V. J.,
Stanley, K., and Winters, F. I. (2010).** On the roles of external
knowledge representations in assessment design. *Journal of Technology,
Learning, and Assessment, 8*(2). Retrieved May 10, 2010, from
http://www.jtla.org.
Rose, D. H., and Meyer, A. (2002). *Teaching every student in the digital age:
Universal design for learning.* Alexandria, VA: ASCD Press.

CHAPTER 8

PERFORMANCE ASSESSMENTS

KEY TOPICS

- *The General Role of Performance Assessments*

- *Performance Assessment in Schools*

- *Developing Performance Assessments*

- *Anecdotal Records, Checklists, and Rating Scales*

- *Rubrics*

- *Portfolios*

- *Validity and Reliability of Performance Assessments*

After reading this chapter, you will be able to:

- Define *checklist, rating scale, rubric, performance criteria,* and other basic terms
- Contrast performance processes and performance products
- Contrast performance assessment with other assessment types
- Contrast performance assessment with learning activity
- Write well-stated performance criteria for a given process or performance
- Apply different scoring approaches for performance assessments
- Construct a scoring rubric
- Discuss portfolios and their use in assessment
- Identify strategies to improve the validity and reliability of classroom performance assessments

THINKING ABOUT TEACHING

In what ways can teachers use the results of assessment to improve student learning?

Performance assessment is a general term used to describe assessments that require students to demonstrate skill and knowledge by producing a formal product or performance. Performance assessment is often described as an alternative to timed tests that employ multiple-choice and short-answer items. Rather than asking students to demonstrate their skills and knowledge by answering a set of short, discrete questions, performance assessments generally require students to work on a product or prepare for a performance over an extended period of time. Unlike a multiple-choice or short-answer test item that focuses on a single learning objective, the product or performance often requires students to demonstrate the achievement of multiple objectives simultaneously. This chapter describes how to develop performance assessments and discusses their pros and cons, including issues of validity and reliability.

THE GENERAL ROLE
OF PERFORMANCE ASSESSMENTS

There are many classroom situations for which valid assessment requires that teachers gather formal information about students' performances or products. Teachers collect student products such as written

TABLE 8.1 EXAMPLES OF FOUR ASSESSMENT APPROACHES			
Selection	**Supply**	**Product**	**Performance**
Multiple-choice	Completion	Essay, story, or poem	Musical, dance, or dramatic performance
True-false	Label a diagram	Research report	Science lab demonstration
Matching	Short-answer	Writing portfolio	Typing test
	Concept map	Diary or journal	Athletic competition
		Science fair project	Debate
		Art exhibit or portfolio	Oral presentation
			Cooperation in groups

SOURCE: *If Minds Matter: A Foreword to the Future*, vol. 2, edited by Arthur L. Costa, James Bellanca, and Robin Fogarty. © 1992 IRI/Skylight Publishing Inc. Reprinted by permission of Skylight Professional Development. www/skylightedu.com

stories, paintings, lab reports, and science fair projects, as well as performances such as holding a pencil, typing, giving a speech, and cooperating in groups. Generally, products produce tangible outcomes—things you can hold in your hand—while performances are things you observe or listen to. Table 8.1 contrasts the selection and supply items discussed in Chapter 6 with typical examples of performance and product assessments.

Performance assessments may also be called alternative or authentic assessments. The term "alternative" is used to describe performance assessments because they serve as an alternative to a multiple-choice or short-answer test. The term "authentic" is used because some performance assessments permit students to show what they can do in real situations (Wiggins, 1992). In all cases, performance assessments present students with a clearly defined task that requires them to apply specific skills and knowledge. Rather than asking a student to demonstrate knowledge by selecting an answer or by describing how a skill should be performed, the student is required to actually apply that knowledge or skill to complete a task. Teachers recognize this distinction between selecting an answer or describing a skill versus actually applying knowledge or demonstrating a skill, as the following comments illustrate.

Performance assessments allow students to demonstrate what they know and can do in a real situation. Performance assessments are also called alternative and authentic assessments.

> I want my students to learn to do math for its own intrinsic value, but also because math is so essential for everyday life. Making change, balancing checkbooks, doing a budget, and many other practical, real-world activities require that students know how to use their math knowledge.

The kids need to learn to get along in groups, be respectful of others' property, and wait their turns. I don't want kids to be able to recite classroom rules, I want them to practice them. These behaviors are just as important for kids to learn in school as reading, writing, and math.

Just because they can write a list of steps they would follow to ensure laboratory safety does not mean that in a given situation they could actually demonstrate that knowledge.

Some types of short-answer test items can be used to provide information about the thinking processes that underlie students' performance. For example, a math problem in which students have to show their work provides insight into the mental processes used to solve the problem. An essay question can show students' organizational skills, thought processes, and application of capitalization and punctuation rules. These two forms of test items can assess what students can do as opposed to the majority of multiple-choice and short-answer test questions that reveal what students know. With most selection and short-answer supply questions, the teacher observes the *result* of the student's intellectual process, but not the thinking process that produced the result. If the student correctly answers a multiple-choice, true-false, matching, or completion item, the teacher *assumes* that the student must have followed the correct process, but there is little direct evidence to support this assumption since the only evidence of the student's thought process is a circled letter or a few written words. On the other hand, essays and other extended-response items provide a product that shows how students think about and construct their responses. They permit the teacher to see the logic of arguments, the manner in which the response is organized, and the basis of conclusions drawn by the student (Bartz et al., 1994). Like stories, reports, or "show-your-work" problems, essays and extended-response test items are important forms of performance assessments. Table 8.2 shows some of the differences between multiple-choice and short-answer test items, essay tests, oral questions, and performance assessments.

Chapters 2 and 4 discussed how teachers observe their students' performance in order to learn about them and also to obtain information about the moment-to-moment success of their instruction. Such observations are primarily informal and spontaneous. In this chapter, we are concerned with assessing more formal, structured performances and products, those that the teacher plans in advance, helps each student to perform, and formally assesses. These assessments can take place during normal classroom instruction (e.g., oral reading activities, setting up laboratory equipment) or in some special situation set up to elicit a performance (e.g., giving a speech in an auditorium). In either case, the activity is formally structured—the teacher arranges the conditions in which the performance or product is demonstrated and judged. Such assessments permit each student to show his or her mastery of the same process or task, something that is impossible with informal observation of spontaneous classroom performance and events.

TABLE 8.2   COMPARISON OF VARIOUS TYPES OF ASSESSMENTS

	Objective Test	Essay Test	Oral Question	Performance Assessment
Purpose	Sample knowledge with maximum efficiency and reliability	Assess thinking skills and/or mastery of how a body of knowledge is structured	Assess knowledge during instruction	Assess ability to translate knowledge and understanding into action
Student's Response	Read, evaluate, select	Organize, compose	Oral answer	Plan, construct and deliver an original response
Major Advantage	Efficiency—can administer many items per unit of testing time	Can measure complex cognitive outcomes	Joins assessment and instruction	Provides rich evidence of performance skills
Influence on Learning	Overemphasis on recall encourages memorization; can encourage thinking skills if properly constructed	Encourages thinking and development of writing skills	Stimulates participation in instruction, provides teacher immediate feedback on effectiveness of teaching	Emphasizes use of available skill and knowledge in relevant problem contexts

SOURCE: Adapted from R. J. Stiggins, "Design and Development of Performance Assessments," *Educational Measurement: Issues and Practice,* 1987, 6(3), p. 35. Copyright 1987 by the National Council on Measurement in Education Adapted by permission of the publisher.

Although the term "assessment" is used as part of the term "performance assessment," it is important to note that a performance assessment is actually a type of test. Recall from Chapter 1 that a test is a formal, systematic procedure used to gather information about student's achievement, behavior, or cognitive skills. As we will see later in this chapter, performance assessments are formal procedures to gather information about students' ability to apply knowledge and demonstrate specific skills or behaviors. Thus, just like a set of multiple-choice or short-answer items, performance assessment is a form of testing.

It is also important to distinguish between performance assessments and learning activities. Tasks such as writing an essay or story, conducting a laboratory experiment, or creating a diagram can be used to help students develop skills and knowledge. For example, before conducting a classroom discussion, a teacher might ask students to write a paragraph about something they read for homework in order to spur their thinking.

The purpose here is not to assess their understanding of the reading, but to help stimulate their thinking prior to a discussion. Similarly, a science teacher may ask students to conduct an experiment to observe what happens when two chemicals are combined. The purpose here is to develop students' understanding by having them observe a chemical reaction. These are examples of learning activities. However, these same activities could also be used to assess students' understanding of the previous night's reading or of chemical reactions. When asking students to engage in an activity, it is important for teachers to decide ahead of time whether the purpose of the activity is to develop students' skill and knowledge or to assess their skill and knowledge. Failing to make this distinction prior to the activity can result in decisions about students that have low validity. After all, if students have not had an opportunity to develop their knowledge and skills, it is unfair to make decisions about the extent to which they are able to exhibit their knowledge and skills.

PERFORMANCE ASSESSMENT IN SCHOOLS

The amount of attention that has recently been focused on performance assessment in states, schools, and classrooms might lead one to believe that performance assessment is new and untried, and that it can solve all the problems of classroom assessment. Neither of these beliefs is true (Madaus and O'Dwyer, 1999). Performance assessment has been used extensively in classrooms for as long as there have been classrooms. Table 8.3 provides examples of five common, long-standing areas of performance assessment in schools.

Performance assessments reflect the recent emphasis on real-world problem solving.

TABLE 8.3   FIVE COMMON DOMAINS OF PERFORMANCE ASSESSMENT

Communication Skills	Psychomotor Skills	Athletic Activities	Concept Acquisition	Affective Skills
Writing essays	Holding a pencil	Shooting free throws	Constructing open and closed circuits	Sharing toys
Giving a speech	Setting up lab equipment	Catching a ball	Selecting proper tools for shop tasks	Working in cooperative groups
Pronouncing a foreign language	Using scissors	Hopping	Identifying unknown chemical substances	Obeying school rules
Following spoken directions	Dissecting a frog	Swimming the stroke	Generalizing from experimental data	Maintaining self-control

Many factors account for the growing popularity of performance assessment (Ryan and Miyasaka, 1995; Quality Counts, 1999). First, performance assessment is being proposed or mandated as part of formal statewide assessment programs. Second, increased classroom emphasis on problem solving, higher-level thinking, and real-world reasoning skills has increased the value of performance and product assessments to demonstrate student learning. Third, performance assessments can provide some students who do poorly on selection-type tests an opportunity to show their achievement in alternative ways.

Performance-Oriented Subjects

Assessing students' understanding of concepts through hands-on demonstrations is becoming more common.

All schools expect students to demonstrate communication skills, so reading, writing, and speaking are perhaps the most common areas of classroom performance assessment. Likewise, simple psychomotor skills such as being able to sit in a chair or hold a pencil, as well as more sophisticated skills such as setting up laboratory equipment or using tools to build a birdhouse, are a fundamental part of school life. Closely related are the athletic performances taught in physical education classes.

There also is a growing emphasis on using performance assessment to determine students' understanding of the concepts they are taught and to measure their ability to apply procedural knowledge. The argument is that if students grasp a concept or process, they should be able to explain and use it to solve real-life problems. For example, after teaching students about money and making change, the teacher may assess learning by having students count out the money needed to purchase objects from the classroom "store" or act as a storekeeper and make change for other students' purchases. Or, rather than giving a multiple-choice test on the chemical reactions that help identify unknown substances, the teacher could give each student an unknown substance and have them go through the process of identifying it.

In addition to measuring cognitive learning goals, performance assessments are also used regularly by teachers to assess students' feelings, values, attitudes, and emotions. When a teacher checks the "satisfactory" rating under the category "works hard" or "obeys school rules" on a student's report card, the teacher bases this judgment on observations of the student's demonstration of these traits. Teachers rely on observations of student performance to collect evidence about important behaviors such as getting along with peers, working independently, following rules, and maintaining self-control.

Most teachers recognize the importance of balancing supply and selection assessments with performance and product assessments, as the following comments indicate.

olc

CHAPTER CASE STUDY

Visit the text Online Learning Center to read the case of teacher Frank Oakley's science lesson. It will give you a feel for the challenges of performance assessment in a high school lab.

www.mhhe.com/ russell7e

It is important for teachers to balance supply and selection assessments with performance and product assessments.

It's not reasonable to grade reading without including the student's oral reading skills or their comprehension of what they read. I always spend some time when it's grading time listening to and rating my students' oral reading and comprehension quality.

My kids know that a large part of their grade depends on how well they follow safety procedures and take proper care of the tools they use. They know I'm always on the lookout for times when they don't do these things and that it will count against them if I see them.

I wouldn't want anyone to assess my teaching competence solely on the basis of my students' paper-and-pencil test scores. I would want to be seen interacting with the kids, teaching them, and attending to their needs. Why should I confine my assessments of my students solely to paper-and-pencil methods?

Early Childhood and Special Needs Students

While performance assessment cuts across subject areas and grade levels, it is heavily used in early childhood and special education settings. Because preschool, kindergarten, and primary school students are limited in their communication skills and are still in the process of being socialized into the school culture, much assessment information is obtained by observing their performances and products. Assessment at this age focuses on gross and fine motor development, verbal and auditory acuity, and visual development, as well as social behaviors. Key Assessment Tools 8.1 illustrates some of the

Early education teachers rely heavily on performance-based assessments because of their students' limited communication skills.

Key Assessment Tools 8.1

EARLY CHILDHOOD BEHAVIOR AREAS

Gross motor development: Roll over, sit erect without toppling over, walk a straight line, throw a ball, jump on one or two feet, skip.

Fine motor development: Cut with scissors, trace an object, color inside the lines, draw geometric forms (e.g., circles, squares, triangles), demonstrate neat and legible penmanship, use left-to-right progression in reading and writing, show eye-hand coordination.

Verbal and auditory acuity: Identify sounds, listen to certain sounds and ignore others (e.g., tune out distractions), discriminate between sounds and words that sound alike (e.g., "fix" vs. "fish"), remember numbers in sequence, follow directions, remember the correct order of events, pronounce words and letters.

Visual development: Find a letter, number, or object similar to one shown by the teacher; copy a shape; identify shapes and embedded figures; reproduce a design given by the teacher; differentiate objects by size, color, and shape.

Social acclimation: Listen to the teacher, follow a time schedule, share, wait one's turn, respect the property of others.

important early childhood behaviors and skills that teachers assess by performance-based means. These examples provide a sense of how heavily the early childhood curriculum is weighted toward performance outcomes.

Many special needs students—especially those who exhibit multiple and severe disabilities in their cognitive, affective, and psychomotor development—are provided instruction focused on self-help skills such as getting dressed, brushing teeth, making a sandwich, and operating household items. Students are taught to carry out these performances through many, many repetitions. Observation of students as they perform these activities is the main assessment technique special education teachers use to identify performance mastery or areas needing further work.

DEVELOPING PERFORMANCE ASSESSMENTS

A diving competition is an instructive example of a skill that is assessed by a performance assessment. Submitting a written essay describing how to perform various dives or answering a multiple-choice test about diving rules would provide little information about one's ability to dive. Rather, a valid assessment of diving ability requires seeing the diver actually perform. And, to make the assessment reliable, the diver must perform a series of dives, not just one.

Diving judges rate dives using a scale that has 21 possible numerical scores that can be awarded (e.g., 0.0, 0.5, 1.0 . . . 5.5, 6.0, 6.5, . . . 9.0, 9.5, 10.0). They observe a very complicated performance made up of many body movements that together take about 2 seconds to complete. The judges do not have the benefit of slow motion or instant replay to review the performance, and they cannot discuss the dive with one another. If their attention strays for even a second, they miss a large portion of the performance. Yet, when the scores are flashed on the scoreboard, the judges usually are in very close agreement. Rarely do all judges give a dive exactly the same score, but rarely is there more than a 1-point difference between any two judges' scores. This is an amazing level of agreement among observers for such a short, complicated performance.

With this example in mind, let's consider the four essential features of all formal performance assessments, whether it be a diving competition, an oral speech, a book report, a typing exercise, a science fair project, or something else. This overview will then be followed by a more extensive discussion of each feature. Briefly, every performance assessment should:

1. Have a clear purpose that identifies the decision to be made based on the performance assessment.
2. Identify observable aspects of the student's performance or product that can be judged.

3. Provide an appropriate setting for eliciting and judging the performance or product.
4. Provide a judgment or score to describe performance.

Define the Purpose of Assessment

Teachers use performance assessment for many purposes: grading students, constructing portfolios of student work, diagnosing student learning, helping students recognize the important steps in a performance or product, providing concrete examples of student work for parent conferences. Whatever the purpose of performance assessment, the purpose should be specified at the beginning of the assessment process. Rather than selecting an activity or task that a teacher believes will be fun for students to perform and then trying to decide what information can be gleaned from that activity, the performance assessment should be developed to meet the predefined purpose. The purpose of assessment will also guide the development of proper performance criteria and scoring procedures.

Performances and products are normally broken down into specific, observable criteria, each of which can be judged independently.

Teachers need to think ahead of time about whether a performance assessment's purposes will be formative or summative because their judgment task and scoring criteria will differ depending on the purpose of assessment. When the goal of assessment is formative, the focus is on giving feedback to students about their strengths and weaknesses. For this reason, the scoring criteria will focus on discrete aspects of the performance so that detailed information about the strengths and weaknesses of a student's performance can be provided. When the goal is summative, the focus is on rating the student's level of achievement. When this is the case, the scoring criteria will focus on the overall quality of the product or performance and will often result in a single score.

Since performance assessments usually require students to apply multiple skills and knowledge, a performance assessment is particularly suited for formative assessments. By focusing on specific aspects or components of a student's performance or product, the strong and weak points of a student's performance can be identified. This information can then be used to target instruction on areas of weakness a student reveals through the performance assessment. Whether a performance assessment is used to make formative or summative decisions, the first step in developing a performance assessment is to answer the following three questions: What is my purpose for this assessment? What decisions will I make based on this assessment? What information will I need to make these decisions?

Performance assessments are particularly suited to diagnosis because they provide information about how students perform each specific criterion in a general performance.

Identify Performance Criteria

Performance criteria are the specific behaviors a student should display when properly carrying out a performance or creating a product.

Performance criteria are at the heart of successful performance assessment, yet they are the area in which most problems occur.

When teachers first think about assessing performance, they tend to think in terms of general performances such as oral reading, giving a speech, following safety rules in the laboratory, penmanship, writing a book report, organizing ideas, keyboarding, or getting along with peers. In reality, such performances cannot be assessed until they are broken down into the more specific aspects or characteristics that compose them. These more narrow aspects and characteristics are the performance criteria that teachers will observe and judge.

The challenge to creating useful performance criteria is identifying the specific aspects or components of a performance that relate to the decisions a teacher will make based on the performance assessment. In an English class, a performance assessment might ask students to write an extended essay about a poem they have read. The teacher might then use the essay to make a variety of different decisions including how well a student: (a) understands a poem; (b) understands and is able to identify specific uses of literary devices; (c) writes an analytic essay; (d) uses proper capitalization, punctuation, and spelling; or (e) presents his or her ideas neatly in writing. Which of these decisions the teacher is interested in making will influence the criteria used to assess the student's essay.

Key Assessment Tools 8.2 shows three sets of criteria for assessing students' performance when (1) working in groups, (2) playing the piano, and (3) writing a book report. Criteria such as these focus teachers' instruction and assessments. Notice how the performance criteria clearly identify the important aspects of the performance or product being assessed. Well-stated performance criteria are at the heart of successful efforts to instruct and assess performances and products.

Performance criteria can focus on processes, products, or both.

To define performance criteria, a teacher must first decide if a process or a product will be observed. Will processes such as typing or oral reading be assessed, or will products such as a typed letter or book report be assessed? In the former case, criteria are needed to judge the student's actual performance of targeted behaviors; in the latter, criteria are needed to judge the end product of those behaviors. In some cases, both process and product can be assessed. For example, a first-grade teacher assessed both process and product when she (1) observed a student writing to determine how the student held the pencil, positioned the paper, and manipulated the pencil and (2) judged the finished, handwritten product to assess how well the student formed his letters. Notice that the teacher observed different things according to whether she was interested in the student's handwriting *process* or handwriting *product*. It is for this reason that teachers must know what they want to observe before performance criteria can be identified.

The key to identifying performance criteria is to break down an overall performance or product into its component parts. It is these parts that will be observed and judged. Consider, for example, a product assessment

---

Key Assessment Tools 8.2

EXAMPLES OF PERFORMANCE CRITERIA

Working in Groups

Reports to group project
    area on time

Starts work on own

Shares information

Contributes ideas

Listens to others

Waits turn to speak

Follows instructions

Is courteous to other group
    members

Helps to solve group
    problems

Considers viewpoints
    of others

Carries out share of
    group-determined activities

Completes assigned tasks
    on time

Playing the Piano

Sits upright with feet on
    floor (or pedal, when
    necessary)

Arches fingers on keys

Plays without pauses or
    interruptions

Maintains even tempo

Plays correct notes

Holds all note values for
    indicated duration

Follows score dynamics
    (forte, crescendo,
    decrescendo)

Ensures that melody can be
    heard above other
    harmonization

Phrases according to score
    (staccato and legato)

Follows score pedal
    markings

Writing a Book Report

States the author and title

Identifies the type of book
    (fiction, adventure,
    historical, etc.)

Describes what the book
    was about in four or
    more sentences

States an opinion of the
    book

Gives three reasons
    to support the opinion

Uses correct spelling,
    punctuation, and
    capitalization

---

of eighth-graders' written paragraphs. The purpose of the assessment is to judge students' ability to write a paragraph on a topic of their choice. In preparing to judge the completed paragraph, a teacher initially listed the following performance criteria:

- First sentence
- Appropriate topic sentence
- Good supporting ideas
- Good vocabulary
- Complete sentences
- Capitalization
- Spelling
- Conclusion
- Handwriting

These performance criteria identify important areas of a written paragraph, but the areas are vague and poorly stated. What, for example, is meant by "first sentence"? What is an "appropriate" topic sentence or "good" vocabulary? What should be examined in judging capitalization, spelling, and handwriting? If a teacher cannot answer these questions, how can he or she provide suitable examples or instruction for students? Performance criteria need to be specific enough to focus the teacher on well-defined characteristics of the performance or product. They must also be specific enough to permit the teacher to convey to students, in terms they can understand, the specific features that define the desired performance or product. Once defined, the criteria permit consistent teacher assessments of performance and consistent communication with students about their learning.

Following is a revised version of the performance criteria for a well-organized paragraph. Note the difference in clarity and how the revised version focuses the teacher and students on very specific features of the paragraph—ones that are important and will be assessed. Before assigning the task, the teacher wisely decided to share and discuss the performance criteria with the students.

- Indents first sentence.
- Topic sentence sets main idea of paragraph.
- Following sentences support main idea.
- Sentences arranged in logical order.
- Uses age-appropriate vocabulary.
- Writes in complete sentences.
- Capitalizes proper nouns and first words in sentences.
- Makes no more than three spelling errors.
- Conclusion follows logically from prior sentences.
- Handwriting is legible.

Cautions in Developing Performance Criteria

Three points of caution are appropriate here. First, it is important to understand that the previous example of performance criteria is not the only one that describes the characteristics of a well-written paragraph. Different teachers might identify varying criteria that they feel are more important or more suitable for their students than some of the ones in our example. Thus, emphasis should not be on identifying the best or only set of criteria for a performance or product, but rather on stating criteria that are meaningful, important, and can be understood by the students.

Very long lists of performance criteria (over 15) become unmanageable and intrusive.

Second, it is possible to break down most school performances and products into many very narrow criteria. However, a lengthy list of performance criteria becomes ineffective because teachers rarely have the time to observe and assess a large number of very specific performance criteria for each student. Too many criteria make the observation process intrusive, with the teacher hovering over the student, rapidly checking off behaviors and often interfering with a student's performance.

For classroom performance assessment to be manageable and meaningful, a balance must be established between specificity and practicality. The key to attaining this balance is to identify the *essential* criteria associated with a performance or product; 6 to 12 performance criteria are a manageable number for most classroom teachers to emphasize.

The key to attaining a balance between specificity and practicality is to identify 6 to 12 performance criteria to emphasize.

Third, the process of identifying performance criteria is an ongoing one that is rarely completed after the first attempt. Initial performance criteria will need to be revised and clarified, based on experience with their use, to provide the focus needed for valid and reliable assessment. To aid this process, teachers should think about the performance or product they wish to observe and reflect on its key aspects. They can also examine a few actual products or performances as bases for revising their initial list of criteria.

The following list shows the initial set of performance criteria a teacher wrote to assess students' oral reports.

- Speaks clearly and slowly.
- Pronounces correctly.
- Makes eye contact.
- Exhibits good posture when presenting.
- Exhibits good effort.
- Presents with feeling.
- Understands the topic.
- Exhibits enthusiastic attitude.
- Organizes.

Note the lack of specificity in many of the criteria: "slowly," "correctly," "good," "understands," and "enthusiastic attitude." These criteria hide more than they reveal. After reflecting on and observing a few oral presentations, the teacher revised and sharpened the performance criteria as shown in the following list. Note that the teacher first divided the general performance into three areas (physical expression, vocal expression, and verbal expression) and then identified a few important performance criteria within each of these areas. It is not essential to divide the performance criteria into separate sections, but sometimes it is useful in focusing the teacher and students.

1. Physical expression
   - Stands straight and faces audience.
   - Changes facial expression with changes in tone of the report.
   - Maintains eye contact with audience.

2. Vocal expression
   - Speaks in a steady, clear voice.
   - Varies tone to emphasize points.
   - Speaks loudly enough to be heard by audience.
   - Paces words in an even flow.
   - Enunciates each word.

3. Verbal expression
- Chooses precise words to convey meaning.
- Avoids unnecessary repetition.
- States sentences with complete thoughts or ideas.
- Organizes information logically.
- Summarizes main points at conclusion.

Developing Observable Performance Criteria

The value of performance assessments depends on identifying performance criteria that can be observed and judged.

The value and richness of performance assessments depend heavily on identifying criteria that can be observed and judged. It is important that the criteria be clear in the teacher's mind and that the students be taught the criteria. The following guidelines should prove useful for this purpose.

1. *Select the performance or product to be assessed and either perform it yourself or imagine yourself performing it.* Think to yourself, "What would I have to do in order to complete this task? What steps would I have to follow?" It isn't a bad idea to actually carry out the performance yourself, recording and studying your performance or product.

2. *List the important aspects of the performance or product.* What specific behaviors or attributes are most important to the successful completion of the task? What behaviors have been emphasized in instruction? Include important aspects and exclude irrelevant ones.

3. *Try to limit the number of performance criteria, so they all can be observed during a student's performance.* This is less important when one is assessing a product, but even then it is better to assess a limited number of key criteria than a large number that vary widely. Remember, you will have to observe and judge performance on each of the criteria identified.

When teachers within a school develop similar performance criteria across grade levels, it is reinforcing to students.

4. *If possible, have groups of teachers think through the important criteria included in a task.* Because all first-grade teachers assess oral reading in their classrooms and because the criteria for successful oral reading do not differ much from one first-grade classroom to another, a group effort to define performance criteria will likely save time and produce a more complete set of criteria than that produced by any single teacher. Similar group efforts are useful for other common performances or products such as book reports and science fair projects.

5. *Express the performance criteria in terms of observable student behaviors or product characteristics.* Be specific when stating the performance criteria. For example, do not write "The child works." Instead, write "The child remains focused on the task for at least four minutes." Instead of "organization," write "Information is presented in a logical sequence."

6. *Do not use ambiguous words that cloud the meaning of the performance criteria.* The worst offenders in this regard are adverbs that end in

ly. Other words to avoid are "good" and "appropriate." Thus, criteria such as "appropriate organization," "speaks correctly," "writes neatly," and "performs gracefully" are ambiguous and leave interpretation of performance up to the observer. The observer's interpretation may vary from time to time and from student to student, diminishing the fairness and usefulness of the assessment.

7. Arrange the performance criteria in the order in which they are likely to be observed. This will save time when observing and will maintain primary focus on the performance.

8. Check for existing performance criteria before defining your own. The performance criteria associated with giving an oral speech, reading aloud, using a microscope, writing a persuasive paragraph, cutting with scissors, and the like have been listed by many people. No one who reads this book will be the first to try to assess these and most other common school performances. One need not reinvent the wheel every time a wheel is needed.

Provide a Setting to Elicit and Observe the Performance

Once the performance criteria are defined, a setting in which to observe the performance or product must be selected or established. Depending on the nature of the performance or product, the teacher may observe behaviors as they naturally occur in the classroom or set up a specific situation in which the students must perform. There are two considerations in deciding whether to observe naturally occurring behaviors or to set up a more controlled exercise: (1) the frequency with which the performance naturally occurs in the classroom and (2) the seriousness of the decision to be made.

Teachers may observe and assess naturally occurring classroom behaviors or set up situations in which they assess structured performances.

If the performance occurs infrequently during normal classroom activity, it may be more efficient to structure a situation in which students must perform the desired behaviors. For example, in the normal flow of classroom activities, students rarely have the opportunity to give a planned 5-minute speech, so the teacher should set up an exercise in which each student must develop and give a 5-minute speech. Oral reading, on the other hand, occurs frequently enough in many elementary classrooms that performance can be observed as part of the normal flow of reading instruction.

Formally structured performance assessments are needed when teachers are dealing with low-frequency behaviors and making important decisions.

The importance of the decision to be made from a performance assessment also influences the context in which observation takes place. In general the more important the decision, the more structured the assessment environment should be. A course grade, for example, represents an important decision about a student. If performance assessments contribute to grading, evidence should be gathered under structured, formal circumstances so that every student has a fair and equal chance to exhibit his or her achievement. The validity of the assessment is likely to be improved when the setting is similar for and familiar to all students.

Multiple observations of student performances provide more reliable and accurate information than a single observation.

Regardless of the nature of the assessment, evidence obtained from a single assessment describes only one example of a student's performance. For a variety of reasons such as illness, family problems, or other distractions, student performance at a single time may not provide a reliable indication of the student's true achievement. To be certain that one has an accurate indication of what a student can and cannot do, multiple observations and products are useful. If the different observations produce similar performance, a teacher can have confidence in the evidence and use it in decision making. If different observations contradict one another, more information should be obtained.

Develop a Score to Describe the Performance

Holistic scoring (a single overall score) is good for such things as group placement or grading; analytic scoring (scoring individual criteria) is useful in diagnosing student difficulties.

The final step in performance assessment is to score students' performance. As in previous steps, the nature of the decision to be made influences the type of scores that will be generated. Judging a performance assessment can result in a single holistic score that provides an overall summary of the performance or multiple analytic scores that focus on discrete components of the performance. In situations such as group placement, selection, or grading, holistic scoring is most useful. To make such decisions, a teacher seeks to describe an individual's performance using a single, overall score. On the other hand, if the assessment purpose is to diagnose student difficulties or certify student mastery of each individual performance criterion, then analytic scoring, with a separate score or rating on each performance criterion, is appropriate. In either case, the performance criteria dictate the scoring or rating approach that is adopted.

Anecdotal records, checklists, rating scales, and portfolios are options to collect and record observations of students.

In most classrooms, the teacher is both the observer and the scorer. In situations where an important decision is to be made, additional observers/scorers may be added. It is common for performance assessments in athletic, music, debate, and art competitions to have more than a single judge in order to control for judgment errors, misinterpretations, or biases. A number of options exist for collecting, recording, and summarizing observations of student performance: anecdotal records, checklists, rating scales, rubrics, and portfolios. The following sections explore these options in detail.

ANECDOTAL RECORDS, CHECKLISTS, AND RATING SCALES

Anecdotal Records

Written accounts of significant, individual student events and behaviors the teacher has observed are called **anecdotal records.** Of all methods for recording and reporting information about a student's performance, an

FIGURE 8.1
*Anecdotal Record
for Lynn Gregory*

STUDENT *Lynn Gregory*	DATE *9/22/2010*
OBSERVER *J. Ricketts*	

Lynn entered the room in an orderly manner and moved directly to her desk. She began preparing for class by taking out her homework and a pencil. Lynn then became interested in a conversation that was occurring between two students beside her. She left her desk and became engaged in the conversation. She quickly became animated and, when the bell rang, had difficulty settling back down. For several minutes, she repeatedly shifted her focus from the teacher to the students beside her, at times whispering to them. Only after being spoken to by the teacher was Lynn able to fully focus on the lesson at hand.

FIGURE 8.1
*Anecdotal Record
for Lynn Gregory*

anecdotal record is the most detailed. However, anecdotal records are also the most time-consuming to produce. As with all methods for recording information about student performance, it is important that clear criteria or aspects of a performance be identified prior to creating an anecdotal record. An anecdotal record is not meant to be a free-flowing description of a student's performance. Instead, it should provide a purposeful, detailed description of the strengths and weaknesses of a student's performance based on prespecified performance criteria. Figure 8.1 shows an example of an anecdotal record of student Lynn Gregory. Notice that the written record states events factually and focuses on the criteria (in this case, the student's ability to transition to a new activity, follow directions, and focus on the task at hand). Also note the lack of judgment or recommendations about how to help Lynn improve her behavior. An anecdotal record is not meant to be a report. Rather, it is intended to provide detailed documentation of a performance that can be used to form a decision. Thus, judgment and recommendations are absent from the record and are made when the record is reviewed at a later time.

Checklists

A **checklist** is a written list of performance criteria. As a student's performance is observed or a product is judged, the scorer determines whether the performance or the product meets each performance criterion included in the checklist. If it does, a checkmark is placed next to that criterion, indicating that it was observed; if it does not, the checkmark is omitted. Figure 8.2 shows a completed checklist for Rick Gray's oral presentation. The performance criteria for this checklist were presented earlier in this chapter.

A checklist, which is a written list of performance criteria, can be used repeatedly over time to diagnose strengths, weaknesses, and changes in performances.

Checklists are diagnostic, reusable, and capable of charting student progress. They provide a detailed record of students' performances, one that can and should be shown to students to help them see where

FIGURE 8.2 *Checklist Results for an Oral Presentation*

NAME: *Rick Gray*   DATE: *Oct. 12, 2010*

I. Physical Expression

✓ A. Stands straight and faces audience.

_____ B. Changes facial expression with changes in tone of the presentation.

✓ C. Maintains eye contact with audience.

II. Vocal Expression

✓ A. Speaks in a steady, clear voice.

✓ B. Varies tone to emphasize points.

_____ C. Speaks loudly enough to be heard by audience.

✓ D. Paces words in an even flow.

_____ E. Enunciates each word.

III. Verbal Expression

_____ A. Chooses precise words to convey meaning.

✓ B. Avoids unnecessary repetition.

✓ C. States sentences with complete thoughts or ideas.

✓ D. Organizes information logically.

✓ E. Summarizes main points at conclusion.

improvement is needed. Rick Gray's teacher could sit down with him after his presentation and point out both the criteria on which he performed well and the areas that need improvement. Because a checklist focuses on specific performances, it provides diagnostic information. The same checklist can be reused with different students or with the same student over time. Using the same checklist more than once is an easy way to obtain information about a student's improvement over time.

There are, however, disadvantages associated with checklists. One important disadvantage is that checklists give a teacher only two choices for each criterion: performed or not performed. A checklist provides no middle ground for scoring. Suppose that Rick Gray stood straight and faced the audience most of the time during his oral presentation, or paced his

Checklists cannot record gradations in performance.

words evenly except in one brief part of the speech when he spoke too quickly and ran his words together. How should his teacher score him on these performance criteria? Should Rick receive a check because he did them most of the time, or should he not receive a check because his performance was flawed? Sometimes this is not an easy choice. A checklist forces the teacher to make an absolute decision for each performance criterion, even though a student's performance is somewhere between these extremes.

A second disadvantage of checklists is the difficulty of summarizing a student's performance into a single score. We saw how useful checklists can be for diagnosing students' strengths and weaknesses. But what if a teacher wants to summarize performance across a number of criteria to arrive at a single score for grading purposes?

One way to summarize Rick's performance into a single score is to translate the number of performance criteria he successfully demonstrated into a percentage. For example, there were 13 performance criteria on the oral presentation checklist and Rick demonstrated 9 of them during his presentation. Assuming each criterion is equally important, Rick's performance translates into a score of 69 percent (9/13 × 100 = 69%). Thus, Rick demonstrated 69 percent of the desired performance criteria. (In Chapter 10 we will discuss how scores like Rick's 69 percent are turned into grades.)

A second, and better, way to summarize performance would be for the teacher to set up standards for rating students' performance. Suppose Rick's teacher set up the following set of standards:

Excellent	12 or 13	performance criteria shown
Good	9 to 11	performance criteria shown
Fair	5 to 8	performance criteria shown
Poor	5 or fewer	performance criteria shown

These standards allow the teacher to summarize performance on a scale that ranges from excellent to poor. The scale could also range from an A to a D, depending on the type of scoring the teacher uses. The same standard would be used to summarize each student's performance. Rick performed 9 of the 13 criteria, and the teacher's standard indicates that his performance should be classified as "good" or "B." Of course, many such standards can be set up and the one shown is only an example. In establishing standards, it is advisable to keep the summarizing rules as simple as possible.

Summarizing performances from a checklist can be done by setting up rating standards or by calculating the percentage of criteria accomplished.

Rating Scales

Although they are similar to checklists, **rating scales** allow the observer to judge performance along a continuum rather than as a dichotomy. Both checklists and rating scales are based on a set of performance criteria, and it is common for the same set of performance criteria to be used in both a rating scale and a checklist. However, a checklist gives the observer two categories for judging, while a rating scale provides a broader range of scores.

Three of the most common types of rating scales are the numerical, graphic, and descriptive scales. Figure 8.3 shows an example of each of these scales as applied to two specific performance criteria for giving an oral presentation. In numerical scales, a number stands for a point on the rating scale. Thus, in the example, "1" corresponds to the student *always* performing the behavior, "2" to the student *usually* performing the behavior, and so on. Graphic scales require the rater to mark a position on a line divided into sections based on a scale. The rater marks an "X" at that point on the line that best describes the student's performance. Descriptive rating scales, also called **scoring rubrics,** require the rater to choose among different descriptions of actual performance (Wiggins and McTighe, 1998; Goodrich, 1997) (We will say more about rubrics in the next section.) In descriptive rating scales, different descriptions are used to represent different levels of student performance. To score, the teacher picks the description that comes closest to the student's actual performance. A judgment by the teacher determines the grade.

Regardless of the type of rating scale one chooses, two general rules will improve their accuracy. The first rule is to limit the number of rating categories. There is a tendency to think that the greater the number of rating categories to choose from, the better the rating scale. In practice, this is not the case. Few observers can make reliable distinctions in performance across more than five rating categories. Adding a larger number of categories on a rating scale is likely to make the ratings less, not more, reliable. Stick to three to five well-defined and distinct rating scale points, as shown in Figure 8.3. The second rule is to use the same rating scale for each performance criterion. This is not usually possible in descriptive rating scales where the descriptions vary with each performance criterion. For numerical and graphic scales, however, it is best to select a single rating scale and use it for all performance criteria. Using many different rating categories requires the observer to change focus frequently and will decrease rating accuracy by distracting the rater's attention from the performance.

Figure 8.4 shows a complete set of numerical rating scales for Sarah Jackson for an oral presentation. Note that its performance criteria are identical to those on the checklist shown in Figure 8.2. The only difference between the checklist and the numerical rating scales is the range of scores available to score each performance criteria.

Rating scales provide a range of categories for assessing a student's performance, and thereby provide detailed diagnostic information. However, when a performance must be summarized by a single score, multiple rating categories complicate the process of summarizing performance across criteria to arrive at a student's overall score. With a

The three most common types of rating scales are numerical, graphic, and descriptive (also called scoring rubrics).

Descriptive rating scales, or scoring rubrics, require the rater to choose among different descriptions of actual performance.

Having too many scales tends to distract the rater from the performance, making the ratings unreliable.

Whereas checklists measure only the presence or absence of some performance, a rating scale measures the degree to which the performance matches the criteria.

FIGURE 8.3   *Three Types of Rating Scales for an Oral Presentation*

Numerical Rating Scale

Directions: Indicate how often the student performs each of these behaviors while giving an oral presentation. For each behavior circle **1** if the student **always** performs the behavior, **2** if the student **usually** performs the behavior, **3** if the student **seldom** performs the behavior, and **4** if the student **never** performs the behavior.

Physical Expression

A. Stands straight and faces audience

       1   **2**   **3**   **4**

B. Changes facial expression with changes in tone of the presentation

       1   **2**   **3**   **4**

Graphic Rating Scale

Directions: Place an **X** on the line that shows how often the student did each of the behaviors listed while giving an oral presentation.

Physical Expression

A. Stands straight and faces audience

    always   **usually**   **seldom**   **never**

B. Changes facial expression with changes in tone of the presentation

    always   **usually**   **seldom**   **never**

Descriptive Rating Scale

Directions: Place an **X** on the line at the place which best describes the student's performance on each behavior.

Physical Expression

A. Stands straight and faces audience

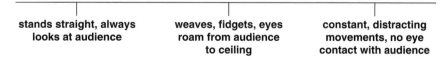

| **stands straight, always looks at audience** | **weaves, fidgets, eyes roam from audience to ceiling** | **constant, distracting movements, no eye contact with audience** |

B. Changes facial expression with changes in tone of the presentation

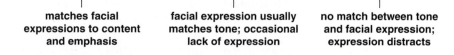

| **matches facial expressions to content and emphasis** | **facial expression usually matches tone; occasional lack of expression** | **no match between tone and facial expression; expression distracts** |

FIGURE 8.4 *Types of Rating Scales*

NAME: *Sarah Jackson*   DATE: *Nov. 8, 2010*

Directions: Indicate how often the student performs each of these behaviors while giving an oral presentation. For each behavior **circle 4** if the student **always** performs the behavior, **3** if the student **usually** performs the behavior, **2** if the student **seldom** performs the behavior, and **1** if the student **never** performs the behavior.

I. Physical Expression

    (4) 3 2 1   A. Stands straight and faces audience

    4 3 (2) 1   B. Changes facial expression with changes in tone of the presentation

    4 (3) 2 1   C. Maintains eye contact with audience

II. Vocal Expression

    (4) 3 2 1   A. Speaks in a steady, clear voice

    4 (3) 2 1   B. Varies tone to emphasize points

    4 3 (2) 1   C. Speaks loudly enough to be heard by audience

    4 (3) 2 1   D. Paces words in an even flow

    4 3 (2) 1   E. Enunciates each word

III. Verbal Expression

    4 3 (2) 1   A. Chooses precise words to convey meaning

    4 (3) 2 1   B. Avoids unnecessary repetition

    (4) 3 2 1   C. States sentences with complete thoughts or ideas

    (4) 3 2 1   D. Organizes information logically

    4 (3) 2 1   E. Summarizes main points at conclusion

checklist, summarization is reduced to giving credit for checked criteria and no credit for unchecked criteria. This cannot be done with a rating scale because performance is judged in terms of *degree,* not presence or absence.

    Numerical summarization is the most straightforward and commonly used approach to summarizing performance on rating scales. It assigns a point value to each category in the scale and sums the points across the performance criteria. For example, consider Sarah Jackson's ratings in

Figure 8.4. To obtain a summary score for Sarah's performance, one can assign 4 points to a rating of "always," 3 points to a rating of "usually," 2 points to a rating of "seldom," and 1 point to a rating of "never." The numbers 4, 3, 2, and 1 match the four possible ratings for each performance criterion, with 4 representing the most desirable response and 1 the least desirable. For the rating scale used to score Sarah's performance, the highest possible score on the rating scale is 52; if a student was rated "always" on each performance criterion, the student's total score would be 52 (4 points × 13 performance criteria). Sarah's total score, 39, can be determined by adding the circled numbers. Thus, Sarah scored 39 out of a possible 52 points. In this manner, a total score can be determined for each student rated. This score can be turned into a percentage by dividing it by 52, the total number of points available (39/52 × 100 = 75%). Thus, high scores indicate good performance.

Note that once Sarah's performance is summarized as a single score, that score no longer conveys information about the strengths and weaknesses of Sarah's performance. Given the richness and instructionally useful information provided by the scores awarded for each individual criterion, before summarizing Sarah's performance into a single score, it is important to closely examine the separate scores to identify areas of weakness so that Sarah can be guided to improve her oral presentations.

RUBRICS

A rubric is a set of clear expectations or criteria used to help teachers and students focus on what is valued in a subject, topic, or activity. A rubric is often similar to a checklist in that it lists multiple criteria for a performance. However, unlike a checklist that simply lists the criteria, a rubric provides a description of the expected level of performance for each criterion. Rubrics lay out criteria for different levels of performance, which are usually descriptive rather than numerical. The descriptions help teachers focus their instruction and their scoring of student work on the important aspects included in the rubric. The descriptions also help students better understand what teachers expect of them for a given performance or product.

Rubrics summarize performance in a general way, whereas checklists and rating scales provide specific diagnostic information about student strengths and weaknesses.

By providing descriptions, and sometime examples, of each level of performance for each performance criterion, rubrics help develop a common understanding of what is valued in a performance. This common understanding increases the reliability of scores awarded by multiple raters by focusing the raters on the same elements of the performance. In addition, this common understanding helps increase the validity of performance assessments by helping students determine the aspects of a performance

FIGURE 8.5
*Rubrics Aid
Teachers and
Students*

Rubrics help teachers by

- specifying criteria to focus instruction on what is important;
- specifying criteria to focus student assessments;
- increasing the consistency of assessments;
- limiting arguments over grading because clear criteria and scoring levels reduce subjectivity; and
- providing descriptions of student performance that are informative to both parents and students.

Rubrics help students by

- clarifying the teacher's expectations about performance;
- pointing out what is important in a process or product;
- helping them to monitor and critique their own work;
- providing informative descriptions of performance; and
- providing clearer performance information than traditional letter grades provide.

on which they should focus. Figure 8.5 lists ways in which rubrics help both the teacher and the student.

Depending on the decision to be made based on a performance assessment, a rubric may be used to make holistic judgments about a student's performance or to provide analytic information that focuses on specific aspects of the performance. A holistic rubric includes a single description for each performance level. This single description generally focuses on the extent to which multiple criteria are met in the performance. Figure 8.6 illustrates holistic scoring for foreign language assessment. There are four scoring levels, each including multiple criteria. The assessor selects the scoring level that best describes the student's overall language proficiency.

An analytic rubric includes a separate description for each performance criterion, and a separate score is awarded for each.

Devising Rubrics

A rubric includes both the aspects or characteristics of a performance that will be assessed and a description of the criteria used to assess each aspect. The following list was developed to inform students about the components of a fifth-grade book report that will be assessed. Note that this list is *not* a rubric, but instead serves as a checklist that students can use to be sure they have included the characteristics that will be assessed.

1. Tell why you chose the book.
2. Describe the main characters of the book.

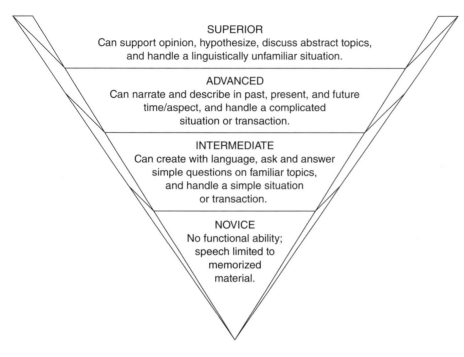

FIGURE 8.6
An Example of Holistic Scoring: ACTEL Proficiency Levels

SOURCE: Adapted from *Oral Proficiency Interview: Tester Training Manual* (n.p.) by the American Council on the Teaching of Foreign Languages. Copyright 1989 by The American Council on the Teaching of Foreign Languages. Adapted by permission.

SUPERIOR
Can support opinion, hypothesize, discuss abstract topics, and handle a linguistically unfamiliar situation.

ADVANCED
Can narrate and describe in past, present, and future time/aspect, and handle a complicated situation or transaction.

INTERMEDIATE
Can create with language, ask and answer simple questions on familiar topics, and handle a simple situation or transaction.

NOVICE
No functional ability; speech limited to memorized material.

3. Explain the plot of the book in three to five sentences.
4. Describe the main place or setting of the book.
5. Explain in three sentences how the main characters have changed through the book.
6. Write in complete sentences.
7. Check spelling, grammar, punctuation, and capitalization.
8. Describe whether or not you enjoyed the book and why.

Based on the characteristics of the book report that will be assessed by the teacher, scoring rubrics are formed by describing the criteria used to categorize each student's book report into a specific level of performance. As seen below, the holistic scoring rubric constructed for the fifth-grade book report contained three levels of performance labeled "excellent," "good," and "poor." Note how a description of the criteria of each characteristic listed above is provided for each level of performance.

Excellent: Student provides two reasons why the book was chosen; describes all main characters with accurate details; describes the plot in a logical, step-by-step sequence; gives detailed description of the place in which the story occurs; describes how each main character changed during the story in five sentences; all sentences are complete; makes no more than a total of five spelling, grammar, punctuation, or capitalization errors; states opinion of the book based on book content.

Good: Student provides one reason why the book was chosen; lists all main characters but descriptions are brief and/or lack details; describes plot but omits one main aspect; provides general description of the book setting; briefly describes how most of the main characters changed during the book; one or more sentences are incomplete; makes more than five spelling, grammar, punctuation, or capitalization errors; states opinion of the book but provides no reference to the book's content.

Poor: Student fails to state why book was chosen; not all main characters are described; provides superficial plot description with key aspects omitted; gives little information about where the book takes place; incorrectly describes changes in the main characters during the book; includes a few nonsentences; makes many spelling, grammar, punctuation, or capitalization errors; provides no opinion of the book.

To score the book report, the teacher reads the report, reflects on the extent to which the report meets the criteria for each performance level, and selects the level that best describes the quality of the report. The selected description determines the "score" for the student's book report.

As discussed above, the number of performance levels, the characteristics that are examined, and the criteria developed for each characteristic will vary across teachers. Often, this variation depends on what learning goals the teacher wants to assess through the performance assessment and the expectations the teacher has for his or her students' performance.

Consider the rubric in Table 8.4 that is used to assess students' responses to journal questions. The rubric has four scoring levels ranging

---

TABLE 8.4 SCORING RUBRIC FOR FIFTH-GRADE RESPONSE JOURNAL QUESTIONS

3—Excellent. Answers are very complete and accurate. Most answers are supported with specific information from the reading, including direct quotations. Sentence structure is varied and detailed. Mechanics are generally accurate, including spelling, use of capitals, and appropriate punctuation.

2—Good. Answers are usually complete and accurate. These answers are supported with specific information from the reading. Sentence structure is varied. Mechanics are generally accurate, including spelling, use of capitals, and appropriate punctuation.

1—Needs improvement. Answers are partially to fully accurate. These answers may need to be supported with more specific information from the reading. Sentence structure is varied, with some use of sentence fragments. Mechanics may need improvement, including spelling, use of capitals, and appropriate punctuation.

0—Poor. Answers are inaccurate or not attempted at all. Sentence structure is frequently incomplete. Mechanics need significant improvement.

SOURCE: Used with permission of Gwen Airasian.

Key Assessment Tools 8.3

GENERAL STEPS IN PREPARING AND USING RUBRICS

1. Select a process or product to be taught.

2. State performance criteria for the process or product.

3. Decide on the number of scoring levels for the rubric, usually three to five.

4. State the description of performance criteria at the highest level of student performance (see "excellent" description of the book report rubric).

5. State descriptions of performance criteria at the remaining scoring levels (e.g., the "good" and "poor" levels of the book report rubric).

6. Compare each student's performance with each scoring level.

7. Select the scoring level closest to a student's actual performance or product.

8. Grade the student.

---

from "excellent" to "poor." Applying the steps in Key Assessment Tools 8.3 to the response journal rubric in Table 8.4, we can trace the steps taken to develop this rubric:

Step 1: Select a performance process or product: journal response questions.

Step 2: Identify performance criteria based on best student performance:
- Answers complete and accurate
- Answers supported with information from readings
- Answers include direct quotations
- Answers show varied and detailed sentences
- Appropriate spelling, capitals, and punctuation

Step 3: Decide on the number of scoring levels: four.

Step 4: State the description of the performance criteria at the highest level: see the "excellent" category in Table 8.4.

Step 5: State descriptions of criteria at the remaining scoring levels: compare the quality of the "excellent" scoring level with the "good," "needs improvement," and "poor" levels.

Step 6: Compare each student's performance with the four scoring levels.

Step 7: Select the scoring level that best describes the level of the student's performance on the response journal.

Step 8: Assign score to student.

An important aspect of developing and using rubrics is the construction of performance levels. When determining how many performance levels to include, consider the number of useful and reliable distinctions that can be made for the performance. If the purpose of the assessment is to identify students who have not mastered a set of skills, creating two or three performance levels will likely suffice. However, if the purpose of the assessment is to inform decisions about placement in one of three math courses, it may be useful to develop three to five performance levels. Three of the levels might reflect the skills and knowledge needed to perform well within each math course. Two additional levels might be used to identify students who possess most, but not all, of the skills and knowledge for the next highest course.

Once the number of performance levels is determined, the criteria that distinguish each performance level must be developed. In most cases, specific criteria should be established for each characteristic that is assessed through the performance. For example, in Table 8.4, notice that in each scoring level except the "poor" one, the same characteristics of the performance criteria are included: completeness and accuracy of answers, support provided from readings, variation in sentence structure, and accuracy of mechanics. Even the "poor" level includes three of the four characteristics. What makes the performance levels different is not the characteristics per se. It is the criteria used to describe each characteristic. For example, in the "excellent" level, answers are *very* complete and accurate; in the "good" level, answers are *usually* complete and accurate; in the "needs improvement" level, answers are *partially* accurate; and in the "poor" level, answers are *inaccurate or not attempted.*

More Examples of Rubrics

Rubrics come in various forms to assess various processes and products. Figure 8.7 shows a small portion of a first-grade report card that is presented as a rubric. The entire report card has a number of such rubrics as well as a cover page sent home to explain the report form to parents. The outcomes reported to parents are the language arts and mathematics outcomes that the district has identified as most crucial for teachers to monitor and for students to achieve. Notice that each desired outcome is defined by specific performances or products at each of the three performance levels: not yet, developing learner, and achieving learner.

Table 8.5 shows a rubric used to assess eleventh-grade history students. There are five scoring levels for each of the two rubrics shown. Can you identify the performance criteria for the two rubrics?

Key Assessment Tools 8.4 shows a general four-level persuasive writing rubric that can be used at varied grade levels. Notice the terms in this rubric that are used to differentiate levels of student performance (e.g., "clearly," "consistently," "thoroughly maintained").

Analytic scoring breaks down the general description of a holistic process or product into separate scores for each criterion. For example,

FIGURE 8.7   *Scoring Rubric Used in First-Grade Report Card*

SOURCE: Reprinted by permission of the Ann Arbor Public Schools, Ann Arbor, Michigan.

NOT YET—1	2	DEVELOPING—3	4	ACHIEVING—5		EXTENDING →

Such as: May demonstrate one or *more* of following:
 	
Identifies the topic but does not identify any details from the book.
Cites information incorrectly.
Draws only from personal experience rather than from evidence in the book.
Identifies details but not topic.
		Such as: May demonstrate one or *more* of following:
		
		Identifies topic and one (1) detail from the book.
		Identifies several details, but needs prompting to clearly state the main topic.
				Criteria: Demonstrates *all* of following:
				
				Identifies from an informational book:
				   topic of book,
				   two or more supporting details.
				
				Such as:
				   "This book is about whales. The blue whale is the largest animal on earth. Whales have babies that are born alive—not hatched."
						Identifies main ideas.
						Identifies background knowledge.
						Distinguishes between what she or he already knew and what was just learned.
						Identifies topic and details of an informational book read by student.

consider the persuasive writing rubric. Unlike a holistic score, analytic scoring provides a score for each of the five performance criteria.

Take a position and clearly state their point of view.

Completely

Generally

Partially

Not at all

Consistently use facts and/or personal information to develop support for their position.

Extensively

Partially

Rarely

Involving Students in the Use of Rubrics

As we have seen above, developing rubrics requires a teacher to identify the characteristics of a student performance that are valued. Developing rubrics also requires a teacher to specify the criteria that distinguish between higher- and lower-quality performances. When using rubrics to score student work, it is important to share them with students before they prepare their performance or product. Doing so allows students to focus their attention on the characteristics that will be assessed and to understand the quality of performance that is expected.

	Level I Minimal Achievement	Level II Rudimentary Achievement	Level III Commendable Achievement	Level IV Superior Achievement	Level V Exceptional Achievement
Communication of Ideas 20	(1–4) Position is vague. Presentation is brief and includes unrelated general statements. Overall view of the problem is not clear. Statements tend to wander or ramble.	(5–9) Presents general and indefinite position. Only minimal organization in presentation. Uses generalities to support position. Emphasizes only one issue. Considers only one aspect of problem.	(8–12) Takes a definite but general position. Presents a somewhat organized argument. Uses general terms with limited evidence that may not be totally accurate. Deals with a limited number of issues. Views problem within a somewhat limited range.	(13–16) Takes a clear position. Presents an organized argument with perhaps only minor errors in the supporting evidence. Deals with the major issues and shows some understanding of relationships. Gives consideration to examination of more than one idea or aspect of the problem.	(17–20) Takes a strong, well-defined position. Presents a well-organized, persuasive argument with accurate supporting evidence. Deals with all significant issues and demonstrates a depth of understanding of important relationships. Examines the problem from several positions.
Knowledge and Use of History 30	(1–6) Reiterates one or two facts without complete accuracy. Deals only briefly and vaguely with concepts or the issues. Barely indicates any previous historical knowledge. Relies heavily on the information provided.	(7–12) Provides only basic facts with only some degree of accuracy. Refers to information to explain at least one issue or concept in general terms. Limited use of previous historical knowledge without complete accuracy. Major reliance on the information provided.	(13–18) Relates only major facts to the basic issues with a fair degree of accuracy. Analyzes information to explain at least one issue or concept with substantive support. Uses general ideas from previous historical knowledge with fair degree of accuracy.	(19–24) Offers accurate analysis of the documents. Provides facts to relate to the major issues involved. Uses previous general historical knowledge to examine issues involved.	(25–30) Offers accurate analysis of the information and issues. Provides a variety of facts to explore major and minor issues and concepts involved. Extensively uses previous historical knowledge to provide an in-depth understanding of the problem and to relate it to past and possible future situations.

SOURCE: California Department of Education, 1990. Reprinted with permission.

Key Assessment Tools 8.4

GENERIC RUBRIC TO SCORE WRITING TO PERSUADE

When describing observables to incorporate in a rubric to assess student responses to a specific prompt, it is important to address all of the specific criteria that were included in the prompt itself. In addition, we need to consider how skillfully the response was crafted and how effectively it addressed the writer's ability to persuade. To assist you with identifying these factors, the following observables are provided at varying score points.

Students at Level 1:
- Take a position and clearly state their point of view.
- Consistently use facts and/or personal information to develop support for their position.
- Organize details in a logical plan that is thoroughly maintained.
- Consistently enhance what they write by using language purposefully to create sentence variety.
- Incorporate appropriate mechanics (spelling, capitalization, punctuation). Any errors that occur are due to risk taking.

Students at Level 2:
- Take a position and adequately attempt to clarify their point of view.
- Frequently use facts and/or personal information to develop support for their position.
- Organize details in a logical plan that is adequately maintained.
- Frequently support their position by providing sufficient information.
- Frequently enhance what they write by using language purposefully to create sentence variety.
- Incorporate appropriate mechanics (spelling, capitalization, punctuation). Most errors that occur are due to risk taking.

Students at Level 3:
- Take a position and make a limited attempt to clarify their point of view.
- Generally use facts and/or personal information that may or may not support their position.
- Organize details in a plan that may or may not be adequately maintained.
- May or may not support their position by providing sufficient information.
- May or may not attend to mechanics (spelling, capitalization, punctuation).

Students at Level 4:
- Usually provide a position and limited information to support the position.
- Minimally organize details that include some support for the position.
- Seldom take their audience into consideration.
- Occasionally choose vocabulary that sufficiently supports the position.
- Seldom enhance what they write by varying sentence structure and incorporating appropriate mechanics (spelling, capitalization, punctuation).

Since some rubrics include examples of desirable responses or correct solutions to a problem, a teacher may need to develop a second more general rubric that is shared with students. Developing a student rubric prevents students from simply copying solutions, while providing them with a clear sense of the level of detail expected. More general student rubrics are useful for performance assessments given to assess mathematics or science skills and knowledge.

In addition to sharing a rubric with students, it may also be useful to share examples of higher- and lower-quality responses. This practice is most common when the performance assessment requires students to create an extended essay, poster, or written report. Such exemplars allow students to develop a better sense of the level of detail and quality of work that the teacher is looking for in the student's product.

Sharing student rubrics and, in some cases, exemplars, lets students know what makes a good product. Knowing the criteria of quality performance before assessment leads to a number of benefits for both students and teacher. First, knowledge of performance criteria provides information to students about what is expected of their work—what characteristics define good work. Second, knowledge of the criteria lends focus and structure to students' performances and products. They know what is expected of them and thus can concentrate on learning and demonstrating the desired knowledge and behaviors. This, in turn, saves the teacher time in scoring students' products or processes because the criteria narrow the breadth of student responses.

Many teachers let students help identify the important performance criteria for a classroom process or product. Involving students in identifying performance criteria gives them a sense of ownership of the rubric as well as an early preview of the important characteristics of the process or product they will be working on. Some teachers provide students with good and poor examples of the process or product they are teaching and ask students to identify what makes a good example. In the process of determining what makes good examples, the students are also identifying relevant criteria for the process or product. Figure 8.5 summarized some of the main advantages of rubrics for students.

To teach students to use rubrics, start with simple rubrics, explain how and why they are used, practice the rubrics, and revise them based on student responses.

It is very important to understand that there is a learning curve for mastering the construction and use of rubrics. It takes time to learn to use rubrics well. Trial and error as well as practice for both students and teachers are needed to help each gain the most from rubrics. Start with simple and limited performance criteria and scoring levels—perhaps three or four criteria and two or three scoring levels. Explain the rubric process to the students: what rubrics are, why we use them, how they can help improve learning and clarify grading. Practice with the students. One approach is to have students use a rubric to revise their work before passing it in. A teacher should expect to revise a rubric a few times before he or she and the students feel comfortable with it.

PORTFOLIOS

Most performance assessments require students to create a single product or performance. A **portfolio** is an extended performance assessment that includes multiple samples of student products or performances. The term *portfolio* derives from the collections that photographers, models, and artists assemble to demonstrate their work. In the classroom, portfolios have the same basic purpose: to collect student performances to show their work and accomplishments over time. Portfolios do not contain haphazard, unrelated collections of a student's work. They contain purposefully selected examples of work. Depending on the purpose of the portfolio, these examples of work may demonstrate the achievement of important learning goals or they may document growth over time. The contents of a portfolio should be closely related to a teacher's learning objectives and should provide information that helps a teacher form decisions about student learning.

A portfolio can be made up of many different student performances or of a single performance. For example, a multi-focused writing portfolio might contain writing samples, lists of books read, journal entries about books read, and descriptions of favorite poems. Conversely, a single-focus portfolio might contain multiple pieces of the same process or product, such as a portfolio containing only book reports, only written poems, or only chemistry lab reports. Key Assessment Tools 8.5 samples the range of materials that can go into a portfolio.

In one first-grade class, students developed a reading portfolio. Every third week the students read a paragraph or two into their audiotape "portfolio." The teacher monitored student improvement over time and students could play back their pieces to measure their reading improvement. Also, periodically the students' reading portfolios were sent home for the parents to listen to their child's reading improvement, an opportunity parents appreciated.

Key Assessments Tools 8.5

WHAT CAN GO INTO A PORTFOLIO

Media: videos, audiotapes, pictures, artwork, computer programs

Reflections: plans, statements of goals, self-reflections, journal entries

Individual work: tests, journals, logs, lab reports, homework, essays, poems, maps, inventions, posters, math work

Group work: cooperative learning sessions, group performances, peer reviews

Work in progress: rough and final drafts, show-your-work problems, science fair projects

Portfolios contribute to instruction and learning in many ways:

- Showing students' typical work.
- Monitoring student progress and improvement over time.
- Helping students self-evaluate their work.
- Providing ongoing assessment of student learning.
- Providing diagnostic information about student performance.
- Helping teachers judge the appropriateness of the curriculum.
- Facilitating teacher meetings and conferences with students, parents, and both students and parents.
- Grading students.
- Reinforcing the importance of processes and products in learning.
- Showing students the connections among their processes and products.
- Providing concrete examples of student work.
- Encouraging students to think about what is good performance in varied subject areas.
- Focusing on both the process and final product of learning.
- Informing subsequent teachers about students' prior work.

A portfolio is a record of specific student work that demonstrates defined learning objectives. These objectives should be determined before the portfolio is created.

A portfolio is not a repository into which all of the work produced by a student is stored. Instead, a portfolio has a defined, specific purpose that reflects the learning objectives. This clearly defined purpose focuses the samples of work that are collected in the portfolio. Too often, teachers defer the question of the portfolio's purpose until *after* students have collected large amounts of their work in their portfolios. At that time the teacher is likely to be confronted with the question of what to do with a vast, undifferentiated collection of student information.

Perhaps the greatest contribution that portfolios provide for learning is that they give students and their parents or guardians a chance to revisit and reflect on the products and processes a student has produced. For many students, life in school is an ongoing sequence of papers, performances, assignments, and productions. Each day a new batch of paperwork is produced and the previous day's productions are tossed away or lost, both mentally and physically. Collecting pieces of students' work in a portfolio retains them for subsequent student review, reflection, demonstration, and grading. With suitable guidance, students can be encouraged to think about and compare their work over time. For example, students might be asked to reflect on the following questions. Which of these portfolio items shows the most improvement and why? Which did you enjoy most and why? From which did you learn the most and why? In what areas have you made the most progress over the year, and what was the nature of that progress? Portfolios allow students to see their progress and judge their work from the perspectives of time and personal development.

As noted, there is a great deal more to successful portfolio assessment than simply collecting bunches of students' work. Portfolio assessment is

> ### Key Assessment Tools 8.6
> ## PORTFOLIO QUESTIONS
>
> 1. What is the purpose of the portfolio?
> 2. What will go into and be removed from the portfolio during its use?
> 3. Who will select the entries that go into the portfolio: teacher, students, or both?
> 4. How will the portfolio be organized and maintained?
> 5. How will the portfolio be assessed?

a type of performance assessment and thus depends on the same four elements that all types of performance assessment require: (1) a clear purpose, (2) appropriate performance criteria, (3) a suitable setting, and (4) scoring performance. A number of questions must be answered in developing and assessing portfolios. Key Assessment Tools 8.6 lists the main questions that guide classroom use of portfolios.

Purpose of Portfolios

The items that go into a portfolio, the criteria used to judge the items, and the frequency with which items are added to or deleted from the portfolio all depend on the portfolio's purpose. If the purpose is to illustrate a student's typical work in various school subjects for a parents' night at the school, the portfolio contents would likely be more wide-ranging than if its purpose is to assess the student's improvement in math problem-solving over a single marking period. In the latter case, math problems would have to be obtained periodically throughout the marking period and collected in the portfolio.

It is important to determine the purpose and guidelines for a portfolio's content before compiling it. Is it to grade, group, instruct, or diagnose students?

If a portfolio is intended to show a student's best work in a subject area, the contents of the portfolio would change as more samples of the student's performance became available and as less good ones were removed. If the purpose is to show improvement over time, earlier performances would have to be retained and new pieces added.

Given the many and varied uses of portfolios, purpose is a crucial issue to consider and define in carrying out portfolio assessment. It is important to determine the purpose and general guidelines for the pieces that will go into the portfolio *before* starting the portfolio assessment. It is also critical that all pieces going into a portfolio be dated, especially in portfolios that aim to assess student growth or development. Without recorded dates for each portfolio entry, it may be impossible to assess growth and improvement.

Allowing students to help determine what goes into their portfolios gives them a sense of ownership.

To promote students' ownership of their portfolios, it is useful to allow students to choose at least some of the pieces that will go into their portfolios. Some teachers develop portfolios that contain two types of pieces: those required by the teacher and those selected by the student. It is also important that all student portfolio selections be accompanied by a brief written explanation of why the student feels that a particular piece belongs in her or his portfolio. This will encourage the student to reflect on the characteristics of the piece and why it belongs in the portfolio.

Performance Criteria

Performance criteria are needed to evaluate each of the individual pieces within a portfolio.

Performance criteria are needed to assess the individual pieces that make up a portfolio. Without such criteria, assessment cannot be consistent within and across portfolios. The nature and process of identifying performance criteria for portfolios is the same as that for checklists, rating scales, and rubrics. Depending on the type of performance contained in a portfolio, many of the performance criteria discussed earlier in this chapter can be used to assess individual portfolio pieces.

If student portfolios are required for all teachers in a grade or if portfolios are to be passed on to the student's next teacher, it is advisable for all teachers who will use information provided by the portfolio to cooperate in formulating performance criteria.

The performance criteria used in evaluating portfolios should align with a teacher's instructional objectives.

It can also be valuable to allow students to help identify performance criteria used for assessing the contents of a portfolio because this can give students a sense of ownership over their performance and help them think through the nature of the portfolio pieces they will produce. Beginning a lesson with a discussion of what makes a good book report, oral reading, science lab, or sonnet is a useful way to get the students thinking about the characteristics of the process or product they will have to develop.

Setting

In addition to a clear purpose and well-developed performance criteria, portfolio assessments must take into account the setting in which students' performances will be gathered. While many portfolio pieces can be gathered by the teacher in the classroom, others pieces cannot. When portfolios include oral speaking, science experiments, artistic productions, and psychomotor activities, special equipment or arrangements may be needed to properly collect the desired student performance. Many teachers underestimate the time it takes to collect the processes and products that make up portfolios and the management and record keeping needed to maintain them.

An important dimension of using portfolios is the logistics of collecting and maintaining student portfolios. Portfolios require space. They have to be stored in a safe but accessible place. A system has to be established for students to add or subtract pieces of their portfolios. Can students go to their portfolio at any time or will the teacher set aside special times when all students modify their portfolios? If the portfolio is intended to show growth, how will the order of the entries be kept in sequence? Maintaining portfolios requires time and organization. Materials such as envelopes, crates, tape recorders, and the like will be needed for assembling and storing student portfolios.

Scoring

Scoring portfolios can be a time-consuming task. Not only does each individual portfolio piece have to be assessed, but the summarized pieces must also be assessed to provide an overall portfolio performance.

Scoring portfolios is a time-consuming process that involves judging each individual piece and the portfolio as a whole.

Summative Scoring

Consider the difference in managing and scoring portfolios that contain varied processes or products compared with portfolios that contain examples of a single process or product. The multi-focused portfolio provides a wide range of student performance, but at a substantial logistical and scoring cost to the teacher. The single-focus portfolio does not provide the breadth of varied student performances of the multi-focused portfolio, but can be managed and scored considerably more quickly.

Figure 8.8 is a narrative description of one student's writing portfolio. When the purpose of a portfolio is to provide descriptive information about student performance for a parent-teacher night or to pass student information on to the next year's teacher, no scoring or summarization of the portfolio contents will be necessary. The contents themselves provide the desired information. However, when the purpose of a portfolio is to diagnose, track improvement, assess the success of instruction, encourage students to reflect on their work, or grade students, some form of summarization or scoring of the portfolio pieces is required.

The purpose of assessing an entire portfolio, as opposed to the individual pieces, is usually summative—to assign a grade. Such holistic portfolio assessment requires the development of a set of summarizing criteria. For example, improvement in writing might be judged by comparing a student's early pieces with later pieces in terms of the following performance criteria: (1) number of spelling, capitalization, and punctuation errors, (2) variety of sentence structures used, (3) use of supporting detail, (4) appropriateness of detail to purpose, (5) ability to emphasize and summarize main ideas, (6) link and flow between paragraphs, and (7) personal

Performance criteria used to assess an entire portfolio are different from those used to assess individual portfolio items.

FIGURE 8.8 *Narrative Description of a Student's Writing Portfolio*

SOURCE: P. A. Moss, et al., "Portfolios, accountability, and an interpretive approach to validity," *Educational Measurement: Issues and Practice,* 1992, *11*(3), p. 18. Copyright 1992 by the National Council on Measurement in Education. Used by permission of AERA.

Date	Genre	Topic	Reason	Length	Drafts
9/??	Self-Reflection	Thinking About Your Writing	Requested	1 page	1 draft
10/17	Narrative/Dramatic	Personal Monologue	Important	1 page	2 drafts
1/16	Response to Literature	On *The Lord of the Flies*	Unsatisfying	1 page	4 drafts
2/??	Self-Reflection	Response to Parent Comments	Requested	1 page	1 draft
2/28	Narrative/Dramatic	"The Tell-Tale Heart"	Free Pick	3 pages	2 drafts
5/22	Response to Literature	On *Animal Farm*	Satisfying	5 pages	2 drafts
6/??	Self-Reflection	Final Reflection	Requested	2 pages	1 draft

As a writer, Barry shows substantial growth from the beginning of the year in his first personal monologue to his last piece, a response to *Animal Farm.* Initially, Barry seems to have little control over the flow and transition of his ideas. His points are not tied together, he jumps around in his thinking, and he lacks specificity in his ideas. By January, when Barry writes his response to *The Lord of the Flies,* he begins a coherent argument about the differences between Ralph's group and Jack's tribe, although he ends with the unsupported assertion that he would have preferred to be "marooned on a desert island" with Ralph. Barry includes three reasons for his comparison, hinges his reasons with transition words, but more impressively, connects his introductory paragraph with a transition sentence to the body of his essay. In the revisions of this essay, Barry makes primarily word and sentence level changes, adds paragraph formatting, and generally improves the local coherence of the piece.

By the end of February when he writes his narrative response to Poe's "The Tell-Tale Heart," Barry displays a concern for making his writing interesting. "I like the idea that there are so many twists in the story that I really think makes it interesting." He makes surface-level spelling changes, deletes a sentence, and replaces details, although not always successfully (e.g., "fine satin sheets and brass bed," is replaced with the summary description "extravagant furniture"). Overall, it is an effective piece of writing showing Barry's understanding of narrative form and his ability to manipulate twists of plot in order to create an engaging story.

Barry's last selection in his portfolio is an exceptional five-page, typed essay on Orwell's *Animal Farm.* The writing is highly organized around the theme of scapegoating. Using supporting details from the novel and contemporary examples from politics and sports, Barry creates a compelling and believable argument. The effective intertextuality and the multiple perspectives Barry brings to this essay result largely from an exceptional revision process. Not only does he attempt to correct his standard conventions and improve his word choices, he also revises successfully to the point of moving around whole clumps of text and adding sections that significantly reshape the piece. This pattern of revision shows the control Barry has gained over his writing.

In Barry's final reflection he describes his development, showing an awareness of such issues as organizing and connecting ideas, choosing appropriate words and details, and making his writing accessible to his readers. "I had many gaps in my writing. One problem was that I would skip from one idea to the next and it would not be clear what was going on in the piece. . . . Now, I have put in more details so you don't have to think as much as you would. I also perfect my transitions and my paragraph form. . . . My reading . . . has improved my vocabulary and it helped me organize my writing so it sounds its best and makes the most sense possible. . . . There are many mistakes I have made throughout the year, but I have at least learned from all of them." I agree with him.

involvement in written pieces. An alternative approach might be for the teacher to rate earlier written pieces using a general scoring rubric and compare the level of early performances with later performances using the same rubric.

Different portfolios with different purposes require different summarizing criteria. For example, how would you summarize a portfolio containing a number of tape recordings of a student's Spanish pronunciation or a portfolio made up of poems a student wrote as part of a poetry unit? What criteria would you use to judge *overall* progress or performance?

Scoring the Pieces

Individual portfolio pieces are typically scored using methods we have discussed: checklists, rating scales, and rubrics. Table 8.6 gives examples. Thus, each story, tape recording, lab report, handwriting sample, persuasive essay, or cooperative group product can be judged by organizing the performance criteria into a checklist, rating scale, or rubric.

Of course, the teacher does not always have to be the one who assesses the pieces. It is desirable and instructive to allow students to self-assess some of their portfolio pieces in order to give them practice in critiquing their own work with respect to the performance criteria. This approach to assessment encourages student reflection and learning.

Individual portfolio pieces are normally judged using performance criteria that have been assembled into some form of checklist, rating scale, or rubric.

Allowing students to self-assess their portfolio encourages student reflection and learning.

TABLE 8.6   ASSESSING INDIVIDUAL PORTFOLIO PIECES

Checklist

Selects correct solution method	Yes	No
Draws and labels diagrams	Yes	No
Shows work leading to solution	Yes	No
Gets correct answer	Yes	No

Rating Scale

Selects correct solution method	Quickly	Slowly	Not at all
Draws and labels diagrams	Completely	Partially	Not at all
Shows work leading to solution	Completely	Partially	Not at all
Gets correct answer	Quickly	Slowly	Not at all

Rubric

Selects correct solution method; draws complete, labeled diagrams; shows all work; gets correct answer

Selects correct solution method; draws complete but poorly labeled diagrams; shows partial work; gets partially correct answer

Selects incorrect solution method; neither draws nor labels diagrams; shows very little work; gets incorrect answer

TABLE 8.7   ADVANTAGES AND DISADVANTAGES OR PERFORMANCE, PRODUCT, AND PORTFOLIO ASSESSMENTS

Advantages

- Chart student performance over time.
- Conduct student self-assessment of products and performances.
- Conduct peer review of products and performances.
- Provide diagnostic information about performances and products.
- Integrate assessment and instruction.
- Promote learning through assessment activities.
- Give students ownership over their learning and productions.
- Clarify lesson, assignment, and test expectations.
- Report performance to parents in clear, descriptive terms.
- Permit student reflection and analysis of work.
- Provide concrete examples for parent conferences.
- Assemble cumulative evidence of performance.
- Reinforce importance of student performance.

Disadvantages

Most disadvantages associated with performance, product, and especially portfolio assessments involve the time they require:

- To prepare materials, performance criteria, and scoring formats.
- To manage, organize, and keep records.
- For teachers and students to become comfortable with the use of performance assessments and the change in teaching and learning roles they involve.
- To score and provide feedback to students.

From the teacher's point of view, clearly there are both advantages and disadvantages to performance, product, and portfolio assessments. Table 8.7 summarizes the major trade-offs.

VALIDITY AND RELIABILITY OF PERFORMANCE ASSESSMENTS

Since formal performance assessments are used to make decisions about students, it is important for them to be valid and reliable. This section describes steps that can be taken to obtain high-quality performance assessments. Scoring performance assessments is a difficult and often time-consuming activity. Unlike multiple-choice items, scoring of performances and products requires teachers' interpretation and judgment. Each student produces or constructs a performance or product that is different from that of other students. The more variation in the products or performances students produce and the more criteria to address, the more time-consuming, fatiguing, and potentially invalid scoring will be.

Further, like essays, performance assessments are subject to many ancillary factors that may not be relevant to scoring but may influence the teacher's judgment of the performance assessments. For example, teachers' scoring of products such as essays or reports often is influenced by the quality of a student's handwriting, neatness, sentence structure and flow, and knowledge of the student being scored. These and similar factors are not key aspects of the product, but they often affect scoring. Teachers can rarely be completely unbiased observers of what their students do, because they know their students too well and have a set of built-in predispositions regarding each one. In each case, there are many irrelevant and distracting factors that can influence the teacher's judgments and the validity and reliability of performance assessments.

Distractions and personal feelings can introduce error into either the observation or judging process, thereby reducing the validity and reliability of the assessment.

The key to improving rating or scoring skills is to try to eliminate the distracting factors so that the assessment more closely reflects the student's actual performance. In performance assessments, the main source of error is the observer, who judges both what is happening during a performance and the quality of the performance. Beyond the issue of distractions, teachers can prepare their students well and ensure validity and reliability in various other ways.

Preparing Students

There are many ways teachers prepare their students for performance assessment. First and foremost, they provide good instruction. Students learn to set up and focus microscopes, build bookcases, write book reports, give oral speeches, measure with a ruler, perform musical selections, and speak French the same way they learn to solve simultaneous equations, find countries on a map, write a topic sentence, or balance a chemical equation. They are given instruction and practice. Achievement depends on students being taught the things on which they are being assessed. One of the advantages of performance assessments is their explicit criteria, which focus instruction and assessment.

In preparing students for performance assessment, the teacher should inform and explain the criteria on which they will be judged (Mehrens, Popham, and Ryan, 1998). In many classrooms, teachers and students jointly discuss and define criteria for a desired performance or product. This helps them to understand what is expected of them by identifying the important dimensions of the performance or product. Another, less interactive way to

Unless students are informed about the performance criteria on which they will be judged, they may not perform up to their abilities.

do this is for the teacher to give students a copy of the checklist or rating form that will be used during their assessment. If performance criteria are not made clear to students, they may perform poorly, not because they are incapable, but because they were not aware of the teacher's expectations and the criteria for a good performance. In such cases, the performance ratings do not reflect the students' true achievement, and the grades they receive could lead to invalid decisions about their learning.

Validity

Validity is concerned with whether the information obtained from an assessment permits the teacher to make an appropriate decision about a student's learning. As discussed previously, either failure to instruct students on desired performances or the inability to control personal expectations can produce invalid information. Another factor that can reduce the validity of formal performance assessment is **bias.** When some factor such as race, native language, prior experience, gender, or disability differentiates the scores of one group from those of another (e.g., English-speaking and Spanish-speaking students, prior experience and inexperience, hearing disability and no hearing disability) we say the scores are biased. That is, judgments regarding the performance of one group of students are influenced by the inclusion of irrelevant, subjective criteria.

When irrelevant, subjective factors differentiate the scores of one group of students from another, the scores are said to be biased.

When an assessment instrument provides information that is irrelevant to the decisions it was intended to help make, it is invalid. Thus, in all forms of assessment, but especially performance assessment, a teacher must select and use procedures, performance criteria, and settings that do not give an unfair advantage to some students because of cultural background, language, disability, or gender. Other sources of error that commonly affect the validity of performance assessments are teachers' reliance on mental rather than written record keeping and their being influenced by prior perceptions of a student. The longer the interval between an observation and the written scoring, the more likely the teacher is to forget important features of students' performances.

Assessing students on the basis of their personal characteristics rather than their performance lowers the validity of the assessment.

Often, teachers' prior knowledge of their students influences the objectivity of their performance ratings. Personality, effort, work habits, cooperativeness, and the like are all part of a teacher's perception of the students in his or her class. Often, these prior perceptions influence the rating a student is given: the likable, cooperative student with the pleasant personality may receive a higher rating than the standoffish, belligerent student, even though they performed similarly. Assessing students on the basis of their personal characteristics rather than their performance lowers the validity of the assessment. Each of these concerns threatens the validity of teacher interpretations and scores. These concerns are particularly difficult to overcome because of the complexity of performance assessment.

Reliability

Reliability is concerned with the stability and consistency of assessments. Hence, the logical way to obtain information about the reliability of student performance is to observe and score two or more performances or products of the same kind. Doing this, however, is not reasonable in most school settings; once a formal assessment is made, instruction turns to a new topic. Few teachers can afford the class time necessary to obtain multiple assessments on a given topic. This reality raises an important problem with the reliability of performance assessments: They may lack generalizability. Performances, products, and portfolios are more complex and fewer in number than selection or short-answer assessments. Because of such discrepancies in the quantity of information obtained from particular assessments, the teacher who employs performance assessments sees fewer examples of student mastery than when more narrow assessment approaches are used. The teacher's question then becomes, "How reliable is the limited information I have obtained from students?" Does a single essay, a few show-your-work problems, or a portfolio provide enough evidence that students will perform similarly on other essays, show-your-work problems, or portfolios? Teachers find themselves on the horns of a dilemma. Because they want their students to learn more than facts and narrow topics, they employ performance assessments to ensure deeper, richer learning. However, by employing an in-depth and time-consuming approach, they often diminish the reliability of the assessment. This is a dilemma faced in classroom teachers' own assessments and in more general, statewide student assessments. There are few easy ways to resolve the dilemma. However, it is better to use evidence from imperfect performance assessments than to make uninformed decisions about student achievement.

Observing a performance more than once increases the reliability of the assessment, but it is time-consuming.

Reliability is also affected when performance criteria or rating categories are vague and unclear, forcing the teacher to interpret them. Because interpretations often vary with time and situation, they introduce inconsistency into the assessment. One way to eliminate much of this inconsistency is to be explicit about the purpose of a performance assessment and to state the performance criteria and rubrics in terms of observable student behaviors. The objectivity of an observation can be enhanced by having several individuals independently observe and rate a student's performance. In situations where a group of teachers cooperate in developing criteria for a student performance, product, or portfolio, it is not difficult to have more than one teacher observe or examine a few students' products or performances to see whether scores are similar across teachers. This practice is followed in performance assessments such as the College Board English Achievement Essay and most statewide writing assessments.

Having more than one person observe and rate a performance increases the objectivity of the assessment.

Key Assessment Tools 8.7

IMPROVING VALIDITY AND RELIABILITY
OF PERFORMANCE ASSESSMENTS

- Know the purpose of the assessment from the beginning.
- Teach and give students practice in the performance criteria.
- State the performance criteria in terms of observable behaviors and avoid using adverbs such as *appropriately, correctly,* or *well* because their interpretation may shift from student to student. Use overt, well-described behaviors that can be seen by an observer and therefore are less subject to interpretation. Inform students of these criteria and focus instruction on them.
- Select performance criteria that are at an appropriate level of difficulty for the students. The criteria used to judge the oral speaking performance of third-year debate students should be more detailed than those used to judge first-year debate students.
- Limit performance criteria to a manageable number. A large number of criteria makes observation difficult and causes errors that reduce the validity of the assessment information.
- Maintain a written record of student performance. Checklists, rating scales, and rubrics are the easiest methods of recording student performance on important criteria, although more descriptive narratives are often desirable and informative. Tape recordings or videotapes may be used to provide a record of performance, so long as their use does not upset or distract the students. If a formal instrument cannot be used to record judgments of student performance, then informal notes of strong and weak points should be taken.
- Be sure the performance assessment is fair to all students.

Key Assessment Tools 8.7 contains guidelines for improving the validity and reliability of performance, product, and portfolio assessments.

CHAPTER SUMMARY

- Performance assessments require students to demonstrate their knowledge by creating an answer, carrying out a process, or producing a product, rather than by selecting an answer. Performance assessments complement paper-and-pencil tests in classroom assessments.
- Performance assessments are useful for determining student learning in performance-oriented areas such as communication skills, psychomotor skills, athletic activities, concept acquisition, and affective characteristics.

- Performance assessments have many uses. They can chart student performance over time, provide diagnostic information about student learning, give students a sense of ownership of their learning, integrate the instructional and assessment processes, foster students' self-assessment of their work, and assemble into portfolios both cumulative evidence of performance and concrete examples of students' work. The main disadvantage of performance assessments is the time required to prepare for, implement, and score them.

- Successful performance assessment requires a well-defined purpose for assessment; clear, observable performance criteria; an appropriate setting in which to elicit performance; and a scoring or rating method.

- The specific behaviors a student should display when carrying out a performance or the characteristics a student product should possess are called performance criteria. These criteria define the aspects of a good performance or product. They should be shared with students and used as the basis for instruction.

- The key to identifying performance criteria is to break down a performance or product into its component parts, since it is these parts that are observed and judged. It is often useful to involve students in identifying the criteria of products or performances. This provides them with a sense of involvement in learning and introduces them to important components of the desired performance.

- The number of performance criteria should be small, no more than 15, to focus on the most important aspects of performance and simplify the observation process. Teacher collaboration on common assessment areas or performances is advisable.

- Ambiguous words that cloud the meaning of performance criteria (e.g., *adequately, correctly, appropriate*) should be avoided; state specifically what is being looked for in the performance or product. Criteria should be stated so explicitly that another teacher could use them independently.

- Performance assessments may be scored and summarized either qualitatively or quantitatively. Anecdotal records and teacher narratives are qualitative descriptions of student characteristics and performances. Checklists, rating scales, and scoring rubrics are quantitative assessments of performance. A rubric describes the level at which a student may be performing a task. Portfolios may include either qualitative, quantitative, or both kinds of information about student performance.

- Checklists and rating scales are developed from the performance criteria for a performance or product. Checklists give the observer only two choices in judging each performance criterion: present or absent. Rating scales provide the observer with more than two

olc
CHAPTER
REVIEW
Visit the Online
Learning Center at
**www.mhhe.com/
russell7e** to
review the case
study referenced
in the chapter.

choices in judging: for example, always, sometimes, never, or excellent, good, fair, poor, failure. Rating scales may be numerical, graphic, or descriptive. Performance can be summarized across performance criteria numerically or with a scoring rubric.

- Portfolios are collections of students' work that show change and progress over time. Portfolios may contain student products or student performances.

- Portfolios have many uses: focusing instruction on important performance activities; reinforcing the point that performances are important school outcomes; providing parents, students, and teachers with a perspective on student improvement; diagnosing weaknesses; allowing students to revisit, reflect on, and assess their work over time; grading students; and integrating instruction with assessment.

- Portfolio assessment is a form of performance assessment that involves four factors: definition of purpose, identification of clear performance criteria, establishment of a setting for performance, and construction of a scoring or rating scheme. In addition to performance criteria for each individual portfolio piece, it is often necessary to develop a set of performance criteria to assess or summarize the entire portfolio.

- To ensure valid performance assessment, students should be instructed on the desired performance criteria before being assessed.

- The validity of performance assessments can be improved by stating performance criteria in observable terms; setting performance criteria at an appropriate difficulty level for students; limiting the number of performance criteria; maintaining a written record of student performance; and checking to determine whether extraneous factors influenced a student's performance.

- Reliability can be improved by multiple observations of performance or by checking for agreement among observers viewing the same performance, product, or portfolio and using the same assessment criteria.

QUESTIONS FOR DISCUSSION

1. What types of objectives are most suitably assessed using performance assessment?
2. How do formal and informal performance assessments differ in terms of student characteristics, validity and reliability of information, and usefulness for teacher decision making?

ACTIVITIES

1. Select a subject area you might like to teach, and identify one objective in that subject matter that cannot be assessed by selection or essay questions. Construct a performance or product assessment instrument for this objective. Provide the following information:
   (a) the objective and a brief description of the behavior or product you will assess and the grade level at which it will be taught;
   (b) a set of at least 10 observable performance criteria for judging the performance or product;
   (c) a method to score student performance;
   (d) a method to summarize performance into a single score.
   The assessment procedure used may be in the form of a checklist or a rating scale. A 2- to 3-page document should provide the needed information. Be sure to focus on the clarity and specificity of the performance criteria and on the clarity and practicality of the scoring procedure.
2. Rewrite in clearer form the following performance criteria for assessing a student's poem. Remember that you are trying to write performance criteria that most people will understand and interpret the same way.
   - Poem is original
   - Meaningfulness
   - Contains rhymes
   - Proper length
   - Well-focused
   - Good title
   - Appropriate vocabulary level

REVIEW QUESTIONS

1. How do performance assessments differ from other types of assessment? What are the benefits of using performance assessment? The disadvantages?
2. What four steps must be attended to in carrying out performance assessment? What happens at each of these steps?
3. Why are performance criteria so important to performance assessment? How do they help the assessor not only with judging students' performance and products but also with planning and conducting instruction?
4. What are the differences between checklists, rating scales, and rubrics? How is each used to assess performance and products?
5. What are the main threats to the validity of performance assessments? How can validity be improved?

6. In what ways is scoring performance assessments similar to scoring essay questions?
7. What makes an effective scoring rubric?
8. What are some pros and cons of portfolios?

REFERENCES

Bartz, D., Anderson-Robinson, S., and Hillman, L. (1994). Performance assessment: Make them show what they know. *Principal, 73,* 11–14.

Goodrich, H. (1997). Understanding rubrics. *Educational Leadership, 54*(4), 14–17.

Madaus, G. F., and O'Dwyer, L. M. (1999). A short history of performance assessment: Lessons learned. *Phi Delta Kappan, 80*(9), 688–695.

Mehrens, W. A., Popham, W. J., and Ryan, J. M. (1998). How to prepare students for performance assessments. *Educational Measurement: Issues and Practice, 17*(1), 18–22.

Quality Counts. (1999). Rewarding results, punishing failure. *Education Week* (January 11, 1999).

Ryan, J., and Miyasaka, J. (1995). Current practices in teaching and assessment: What is driving the change? *NAASP Bulletin, 79,* 1–10.

Wiggins, G. (1992). Creating tests worth taking. *Educational Leadership, 44*(8), 26–33.

Wiggins, G., and McTighe, J. (1998). *Understanding by design.* Alexandria, VA: Association for Supervision and Curriculum Development.

CHAPTER 9

GRADING

KEY TOPICS

- *Rationale and Difficulties of Grading*

- *Grading as Judgment*

- *Four Types of Comparison for Grading*

- *Grading for Cooperative Learning and Students with Disabilities*

- *Deciding What to Grade*

- *Summarizing Varied Types of Assessment*

- *Two Approaches to Assigning Grades*

- *Other Methods of Reporting Student Progress*

CHAPTER OBJECTIVES

After reading this chapter, you will be able to:

- Define basic terms such as *norm-referenced, criterion-referenced,* and *grading curve*
- Contrast the characteristics of norm- and criterion-referenced grading
- Identify principles of grading and explain their importance
- Describe approaches for grading cooperative learning and students with disabilities
- State strategies for conducting effective parent-teacher conferences

THINKING ABOUT TEACHING

How do you think you will feel about grading students? What will be your grading model?

Grading is the process of judging the quality of a student's performance by comparing it with some standard of good performance.

We have seen that teachers use a variety of techniques to gather information about their students' learning. But teachers must do more than just gather samples of students' performances; they also must make judgments about their quality. The process of judging the quality of a student's performance is called **grading.** It is the process that translates test scores and descriptive assessment information into marks or letters that indicate the quality of each student's learning and performance. Assigning **grades** to students is an exceptionally important professional responsibility, one that has important consequences for students. Grades are the most common and important product of classroom assessment that most students and parents experience.

A teacher can provide a grade for a single assessment or can use a grade to summarize performance across a group of assessments. When a student says, "I got a B on my book report," or "I got an A on my chemistry test," the student is focusing on a grade for a single assessment. Report card grades, on the other hand, represent a student's performance across a variety of assessments that were completed during a term or grading period. Some people refer to the former process as "assigning grades" and the latter as "assigning marks," but the basic processes are similar, so we shall use the term "grading." Hence, grading is the process of judging the quality of performance on a single assessment or multiple assessments over time.

In order to judge the quality of a student's performance, it must be compared with something or someone. There is no grading without comparison. When a teacher grades, he or she is making a judgment about the quality of a student's performance by comparing it with some standard of good performance. Suppose that Jamal got a score of 95 on a test. His score *describes* his performance—95 points. But does 95 indicate excellent, average, or poor achievement? This is the grading question—what is Jamal's performance worth? To answer this question, we need more than Jamal's test score. For example, we might want to know how many items were on Jamal's test and how much each item counted. A score of 95 does not provide this information. It would probably make a difference in the way Jamal's performance was judged if he got 95 out of 200 items right as opposed to 95 out of 100 items right. Or we might like to know how Jamal did in relation to other students in the class. A score of 95 does not tell us this. It might make a difference in grading to know whether Jamal's score was the highest or the lowest in the class. Finally, we might like to know whether Jamal's 95 represents an improvement or a decline compared with his previous test scores. A score of 95 does not tell us this. Some form of comparison is needed to form a judgment about performance and then to assign a grade based on this judgment.

RATIONALE AND DIFFICULTIES OF GRADING

The purpose of this chapter is to raise the questions teachers face when grading and to help answer these questions. While the main focus is on the process of assigning report card grades in academic subjects, the principles discussed are also appropriate for grading single tests or assessments. A logical place to begin discussion is with the question "Why grade?"

Why Grade?

The simplest and perhaps most compelling reason that classroom teachers grade their students is that they have to. Grading is one type of official assessment that nearly all school teachers are required to carry out. Virtually all school systems demand that classroom teachers make periodic judgments about their students' performance.

Grading is an official assessment required of teachers.

The form of these written judgments varies from one school system to another and from one grade level to another. Some schools require teachers to record student performance in the form of letter grades (e.g., A, A−, B+, B, B−, C+); some in the form of standards-based achievement categories (e.g., excellent, good, fair, poor); some in the form of percentage or other numerical grades (e.g., 100–90, 89–80); some in the form of pass-fail; some in the form of a checklist of specific skills or objectives that are graded individually; and some in the form of teachers' written narratives describing students' accomplishments and weaknesses. The most widely used systems are letter grades, which are the main grading system in upper elementary, middle, and high schools; and skill-based or objective-based ratings, which are used mainly in kindergarten and the primary grades.

Some school systems also require teachers to write comments about each student's performance on the report card, while others require teachers to grade performance in both academic subjects and social adjustment areas. There are many different varieties of grading forms, and Figures 9.1, 9.2,

Regardless of the grading system or reporting form used, grades are always based on teacher judgments.

FIGURE 9.1 *Example of an Elementary School Report Card*

ALLSTON PUBLIC SCHOOL
Grades 1–3

NAME_____ GRADE_____ SCHOOL YEAR_____

SCHOOL _____ HOMEROOM TEACHER_____

KEY	
C Commendable	✓ denotes an area of weakness
S Satisfactory	M denotes modified program
N Needs Improvement	+ or - may be used to modify **S**

ATTENDANCE RECORD

TERM	I	II	III	IV	TOTAL
ABSENT					
TARDY					
DISMISSED					

READING GRADE	1	2	3	4
Effort				
Connects literature with other experiences				
Learns and applies vocabulary				
Comprehends teacher read selections				
Understands story structure				
Uses word attack skills				
Applies appropriate reading strategies and skills				
Reads with fluency				
Reads with understanding				
Makes good use of independent reading time				
LANGUAGE GRADE				
Effort				
Organizes and expresses ideas orally				
Expresses ideas through writing				
Develops and organizes ideas in written work				
Writes with correct usage and mechanics				
Edits and revises as necessary				
SPELLING GRADE				
Effort				
Masters assigned spelling words				
Spells correctly in written work				
HANDWRITING GRADE				
Effort				
Forms letters correctly				
Writes neatly and legibly				
MATHEMATICS GRADE				
Effort				
Understands concepts				
Masters basic facts				
Works with accuracy				
Interprets information to solve problems				

SOCIAL STUDIES (grade 3 only) GRADE	1	2	3	4
Effort				
Demonstrates geographic awareness				
Understands cultural similarities and differences				
Understands historical concepts and ideas				
COMPUTERS GRADE				
Effort				
Conduct				
Understands concepts and ideas				
WORK HABITS GRADE				
Listens attentively				
Works cooperatively in a group				
Participates in class				
Completes homework				
Completes work independently				
Uses time efficiently				
Has a positive attitude toward learning				
Follows directions				
Seeks help when needed				
Organizes work and materials				
Uses study skills				
CONDUCT GRADE				
Follows classroom rules				
Follows school rules				
Demonstrates self control				
Respects rights, opinions and property of others				

and 9.3 show three examples. Often, there are heated debates over the form of the report cards used in a school district, with some parents wanting the product-oriented A, B, C, D, and F grades and others wanting the more process-oriented checklist. Regardless of the particular system or report form used, grades are always based on teacher judgments.

FIGURE 9.2 *Example of a High School Report Card*

STUDENT NAME		YEAR OF GRAD 2007	HOME ROOM	SEMESTER 1 2006 – 2007
		STUDENT I.D.	TELEPHONE	PREV. CREDITS 62.00

SEMESTER SCHOLARSHIP REPORT

NO.	COURSE	TEACHER	1ST GRADE	1ST MISSED	2ND GRADE	2ND MISSED	EXAM	FINAL GRADE	CREDITS EARNED
11	HEALTH	Mr. Fleagle	A	1	A–		B	A–	1.00
133	ENGLISH	Mr. Turcotte	B	2	B+		B	B+	2.50
221	AP EUR HIS	Mrs. Golden	B	1	B+		B	B	2.50
321	GEOMETRY	Ms. Franklin	B	2	C+		C+	B–	2.50
433	PHYSICS	Mr. Wind	B–		B	1	B–	B	3.00
737	INTRO LAW	Mr. Tarot	B+	1	A–	2	B+	A–	2.50
	MERITS		100		100				

CREDITS TO DATE 76.00

ATTENDANCE	THIS GRADING PER.	TOTAL THIS YEAR
DAYS ABSENT	0	0
TIMES TARDY	0	0
TIMES DISMISSED	1	1

ATTENDANCE IS RECORDED AS OF 01–19–05

FELTON HIGH SCHOOL
47 WEST STREET
WILSON, MASS. 01760

GUIDANCE COUNSELOR
TELEPHONE

PARENT / STUDENT
PLEASE SEE REVERSE SIDE FOR EXPLANATION OF GRADES

FIGURE 9.3 *Example of a Kindergarten Report Card*

SOURCE: Reprinted by permission of Our Lady of Lourdes School, Jamaica Plain, MA.

KINDERGARTEN PROGRESS REPORT	Student's Name	School Year
Our Lady of Lourdes School	Teacher's Name	
54 Brookside Avenue	ATTENDANCE	EVALUATION KEY
Jamaica Plain, MA 02130		G - Good S - Satisfactory
542-6136		I - Needs Improvement
		N - Not expected at this time

READING READINESS	D	M	J
Recognizes own name			
Knows alphabet in sequence			
Recognizes uppercase letters			
Recognizes lowercase letters			
Associates sounds with letters			
Is able to blend sounds into words			
Works from left to right			
Shows interest in books/stories			

LANGUAGE DEVELOPMENT			
ORAL	D	M	J
Speaks clearly			
Expresses ideas and feelings well			
Shares ideas and feelings well			
Uses adequate vocabulary			
Speaks in complete sentences			
Tells story in sequence			
WRITTEN			
Can print full name			
Prints alphabet			

MATH READINESS	D	M	J
Can count in order			
Recognizes numbers to 10			
Recognizes numbers above 10			
Writes numbers clearly			
Applies knowledge of numbers			
Identifies basic shapes			
Understands math items			
Visually discriminates among likenesses and differences			

PHYSICAL DEVELOPMENT			
SMALL MUSCLE	D	M	J
Dresses self			
Buttons			
Zips			
Laces			
Controls pencil well			
Can cut well			
Colors neatly			
Pastes neatly			
LARGE MUSCLE			
Runs and jumps well			
Can catch, bounce, and throw ball			
Shows partiality to left or right			

DEVELOPMENT IN ART AND MUSIC			
Is eager to explore art materials			
Is imaginative with art materials			
Identifies colors, shapes, and sizes			
Shows enthusiasm for music			
Enjoys singing			

RELIGIOUS DEVELOPMENT			
Is learning to pray and talk to God			
Is learning about God and His creation			

ATTENDANCE

	D	M	J
Absent			
Tardy			

SOCIAL DEVELOPMENT	D	M	J
Accepts responsibility			
Respects others' property			
Respects others' feelings			
Respects authority			
Works well with others			
Plays well with others			
Listens when others talk			

WORK HABITS			
Observes rules and regulations			
Listens carefully			
Follows directions			
Has good attention span			
Completes activities promptly			
Works well independently			
Uses materials correctly			
Takes care of materials			
Cleans up after work period			
Finishes what has been started			
Values own work			
Is observant			

PERSONAL			
Knows full name			
Knows address			
Knows phone number			
Knows age and birthday			

254

The purpose of all grades is to communicate information about a student's academic performance to students, parents, and others. Within this general purpose are four more specific grading purposes: administrative, informational, motivational, and guidance.

Administratively, grades help determine such things as a student's rank in class, credits for graduation, and suitability for promotion to the next level. They may also be used to judge different teaching approaches and the quality of both teachers and administrators.

Administrative reasons for grading include determining a student's rank in class, credits for graduation, and readiness for promotion.

Informationally, grades are used to inform parents, students, and others about a student's academic performance and effort or lack of effort. Grades represent the teacher's summary judgment about how well students have mastered the content and processes taught in a subject area during a particular term or grading period. Because report card grades are given only four or five times a year, the judgments that they contain are summary. Grades rarely provide diagnostic information about student accomplishments and shortcomings. Teachers recognize this limitation (Hubelbank, 1994), but it does not diminish the importance of grades for students and parents. Grades are important, but bear in mind that grades are only one means of communicating with students and parents. Other methods such as parent conferences can provide more detailed information about a student's progress, and will be described later in this chapter.

Grades are also used to motivate students to study. A high grade is a reward for a good performance. This motivational aspect of grading is, however, a two-edged sword. Student motivation may be enhanced when grades are high, but may be diminished when grades are lower than expected or when the same students continually get low grades. Moreover, it is not desirable to have students study solely to get a good grade, so teachers should try to balance grading rewards with other kinds of rewards.

Lastly, grades are used for guidance. They help students, parents, teachers, and counselors to choose appropriate courses and course levels and to group students. They help identify students who may be in need of special services and they provide information to colleges about the student's academic performance in high school. Table 9.1 summarizes these various purposes.

Grades are used to motivate students to study and to guide them toward appropriate courses, course levels, colleges, and special services.

While there are periodic calls to abolish grades, it is difficult to envision schools in which judgments about students' performance would not be made by teachers and communicated to various interested parties. The basis on which teacher judgments are made may change, the format in which the grades are reported may be altered, and the judgments may no longer be called "grades," but the basic process of teachers judging and communicating information about student performance—that is, "grading"—will still occur.

Grades in whatever form are potent symbols in our society, symbols that are taken very seriously by teachers, students, parents, and the public at large. Regardless of your personal feelings about the value and usefulness of grades and grading, it is necessary to take the grading

TABLE 9.1 PURPOSES OF GRADING

Administrative	Determine student's suitability for promotion or graduation. Determine student's rank in class. Determine quality of teachers and teaching approaches. Determine quality of administration.
Informational	Judge and inform parents, student, and others about student's academic performance.
Motivational	Judge level of student effort. Reward good motivation. Motivate parents and student to improve student's effort.
Guidance	Help students, parents, and counselors to choose appropriate courses and levels. Help teachers to group students by level of performance or need.

Because grades can affect students' chances in life, teachers are ethically bound to be as fair and objective as possible when grading.

process seriously. That means you should devise a grading system for your students that (1) is fair to your students and (2) delivers the message about student performance you wish to convey. Teachers have a responsibility to be objective and fair in assigning grades and should never use grades to reward or punish students the teacher likes or dislikes.

The Difficulty of Grading

Grading can be a very difficult task for teachers for four reasons: (1) Few teachers have had formal instruction in how to grade their students (Brookhart, 1999); (2) school districts and principals provide little guidance to teachers regarding specific grading policies and expectations (Hubelbank, 1994); (3) teachers know that grades are taken seriously by parents and students and that the grades a student gets will be scrutinized and often challenged; and (4) the awareness of each student's needs and characteristics that teachers must have to provide good instruction is difficult to ignore when the teacher determines grades.

The helping relationship that teachers have with their students makes it difficult to judge them on a completely objective basis.

When determining grades, questions regarding fairness in grading inevitably arise. Must teachers focus only on the grades and test scores they have collected during a term to calculate a student's grade, or should teachers also take into account a student's unique needs, circumstances, and problems? The special helping relationship that teachers have with their students makes it difficult for teachers to judge them on a solely objective or dispassionate basis (Hubelbank, 1994). This is especially so for grading, because the judgments made about students are public, taken very seriously, have real consequences for students, and can influence the student's educational, occupational, or home status.

The following remarks indicate some of the ambivalence teachers feel about grading:

Report card time is always difficult for me. My students take grades seriously and talk about them with one another even though I warn them not to. They're young (fourth-graders) and some let their grades define their self-images, so grades can have a negative effect on some. Still, I guess it doesn't do a kid much good to let him think everything's great in his schoolwork when it really isn't . . . but putting it down on a report card makes it final and permanent . . . I agonize over the grades I give.

The first report card of the year is always the toughest because it sets up future expectations for the child and his or her parents.

At the high school level where I teach, grades are given more "by the book" than I think they are in the elementary school. Here we don't get to know our students as well as elementary school teachers and so we can be more objective when grading. I have to admit, though, that I do recognize differences in student interest, effort, and politeness that probably influence my grades a little bit.

Sitting in judgment of students is always difficult, but report card grades are especially so for me. Subject matter grades are supposed to reflect only academic performance, so some good and desirable qualities of students get left out. Yet parents and many kids take these incomplete indicators very, very seriously. I try to cover each student's good, nonacademic qualities in my written report card comments. Another reason report card grades are so difficult for me is because my grade is the first one in which students receive letter grades in subject areas. Every time I give a report card grade, I am aware that I'm setting expectations for the student, the student's parents, and future teachers.

These comments indicate that grading is a difficult, time-consuming process that demands considerable mental and emotional energy from teachers. The demands placed on teachers when assigning grades result, in part, because grades have important consequences for students and others. Grading is further complicated by the lack of uniformly accepted strategies for assigning grades. Grading systems are not comparable from school to school or from teacher to teacher, so each teacher must find his or her own answer to the many questions associated with the grading process. Table 9.2 summarizes some of the more difficult considerations teachers face when assigning grades to their students.

There are no uniformly accepted strategies for assigning grades.

TABLE 9.2   DIFFICULTIES OF GRADING

- Teacher's dual role: judgmental, disciplinarian relationship versus helping relationship
- Preventing student's personal circumstances, characteristics, and needs from distorting judgment regarding academic achievement
- Judgmental, subjective nature of grading; evidence always inconclusive
- Lack of formal training in grading
- Lack of universally accepted strategies for grading

GRADING AS JUDGMENT

The most important aspect of the grading process is its dependence on teacher judgments.

Although there are general guidelines to help develop a classroom grading system, all such systems rely on teacher judgment. Consequently, in assigning grades, teachers are granted considerable discretion and autonomy.

Teacher judgments require two things: (1) information about the person being judged (e.g., test scores, book reports, performance assessments) and (2) a basis of comparison that can be used to translate that information into grading judgments (e.g., what level of performance is worth an A, B, C, D, or F). Information provides the basis for judgment, but note that judgment is different from mere guessing. Guessing is what one does when there is no information or evidence to help make a judgment: "I have no information, so I'll just have to guess." To *judge* implies that the teacher has some evidence to consider in making the judgment. Thus, a teacher gathers evidence of various kinds to help make judgments and decisions about student learning.

A judgment is neither a guess nor a certainty but is based on evidence the teacher deems valid and reliable.

But judgment also implies uncertainty, especially in the classroom setting. When there is complete certainty, there is no need for a teacher to judge. For example, when teachers state "Gerhard is a boy," "Svetlana's parents are divorced," or "Sigmund got the highest score on the math test," they are stating facts, not making judgments. Judgment, then, falls between guessing and certainty. Because the evidence for assigning a grade is rarely conclusive or complete, teachers are required to make a judgment. Using greater amounts of information can reduce, but rarely eliminate, the need for teachers to make judgments when grading. Because assessment evidence is always incomplete, teachers must be concerned about the validity and reliability of judgments made from it.

To summarize our discussion of purpose, the goal of grading is to obtain enough valid evidence about student accomplishments to make a grading judgment that is fair, communicates the level of a student's academic performance, and can be supported with evidence. Because grades are important public judgments, they should be based mainly on formal evidence such as tests, projects, and performance assessments. The concreteness of these evidence types not only helps the teacher to be objective in awarding grades, but also can help to explain or defend a grade that is challenged. Bearing this in mind, there are three main questions to answer when developing a **grading system:**

olc

CHAPTER
CASE STUDY

Visit the text Online Learning Center to read the case of Sarah Hanover, a high school math teacher who is confronted by angry parents about her grading practices.

www.mhhe.com/ russell7e

- Against what standard shall I compare my students' performance?
- What aspects of student performance shall I include in my grades?
- How should different kinds of evidence be weighted in assigning grades?

Embedded in these three questions are other questions that all teachers must address when grading. Unfortunately, few school districts have explicit grading policies that tell a teacher how to answer these questions.

Most districts have particular grading formats teachers must use (e.g., A, B, C; good, satisfactory, poor), but teachers must work out the specific details of their grading systems for themselves. They must answer questions such as "What level of performance is A work and what is D work?" "What is the difference between good and satisfactory performance?" and "Should students be failed if they're trying?" Even if a teacher does not consciously ask such questions when grading, he or she must implicitly answer them, because otherwise grades cannot be assigned.

FOUR TYPES OF COMPARISON FOR GRADING

As noted earlier, a grade is a judgment about the quality of a student's performance. But it is impossible to judge performance in the abstract. Comparison must be involved. Recall the difficulty we had in judging how good Jamal's test score of 95 was when that was our only piece of information. We needed to seek additional information that would allow us to compare Jamal's performance with some standard of goodness or quality. Without comparison, there can be no grading.

Many bases of comparison can be used to assign grades to students. Those most commonly used in classroom grading compare a student's performance with:

A student's performance is most commonly compared with the performance of other students or to predefined standards of good and poor performance.

- The performance of other students.
- Predefined standards of good and poor performance.
- The student's own ability level.
- The student's prior performance (improvement).
- The standards of state assessments.

The vast majority of teachers use one of the first two comparisons in assigning grades to their students (Brookhart, 1999). Grades based on a student's own ability or improvement often prove problematic since the basis for comparison differs for each student in the class. In addition, these strategies also require teachers to defend both the quality of assessment information they use when forming judgments about changes in a student's ability or their improvement as well as their judgments about the starting point for a student's ability or performance level.

Norm-Referenced Grading (Comparison with Other Students)

Assigning grades to students based on a comparison with other students in the class is referred to as **norm-referenced grading.** Other names for this type of grading are "relative grading" and "grading on the curve." A high grade means that a student scored higher than most of his or her classmates, while a low grade means the opposite. When a teacher says

Norm-referenced grading is based on a student's comparison with other students.

things like "Garth is smarter than Omar," "Rowanda works harder in social studies than Tiffany and Tamika," and "Maria completes her math worksheets faster than anyone else in the class," the teacher is making norm-referenced comparisons. In norm-referenced grading, not all students can get the top grade, no matter how well they perform. The system is designed to ensure that there is a distribution of grades across the various grading categories. In norm-referenced grading, the grade a student receives provides no indication of how well or poorly the student actually performed. Students get A grades for having higher scores than their classmates. If a student answered only 40 out of 100 test questions correctly, but was the highest scorer in the class, he or she would receive an A grade in norm-referenced grading, despite answering only 40 items correctly. The opposite can occur at the other end of the scoring range: A student may answer 97 out of 100 questions correctly but get a C because many students in the class got 98's, 99's, and 100's. Compared with classmates, a score of 97 falls in the middle of the group, even though, in absolute terms, it is very high performance.

A grading curve sets up quotas for each grade.

In norm-referenced grading, teachers establish a **grading curve** that defines what percentage of the students can get A's, B's, C's, and so on. This curve, which varies from teacher to teacher and is established before an assessment is given, sets up quotas for each grade. Following are two examples of grading curves:

A	Top 20 percent of students	A	Top 10 percent of students
B	Next 30 percent of students	B	Next 40 percent of students
C	Next 30 percent of students	C	Next 45 percent of students
D	Next 10 percent of students	D	Last 5 percent of students
F	Last 10 percent of students		

If the curve on the left were applied to grading a chapter or unit test, the teacher would administer the test, score it, and arrange the students in order of their scores from highest to lowest. The highest-scoring 20 percent of the students (including ties) would get an A grade; the next 30 percent, a B grade; the next 30 percent, a C grade; and so on. If the same curve were to be applied when giving report card grades, the teacher would first have to summarize the varied information about student performance that was gathered over the entire term. The list of summary scores for each student would be arranged in order from highest to lowest, and the percentages in the curve would be applied to allocate grades.

There is no single best grading curve that should be used in every norm-referenced grading situation. Some teachers give mostly A's and B's, while others give mainly C's. Some teachers do not believe in giving students F's, while others give many F's. Teacher discretion determines the nature of the grading curve. However, if a teacher's curve gives too many high grades to mediocre students, students will not respect it. If it is too difficult even for bright, hardworking students to get an A, they will give up. In the end, one seeks a grading curve that is fair to the students and that represents academic standards that the teacher feels are appropriate and realistic for the students.

The type of comparison that is used to assign grades to students can influence their effort and attitude. For example, norm-referenced grading tends to undermine the learning and effort of students who repeatedly score near the bottom of the class, since they continually receive poor grades. Norm-referenced grading poses a lesser threat to the top students in the class, although it can spur competition among students for the high grades. Competitive, norm-referenced approaches that make a student's success or failure dependent on the performance of classmates can also reduce student cooperation and interdependence, because success for one student reduces the chance of success for other students.

Norm-referenced grading makes a student's grade dependent on the performance of classmates, which can reduce student cooperation.

Criterion-Referenced Grading (Predefined Standards)

Instead of grading by comparing one student with others, a teacher can compare a student's performance with preestablished performance standards. **Performance standards** define the level or score that a student must attain to receive a particular grade. All students who reach a given level get the same grade, regardless of how many students reach that level. The test for a driver's license is a simple, pass–fail example of performance standards. In many states, the driver's test contains two parts, a written section covering knowledge of the rules of the road and a performance section in which the applicant must actually drive an automobile around local roads. (Notice how paper-and-pencil tests *and* performance assessments are combined in driver's tests to make certain the all-important knowledge and skills of safe driving are assessed. This is a good example to keep in mind for your own classroom assessments.)

The written portion of the driver's test usually contains 20 multiple-choice items that must be passed before the performance portion is attempted. The written test is administered to groups of applicants in much the same way paper-and-pencil tests are administered in schools. In most states, passing the test depends on getting 70 percent of the items correct. In this case, 70 percent is the performance standard. Whether any single applicant passes or fails depends only on how he or she compares with the performance standard of 70 percent. Passing has nothing whatsoever to do with the performance of other applicants taking the test because applicants' scores are not compared with one another. They are compared with the predetermined 70 percent performance standard. In this system it is possible for all or none of the applicants to pass.

Grading that compares a student's achievement with preestablished standards rather than to other students' achievement is called criterion-referenced grading.

Grading that compares a student's achievement with predefined performance standards is called **criterion-referenced grading** or absolute grading. As in the driver's test, each student is graded on the basis of his or her own performance. Since students are not compared with one another and do not compete for a limited percentage of high grades, it is possible for all students to get high or low grades on a test. Criterion-referenced grading is the most commonly used grading system in schools. The criteria used to determine performance standards can be either performance-based or percentage-based.

Performance-Based Criteria

Performance-based criteria spell out in detail the specific learning students must demonstrate to receive a particular grade. For example, in some classrooms teachers use contract grading in which the student and teacher negotiate the quality and amount of work the student must satisfactorily complete to receive a particular grade. If the student meets the negotiated performance standard by the end of the semester, he or she receives the promised grade. Alternatively, a more narrow performance standard could be set up to grade each student who must give an oral speech. The teacher would observe the speech, concentrating on the specific activities listed in the oral speech performance standards. At the end of the speech, the teacher would refer to the performance standards or rubric and assign a grade to each student. A sample rubric based on preset performance standards for an oral speech is presented below. Again, notice that each student's grade depends on how he or she performs in comparison with the standard, not in comparison with other students.

In criterion-referenced grading, there is no limit to the number of students who can receive a particular grade.

A   Student consistently faces audience, stands straight, and maintains eye contact; projects voice well and clearly; pacing and tone variation appropriate; well-organized points logically and completely presented; brief summary at end.

B   Student usually faces audience, stands straight, and makes eye contact; voice projection good, but pace and clarity vary during talk; well organized but repetitive; occasional poor choice of words; incomplete summary.

C   Student fidgety; some eye contact and facial expression change; uneven voice projection, not heard by all in room, some words slurred; loosely organized, repetitive, contains many incomplete thoughts; poor summary.

D   Student's body movements distracting, little eye contact or voice change; words slurred, speaks in monotone, does not project voice beyond first few rows, no consistent or logical pacing; rambling presentation, little organization with no differentiation between major and minor points; no summary.

Percentage-Based Criteria

This second, more common type of criterion-referenced standard uses cut-off scores based on the percentage of items answered correctly. In the case of report card grading, an overall or average percentage of mastery across many individual assessments is determined. The following cutoff percentages represent perhaps the most widely used standard of this type:

90 to 100 percent of items correct = A
80 to 89 percent of items correct = B
70 to 79 percent of items correct = C
60 to 69 percent of items correct = D
Less than 60 percent of items correct = F

Any student who scores within one of the above performance standards will receive the corresponding grade. There is no limit on the number of students who can receive a particular grade, and the teacher does not know what the distribution of grades will be until after the tests are scored and graded. Note that this is not the case in the norm-referenced approach.

Many teachers use percentage-based cutoff scores other than those shown here; some use 85 percent and higher as the cutoff for an A grade and readjust the cutoffs for the remaining grades accordingly. Others refuse to flunk a student unless he or she gets less than half (50 percent) of the items incorrect. Like the curve in norm-referenced grading, the grading standards used in criterion-referenced grading are based on a teacher's judgment about what is suitable and fair for his or her class. Standards should be reasonable given the ability of the class and the nature of the subject matter, and they should be academically honest and challenging for the students.

Interpreting and Adjusting Grades

A criterion-referenced grading system is intended to indicate how much a student has learned of the things that were taught. Grades based on poor instruction, invalid assessments, or assessments that fail to cover the full range of what students were taught will convey an incorrect message about student learning. Of course, good instruction and valid instruments that fully assess what students have been taught should always be used, regardless of the grading approach. However, the focus on content mastery in criterion-referenced grading makes it especially crucial that teachers provide good instruction and develop assessments that are fair and that cover the full range of objectives taught.

In criterion-referenced grading, getting an invalid or unclear test item wrong can have major implications for student grades. Suppose that 2 out of 10 items on a teacher's test were not taught to students and as a consequence many students answered these two items incorrectly. The highest score the students could get would be 80 percent. If they made

These days, students are being graded not only by their teachers, but also by statewide assessments.

no other mistakes and were being graded on performance standards in which 80 percent or higher is a B grade, the highest grade these students could receive would be a B, even though the two items that they got wrong were not their fault.

Thus, before using assessment information to grade students, the quality of that information should be considered. Grades are only as meaningful as the information on which they are based. If grades are assigned subjectively, if scoring criteria change from student to student, if there are no established grading criteria, or if the teacher's attention wanders during scoring, grades will not accurately reflect student achievement. If unit tests are unfair to students or do not test a representative sample of what was taught, the scores students attain will not be valid indicators of their achievement. It is important for teachers to examine assessment results that are unusual or unexpected. Typically, unexpectedly low results provoke teacher concern and attention. Teachers ask themselves: Do these low scores indicate a problem with the test or instruction, or a problem with the effort students put into preparing for the test? How should this result be handled in grading?

Suppose a teacher's test produced lower than usual scores for most students. When he compared the test items with what he had taught, he found that the test contained items on a section of the unit he had not taught. Thus, the match between the unit test and classroom instruction was not good. Students were being penalized because the teacher's instruction failed to cover many concepts included in the test. Thus, the scores provide a distorted picture of the students' actual achievement, reducing the validity of their grades.

To resolve this problem, the teacher decided to change the students' scores on the test to better reflect their achievement. He estimated that about 20 percent of the items on the test were from the section he had not taught. After determining that most students had done poorly on these items, the teacher decided to increase each student's test score by 20 percentage points to adjust for the invalid items. He correctly reasoned that the increased scores would provide a better indication than the original scores of what students had learned *from the instruction provided.*

It is important to reiterate the critical need to make such adjustments when criterion-referenced grading is used. It is also important to note that the teacher adjusted the low scores on the test only *after* reexamining both the test and his instruction. He did not raise the scores to make the students feel better about themselves or to have them like him more. In this instance the test scores were raised to provide a more valid indication of how well students had learned from the instruction. The raised grades better reflected the students' mastery of the subject matter.

If a grading standard or curve proves to be inappropriate or unfair, it should be changed before grades are assigned.

Regardless of whether one employs a norm- or a criterion-referenced grading system, the grading curve or performance standards should be determined before assessment is carried out. Doing this helps teachers to think about expected performance and allows them to inform students of what will be needed to get high grades. When properly defined, a grading system tells students what constitutes high and low achievement. However, judgments are sometimes incorrect and need to be adjusted. Consequently, once established, performance standards and grading curves need not be set in stone. If, for some reason, a standard or grading curve turns out to be inappropriate or unfair, it can and should be changed before grades are assigned. While changes in performance standards or grading curves should not be made frivolously, it is better to make changes than to award incorrect and invalid grades. Usually, increased experience with a class helps a teacher arrive at a set of standards or a grading curve that is appropriate and fair. The classroom teacher can make changes in grading curves and standards when he or she judges them to be invalid for some reason. Teacher discretion is at the heart of good grading.

Having made this point, it must also be emphasized that fairness to students does not mean selecting standards or curves to ensure that everyone gets high grades. Lowering standards or grading curves to guarantee high grades discourages student effort and diminishes the validity of the grades. Fairness means fully assessing what students were taught, using assessment procedures appropriate to the grade level and type of instruction used, and establishing performance standards or grading curves that are realistic if students work hard. These are the teacher's responsibilities in integrating instruction, assessment, and grading. Table 9.3 compares the main features of norm- and criterion-referenced grading.

Fairness means assessing what pupils were taught, using appropriate assessment procedures, and establishing realistic performance standards or grading curves.

Comparison with a Student's Ability

Teachers frequently make remarks such as "Dwayne is not working up to his ability," "Maurice is not doing as well as he can," or "Jaklyn continues to achieve much higher grades than I expected she would." When

---

TABLE 9.3   COMPARISON OF NORM-REFERENCED AND CRITERION-REFERENCED GRADING

	Norm-Referenced	**Criterion-Referenced**
Comparison made	Student with other students	Student with predefined criteria
Method of comparison	Grading curve; percentage of students who can get each grade	Standard of performance; scores students must achieve to get a given grade
What grade describes	Student's performance compared with others in the class	Student's percentage mastery of course objectives
Availability of a particular grade	Limited by grading curve; not all students can get an A	No limit on grade availability; all students could get an A

teachers make such statements, they are comparing a student's actual performance with the performance they expect, based on their judgment of the student's ability. The terms "overachiever" and "underachiever" are used to describe students who do better or worse than teacher expectations for what they should be doing. Many teachers assign grades by comparing a student's actual performance with their perception of the student's ability level.

In this ability-based grading approach, students with high ability who do excellent work would receive high grades, as would students with low ability who were perceived by the teacher to be achieving "up to their potential." Even though the actual performance of the low-ability students may be well below that of the high-ability, high-achieving students, each group would receive the same grade if each were perceived to be achieving up to their ability. Conversely, students with high ability who were perceived by their teacher to be underachieving—that is, performing below what the teacher thinks they are capable of performing—would receive low grades. An argument advanced in defense of this grading approach is that it motivates students to do their best and perform at their ability. It also punishes lazy students who do not work up to their perceived ability.

However, grading based on student ability is not recommended for a number of reasons (Kubiszyn and Borich, 2003). First, the approach depends on the teacher having an accurate perception of each student's ability. In reality, teachers rarely know enough about their students to permit valid and precise assessments of their abilities. Teachers do have a general sense of students' abilities from their early assessments and the students' classroom performance, but this information is too imprecise to form an accurate understanding of a student's ability. Similarly, formal tests designed to measure ability are rarely precise enough to accurately predict a student's capacity for learning. Even for experts, it is all but impossible to make valid predictions about what a student of a certain general ability level is capable of achieving in a specific subject area.

Even formal tests designed to measure ability are rarely precise enough to accurately predict a student's capacity for learning.

Second, teachers often have a difficult time differentiating a student's ability from other student characteristics such as self-assurance, motivation, or responsiveness. This is especially problematic in light of recent thinking that students have numerous types of abilities or intelligences, not just one (Gardner, 1995). Given these multiple abilities or intelligences that help students learn and perform in different modalities (e.g., oral, visual, written), which ones should a teacher focus on to judge a student's ability?

Teachers should not assign grades by comparing a student's actual performance with their perception of the student's ability level.

Third, grades comparing performance against expectations are confusing to people outside the classroom, especially parents. For example, a high-ability student who attained 80 percent mastery of the instruction might receive a C grade if perceived to be underachieving, while a low-ability student who attained 60 percent mastery might receive an A grade for exceeding expectations. An outsider viewing these two grades would probably think that the low-ability student mastered more of the course, because that student got the higher grade. Yet, when grades are based on a comparison with a student's perceived ability, there is little correlation between grades and student mastery of course content.

Together, these reasons argue strongly against the use of a grading system that compares actual and predicted achievement. Some report cards do allow separate judgments about student achievement and ability. The teacher can record a subject matter grade based on the student's actual achievement, and then, in a separate place on the report card, indicate whether he or she thinks the student is working up to expectations. Usually, the teacher writes comments or checks boxes to show whether the student "needs improvement," "is improving," or "is doing his best" relative to his or her ability. Even in this approach, teachers must be cautious about putting too much faith in their estimates of student ability and potential.

Comparison with Student Improvement

Basing grades on student improvement over time creates problems similar to those of awarding grades based on comparing actual performance with perceived ability. Student improvement is determined by comparing a student's early performance with his or her later performance. Students who show the most progress or growth receive high grades, and those who show little progress or growth receive low grades. An obvious difficulty with this approach is that students who do well early in the grading period have little opportunity to improve, and thus have little chance to get good grades. Low scorers at the start of the term have the best chance to show improvement, and thus tend to get high grades. It is not surprising that students graded on improvement quickly realize that it is in their best interests to do poorly on the early tests. They intentionally perform poorly so early performance will be low and improvement can be shown easily.

As with comparisons of actual and predicted performance, grading on the basis of improvement causes problems with grade interpretation. A student who improves from very low achievement to moderate achievement may get an A, while a student who had high achievement at the start and therefore improved little may get a B or a C, when it was the latter student who mastered more of the subject matter than the student who received the A grade.

There is little correlation between grades and student mastery of course content in ability-based grading systems.

Some teachers recognize this difficulty and propose the following solution: Give the students who achieve highly throughout the term an A grade for their high performance, but also give A grades to students who improve their performance a great deal over time. While this suggestion overcomes the problem noted above, it creates a new problem. In essence, these teachers are proposing to use two very different grading systems, one

The same grading system must be applied to all students in the class in order to convey a consistent and understandable message about classroom standards.

based on high achievement and the other on high student improvement. This approach provides rewards for both groups of students but confuses the meaning of their grades, since the grades can mean two different things: achievement or improvement. Thus, grading systems based on improvement and ability, and grading systems based on combinations of these two, are not recommended. Grades can convey a consistent, understandable message only if the same approach is applied to all students.

GRADING FOR COOPERATIVE LEARNING AND STUDENTS WITH DISABILITIES

Grading in Cooperative Learning

The main purpose of cooperative learning is to have students learn to work together to arrive at a single, group-generated solution.

Classrooms at all levels of education are increasingly emphasizing group-based or cooperative learning strategies. In cooperative learning, small groups of two to six students are presented with a task or problem situation that they must solve together. While the problem given in a cooperative group can be posed in virtually any subject area.

In grading cooperative learning, teachers are usually concerned with assessing three important outcomes: (1) the interactive, cooperative processes that go on within the group, (2) the quality of the group's solution, and (3) each member's contribution to and understanding of that solution. While the assessment of the group processes is important, assessment of subject matter learning is equally important. However, conducting assessment of each individual group member is difficult because the group turns in a single, cooperatively reached product. At issue is how a teacher should assign individual student grades on the basis of a single group production.

Teachers must decide how to grade a group project: Will all members get the same grade, or will each member get an individual grade?

The most common grading practice in cooperative learning is to assign a single grade to a group's solution and to give that grade to each group member. The difficulty with such a strategy is that it assumes equal contributions and understanding on the part of each group member. Both the student who contributed and learned a great deal and the student who contributed and learned very little receive the same grade. On the other hand, to push too hard for individual student solutions and contributions can destroy many of the benefits of cooperative problem solving. Thus, for many teachers, grading in cooperative learning situations creates problems not encountered in grading individual student performance.

There is no single acceptable solution to these problems. Many teachers see no difficulty in assuming equal contributions and learning from each group member and give identical grades to all of them. Other teachers combine assessment of the group process with assessment of the group product, relying on their observations and interactions with students to provide them with an indication of the contribution and comprehension of each group member. Teachers then adjust individual grades according to their observations of student participation, contribution, and understanding. Still other teachers let the students self-assess their own contributions and understanding by grading themselves. This approach is less than ideal because students' self-assessments will often be based as much on their self-perceptions and self-confidence as on their actual contributions and learning.

Another strategy that has some advantages over the preceding ones combines group and individual grades. All members of the group receive the same grade for their single, group-based solution or product. To assess the contributions and participation of each individual, students are asked to self-assess their own contributions and those of their group members. These self- and peer assessments are then used in conjunction with the teacher's own observations to form a participation or individual contribution grade. Subsequently, if a teacher wants to assess the learning of each individual, the teacher requires each student to individually answer or perform follow-up or application activities related to the group problem or task. The purpose of these follow-up activities is to determine how well each student understands and can apply the group solution in solving similar types of problems. This approach blends both participation and contribution with subject matter learning in a way that helps the teacher know what each student has learned.

Teachers can use follow-up activities with individual students to determine how well they understand the processes used in a group-based solution.

Grading Students with Disabilities

In previous chapters, we discussed issues of instructing and assessing students with disabilities. We saw that more and more students with learning disabilities are being integrated into or "included" in regular education classrooms. While some learning disabilities make it difficult for students to perform at a level similar to their non-disabled classmates in some areas, the intellectual and social benefits of inclusion warrant placing students who have disabilities with their non-disabled peers. However, because of the disparities in academic performance that often occur between some disabled and non-disabled students, grading can present classroom teachers with a variety of concerns. Indeed, one of the questions asked most frequently by classroom teachers is "How should I assign grades to my included students with disabilities?"

The Nature of the Problem

Embedded in the question above is a host of other questions. For example, who should be responsible for grading an included student: the classroom teacher, a special education teacher, or these two in combination?

Should the same standards be used to assess students with and without disabilities? How should an included student's Individual Education Plan (IEP) enter into the grading process? What is the best way to report the performance of students with disabilities? These and many other questions face the classroom teacher who must grade students with disabilities (Guskey and Bailey, 2001). In this section, we examine issues associated with grading students with disabilities placed in regular classrooms. We will consider a variety of ways in which such grading can be done and the limitations of these methods. We will also identify the primary problem that confronts teachers who must grade students with disabilities and suggest how that grading can be made more manageable and informative.

Consider the question of who should be responsible for grading students with disabilities. The answer to this question depends on the extent of a student's inclusion in regular classrooms. Students with various disabilities often spend different amounts of time in regular classrooms—from full-time inclusion, to part-time inclusion for instruction in particular subject areas, to no inclusion at all. Generally, the teacher who delivers the instruction in a subject area should be responsible for grading a student in that subject area. Thus, fully included students with disabilities should be graded by the regular classroom teacher, as should partially included students who take particular courses from a classroom teacher. Subject areas taught by special education teachers in separate classrooms should be graded by the special education teacher. Our focus here is on the issues related to grading students with disabilities who are included part- or full-time in a regular classroom.

The main problem teachers can face when grading students with disabilities is the disparity in achievement of some students with disabilities compared with non-disabled students. Not all disabilities hamper a student's ability to achieve at a level comparable with non-disabled peers, but some disabilities do. Teachers often ask two questions: (1) "Should grading standards be the same for all students in my class?" and (2) "How can I take into account a student's disability when I assign grades to my class?"

If a teacher applies the same grading standard to all students, many of the students with disabilities will receive low grades. If the teacher uses different standards for students with and without disabilities, the same grade will mean different things depending on which grading standard was applied to a given student. Notice that this is a problem whether a norm-referenced or criterion-referenced grading system is used. However, it is especially a problem for students with disabilities in criterion-referenced grading where the performance standards are rigid and inflexible (Polloway et al., 1994). The problem is heightened because students who are moved from special education classrooms to regular classrooms previously were graded on standards different from those used in regular classrooms (Valdes, Williamson, and Wagner, 1990), thereby creating more confusion about the meaning of a grade.

Some Possible Strategies

Many alternative grading strategies have been adopted to grade students with disabilities (Salend, 2001). All of the approaches are based on the objectives and learning strategies described in a student's IEP. Most of the approaches are based on establishing and applying standards that are unique to each student, so that a student is compared with her- or himself in some way. An individual student grading strategy is often developed by a team, which may include the classroom teacher, the student, his or her parents, and special education experts (Munk and Bursuck, 2003). Following are explanations of some of these alternative strategies.

- **Contract grading:** The teacher and the student jointly determine the type and quality of work a student will complete in order to receive a particular grade. The contract spells out the amount of work at a given level of quality that is needed for a student to receive an A, B, C, and so on. The amount and level of work required for a given grade will vary by student. As a student progresses through the year, the terms of the contract may evolve such that the student is expected to do more work at a higher level.
- **IEP-based grading:** Students are graded on the percentage of objectives in their IEP that they achieve in a term or marking period. The grading standards would be criterion-referenced with different percentages of completion resulting in different grades (i.e., 80 percent or more completion is an A, 70 to 79 percent completion is a B, and so on). This approach is similar to grading a student based on her or his improvement over time.
- **Multiple grading:** The student receives different grades for different performances rather than a single, overall grade. For example, a student could receive separate grades for effort, participation, achievement, and progress. Such an approach allows the teacher to make some distinctions in the student's overall performance and to show areas of strength and weakness. A similar approach is to adjust grading weights for different students by, for example, counting written assignments or projects more than test results. Report cards that are similar in form to checklists or rating scales permit more detailed descriptions of student performances and enable a teacher to distinguish between a student's level of effort, participation in learning, and level of achievement.
- **Level-based grading:** Students are given grades that indicate both their achievement level and curriculum level. This strategy is particularly useful for students who are performing below grade level and thus are focusing on achieving standards and objectives for a previous grade level. For example, a student who shows B-level achievement on the fourth-grade curriculum can be graded B(4), while a student

who shows B-level achievement in a below-grade-level curriculum can be graded B(3). The number in parentheses represents the grade level of the curriculum in which a student is performing. This approach allows a teacher to apply standards and expectations consistently across all students, but to distinguish the grade level at which the student is meeting expecations.

- **Narrative grading:** The teacher does not assign a grade per se, but provides a substantial written or oral description of the student's performance, achievements, strengths, and weaknesses based on the teacher's observations and assessments of the student. Note that this is an informative, but time-consuming, grading approach.

A survey of non–special education teachers (Bursuck et al., 1996) indicates that classroom teachers use many of these strategies in grading students *both* with and without disabilities. The survey also showed that teachers use some strategies more than others in grading students with disabilities. Among the commonly used strategies are grading on the basis of improvement in IEP objectives; awarding separate grades for process (effort, participation) and achievement (test results); weighting student process more than product in grading; and using contract grading. For students with disabilities, teachers were less likely to change their grading standards, pass students just for high effort, or pass them no matter what their performance. While all of the above strategies are used by teachers, none avoid the grading problems of measuring improvement, determining ability, and applying differing grading standards.

The Need for Different Messages

The main problem most teachers face in grading classes that contain students both with and without disabilities is the inability of any single type of grade to convey the many important messages to the many different audiences interested in grades.

The most common grading system used in schools is the A, B, C, D, and F letter grade system (Polloway et al., 1994; Friedman and Frisbie, 1993). This system limits the information that can be conveyed in a grade because all a teacher can record for a student's grade is a single letter, perhaps with a plus or minus added. A, B, C, D, F grading conveys little of the specifics of what the student can or cannot do and has or has not learned. Letter grades create particular problems for teachers who want to take a student's disability into account when awarding a grade. As noted previously, regardless of whether teachers use a norm- or criterion-referenced grading system, many students with disabilities are likely to receive low grades. On the one hand, if teachers raise a grade because of a student's disability, they are constrained to do it within the letter grading system. This means that although a student with a disability performed less well than another student, both students were given the same grade. People who see the two grades will assume that they represent the same level of achievement. However, if teachers do not take the disability into account, many students with disabilities will continually receive low grades. This is the teacher's grading dilemma.

Reporting systems that allow teachers to provide more information about a student's grade than a single letter or number can help teachers with this dilemma. Systems such as the level-based and narrative grading approaches allow the teacher to provide important information about the meaning of the student's performance. The ability to describe a student's specific learning outcomes, the grade level of student performance, the amount of improvement, the weight given to effort and achievement, the availability of an aide for a student, or other pertinent factors related to student performance can help teachers grade a student with a disability. Employing such information takes a student's disability into account in the grades given and also provides the desired perspective on the meaning of the grades.

DECIDING WHAT TO GRADE

Once the comparative basis for assigning grades is decided on, it is necessary to select the particular student performances and products that will be used to award grades. If a teacher is grading a single test or a project, there is obviously only one performance to be considered. If a teacher is assigning report card grades, many types of performances and behaviors could be considered. These can include both formal academic achievement and the less formal area of "affective performance"—motivation, behavior, interest, and so forth.

The quantity and the nature of the assessment information available to a teacher varies depending on the grade level and subject area. For example, assigning a term grade in spelling simply involves combining the results of each student's performance on the Friday spelling tests. In American history or social studies, however, a teacher may have information from quizzes, tests, homework, projects, reports, portfolios, and worksheets. High school math teachers have homework papers, quizzes, portfolios, and test results to consider in assigning grades, while English teachers have tests, essays, oral reports, homework, quizzes, portfolios, projects, and class discussion to consider. In addition to these formal indicators of achievement, teachers have informal perceptions of students' effort, interest, participation in class discussions, motivation, helpfulness, and behavior. Each teacher must decide which of the available information will be used in determining report card grades. This decision is critical, because the performances that are included define what the grade really means.

Teachers must choose from many formal and informal sources of information in determining a report card grade.

Since grades serve as a motivator for many students, determining which performances and behaviors are included in a term grade sends an important message about what a teacher values. By including behaviors such as participation in classroom discussions or being on time to class, a teacher can encourage students to participate more actively or be more timely. Conversely, by excluding behaviors, a teacher may inadvertently send a message that the behavior is not valued. Thus, deciding what to include and what to exclude from a grade provides an important opportunity for a teacher to convey his or her values and encourage students to adopt or modify specific behaviors or types of performances.

Three questions teachers have to ask about grading are "What do I want my grades to convey about student performance?" "Which types of behaviors and performances do I want to promote or discourage?" and "Do the assessments I've included in the grade reflect what I want to convey?" When answering these questions, a teacher may realize that not all of the performances, activities, or types of behaviors that students exhibit in a classroom are necessary to include in a grade. Most often, however, a teacher's grading system will include a combination of academic achievement and affective behaviors.

Academic Achievement

Subject matter grades should reflect a student's academic achievement rather than such things as motivation, cooperation, and attendance.

Grades are usually viewed as an indication of how much students have learned from instruction. Formal assessments of students' achievement of the course objectives should be the major component of subject matter grades. Affective performances should *not* be a major determinant of subject matter grades because affective characteristics pertain to student processes, not student learning. To judge students' academic achievement we look at the *results* of affect (effort, motivation, interest), as demonstrated in formal assessments.

Formal subject matter assessments such as teacher-made tests and homework provide the hard evidence to explain or defend a grade.

Formal subject matter assessments such as teacher-made and textbook tests, papers, quizzes, homework, projects, worksheets, portfolios, and the like are the best types of evidence to use in assigning report card grades. They are suitable in two respects. First, they provide information about students' academic performance, which is what grades are intended to describe. Second, as tangible products of students' work, they can be used to explain or defend a grade if the need arises. It is defensible to say to a student, "I gave a C grade because when I compared your test scores, projects, and homework assignments in this marking period with my grading standards, you performed at a C level." It is indefensible to say, "I gave a C grade because I had a strong *sense* that you were not working as hard as you could and because I have a negative *general perception* of your daily class performance." This second rationale would be difficult to defend or explain to students, parents, or principals.

Because formal assessments of student achievement should be accorded major weight in assigning grades, it is important to stress that grades will be only as good as the instruction and formal assessments on which they are based. Grading as a process cannot be separated from the quality of the instruction and assessment information teachers collect prior to grading. Just as good instruction can be undermined by invalid assessment, good grading can be undermined by poorly constructed, invalid, and unreliable assessments. Irrelevant, invalid evidence about student achievement will produce irrelevant, invalid grades. The guidelines for constructing valid assessments described in Chapters 5 through 8 should underlie the assessments teachers construct and use in their grades.

As the culminating step in the process of assessing students' academic achievement, grading should be based on a varied assortment of valid and reliable evidence. A general rule of grading is to draw on several different types of information rather than a single type, because this provides a fuller understanding of what students have achieved. By including information from tests, class assignments, papers, term projects, and other activities that require students to demonstrate their achievement, a term grade is less likely to be influenced by a single type of assignment that may misrepresent a student's achievement. As an example, some students simply do not perform well on formal tests, but are able to demonstrate their achievement more accurately through projects, papers, and other types of classroom assignments. By including multiple types of performances, teachers can ensure that poor performances on tests that misrepresent the student's achievement level are balanced by the other types of information. Also, since students are required to remember, understand, and apply most subject areas, varied procedures are needed to assess all important outcomes of instruction.

olc
CHAPTER CASE STUDY
Visit the text Online Learning Center to read the case of Leigh Scott, a high school social studies teacher. Leigh is confronted by an angry student who wants her to explain how she arrived at his report card grade.
www.mhhe.com/russell7e

Students are given greater opportunity to demonstrate achievement when grades are based on several types of assessment information.

Affective Performances

Affective characteristics should not be major factors in report card grades, but teachers' perceptions of their students' affective characteristics often enter into grading decisions. A common situation in which student motivation, interest, and effort enter into grades is their use in giving borderline students the benefit of the doubt. When a teacher awards a B+ to a student whose academic performance places her between a B and a B+ grade, but who is motivated, participates in class, and works diligently, the teacher is taking into account more than just formal assessments of achievement.

Teachers often nudge upward the grades they give to conscientious, participating students in order to keep them motivated. Strictly speaking, such adjustments distort the intended meaning of a grade, but most teachers do make them based on their knowledge of particular student characteristics and needs. Grading is a human judgmental process, and

Student effort and participation can be used to adjust a grade but should not be the main determiner of the grade.

it is virtually inevitable that such teacher adjustments will be made. These borderline decisions usually operate for the benefit of the student.

A teacher should guard against allowing effort, motivation, interest, or personality to become the dominant factors in determining grades. If that happens, grades are distorted, providing little useful information about the student's academic achievement.

For example, to give an A grade to a student who is academically marginal but very industrious and congenial would be misleading to the student, parents, and others who would interpret the grade as indicating high achievement. Students who work hard, are cooperative, and show great motivation and interest are desirable to have in class and deserve to be rewarded, but subject matter grades are not the proper arena for such rewards. Nor should grades be used to punish students for behavioral problems or late work unless timeliness is part of the formal performance criteria. Although few teachers can ignore nonacademic evidence like students' ability, effort, and improvement when they grade, most correctly use such evidence as a basis for adjustments in students' grades, not as the central determiner of grades (Brookhart, 1992; Griswold and Griswold, 1992; Nava and Loyd, 1992).

As we have seen in this chapter, teachers must decide what standards of comparison to use in assigning grades. This means deciding on either a norm-referenced or a criterion-referenced standard. Once this decision has been made, the teacher must establish a grading curve in the norm-referenced approach or a set of performance standards in the criterion-referenced approach. Next, the teacher must determine what performances will be included in the grade. Because grades are mainly intended to convey information about students' mastery of subject matter rather than their personal qualities, grades should be based primarily on formal assessments of student achievement. Although teachers' subjective perceptions and insights inevitably influence the grading process to some extent, they should not be allowed to greatly distort the subject matter grade.

Using Discretion When Assigning Grades

If term grades were assigned by computers, it would be easy to grade solely on formal assessments of student achievement. We could simply determine which performances would be included in the grade and how much weight each performance would receive, and then a computer could calculate the grades. Although a teacher's grading system will often specify which types of performances and behaviors will be included in a term grade and how much weight different types of performances and behaviors will receive, teachers know a great deal more about their students than this limited set of performances and behaviors can reveal. Teachers know their students as whole persons, not one-dimensional scores or achievers. Teachers understand students' home backgrounds and know the effects grades will have on students and their parents. Because of this, teachers rarely can be completely objective and dispassionate dispensers of report card grades. Instead, as the following excerpts illustrate, teachers often struggle with whether and how to adjust grades so that they reflect other pieces of information that the teacher knows about an individual student.

> Peter works harder than any student in my class, but he cannot seem to overcome his lack of ability. No one tries harder, yet his tests and projects are all failures. But I just can't in good conscience give Peter a failing grade because he tries so hard and an F would destroy him.

> Brianne had a terrible term. Her test scores dropped off, her attention during instruction was poor, and she failed to complete many homework assignments. The reason for these behaviors is in her home situation. Her father left the home, her mother had to find a job, and Brianne had to assume most of the household and babysitting responsibilities because she is the oldest child. How can I not take this into account when I grade her this term?

> Jermaine is the ultimate itch: constant motion, inattention, socializing around the classroom at inappropriate times. He drives me crazy. However, his classwork is well done and on time. When I sit down to grade him, I have to refrain from saying "OK, Jermaine, now I'm going to get you for being such a distraction." I have a hard time separating his academic performance from his classroom behavior.

Determining how to incorporate specific information about a student into a grade requires discretion. A teacher must balance how the inclusion of such information will affect the meaning and interpretation of the grades they receive against the effect the grade may have on the student.

In the case of Peter, above, the teacher must balance the potential effect of discouraging Peter from trying if he is given an F versus the potential that some people may interpret that Peter has achieved at an adequate level if he is given a higher grade that factors in his effort level. Similarly, the teacher must decide whether Brianne's home situation contributed to an anomalous performance and how her future effort level might be affected if a low grade is given based on an anomaly. On the other hand, if Brianne's home situation is likely to be lasting and she is the type of person who rises to a challenge, giving a lower grade that reflects her achievement level during the current marking period may serve as a motivator that helps her overcome the challenges she is facing at home. Finally, although Jermaine is able to perform well himself, the teacher must consider whether allowing his behavior in class to continue may send a message that such behavior is acceptable and whether such behavior will likely have a negative effect on him in the long term. Depending on the teacher's answer to these questions, it may be advisable to ignore the behavior when awarding a grade or to factor it into the grade so as to motivate Jermaine to modify his classroom behavior. In all cases, teachers must apply discretion when incorporating additional information into a student's grade and consider both the short-term and long-term effects that an adjusted grade are likely to have on the student's future achievement.

SUMMARIZING VARIED TYPES OF ASSESSMENT

Report card grades require teachers to summarize each student's performance on the many individual assessments gathered during the marking period. To assist in keeping track of student performances over a period of time, it is very important that teachers maintain grade books and that they be carefully guarded to ensure confidentiality of student grades. Regardless of whether the grade book is maintained on paper or on a computer, it is recommended that teachers keep two copies of the grade book, one kept in the classroom and one at home. Losing your only copy of a grade book leaves you with the difficult task of reconstructing it in order to grade.

Figure 9.4 shows a page from a fifth-grade teacher's actual grade book for the first 5 weeks of term 2 in geography. At the bottom of the figure is a list of all the assessments the students were expected to complete. Each student is assigned a grade for each of the assessments. Grades that have an empty circle indicate that the student has not yet turned in that assessment. Assessment topics that have no grades listed for all students, such as "Around the World in 26 Letters," indicate assessments that are in process but not completed.

At the end of the term, teachers must synthesize the information they maintain in their grade books into a single grade. Most often, teachers begin the process of determining term grades by using information from the grade book to calculate a score that summarizes each student's overall performance. In some subject areas, summarization across a term is easy and straightforward. As an example, determining a grade for spelling may be as simple as calculating the average score a student received on all of the weekly spelling tests given during the term. However, for a more complex subject area, such as social studies, the teacher may need to combine information from homework assignments, quizzes, tests, and projects to form a single term grade. While one strategy is to calculate the average score across all of these assignments, the social studies teacher may want to apply more weight to tests and projects, thus making the process of summarizing student performances more complex.

Calculating each student's overall performance has been made easier with the use of spreadsheets and varied computer grading programs. Table 9.4 shows the results of a computer grading program. The scores for each assessment are shown in the columns numbered 1 to 13. The average of each student's assessments is shown on the left of the table under "Average." Scores shown in bold in the "Average" column indicate students who have not completed all the term assessments. Note that synthesizing students' term performance as shown does not produce student grades. The teacher must still apply grading standards to the scores to determine student grades.

Returning to the task of assigning report card grades for spelling, suppose there were 11 spelling tests for each student, each scored on the basis of 100 points. The scores for each student are averaged and the resulting

FIGURE 9.4 *Fifth-Grade Teacher's Grade Book*

Subject Geography / Section 02	Assignment	M	T	W	T	F	M	T	W	T	F	M	T	W	T	F	M	T	W	T	F	M	T	W	T	F
		1	2 (+3)	3 (+2)	4		5 (+3)					6	7	8 (Sit Report)			9	10								
Month		1st week					2nd week					3rd week					4th week					5th week				
Students																											
Abra, G.	1	70	92	79	99	ı	91	ı		√+		81	60	47	√		80	82	85							
Avakian, P.	2	50	95	79	92	ı	90	ı		√+		100	60	86	√+		100	91	100							
Bornstein, E.	3	40	82	47	○	ı	74	ı		○		80	40	ı			80	64	55							
Brooks, P.	4	70	76	89	86	ı	82	ı		√+		93	80	79	√+		90	99	100							
Chang, M.	5	54	84	47	88 88	ı	67	-10		89 39			62				55	66	80							
Chou, C.	6	60	91	84	100	ı	85	ı		√+		91	70	87	√		100	100	95							
Davis, L.	7	49	67	47	○	ı	55	ı		√+		59	40	58	√			68	80							
Garcia, G.	8	70	94	89	100	ı	86	ı		√+		92	40	93	√+		97	100								
Haley, N.	9	69	68	100	83	ı	88	ı		√+		89	80	87	√+			100	90							
Katz, W.	10	30	73	74	100	ı	99	ı		√+		0	20	73			80	77	80							
Morgan, J.	11	39	73	47	98	ı	62	ı		√+		90	70	46			70	100	80							
Nguyen, T.	12	70	76	89	92	ı	78	ı		√+		88	70	67	√		80	99	100							
Ortiz, J.	13	—																								
Rodriguez, H.	14	68	62	79	81	ab	69	ı		√+		31	ab	59	√		70	94	80							
Schmitt, O.	15	63	79	74	98	ı	79	ı		√+		77	80	60	√		95	99								
Vance, N.	16	59	34 60	58	92	ı	75	-10	0			86	100	67	ı			82	80							
Winston, D.	17	71	87	100	85	ı	95	-10				89	100	59	√+		100	100	75							
Zang, E.	18	80	79	100	83	ı	74	-10		√+		6	100	53	√+		95	80	95							
	19																									
	20																									

Assignment labels (columns, written vertically):
Weekly Geo #8 (10) — Oct; Current Event — Oct; Pictonitions Quiz (19); Weekly Geo #9 (14); Around World in 26 Letters (25); Current Event — Nov; Mystery Post Card; American Squares; Weekly Geo #10 (18); Sec 2 Quiz (10) P 26-30; Weekly Geo #11 (15); December Cities; Around World in 20 cards; Weekly Geo #12 (11)

number is used to assign a report card grade. This is a relatively easy task, since each test was scored on the basis of 100 total points and each test was worth the same amount. To calculate the mean or average score, the 11 test scores are summed and then divided by 11.

Let us assume a teacher decided to assign spelling grades using a criterion-referenced approach with the following performance standards: 90 to 100 = A, 80 to 89 = B, 70 to 79 = C, and below 70 = D. The teacher

Student Name	Average	13	12	11	10	9	8	7	6	5	4	3	2	1
Achebe, K.	85.40	95	95	100	100	83	49	35	91	91	96	88	88	88
Ansary, T.	92.20	95	95	88	100	87	100	80	90	91	100	88	95	94
Chapman, G.	**85.16**		95		80	58	88	85	94	82	89	50	85	94
Cunningham, P.	94.40	95	95	100	100	82	88	85	98	100	100	88	95	94
Garcia, W.	86.53	92	92	88	90	75	98	80	83	55	100	100	85	94
Gaspari, F.	95.40	95	95	100	100	92	98	85	100	87	96	94	95	94
Griffiths, C.	74.93	85	95	88	65	82	88	25	76	36	71	88	85	88
Hussein, K.	94.87	95	95	100	100	92	100	85	92	100	100	94	92	94
Jones, T.	91.33	95	95	100	100	88	88	85	83	87	100	94	95	94
Jones, W.	77.67	95	88	100	90	87	63	85	45	64	82	88	88	100
Kelley, W.	77.60	95	95	87	50	58	87	95	63	73	100	56	85	94
Lee, J.	89.13	95	95	100	90	83	75	80	89	73	96	88	95	100
Mulera, R.	80.13	95	92	74	90	81	67	70	75	60	71	88	95	94
Pitzer, S.	82.13	95	95	100	70	83	100	60	65	64	100	88	82	100
Schell, M.	**75.01**		85	100	70	49	56	40	72	73	100	63	85	94
Sickafoose, T.	**89.24**	95	95	99	100	81	99	85	72	91	100	88		100
Stockbridge, J.	90.40	95	100	100	80	91	100	75	80	96	100	100	88	91

TABLE 9.4   COMPUTER GRADING PROGRAM 2004, GEOGRAPHY, TERM I

also decided not to flunk any students in the first term and not to award pluses and minuses, but instead to use only A, B, C, and D as possible grades. It is important to recognize that not all teachers would have made the same decisions. Some might have used a norm-referenced grading system, selected different performance standards, or made adjustments based on effort and motivation. There is no best way to assign grades in all classrooms; we can only discuss the topic in terms of examples that allow us to look at basic issues that should be considered in all grading situations. In this example, the teacher would compare each student's spelling average with the performance standards and then award the corresponding letter grade: All students whose average scores were between 90 and 100 would be given an A, all between 80 and 89 a B, and so on.

This example provides a basic frame of reference for understanding the grading process. It shows how standards come into play in allocating grades, how formal assessment evidence is recorded in a marking book, and how individual scores are averaged to provide a summary of student performance for report card purposes. However, most grading situations are not as simple as this example. Consider the more typical example of Ms. Fogarty's marking book for social studies, shown in Figure 9.5. Notice two important differences between the information Ms. Fogarty has available

FIGURE 9.5 *Marking Book for Social Studies Assessments*

SOCIAL STUDIES

TERM # 1

	HW #1	HW #2	HW #3	HW #4	quiz	quiz	test unit 1	test unit 2	test unit 3	test unit 4	proj. Explor. Amer.	proj. Colon.
Avadis, P.	✓	✓	✓	✓−	85	90	80	85	50	80	B+	B
Babcock, W.	✓	✓	✓	✓−	90	90	85	80	60	80	B	B
Cannata, T.	✓	✓−	✓	✓	80	75	70	70	45	75	C−	C
Farmer, P.	✓+	✓+	✓+	✓	100	95	90	85	70	95	A−	A−
Foster, C.	✓+	✓+	✓	✓	90	80	85	90	65	80	B	B+
Gonzales, E.	✓	✓−	✓−	✓−	70	75	60	70	55	70	C	B−
Grodsky, F.	✓−	✓−	✓−	✓−	65	65	65	60	35	60	C	C
Miarka, S.	✓	✓	✓	✓	80	90	70	85	65	85	C	B
Picardi, O.	✓	✓	✓	✓	75	80	85	75	65	80	B	B−
Ross, O.	✓+	✓	✓	✓	85	80	90	90	75	95	A	A−
Sachar, S.	✓−	✓	✓	✓+	80	85	75	80	40	80	B+	B
Saja, J.	✓	✓	✓	✓	75	80	85	85	50	80	B	B+
Stamos, G.	✓	✓+	✓+	✓	70	60	75	85	50	70	B−	B
Whalem, W.	✓	✓	✓	✓	70	70	50	60	60	70	B−	B−
Yeh, T.	✓+	✓+	✓+	✓+	95	100	95	95	75	95	A	A−

to grade social studies and the information that was available in the spelling example. In spelling, the only formal assessments were the weekly spelling tests. In social studies, Ms. Fogarty has collected many different kinds of assessment information. Four homework assignments, two quiz results, four unit test results, and two projects make up the information Ms. Fogarty can use to assign grades in social studies. In spelling, all test results were expressed numerically, on a scale of 0 to 100. In social studies, different grading formats are used for different assessments: Homework assignments are rated + or −; quizzes and tests are recorded on a scale of 0 to 100; and the two projects are recorded as letter grades. Grading social studies will be a more complicated process than grading spelling.

Despite their differences, both grading processes start out with the same concerns. First, what standard of comparison will be used to award grades? Second, what specific performances will be included in the grade? Let us assume that, in social studies, Ms. Fogarty wishes to use a criterion-referenced grading approach and that she wishes to use pluses and minuses. With this decision made, she must next determine which of the four different kinds of assessment information available to her will be included in the grade. She must not only decide which of these to include, but determine how much each kind of information will count in determining the grades. For example, should a project count as much as a unit test? Should two quizzes count as much as one unit test or four homework assignments? These are questions all teachers face when they try to combine different kinds of assessment information into a single indicator. The following sections contain suggestions for answering such questions.

What Should Be Included in a Grade?

Figure 9.5 shows four different formal indicators of Ms. Fogarty's students' academic performance: homework, quizzes, unit tests, and projects. In addition to these formal indicators, Ms. Fogarty also has many informal, unrecorded perceptions about each student's effort, participation in class, interest, behavior, and home situation. Should all the formal and informal information be included in her students' grades?

Almost all teachers would include the unit tests and the project results in determining their students' grades. These are formal, summative indicators of student achievement that should be reflected in the grade a student receives. Most teachers rightly assign grades based mainly on formal assessments. Many teachers would also include quiz results and homework, although there would be less unanimity among teachers on this point. For some teachers, the purpose of giving quizzes and homework is to provide students with practice activities that are more closely tied to instruction than to assessment. For other teachers, the purpose of homework and quizzes is to assess how well students have learned their daily lessons. When the purpose for assigning homework and quizzes focuses on instructional activities, then it makes sense not to count them as part of a grade. However, when the purpose for assigning homework and quizzes is to provide assessment information, then it is logical to include them as part of a grade.

Some teachers view quizzes and homework as more closely tied to the instructional process than to the grading process.

Let us assume that Ms. Fogarty has decided to include three types of formal assessment information in her students' social studies grades: tests, projects, and quizzes. Let us also assume that she has decided not to include a formal rating of each student's effort, participation, interest, and behavior. Having decided what student performances will be included, she now must determine whether each kind of information will count equally or whether some kinds should be weighted more heavily than others.

Selecting Weights for Assessment Information

An immediate concern in summarizing student performance on different kinds of evidence is how each should be weighted. In general, teachers should give the more important types of student performance (e.g., tests, projects, and portfolios) more weight than short quizzes or homework assignments, since the former provide a more complete, integrated and valid view of students' subject matter learning. Ms. Fogarty decided that unit tests and projects should count equally and that both should count more than quiz results. She was fairly certain that she had used valid tests that reflected the important aspects of her instruction and that the projects assigned required students to integrate their knowledge about the topic. Thus, she was confident in using tests and projects as the main components of her social studies grade. Finally, she decided that the two quizzes would count as much as one unit test.

Although many teachers do not count homework directly in determining grades, they often warn students that if more than three or four homework assignments are not turned in, their report card grade will be lowered. Used this way, homework becomes more an indicator of effort or cooperation than of subject matter mastery. This lowers the validity and clarity of the grade. Some teachers do not actually compute student homework averages, but rely instead on an informal "sense" or "intuition" of how a student has performed. Although timesaving, this practice allows subjective factors such as the student's behavior or interest in the subject matter to influence the teacher's judgment. Neither lowering student grades for missed homework assignments nor determining grades on the basis of an informal sense of student performance is recommended.

Regardless of how a teacher weights each kind of assessment information, it is strongly suggested that the weightings be simple. It is better to weight some things twice as much as others than to weight some five times as much and others seven times as much. Except in rare cases when a student's performance varies widely across different types of assessment information, the final grades arrived at by using a simple weighting scheme will not differ greatly from those arrived at by using a more complex, cumbersome weighting scheme.

Methods for weighing the various types of assessment information should be kept simple.

After deciding on her weightings for quizzes, unit tests, and projects, Ms. Fogarty identified seven pieces of information that she would combine to determine her students' report card grades in social studies:

- One overall assessment of quiz results
- Four scores from the unit tests
- Two project grades

In the final weightings, quiz results count one-seventh of the grade, unit tests count four-sevenths of the grade, and projects count two-sevenths of the grade. Ms. Fogarty next had to combine the available information according to the selected weights.

Combining Different Assessment Information

Figure 9.5 shows that student performance on different assessments often is represented in different ways. Somehow Ms. Fogarty must combine the selected scoring formats into a single summary score that includes performance on tests, projects, and quizzes. Some of the information shown in Figure 9.5 will have to be changed into another format, preferably a numerical one. This means that the project letter grades will have to be converted into numerical scores on a scale of 0 to 100 percent, so that they will correspond to the scores for the quizzes and unit tests.

It is important to stress that all performance indicators should be expressed in terms of the same scale, so that they can be combined meaningfully. As another example, suppose a teacher gave two tests, one with 50 items and one with 100 items, and that the teacher wanted each test to count equally in determining a student's grade. Now suppose that two students, Terence and Marcus, each got a perfect score on one of the tests and a zero score on the other: Marcus got his perfect score on the 50-item test and Terence got his on the 100-item test. Because the tests are to count equally, one would think that the students' grades should be the same regardless of the number of items on each test. However, if the teacher calculates the average performance for Marcus and Terence using the number of items they got right across both tests, the resulting averages will be quite different: Marcus's average would be 25 (50 + 0)/2 = 25) and Terence's average would be 50 (0 + 100)/2 = 50). Terence would get a higher grade than Marcus, even though they each attained a perfect score on one test and a zero score on another and the tests were to count equally. Clearly, combining raw scores (or numbers of items correct) and finding their average does not give equal weight to each test.

Each type of assessment information should be expressed in terms of the same scale so that all can be combined into a composite score.

The problem in the preceding example is that the teacher did not take into account the difference in the number of items on the two tests; the teacher did not put the two tests on the same scale before computing an average. If the teacher had changed the scores from number of items correct to percentage of items correct *before* averaging, Marcus and Terence would have had the same overall performance [Marcus = (100 + 0)/2 = 50; Terence = (0 + 100)/2 = 50]. Or if the teacher had expressed performance on both tests in terms of the 100-point test, the averages would have been the same, since Marcus's perfect score on a 50-item test would be worth 100 points on a 100-point scale. Once again, if scores are not expressed in a common scale, student performance will be distorted and grades will not reflect actual achievement.

Returning to Ms. Fogarty's grading task, a way must be found to express project performance on a scale that corresponds to the 0-to-100-percent scale used for quizzes and unit tests. She decided that for project grades, the following scale would be used to assign numerical scores to the projects: 95 = A, 92 = A−, 88 = B+, 85 = B, 82 = B−, 78 = C+, 75 = C, 72 = C−, 68 = D+, 65 = D, 62 = D−, less than 60 = F. If, for example, a student got a B− on one of the projects, that student's numerical score on the project would be 82. When Ms. Fogarty applied these values to the projects, she ended up with the information shown in Table 9.5. It is important to note that Ms. Fogarty's method is not the only way that the different scores could be put on the same scale. It is, however, one way

	Quiz 1	Quiz 2	Test 1	Test 2	Test 3	Test 4	Proj. 1	Proj. 2
TABLE 9.5	SOCIAL STUDIES ASSESSMENT SCORES PLACED ON THE SAME SCALE, SOCIAL STUDIES, TERM 1							
Avadis, P.	85	90	80	85	50	80	88	85
Babcock, W.	90	90	85	80	60	80	85	85
Cannata, T.	80	75	70	70	45	70	72	70
Farmer, P.	100	95	90	85	70	95	92	92
Foster, C.	90	80	85	90	65	80	85	88
Gonzales, E.	70	75	60	70	55	70	75	82
Grodsky, F.	65	65	65	60	35	60	75	75
Miarka, S.	80	90	70	85	65	85	75	85
Picardi, O.	75	80	85	75	65	80	85	82
Ross, O.	85	80	90	90	75	95	95	92
Sachar, S.	80	85	75	80	40	80	88	85
Saja, J.	75	80	85	85	50	80	85	88
Stamos, G.	70	60	75	85	50	70	82	85
Whalem, W.	70	70	50	60	60	70	82	82
Yeh, T.	95	100	95	95	75	95	95	92

she could accomplish her task with a method she felt comfortable using. With this task completed, Ms. Fogarty has to confront one additional issue prior to computing grades.

Validity of the Information

Before combining assessment information into a grade, the quality of that information must be considered. Grades will be only as meaningful as the information on which they are based. If the project grades were assigned subjectively, with no clear criteria in mind and with shifting teacher attention during scoring, they will not accurately reflect student achievement. If the unit tests were unfair to students or did not test a representative sample of what was taught, the scores students attained will not be valid indicators of their achievement. In this regard, Ms. Fogarty should examine the results of the unit 3 test, since they were much lower than scores on the other unit tests (see Figure 9.5). Do these scores indicate a problem with the test or a problem with the effort students put into preparing for the test? How should this result be handled in grading? These questions must be answered before information can be combined and used for grading.

Grades are only as meaningful (valid) as the information on which they are based.

Most teachers assume that unexpectedly low test scores are the result of a faulty assessment instrument, while unexpectedly high scores are the result of superior teaching.

Ms. Fogarty noticed the poor performance on the unit 3 test when she scored the test, and no doubt asked herself why the scores were so low. Normally, questions about the match between an assessment instrument and the things students were taught occur *before* an assessment instrument is used. Sometimes, however, mismatches are overlooked or do not become apparent until after the instrument is administered and scored. When Ms. Fogarty looked over the items in the unit 3 test (a textbook test), and compared the items with the topics and skills she had taught in that unit, she found that a large number of the test items had come from a section of the textbook that she had decided not to teach. By oversight she had failed to remove the items. Thus, the match between the unit test and classroom instruction was not good, and her students had been penalized by being asked questions about material they had not been taught. Clearly, the unit 3 test scores did not reflect her students' actual achievement and, if used in grading, would reduce the validity of the grades.

If unexpectedly low scores on some part of a test indicate a mismatch with instruction, then grading adjustments should be made.

To avoid this, Ms. Fogarty decided to change the students' scores on the unit 3 test to better reflect their achievement. This change made her grades better reflect her students' subject matter mastery. Low assessment scores should not be raised simply because they are low or because the teacher is disappointed with them.

Computing Overall Scores

Having decided on score equivalents for the project assessments and having adjusted scores on the unit 3 test to correct the partial mismatch between instruction and assessment, Ms. Fogarty is ready to compute her students' social studies grades. To do this, she must (1) give each kind of assessment information the weight she decided on, (2) sum the scores, and (3) divide by 7, which is the number of assessment items she is using to grade (one overall quiz score, four unit test scores, and two project scores). This computation will provide an average social studies score for each student's marking period. Table 9.6 shows the seven components to be included in each student's grade, their total, and their average. To make her task simpler, Ms. Fogarty decided that all fractions would be rounded off to the nearest whole number.

Strictly speaking, the actual weight that a particular assessment carries in determining a grade depends on the spread of scores on that assessment compared with the spread of scores on other assessments (Frisbie and Waltman, 1992). The greater the spread of scores on an assessment, the greater the influence that assessment will have on the final grade when averaged with other assessments. Fairly simple and straightforward techniques are available for equalizing the influence of assessments whose scores are widely spread. However, this is not a major problem with most classroom assessments because they are similar in format, are given to the same group of students, cover topics taught in instruction, and are scored

	Quizzes	Test 1	Test 2	Test 3	Test 4	Proj. 1	Proj. 2	Total Score	Average
Avadis, P.	88	80	85	70	80	88	85	576	82
Babcock, W.	90	85	80	80	80	85	85	585	84
Cannata, T.	78	70	70	65	70	72	70	495	71
Farmer, P.	98	90	85	90	95	92	92	642	92
Foster, C.	85	85	90	85	80	85	88	598	85
Gonzales, E.	73	60	70	75	70	75	82	505	72
Grodsky, F.	65	65	60	55	60	75	75	455	65
Miarka, S.	85	70	85	85	85	75	85	570	81
Picardi, O.	78	85	75	85	80	85	82	570	81
Ross, O.	83	90	90	95	95	95	92	640	91
Sachar, S.	83	75	80	60	80	88	85	551	79
Saja, J.	78	85	85	70	80	85	88	571	82
Stamos, G.	65	75	85	70	70	82	85	532	76
Whalem, W.	70	50	60	80	70	82	82	494	71
Yeh, T.	98	95	95	95	95	95	92	665	95

TABLE 9.6   COMPUTATION OF STUDENTS' SOCIAL STUDIES GRADES, SOCIAL STUDIES, TERM I

in the same way. Under these conditions, the spread of scores on different assessments will usually be close enough so that adjustments need not be made. Table 9.6 shows that the difference between the highest and lowest score on each of the seven assessments is 33 for the quiz score; 45, 35, 40, and 35 for the four unit tests; and 23 and 22 for the two projects. These ranges are similar enough to permit the seven components to be added and averaged to determine an overall student score.

Table 9.6 shows the final average of each student after each piece of assessment information was weighted in the way Ms. Fogarty chose. Consider P. Avadis's scores in the table. This student received a total quiz score of 88, based on the average of two quizzes rounded off to a whole number. The four test scores—with 20 points added to the unit 3 score—are shown in the table. The two project grades are expressed in terms of the numerical equivalents Ms. Fogarty selected. Adding these scores gives a total score of 576, which, when divided by 7 (for the seven pieces of information that were combined), gives an average performance of 82. The average for each student gives an indication of the proportion of social studies objectives each student achieved in the marking period. Notice that this interpretation is only appropriate if Ms. Fogarty's various assessments are scored in terms of percentage mastery and if they are a fair and representative assessment of the things that were taught. Ms. Fogarty can now apply her performance standards to award students' grades.

TWO APPROACHES TO ASSIGNING GRADES

Here we return again to our basic distinction between norm- and criterion-referenced grading.

A Criterion-Referenced Example

Ms. Fogarty decided to assign grades based on a criterion-referenced approach because she felt that this approach gave each student a chance to get a good grade if he or she mastered what was taught. The performance standards Ms. Fogarty adopted for her social studies grades follow:

A	= 94 or higher	C	= 74 to 76
A−	= 90 to 93	C−	= 70 to 73
B+	= 87 to 89	D+	= 67 to 69
B	= 84 to 86	D	= 64 to 66
B−	= 80 to 83	D−	= 60 to 63
C+	= 77 to 79	F	= less than 60

Looking at the overall semester averages as shown in Table 9.6, Ms. Fogarty can apply her performance standards to award grades. At this juncture she is likely to consider students' nonacademic characteristics. For example, she may say to herself, "This student has worked so hard this term despite an unsettled home situation that it's amazing she was able to focus on her schoolwork at all," or "There is so little positive reinforcement in this child's life right now that a failing grade would absolutely crush him, even though his performance has been very poor." In short, Ms. Fogarty, like most teachers, is aware of her responsibility to grade students primarily on their academic performance, but allows herself some room for small individual adjustments. Opinions will always differ about making such grading adjustments, as the following excerpts show.

I grade strictly by the numbers. I calculate each student's average and assign grades based strictly on that average. A 79.4 average is not an 80 average, and thus will get a C+. This is the only way I can be fair to all students.

I calculate the averages based on tests and assignments just like the books say to. But when it comes time to assign the grade, I know I'm not grading an average, I'm grading a kid I know and spend time with every day. I know how the kid has behaved, how much effort has been put into my class, and what effect a high or low grade will have on him or her. I know about the pressure the kid gets from parents and what reaction they will have to a particular grade. If I didn't know about these things, grading would be much easier.

When Ms. Fogarty applied her performance standards to her class averages, the grades awarded to each student were as follows:

Name	Average	Grade	Name	Average	Grade
Avadis, P.	82	B–	Picardi, O.	81	B–
Babcock, W.	84	B	Ross, O.	91	A–
Cannata, T.	71	C–	Sachar, S.	79	C+
Farmer, P.	92	A–	Saja, J.	82	B–
Foster, C.	85	B	Stamos, G.	76	C
Gonzales, E.	72	C–	Whalem, W.	71	C–
Grodsky, F.	65	D	Yeh, T.	95	A
Miarka, S.	81	B–			

Notice that students Sachar and Stamos are within one point of the performance standard for the next higher grade. It is for students who are close to reaching the next higher grade that the teacher's judgments about nonacademic characteristics usually enter into grading.

Teachers' judgments about nonacademic characteristics often enter into grading when the student is close to reaching the next higher grade level.

To summarize, Ms. Fogarty had to make many decisions to arrive at these grades. She had to decide whether to use a norm-referenced or a criterion-referenced grading approach. Having selected the criterion-referenced approach, she had to decide on performance standards for awarding grades. Next she had to decide on the kinds of assessment information that would be included in her grades and how to weight each kind. Ms. Fogarty then had to decide how to put all assessment scores on the same scale because some information was expressed in percentage scores and other information as letter grades. Then she had to decide whether to adjust any scores because of faulty instruments. Finally, she had to decide whether to base her grades solely on the students' average academic performance or to alter them slightly because of affective or personal characteristics (Borich, 2003; Tombari and Borich, 1999). Teachers with different classes and in different schools likely would have made different decisions from Ms. Fogarty, but all would have had to confront the same issues. Key Assessment Tools 9.1 summarizes the steps in the grading process.

A Norm-Referenced Example

Consider how Ms. Fogarty would have assigned grades if she had chosen a norm-referenced grading approach. In this case, she would have decided in advance on a grading curve that identified the percentage of students that she wanted to receive each grade. Suppose she used a norm-referenced curve that gave the top 20 percent of the students an A, the next 20 percent a B, the next 40 percent a C, and the last 20 percent a D.

In norm-referenced grading, a teacher decides in advance the percentage of students receiving each grade.

Key Assessment Tools 9.1

STEPS IN THE GRADING PROCESS

1. Select a standard of comparison (norm-referenced or criterion-referenced).
2. Select types of performances (tests, projects, etc.).
3. Assign weights for each type of performance.
4. Record the number of points earned out of the total possible points for *each individual performance* graded.
5. Total the points earned for *each type of performance* and divide this by the total number of possible points. This gives a percentage for each type of performance.
6. Multiply each of these percentages by the weights assigned.
7. Sum the totals and apply the chosen standard of comparison with the totals.
8. Review the grades and make adjustments if necessary.

To assign grades using this norm-referenced curve, Ms. Fogarty must first arrange the students from highest to lowest average score. The norm-referenced ordering for Ms. Fogarty's class follows:

Name	Score	Name	Score
Yeh, T.	95	Miarka, S.	81
Farmer, P.	92	Sachar, S.	79
Ross, O.	91	Stamos, G.	76
Foster, C.	85	Gonzales, E.	72
Babcock, W.	84	Cannata, T.	71
Avadis, P.	82	Whalem, W.	71
Saja, J.	82	Grodsky, F.	65
Picardi, O.	81		

In norm-referenced grading, two students who achieve the same score must receive the same grade, regardless of the curve used.

Because there are 15 students in the class, 20 percent of the class is three students. Thus, Yeh, Farmer, and Ross, the three highest-scoring students, received A grades. The next 20 percent of the students—Foster, Babcock, and Avadis—received B grades. The next 40 percent of the class (six students) were given C grades. Finally, the last 20 percent of the class—Cannata, Whalem, and Grodsky—received D grades. In assigning grades by the norm-referenced approach, it is important to bear in mind that two students who attain the same score must receive the same grade, regardless of the curve being used. Notice the differences in the grade distributions under the norm-referenced and the criterion-referenced approaches. Remember that these differences are mainly the result of decisions made about the grading curve or performance standards that are used. Regardless of the method of grading adopted, it is extremely important for the teacher to be able to explain the grading process to students, parents, and administrators. Key Assessment Tools 9.2 lists the guidelines for grading.

Software can help teachers keep grade books, calculate grades, and store and organize test items.

Key Assessment Tools 9.2

GUIDELINES FOR GRADING

- The chosen grading system is consistent with the purpose of grading.
- Data for grading are gathered throughout the grading period.
- Varied pieces of data are collected (tests, projects, quizzes, etc.).
- Students are informed about the system used to grade them.
- The grading system separates subject matter achievements from nonacademic performance (effort, motivation, etc.). Nonacademic performance is evaluated independently of subject matter performance.
- Grading is based on valid and reliable assessment evidence.
- Important evidence of achievement is weighted more than less important evidence (e.g., tests weighted more than quizzes).
- The grading system is applied consistently across all pupils.

OTHER METHODS OF REPORTING STUDENT PROGRESS

Report card grades are the most common way that students and their parents are kept informed of how things are going in the classroom. But the functionality of grades is limited because they are usually provided infrequently, provide little *specific* information about how a student is performing, and rarely include information about the teacher's perceptions of a student's effort, motivation, cooperation, and classroom demeanor. Moreover, since report card grades usually reflect student performance on a variety of assessment tasks, it is quite possible for two students to receive the same grade but have performed very differently on the assessments used to determine the grade. Because of these limitations, other approaches for reporting students' school progress also are needed and used by teachers. Key Assessment Tools 9.3 lists the many ways teachers can communicate and interact with parents. Each of these forms of communication can provide important supplementary information that rounds out the picture of a student's life at school.

Grades are the most common device by which students and parents are kept informed about how things are going in the classroom.

To have a complete and specific picture of their child's school performance, parents must receive more than the report card.

Parent-Teacher Conferences

Unlike the one-way communication provided by report cards, parent-teacher conferences allow flexible, two-way communication. Conferences permit discussion, elaboration, and explanation of student performance. In addition to providing information to parents about their child's performance in school, the teacher can acquire information from the parents about their concerns and perceptions of their child's school experience. Information can also be obtained about special problems the student is

Unlike grades, parent-teacher conferences provide flexible, two-way communication.

Key Assessment Tools 9.3
OPTIONS FOR PARENT-TEACHER COMMUNICATION

- Report cards
- Weekly or monthly progress reports
- Parents' nights
- School visitation days
- Parent-teacher conferences
- Phone calls
- Letters
- Class or school newsletter
- Papers and work products

---

having, from physical and emotional problems to problems of classroom adjustment. Parents can inform the teacher of their concerns and ask questions about their child's classroom behavior and about the curriculum being taught. Preschool teachers or those who teach the last grade of elementary or middle school will often be asked by parents to recommend the type of school, teacher, or academic program that is most suitable for their child. Certainly a parent-teacher conference can address a broader range of issues and concerns than a report card grade can.

Parents indicate that parent-teacher conferences are vastly more useful than report cards in understanding children's progress in school.

Moreover, parents learn a great deal about their children's performance from parent-teacher conferences. A study by Shepard and Bliem (1995) based on information obtained from a sample of elementary school parents examined the usefulness of report cards, parent-teacher discussions, standardized tests, and graded examples of students' schoolwork for parents' understanding of their child's progress in school. Ninety-four percent of the parents indicated that discussions with teachers were useful or very useful in understanding their child's progress, and 90 percent also said that receiving graded examples of their child's work was useful or very useful. Only 76 percent of the parents felt that report cards were useful or very useful for informing them about their child's school progress. Thirty-six percent cited standardized tests as useful or very useful for informing them about progress. Clearly, parents value information beyond report cards to indicate how their children are performing in school.

It is natural for teachers to feel somewhat uneasy at the prospect of a conference with parents. Teachers will want to be respected by the parents, will not want a confrontational experience, and may have to tell parents some unpleasant things about their child. Because teachers will have certain things they want the parents to know and because there is always an element of uncertainty about the way the conference will go, it is recommended that teachers prepare an agenda of the things they want to cover. Parents will probably do this also. For example, most teachers will want to provide a description of the student's academic and social classroom performance. They will also want to ask the parents questions such as

"Does your child act this way at home?" and "What does he say about the workload in school?" Certainly teachers will want to give parents the opportunity to ask questions. Parents are most likely to ask questions such as "What are my child's current levels in reading and math?" "How is my child's behavior in class?" "Does she get along with her classmates?" or "Why did my son get a C– in math?" Finally, teachers, in conjunction with the parents, may want to plan a course of action to help the student. The course agreed on should prescribe actions to be performed by teachers, parents, and students. Teachers may want a counselor or administrator to attend the conference if it is likely to be confrontational.

Planning conferences is necessary to accomplish such agendas. The individual teacher will want to gather samples of the student's work—perhaps in a portfolio—and identify (with examples) particular behavioral or attitudinal issues that should be raised. If there is a major existing or potential problem, the teacher ought to look over the student's permanent record file in the school office to see whether the problem surfaced in other grades. All of this preparation should be done before the conference.

Finally, the teacher will want to locate a comfortable, private spot to hold the conference. Usually this means before or after school in the teacher's classroom, when students are not present. If this is the case, provide suitable, adult-sized chairs for the parents. The authors are veterans of many elementary school conferences in which the teacher sat comfortably behind his or her desk and the authors were scrunched down in a primary-sized student chair, knees near their chin, trying to get comfortable while participating in a productive conference. Conferences work better when they are private and undisturbed, and when all parties are comfortably situated.

Conferences should be private, undisturbed, and well planned.

Tips for a Successful Parent-Teacher Conference

The following tips can help the actual parent-teacher conference proceed successfully.

1. *Set a proper tone.* This means making parents feel welcome, maintaining a positive attitude, and remembering that a student is not "their" concern or "your" concern, but a mutual concern. If possible, find out what parents want to know before the conference so that you can prepare for their questions. Don't do all the talking; be a good listener and use the conference to find out parents' perceptions and concerns. Talk in terms parents will understand; avoid educational jargon, such as "discovery learning," "rubrics," "higher-order thinking skills," or "prosocial behavior," which will confuse rather than clarify discussion. Providing examples of student work from portfolios, performance assessments, and scoring rubrics can help parents understand classroom expectations and student performance.

2. *Be frank with parents, but convey both the student's strengths and weaknesses.* Do not hold back unpleasant information because you think the parents will become confrontational. The aim of parent-teacher conferences is for each party to understand and help the student. It is the

Teachers must maintain their professional demeanor during parent-teacher conferences.

teacher's responsibility to raise issues with parents that will help the student, even though discussion of those issues might be unpleasant. If you do not know the answer to a question, do not bluff. Tell the parents you do not know the answer, then research it after the conference and follow up by relaying it to the parents.

3. *Do not talk about other students or colleagues by name or by implication.* Never belittle colleagues or the principal in front of parents, no matter what your feelings. Saying things like "Last year's teacher did not prepare Rosalie well in math" or "Teachers get so little support for their ideas from the principal" is inappropriate. True or not, it is not professional to discuss such issues with parents. Do not compare a child with other students by name or show parents other students' work, test scores, or grades. Teachers are professionals and they have an obligation to act professionally. This means being truthful with parents, not demeaning colleagues in front of parents, concentrating discussion only on the parents' child, and not discussing information from the conference with other teachers. This caution is appropriate for all forms of parent-teacher interaction.

4. *If a course of remedial action for the student seems appropriate, plan the action jointly with the parents.* Make both parties responsible for implementing the plan: "I will try to do these things with Janessa in class, and you will try to do these other things with her at home."

5. *Finally, summarize the conference before the parents leave.* Review the main points and any decisions or courses of action that have been agreed on.

Key Assessment Tools 9.4 supplements these guidelines with other useful suggestions.

Parent-teacher conferences can be very useful to both teachers and parents if planned and conducted successfully. They allow the teacher to supplement his or her information about the student and the parents to obtain a broader understanding of their child's school performance. The main drawback to parent-teacher conferences is that they are time-consuming. Recognizing the value of conferences as well as the time required to hold productive conferences, many school districts set aside a day or two in the school calendar specifically for parent conferencing.

Additional Reporting Methods

A common method of informing parents about their child's school performance is to either send examples of schoolwork home or to collect it in a portfolio to be examined during a parent-teacher conference or school open house. Periodic newsletters, often written and assembled by students, can be sent home. If a teacher has developed or selected a scoring rubric, a copy of the rubric with the student's level of performance circled can be used to provide information about an area of the student's learning.

Key Assessment Tools 9.4

PARENT-TEACHER CONFERENCES

1. Prepare for the conference by gathering samples of the student's work and identifying issues to discuss with parents; if possible, find out what parents want to know before the conference.

2. Find a private, comfortable location for the conference.

3. Set a proper tone by:

   a. Remembering that the student is of mutual concern to you and the parents

   b. Listening to the parents' perspectives and concerns

   c. Avoiding educational jargon, yet giving concrete examples

   d. Being frank with parents when conveying the student's strengths and weaknesses

4. Admit to not knowing the answer to a question and be willing to find out; do not try to bluff parents.

5. Do not talk about or belittle other colleagues or students by name or implication; do not compare one student with another by name.

6. If a remedial action is agreed on, plan the action jointly with parents and make each party responsible for part of the plan.

7. Orally review and summarize decisions and planned actions at the end of the conference.

8. Write summary notes of the conference.

Letters and phone calls to parents are used mainly to inform parents of a special problem that has occurred and, as such, should be used infrequently by teachers. Regular written or phone communication between a teacher and a parent is very rare and occurs only if the parent specifically requests frequent written progress reports and the teacher agrees to provide them.

With increasing access to e-mail in schools and in homes, e-mail is fast becoming a useful tool for communicating with parents. While writing e-mails may require more time than a phone call, e-mail has several advantages. First, it allows the teacher and the parent time to reflect on each other's questions and comments before responding. Second, e-mail provides opportunities for a teacher to consult other people in the school, be they counselors, school psychologists, colleagues, or the principal, before responding to a parent's inquiry. Third, e-mail provides a concrete paper trail of what was said and what was decided. Finally, e-mail can allow a teacher with limited time during the school day to connect with a parent whose schedule also may be busy during the day. When writing to parents, whether it be in the form of a traditional letter or e-mail, it is extremely important that your message be accurate, professional, and follow appropriate writing conventions (i.e., be free of spelling and grammatical errors and not use slang terms). A poorly written communication can lead a parent to form a negative impression of a teacher and undermine the substantive message the teacher was trying to convey to the parent.

CHAPTER SUMMARY

- The process of judging the quality of a student's performance is called grading. The single most important characteristic of the grading process is its dependence on teacher judgment, which is always subjective to some degree.
- Grading is a difficult task for teachers because they have had little formal instruction in grading; they must make judgments based on incomplete evidence; they have conflicting classroom roles; they must not allow students' personal characteristics and circumstances to distort subject matter judgments; and there is no single, universally accepted grading strategy.
- When grading, the teacher's prime aims are to be fair to all students and to reflect students' learning of the subject matter.
- The main purpose of report card grades is to communicate information about student achievement. Grades serve administrative, informational, motivational, and guidance functions.
- All grades represent a comparison of student performance with some standard of excellence or quality.
- Norm-referenced grades compare a student's performance with that of other students in the class. Students with the highest scores receive the designated number of high grades as defined by the grading curve.
- Criterion-referenced grades compare a student's performance with a predefined standard of mastery. There is no limit on the number of students who can receive a particular grade.
- Basing grades on comparisons between a student's performance and the student's perceived ability or record of improvement is not recommended.
- After selecting the comparative basis for grading, the teacher next must decide which student performances will be considered in awarding grades. For subject matter grades it is recommended that student performances that demonstrate mastery of the subject matter be included in the grade. Effort, motivation, participation, and behavior should not be major parts of subject matter grades.
- Grading requires teachers to summarize many different types of information into a single score. More important types of student performance such as tests and projects should be weighted most heavily in arriving at a grade.
- To summarize various types of information, each type must be expressed in the same way and on the same scale, usually a percentage scale.
- Before combining information into a grade, the quality of each piece of selected assessment information should be reviewed and adjustments made if invalid assessment information is found. Grades will be only as valid as the assessment information on which they are based.

- Grading information should be expanded and supplemented by other means of parent-teacher communication, such as conferences, open houses, progress reports, and papers and projects sent home.

QUESTIONS FOR DISCUSSION

1. What are the purposes of giving grades to students? How well do different grading formats fulfill these purposes?
2. What are a teacher's responsibilities to students when assigning grades on a paper, test, or project? What additional responsibilities to students do teachers have when they assign report card grades?
3. Is the task of assigning report card grades the same for elementary and high school teachers? How might the process of assigning grades differ at the two levels?
4. How can the information on report cards be supplemented and made more informative for parents and students?
5. What are possible impacts, both good and bad, of grades on students? What can be done to lessen the detrimental impact of grades?

ACTIVITY

Table 9A contains information that a teacher accumulated about her students during a marking period. Use this information to assign a report card grade to each student. Answer the questions that follow the table.

TABLE 9A   GRADING ACTIVITY

Student	Test 1	2	3	4	Project	Class Participation	General Effort	Quizzes and Homework	Behavior	Student's Ability (Estimate)
Malcolm	40	60	55	100	A–	Good	G	G	G	M
Tiffany	90	95	45	85	A	Excellent	Ex	Ex	Ex	H
Jason	70	65	20	30	C	Excellent	G	P	P	M
Thomas	85	80	50	85	B–	Poor	P	G	P	H
Gretta	70	70	15	65	D	Good	Ex	P	Ex	L
Susan	45	75	45	100	C	Excellent	Ex	G	G	M
Maya	75	80	45	75	B–	Good	G	G	G	M
Maria	70	75	30	70	A	Excellent	G	G	G	M
Oscar	80	90	45	85	C	Poor	P	P	P	M
Angelina	30	40	10	40	D–	Poor	Ex	P	Ex	L
James	60	60	15	45	D	Poor	P	P	P	H

1. Will you use a norm-referenced or a criterion-referenced grading approach? Why?
2. Will you include all the information in the table in determining a grade or only some of the information? State what you will and will not include and explain why.
3. Will all the pieces of information you have decided to include count equally, or will some things count more than others?
4. How will you take into account the different representation of student performance on different pieces of information (e.g., percentages, letter grades, excellent-good-poor, high-middle-low)?
5. What, if anything, will you do about test 3?
6. How will you summarize the different pieces of information into a single score or rating?
7. What will be your grading curve (norm-referenced) or performance standards (criterion-referenced) for awarding grades?
8. What grade would each student receive?
9. In what ways is this exercise artificial? That is, would there be a difference between the way you graded these students and the way a teacher who had actually taught them for the marking period would grade them?
10. If you graded the students in a norm-referenced way, go back and regrade using a criterion-referenced approach. If you graded the students using a criterion-referenced approach, go back and regrade using a norm-referenced approach.
11. What are the strengths and weaknesses of the grading system you have developed?

REVIEW QUESTIONS

1. What are grades, and why are they important? Why do schools and teachers give grades?
2. What questions must a teacher answer in order to carry out the grading process? What teacher judgments must be made in the grading process? Why is there no single best way to assign grades to students?
3. In what way is all grading based on comparison? What common methods of comparison are used in grading and how do they differ? What is the difference between norm- and criterion-referenced grading? Which method would you use and why?
4. What are the advantages and disadvantages of norm- and criterion-referenced grading? What are the advantages and disadvantages of grading accommodations made for students with disabilities?
5. Why should grades be determined mostly by the academic performances of students, rather than other information a teacher has about students?
6. What information should a teacher provide students about the grading process?
7. What other methods exist for reporting student progress?

REFERENCES

Borich, G. D. (2003). *Effective teaching methods,* 5th ed. Englewood Cliffs, NJ: Prentice-Hall.

Brookhart, S. M. (1992). *Teachers' grading practices: Meaning and values.* Paper presented at the annual meeting of the American Educational Research Association, San Francisco.

Brookhart, S. M. (1999). Teaching about communicating assessment results and grading. *Educational Measurement: Issues and Practice, 18*(1), 5–13.

Bursuck, W. D., Polloway, E. A., Plante, L., Epstein, M. H., Jayanthi, M., and McConeghy, J. (1996). Report card grading adaptations: A national survey of classroom practices. *Exceptional Children, 62*(4), 301–318.

Friedman, S. J., and Frisbie, D. A. (1993). *The validity of report cards as indicators of student performance.* Paper presented at the annual meeting of the National Council on Measurement in Education, Atlanta.

Frisbie, D. A., and Waltman, K. K. (1992). Developing a personal grading plan. *Educational Measurement: Issues and Practice, 11*(3), 35–42.

Gardner, H. (1995). *Frames of mind: The theory of multiple intelligences.* New York: Basic Books.

Griswold, P. A., and Griswold, M. M. (1992). *The grading contingency: Graders' beliefs and expectations and the assessment ingredients.* Paper presented at the annual meeting of the American Educational Research Association, San Francisco.

Guskey, T. R., and Bailey, J. M. (2001). *Developing grading and reporting systems for student learning.* Thousand Oaks, CA: Corwin Press.

Hubelbank, J. H. (1994). *Meaning of elementary school teachers' grades.* Unpublished dissertation, Boston College, Chestnut Hill, MA.

Kubiszyn, T., and Borich, G. (2003). *Educational testing and measurement,* 7th ed. New York: Wiley.

Munk, D. D., and Bursuck, W. D. (2003). Grading students with disabilities. *Educational Leadership, 61*(2), 38–43.

Nava, F. J., and Loyd, B. (1992). *The effect of student characteristics on the grading process.* Paper presented at the annual meeting of the National Council on Measurement in Education, San Francisco.

Polloway, E. A., Epstein, M. H., Bursuck, W. D., Roderique, T. W., McConeghy, J. L., and Jayanthi, M. (1994). Classroom grading: A national survey of politics. *Remedial and Special Education, 15*(3), 162–170.

Salend, S. J. (2001). *Creating inclusive classrooms: Effective and reflective practices,* 4th ed. Upper Saddle River, NJ: Merrill/Prentice-Hall.

Shepard, L., and Bliem, C. (1995). Parents' thinking about standardized tests and performance assessment. *Educational Researcher, 24,* 25–32.

Tombari, M., and Borich, G. (1999). *Authentic assessment in the classroom.* Upper Saddle River, NJ: Prentice-Hall.

Valdes, K. A., Williamson, C. L., and Wagner, M. M. (1990). *The national longitudinal transition study of special education students,* Vol. 1. Menlo Park, CA: SRI International.

CHAPTER 10

COMMERCIAL STANDARDIZED ACHIEVEMENT TESTS

KEY TOPICS

- *How Commercial Achievement Tests Are Created*

- *Administering the Test*

- *Interpreting Scores*

- *Types of Standardized Test Scores*

- *Three Examples of Test Interpretation*

- *The Validity of Commercial Achievement Tests*

After reading this chapter, you will be able to:

- Define terms related to standardized testing
- State differences between teacher-made, commercial, and statewide tests in terms of objectives, construction, and scoring
- Interpret commercial achievement test results
- Identify factors that influence the validity and reliability of commercial and statewide achievement tests

THINKING ABOUT TEACHING

How can information from commercial standardized tests be used to inform instruction?

eachers do not create or have the freedom to modify all of the assessments that their students are required to take. **Standardized assessments** are designed to be administered, scored, and interpreted in a consistent way across many classrooms and schools. Statewide assessments (discussed in Chapter 3) are one example.

Nationally published **commercial achievement tests,** another example of standardized assessments, are the focus of this chapter. Private testing companies construct and sell these tests to school systems, and the classroom teacher is unable to alter the content or form of these tests. Some of the most widely used commercial achievement tests are listed below:

California Achievement Tests
Comprehensive Tests of Basic Skills
TerraNova
Iowa Tests of Basic Skills
Metropolitan Achievement Tests
Sequential Tests of Educational Progress
SRA Achievement Series
Stanford Achievement Tests

In general the commercial achievement tests have three main purposes: (1) to compare the performance of local students with that of similar students nationwide, (2) to provide developmental information about student achievement over time, and (3) to identify areas of student strengths and weaknesses.

Table 10.1 compares these commercial tests with teacher-made and state-mandated tests. We should begin by acknowledging that many

Standardized tests are designed for use across many different classrooms and schools and therefore are administered, scored, and interpreted the same way, no matter where or when given.

Commercial achievement tests are usually given each year. They provide information about student performance over time, and identify strengths and weaknesses.

Commercial achievement tests compare the performance of local students with that of similar students from across the nation.

TABLE 10.1 COMPARISON OF TEACHER-MADE, STATE-MANDATED, AND COMMERCIAL ACHIEVEMENT TESTS

	Teacher-Made	State-Mandated	Commercial Achievement
Content and/or objectives	Specific to class instruction; picked or developed by the teacher; narrow range of content tested, usually one unit or chapter of instruction in a subject	Topics commonly taught or desired to be taught in schools of a state or district; broad range of content covered in a subject area, often covering many years of instruction in a subject	Topics commonly taught in many schools across the nation; broad range of content covering a year of instruction in a subject
Item construction	Written or selected by the classroom teacher	Professional item writers	Professional item writers
Item types	Various	Multiple-choice and performance	Mainly multiple-choice
Item selection	Teacher picks or writes items as needed for test	Many items written and then screened; best items chosen for test	Many items written and then screened and tried out on pupils before few best items chosen for test
Scoring	Teacher	Machine and scorers	Machine
Scores reported	Number correct, percent correct	Usually pass-fail for individuals; percent or proportion of mastery for groups	Percentile rank, stanine, grade-equivalent scores
Interpreting scores	Norm- or criterion-referenced, depending on classroom teacher's preference	Criterion-referenced	Norm-referenced and developmental

teachers have mixed reactions to achievement tests. The following comments provide a sense of the main issues that concern them.

The commercial tests are inappropriate for my class because our curriculum doesn't cover some of the test content.

Many parents put more faith in a 50-item commercial standardized test than in my judgment based on months of observing their child in school. These tests are treated like the Good Housekeeping Seal of Approval of a kid's learning. Too much emphasis is placed on these short, general, one-shot tests.

My principal puts a great deal of emphasis on our school's performance on the commercial tests. He's very concerned about how we do compared with neighboring schools when the results are published in the local paper.

It's hard to know what to do with the commercial test results. They give a sense of how students are doing, but they mainly corroborate what I already know about the students. Occasionally a student will perform very differently than I expected and this forces me to look more carefully at my initial impression of the student. But for the most part, I don't need a commercial standardized test to tell me how students are doing.

The reality is that these standardized tests aren't created to serve the immediate needs of the classroom teacher. They're more for the use of administrators and curriculum planners. But they do contribute to the quality of the school system and thus indirectly to the student's education. In addition, the information the tests provide about an individual student can be useful as a check on the teacher's own decisions about student learning based on classroom assessment. Therefore, it is important that teachers and students take these standardized tests seriously.

Most teachers do not think standardized tests are important to the day-to-day functioning of their classrooms, but parents often view the results with great seriousness.

In this chapter we will mainly acquaint you with how such tests are constructed and standardized, equip you to administer them, and prepare you to interpret them for your own knowledge and for explaining them to parents. We will also discuss issues of validity.

HOW COMMERCIAL ACHIEVEMENT TESTS ARE CREATED

There are two key points to remember about commercial achievement tests: (1) They are usually norm-referenced, and (2) their main function is to compare a student's performance with that of a national group of similar students. The tests make possible statements such as "John scored higher than 87 percent of seventh-graders nationwide in math"; "Maria is in the third grade, but her grade equivalent score on the commercial test was sixth grade, third month"; "Kerry scored above average in science compared with eighth-graders in the United States"; and "Compared with second-graders across the country, Sam was in the bottom quarter in reading." In each case, a student's test performance was obtained by comparing it with a group of similar students across the country. Commercial achievement tests are used in schools mainly because they provide comparisons of student achievement beyond the confines of their classroom. Such comparisons are not possible with teacher-made tests.

Commercial achievement tests are usually norm-referenced.

The most commonly used commercial achievement tests are published in the form of test batteries. A **test battery** is a collection of tests in many different subject areas that are administered together. Rather than constructing one test for math, a totally separate test for reading, and yet another for science, most commercial test publishers construct a single test battery that contains many different subject area tests. For example, the Iowa Tests of Basic Skills battery for the fifth grade is made up of the following 13 subject tests, or, as they are commonly called, **subtests:**

Vocabulary	Reference materials
Reading comprehension	Math concepts and estimation
Spelling	Math problem solving and
	data interpretation
Capitalization	Math computation
Punctuation	Social studies
Usage and expression	Science
Maps and diagrams	

A test battery provides a general picture of a student's school performance and compares performance across subject areas.

A student receives a separate score on each subtest. The entire battery consists of 458 items that take over 5 hours to complete. The main advantages of a test battery are that (1) its broad content coverage provides a general picture of a student's school performance and (2) a student's score on one subtest can be compared with his or her score on other subtests, allowing teachers to identify areas of relative strength or weakness.

Test Construction

A well-constructed commercial achievement test has three characteristics: (1) It is carefully constructed, with pilot testing, analysis, and revision occurring before the final version of the test is completed; (2) there are written directions and procedures for administering and scoring the test; and (3) score interpretation is based on the test having been administered to a carefully selected sample of students from across the nation. Local student performance is compared with the performance of this national sample, or **norm group.** Figure 10.1 compares the steps in constructing a teacher-made achievement test with the steps in constructing a commercial achievement test.

Choosing Objectives

Commercial tests try to assess objectives that are taught nationally in classrooms at a particular grade level.

A teacher-made test and a national commercial standardized achievement test both start with educational objectives. In the teacher-made test, the objectives that have been emphasized during instruction are assessed. The commercial test constructor, on the other hand, seeks to assess only objectives that are commonly taught across the nation in nearly all classrooms at a particular grade level. These objectives are found by examining widely used textbooks and state curriculum guidelines. The objectives and skills that are *common* across textbooks and guidelines are selected for inclusion in the test. This means that some of the objectives that a particular classroom teacher emphasizes may not be assessed by a commercial achievement test.

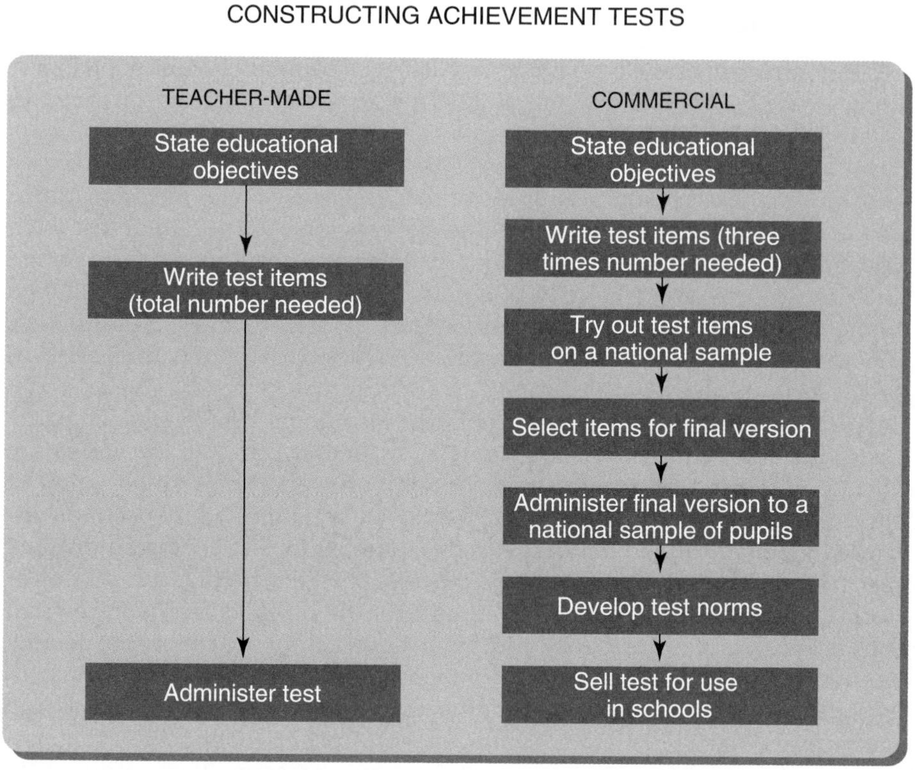

CONSTRUCTING ACHIEVEMENT TESTS

FIGURE 10.1
Steps in Constructing Teacher-Made and Commercial Tests

TEACHER-MADE

State educational objectives

↓

Write test items (total number needed)

↓

Administer test

COMMERCIAL

State educational objectives

↓

Write test items (three times number needed)

↓

Try out test items on a national sample

↓

Select items for final version

↓

Administer final version to a national sample of pupils

↓

Develop test norms

↓

Sell test for use in schools

Writing and Reviewing Items

Once the objectives are identified, the commercial test publisher, like the classroom teacher, must construct or select test items. Unlike the classroom teacher, who writes just as many items as are needed for a test, the commercial test publisher generates two or three times as many items as are needed on the final test. A staff of professional item writers, most of them experienced teachers, research and write items and passages to be piloted.

The selected items go through several cycles of review and revision before being accepted for use. Curriculum specialists study the items to be sure they assess the intended objectives. Test construction specialists review them to be sure they are well written, without ambiguity or clues to answers. Other groups review the items to determine whether they are biased in favor of particular student groups. At the end of this stage of test construction, a large group of items that have been screened by many groups are available to the test publisher. Each item and subtest is reviewed and edited for content, style, and appropriateness for measuring the objective, as well as for ethnic, cultural, racial, and gender bias (The Psychological Corporation, 1984, 1-1).

Commercial test items are reviewed and edited for content, style, and validity, as well as for ethnic, cultural, racial, and gender bias.

Pilot Testing Items

Since no test constructor—classroom teacher or commercial test publisher—knows how well any item will work until it actually is tried on a group of students, the publisher pilot tests the items on a sample of students similar to those for whom the final test is intended. The communities chosen for these tryouts represent different sizes, geographical locations, and socioeconomic levels. The trial test forms look like the final test form and are administered by classroom teachers so that the administrative situation during the tryout is as similar as possible to the way that the final, published test will be administered. A set of items that provides the most valid and reliable information is selected for the final version of the test.

After tests are piloted, commercial test items are statistically analyzed to ensure that they provide the necessary spread among scores for a norm-referenced test.

There are two reasons for trying out test items before finalizing the test. First, the test constructor wants to make sure that all the items are clearly written and understood by students. By examining student responses after the tryout, unclear items can be identified, revised, or discarded. Second, test items that ensure a spread of test scores among the test takers must be selected. After the tryout, the statistical properties of each item are analyzed to make certain the final test contains items that differentiate among test takers. This differentiation permits the desired norm-referenced comparisons in the commercial achievement tests.

Item difficulty indicates the proportion of test takers who answered the item correctly. Item discrimination compares overall test scores on a particular item.

Two important indices for judging test items are item difficulty and discrimination. The **difficulty index** of a test item indicates the proportion of test takers who answered the item correctly. Thus, a difficulty index of 90 means that 90 percent of the students answered the item correctly, while an item with a difficulty index of 15 was answered correctly by only 15 percent of the test takers. The **discrimination index** indicates how well students who scored high on the test as a whole scored on a particular item. An item that discriminates well among test takers is one that high test scorers get correct, but low test scorers get incorrect. That is, the item discriminates between students in the same way as the whole test.

To differentiate among students, commercial tests contain many items that approximately one-half of the test takers get right and one-half get wrong.

When developing a norm-referenced test, the test constructor's purpose is to differentiate among students according to their levels of achievement. The test constructor is not likely to select final items for the test that all students got right or wrong during piloting, because these items do not help differentiate high from low achievers. To accomplish the desired norm referencing among test takers, the test must consist of items that between 30 and 70 percent of students get correct and that discriminate among students in the same way as the test as a whole. Only then does the test differentiate students across the possible scoring range and permit the desired norm-referenced comparisons among test takers. Pilot testing provides the information needed to select items for the final test version.

The preceding steps accomplish three important aims: (1) They identify test objectives that reflect what most teachers across the nation are teaching; (2) they produce test items that assess these objectives; and (3) they identify a final group of items that will produce the desired norm-referenced comparisons among test takers. The final version of the test, including the selected test items, directions for administration, separate answer sheets, and established time limits, must then be "normed."

Norming the Test

In order to provide information that allows comparison of an individual student's performance with that of a national sample of similar students, the final version of the test must be given to a sample of students from across the nation. This process is called norming the test. **Test norms** describe how a national sample of students who took the test actually performed on it.

Test norms describe how a national sample of students who are representative of the general population perform on the test.

Suppose that a commercial test publisher wishes to norm the final version of an achievement test for fifth-graders. To do this, the publisher needs to obtain information about how fifth-graders from across the nation perform on the test. The publisher (1) selects a representative sample of fifth-graders from across the country, (2) administers the test to this sample, (3) scores the test, and (4) uses the scores of the sample to represent the performance of all fifth-graders across the country. Assuming the sample of fifth-graders was well chosen, the scores made by the sample are a good indication of how all fifth-graders would perform on the test.

Obviously, the representativeness of the sample determines how much confidence a teacher can have in the comparisons made between individual students and the "national average." The development of norms is a critical aspect of constructing these tests. Commercial test publishers recognize this and strive to select samples that are representative of the group for whom a test is intended. As one commercial publisher noted:

A test is standardized nationally by administering it under the same conditions to a national sample of students. The students tested become a norm or comparison group against which future individual scores can be compared . . . The sample should be carefully selected to be representative of the national population with respect to ability and achievement. The sample should be large enough to represent the many diverse elements in the population. (Riverside Publishing Company, 1986, 11)

People often describe a student's performance on a norm-referenced test relative to other students in the nation. In reality, however, a norm-referenced test score does not compare a student's performance with all other students who took the test. Instead the comparison is to the students who formed the norm group. Each year a test is given, every student's performance is expressed relative to the norm group. For this reason, forming a norm group is critically important to creating a norm-referenced test that provides valid scores.

Four criteria are used to judge the adequacy of the test norms: sample size, representativeness, recentness, and description of procedures (Popham, 2000). In general, a large sample of students in the norm group is preferable to a small sample; other things being equal, we would prefer a norming sample of 10,000 fifth-graders to one of 1,000 fifth-graders. But size alone does not guarantee representativeness. If the 10,000 students in the norming sample were all from private schools in the same state, the sample would not provide a good representation of the performance of students nationwide. Given a trade-off between sample size and representativeness, it is more important that there be evidence that the norming sample is representative of the national group for whom the test is intended than that the sample contain a very large number of students.

It is more important that the norming sample is representative of the national group than that the sample contain a very large number of students.

School curricula change over time as new topics are added and others are dropped. For this reason, it is important to renorm commercial norm-referenced tests about every 7 to 9 years to keep up with these changes. It is unfair to compare today's students with a norm group that was taught a different curriculum.

The final criterion for judging the adequacy of standardized test norms is the clarity of the procedures used to produce them. The clearer and more detailed the description of the procedures followed in test construction, the better the test user can judge the appropriateness of the test for his or her needs. Publishers provide different kinds of manuals that provide information about their tests. A *technical manual*, for example, provides information about the construction of the test, including selection of objectives, item writing and review, item tryout, and norming. A *teacher's manual* provides a description of the areas tested, as well as guidelines for interpreting and using the results of the test. These manuals should be used by classroom teachers to help them understand and use the test results. Another source of information about published tests is the *Mental Measurement Yearbooks* (Plake, Impara, and Spies, 2003), which provide reviews written by experts in the field.

Commercial test manuals provide information about test construction and interpretation.

ADMINISTERING THE TEST

Once a test is normed, it is ready to be sold to school systems. School systems usually base their selection of a particular test on the judgment of a district administrator or a joint administrator-teacher committee. Once the testing program is selected, other decisions have to be made. In what grades will students be tested? Will all subtests of the achievement battery be administered? What types of score reports are needed? Should students be tested at the start of the school year or at the end of the year? Different school systems answer these questions differently. Whatever the ultimate decisions, it is usually the classroom teacher who is given the task of administering the tests.

The Need for Consistent Administration

A commercial test is meant to be administered to all students under the same conditions whenever and wherever it is given. The reason for standardizing administrative conditions is to allow valid comparisons between local scores and those of the national norm group. If a student takes the test under conditions different from those of the national norm group, then comparisons of the student's performance with the norm group are misleading. It is misleading to compare the performance of a student who was given 40 minutes to complete a test with others who were given only 30 minutes. It is misleading to compare a student who received coaching during testing with students who did not. Thus, every national commercial test comes with very specific and detailed directions to follow during test administration.

Commercial tests must always be administered under the same conditions in order to allow valid comparisons between local scores and those of the national norm group.

The directions spell out in great detail how the room should be set up, what to do while the students are taking the test, how to distribute the tests and answer sheets, and how to time the tests. In addition, the directions suggest ways to prepare students for taking the test. Finally, the directions provide a script for the teacher to read when administering the test.

Every teacher who administers a commercial test is expected to use its accompanying script and not deviate from it. If the conditions of administration vary from the directions provided by the test publisher, comparisons with the norm group and interpretations of students' performances may be invalid.

Accommodations for Disabilities

While standard administration is the rule, commercial achievement test publishers are required to grant accommodations for students with certain disabilities. The Americans with Disabilities Act (ADA) and similar federal legislation require that reasonable test accommodations be made for students with disabilities, unless:

1. The student refuses the accommodation.
2. Providing an accommodation would burden the testing agency with undue hardship.
3. The area of impairment is what is being measured.
4. Accommodation would fundamentally distort the measurement.

Reasonableness implies that cases need to be judged individually, but testing publishers do provide guidelines. If a teacher is uncertain about whether an accommodation is allowed, he or she should receive advice from school administrators or other responsible parties.

Accommodations can be made for learning-disabled high school students taking the SAT or ACT as part of college admissions. Accommodations are also often allowed for tests given at lower grades. However, the nature and extent of accommodation is usually carefully specified, and teachers are not free to improvise outside the guidelines that the testing authority provides. As is done at some universities where accommodations are made for students with disabilities taking a graduate record examination, it is often necessary to request permission to make an accommodation and to register students for whom the accommodation is granted. Permission to accommodate may also depend on professional diagnosis of a disability, the existence of an Individual Education Plan (IEP) or official designation of the student as having limited English proficiency (LEP).

Scores for students who genuinely need accommodations are almost certain to be more valid. However, there is one disadvantage. Typically, when the scores of students who receive accommodation are reported, they are flagged to indicate that some accommodation was made, and the flagging may cause some interpreters to discount the student's performance (Heaney and Pullin, 1998).

INTERPRETING SCORES

Four to 8 weeks after test administration, results are returned to the school. It is important to remember that the tests usually are norm-referenced and compare a student's performance with those of a reference group of students. The most common comparisons are of a student against a national sample of students in the same grade or of a student against his or her own performance in different subtest areas. Although national norms are the most commonly reported and used, most commercial test publishers can provide more specific standardized test norms according to geographic location, type of community (rural, suburban, urban), type of school (public, private), and particular school system.

For example, suppose a school district is in an urban sector and serves a large, multi-racial, multi-ethnic population. The information sought for this school is likely to be how students compare with a national sample drawn from similar urban-sector school districts. Or suppose that a school district is in an affluent suburban area. Past experience has shown that when students in the district are compared with a representative national sample, they generally do very well. Here the information sought is likely to be how students in the district do in comparison with similar students in other affluent suburban districts. Sometimes school districts are interested in comparing student performance within that district. Norms that compare students in a single school district are called **local norms.**

A student's test results may appear quite different depending on the norm group to which he or she is compared.

A student's test performance may appear quite different depending on the choice of norm group to which he or she is compared: a representative national sample, a sample of students in urban schools, a sample of students in suburban schools, or a sample of students from his or her own school district.

TYPES OF STANDARDIZED TEST SCORES

Commercial achievement tests provide the classroom teacher with many different kinds of scores. In interpreting these tests, the number of items a student got correct, called the **raw score,** is not useful in itself. The teacher needs to know how that raw score compares with the chosen norm group, and special types of scores provide this information. Since there are so many types of scores available, discussion here is confined to the three most common types: percentile rank, stanine, and grade equivalent score. If there is a question about the meaning and interpretation of scores not discussed here, the teacher's manual that accompanies a test contains the desired explanation.

The raw score, which is the number of items a student answered correctly, does not provide a basis for comparing commercial test scores.

Percentile Rank Scores

Probably the most commonly used score is the **percentile rank.** Percentile ranks range from 1 to 99 and indicate what percentage of the norm group the student scored above. If Tawon, a seventh-grader, has a percentile rank of 91 on a commercial science test, she scored higher on the test than 91 percent of the national sample of seventh-grade students who made up the norm group. If Josh has a percentile rank of 23 in reading, he scored higher on the reading test than only 23 percent of the students in the norm group. Percentile ranks do not refer to the percentage of items a student answered correctly; they refer to the percentage of students in the norm group who scored *below* a given student.

The most commonly used score is the percentile rank, which indicates what percentage of the norm group a student scored above.

The composition of the norm group defines the comparison that can be made. Thus, Tawon's percentile rank of 91 based on national norms means that she did better than 91 percent of the seventh-graders in the national norm group. This does not necessarily mean that she would have a percentile rank of 91 if compared with seventh-graders in her own school district. A student's percentile rank can vary depending on the group to which he or she is compared. For this reason it is important to know the norm group on which a percentile score is based.

Stanine Scores

The **stanine** is a second type of standardized test score. Stanines are a nine-point scale, with a stanine of 1 representing the lowest performance and a stanine of 9 the highest. These nine numbers are the only possible stanine scores a student can receive. Like a percentile rank, stanines are designed to indicate a student's performance in comparison with a larger norming sample. Table 10.2 shows the approximate relationship between percentile ranks and stanines.

Stanines are a nine-point scale with 1 representing the lowest category and 9 the highest.

TABLE 10.2 APPROXIMATE PERCENTILE RANKS CORRESPONDING TO STANINE SCORES	
Stanine Score	**Approximate Percentile Rank**
9	96 or higher
8	89–95
7	77–88
6	60–76
5	40–59
4	23–39
3	11–22
2	4–10
1	below 4

Although there is comparability between stanine scores and percentile rank scores, most teachers use stanines to represent general achievement categories, with stanine scores of 1, 2, and 3 considered below average; 4, 5, and 6 considered average; and 7, 8, and 9 considered above average. While stanines are not as precise as percentile ranks, they are easier to work with and interpret. As with the percentile rank, a student's stanine score in one subject can be compared with his or her stanine performance in another subject on the same test battery to identify strong and weak areas of the student's achievement.

Grade Equivalent Scores

A grade equivalent score is an estimate of the student's development level, but is not indicative of the grade in which a student should be placed.

While stanines and percentile ranks provide information about a student's performance compared with the norm group, other types of standardized test scores seek to identify a student's development across grade levels. They are intended to compare student performance with a series of reference groups that vary developmentally. The most common developmental scale is the **grade equivalent score,** which is intended to represent students' achievement in terms of a grade and month in school. A grade equivalent score of 7.5 stands for seventh grade, fifth month of school. A grade equivalent score of 11.0 stands for the beginning of the eleventh grade. On some tests, the decimal point is omitted in grade equivalent scores, in which case a grade equivalent score of 43 stands for fourth grade, third month and a score of 108 stands for tenth grade, eighth month.

Grade equivalent scores are easily misinterpreted. A scoring scale that is organized in terms of grade and month in school can seduce test users into making incorrect interpretations of scores. Consider Luisa, who took a commercial achievement test battery at the start of the fifth grade. When her teacher received the results, he saw that Luisa's grade equivalent score in mathematics was 7.5. What does this score indicate about Luisa's mathematics achievement?

If we asked a group of teachers to explain what they believed Luisa's grade equivalent score in math meant, some of them would give one of the following *incorrect* intepretations:

- Luisa does as well in mathematics as a seventh-grader in the fifth month of school.
- Luisa can do the mathematics work of a seventh-grader.
- Luisa's score indicates that she can succeed in a seventh-grade mathematics curriculum.

Except under very rare conditions, each of these interpretations is incorrect or unsubstantiated. Remember, Luisa took a *fifth-grade* mathematics test, which contains mathematics items commonly taught in the fifth grade. Luisa did not take a seventh-grade mathematics test, so we have no way of knowing how she would do on seventh-grade math material. Certainly she wouldn't have had the benefit of math normally taught in the sixth grade. All we know is how Luisa performed on a fifth-grade test, and this tells us nothing about how she might perform on tests for a higher grade level.

If all of the preceding interpretations are inappropriate, what is the correct interpretation of Luisa's grade equivalent score of 7.5? The most appropriate interpretation is that *compared with other fifth-graders,* Luisa is well above the national average in fifth-grade mathematics. Developmentally, she is ahead of the "typical" fifth-grader in mathematics achievement. Caution must be exercised when interpreting grade equivalent scores more than one grade level above or below that of the test taker. Commercial test publishers warn against misinterpretations of grade equivalent scores in their manuals. One test publisher includes the following caution regarding grade equivalent scores in the Test Coordinator's Handbook:

> Grade equivalents are not appropriate for placing students in school grades corresponding to the test scores. A second-grade student who scores above 4.0 in reading should not be advanced to the fourth-grade reading class as a result of the test score alone. This score of 4.0 is a good indication that the student reads considerably better than the average second-grade student. However, if this student had taken a reading test designed for the fourth grade, it is possible that he or she would not have scored at 4.0. Because misinterpretation can easily result if thorough explanation does not accompany the score, it is strongly recommended that grade equivalents not be used in reporting a student's scores to parents or other persons with no training in testing. (CTB/McGraw-Hill, 1986a, p. 88)

Another use of the grade equivalent score is to assess a student's academic development over time. The change in a student's grade equivalent score over time provides an indication of whether the student is making "normal progress" in his or her learning. For example, if a student's grade equivalent score is 8.2 when tested in the eighth grade, one might expect the student's grade equivalent to be around 9.2 if tested at the same time in the ninth grade. However, it is important to recognize that development

olc
CHAPTER
CASE STUDY

Visit the text Online Learning Center to read the case of Melinda Grant, a first-year elementary school teacher who worries about being held accountable for her students' year-end standardized test scores.

www.mhhe.com/
russell7e

TABLE 10.3   COMPARISON OF THREE COMMON STANDARDIZED TEST SCORES

	Percentile Rank	Stanine	Grade Equivalent Score
Format of score	Percentage	Whole number	Grade and month in school
Possible scores	1 to 99 in whole numbers	1 to 9 in whole numbers	Prekindergarten to 12.9 in monthly increments
Interpretation	Percent of students a given student did better than	1 to 3 below average; 4 to 6 average; 7 to 9 above average	Above average, average, below average compared with students in the same grade
Special issues	Small differences often over-interpreted	General index of student achievement	Frequently misinterpreted and misunderstood

is an irregular process that may move ahead rapidly at certain times but remain static at others. Thus, small deviations from so-called normal growth of one grade equivalent per year should not be interpreted as representing a problem.

Table 10.3 compares the characteristics of percentile rank, stanine, and grade equivalent scores. For more discussion of the terms and concepts in this section, see Appendix D, "Statistical Applications for Classroom Assessment."

THREE EXAMPLES OF TEST INTERPRETATION

Commercial tests usually report percentile rank, stanine, and grade equivalent scores.

Although many types of commercial test scores can be provided by test publishers, the percentile rank, stanine, and grade equivalent are most often used. The following three examples show how commercial achievement tests are reported to classroom teachers.

Example 1: Student Performance Report

Figure 10.2 shows Brian Elliott's test results on the Metropolitan Achievement Test battery. The extreme top of the report tells us that Brian was administered the Metropolitan Achievement Tests. The top of the form also tells us that Brian's teacher's last name is Smith, his school is Lakeside Elementary School, and the school is part of the Newtown school district.

FIGURE 10.2 *Standardized Test Report for an Individual Pupil*

SOURCE: Metropolitan Achievement Tests: 7th edition. Copyright © 1992 by Harcourt Brace & Company. Reproduced by permission. All rights reserved. "Metropolitan Achievement Tests" is a registered trademark of The Psychological Corporation.

MAT METROPOLITAN ACHIEVEMENT TESTS
SEVENTH EDITION

INDIVIDUAL REPORT FOR Brian Elliott
AGE 09 YRS 10 MOS

TEACHER: SMITH	
SCHOOL: LAKESIDE ELEMENTARY GRADE: 04	
DISTRICT: NEWTOWN	TEST DATE: 05/05

OLSAT: E 2
MAT/ NATIONAL: ELEM 2 S
NORMS: 2004 SPRING LEVEL: ELEM 2 FORM: S

TESTS	NO. OF ITEMS	RAW SCORE	SCALED SCORE	NATL PR-S	NATL NCE	GRADE EQUIV	ACC RANGE
Total reading	85	66	632	68-6	59.9	5.9	MIDDLE
Vocabulary	30	27	667	90-8	77.0	8.4	HIGH
Reading comprehension	55	39	618	53-5	51.6	5.0	MIDDLE
Total mathematics	64	43	602	55-5	52.6	5.1	MIDDLE
Concepts and problem solving	40	29	617	68-6	59.9	6.0	MIDDLE
Procedures	24	14	579	37-4	43.0	4.3	LOW
Language	54	33	609	51-5	50.5	4.8	MIDDLE
Prewriting	15	10	606	47-5	48.4	4.7	MIDDLE
Composing	15	8	602	43-5	46.3	4.5	LOW
Editing	24	15	614	56-5	53.2	5.3	LOW
Science	35	25	628	65-6	58.1	5.9	MIDDLE
Social studies	35	25	630	69-6	60.4	6.0	MIDDLE
Research skills	36	29	635	73-6	62.9	6.5	MIDDLE
Thinking skills	83	56	615	61-6	55.9	5.7	LOW
Basic battery	203	142	617	60-6	55.3	5.4	MIDDLE
Complete battery	273	192	619	62-6	56.4	5.5	MIDDLE

NATIONAL GRADE PERCENTILE BANDS (1 10 30 50 70 90 99)

OTIS-LENNON SCHOOL ABILITY TEST		RAW SCORE	SAI	AGE PR-S	AGE NCE	SCALED SCORE	NATL GRADE PR-S	NATL GRADE NCE
Total	72	49	112	77-7	65.6	632	81-7	68.5
Verbal	36	25	114	81-7	68.5	637	85-7	71.8
Nonverbal	36	24	109	71-6	61.7	627	76-6	64.9

315

The middle portion at the top of the form tells us that Brian is in the fourth grade and that he took the Metropolitan Achievement Tests in May 2005. This is near the end of the school year, which has an important bearing on the national norming group against which Brian's performance is compared.

Suppose that Brian took the test in October, at the beginning of the school year. How would his performance in October probably compare with his performance in May? In October, Brian was just starting the fourth grade and had not had much instruction on fourth-grade objectives. By May, Brian had 9 months of instruction on fourth-grade objectives, so it is likely that he would test higher in May than he would have tested in October. The time of the year that a student takes a commercial achievement test makes a considerable difference in his or her performance and will affect his or her standing relative to the norm group. Thus, when examining a student's norm-referenced test score, it is important to know the time of year when the student took the test and the time of year when the norm group was administered the test.

Commercial achievement test constructors recognize this fact and take it into account when they norm their tests. They develop different norms for tests in the fall and the spring, so that students who are tested in the fall can be compared with the fall norm group and students who take the test in the spring can be compared with the spring norm group. At the top of Brian's report form under "Norms" is the entry "Spring," which means that Brian, who was tested in May, was compared with a national sample of fourth-graders who were tested in the spring.

Finally, the top of the form describes the level and form of the test Brian took. The **level** of a test describes the grade level for which the test is intended. On the Metropolitan Achievement Tests the level called "Elem 2" is intended for the fourth grade. The **form** of the test refers to the version of the test administered. Often standardized test constructors will produce two interchangeable versions of a test to allow schools that wish to test more than once a year to use a different but equivalent version of the test each time.

Below this general information are Brian's actual test results. First, marked by the circled A, is a list of all the subtests that make up the Metropolitan Achievement Tests battery and the number of items in each. The subtest list starts with total reading and ends with thinking skills. Each of these subtests assesses performance in a distinct curriculum area. Subtest results can be grouped to provide additional scores. For example, the total reading score of 85 is made up of the combined performance on the vocabulary and reading comprehension subtests. What three subtests are combined to make the total language score? The basic battery total includes all subtests except science and social studies, while the complete battery total includes these two subtests.

What kind of information is provided about Brian's performance on the Metropolitan subtests? The six-column section marked with a circled B lists raw scores; scaled scores (a score used to measure year-to-year growth in student performance); national percentile ranks and national stanines (NATL PR-S); national normal curve equivalents (NATL NCE), a score similar to the percentile rank; grade equivalent scores; and an achievement-ability comparison labeled ACC. The raw score tells how many items Brian got correct on each subtest. He got 27 of the 30 items on the vocabulary subtest and 29 of the 40 items on the concepts and problem-solving subtest correct. Because different subtests have different numbers of test items, raw scores are *not* useful in interpreting or comparing student performance on the subtests. Also, since scaled scores are difficult to interpret and normal curve equivalents are similar to percentile ranks, we shall not describe them here. More detailed information about these and other standardized test scores can be found in the interpretive guides for teachers that are available for most commercial achievement tests.

The score column labeled "NATL PR-S" shows Brian's national percentile rank and corresponding stanine score on each subtest. How should Brian's performance of 56-5 on the editing subtest be interpreted? Brian's percentile rank of 56 means that he scored higher than 56 percent of the fourth-grade national norm group on the editing subtest. His stanine score of 5 places him in the middle of the stanine scores and indicates that his performance is average compared with fourth-graders nationwide.

Compare Brian's performance in reading comprehension and composing. In terms of percentile rank, Brian did better in reading comprehension (53rd percentile rank) than in composing (43rd percentile rank), but in terms of stanines, Brian's performance on the two subtests was the same (stanine 5). The apparent difference in the percentile rank and stanine scores illustrates two points. First, the stanine score provides a more general indication of performance than the percentile rank. Second, and more important, fairly large differences in percentile ranks, especially near the middle of the percentile rank scale, are not different when expressed as stanines.

Many teachers and parents forget that all test scores contain some unreliability. Unfortunately, people who ignore this fact mistakenly treat small differences in percentile ranks (up to eight or so percentile ranks) as indicative of meaningful difference in performance. Sometimes answering only one or two more items correctly can change a student's score by 8 to 10 percentile ranks, yet not alter a student's stanine score. This should caution Brian's teacher not to read too much into the percentile rank differences in these two areas.

No test score, not even one from a published commercial test, can be assumed to provide an exact, error-free assessment of a student's performance.

The achievement-ability comparison (ACC) shown in Figure 10.2 is provided by many test publishers when the school testing program includes both a commercial achievement test and a commercial ability test. In essence, the comparison provides information about how a student performs on the achievement test compared with a national sample of students who have a similar ability level. Problems associated with interpreting and using the achievement-ability comparison in a meaningful way are similar to those raised in the discussion of grading students based on their ability:

1. There are problems in accurately assessing ability.
2. The error in the two tests used in the comparison increases the imprecision of the decision.
3. Information about an achievement-ability comparison is difficult to translate into meaningful, instructionally related practices.
4. The information may label a student or influence a teacher's expectations for the student.
5. Many different types of ability affect learning in addition to those that can be elicited with paper-and-pencil tests.

For these reasons, achievement-ability comparisons can be misleading and should be interpreted and used with caution.

The area marked with a circled *C* in Figure 10.2 shows the national percentile bands for Brian's performance on each subtest. Presenting Brian's performance in this way is useful, not only because it provides a graphic contrast to the numerical scores, but also because it reminds the test user about the unreliability in all test scores. In essence, the **percentile bands** tell us that no score is error-free, so it is wrong to treat a score as if it were precise and infallible. It is best to think of a score not as a single number, but as a range of numbers, any one of which could be the student's true performance on an error-free test. Thus, looking at the percentile bands, it is more appropriate to say that Brian's true performance on the total reading subtest falls somewhere between about the 62nd and 80th percentile rank, not exactly and precisely the 68th percentile. His true performance on the math procedures subtest is best interpreted to be between a percentile rank of about 22 and 45, rather than exactly 37. Thinking of test performance in terms of a range of scores prevents overinterpretation of test results based on small score differences. Even if percentile bands are not provided, it is important to think of all types of test scores as representing a range of performance, not a single point.

What does all of this information indicate about how Brian performs in his fourth-grade classroom? By itself, it tells very little. However, in conjunction with the teacher's own classroom observations and assessments, commercial achievement test results provide information about (1) how a student compares with a national sample of students in the same grade, (2) the student's developmental level, and (3) the student's strengths and weaknesses in important subject areas. The tests do not tell how the student does in the day-to-day activities in his or her own classroom. Commercial achievement tests scores should not be interpreted without also considering information about the student's daily classroom performance.

Sometimes commercial test publishers provide information on students' performance on specific skill areas within a subtest. For example, the vocabulary subtest can be broken down into smaller skills such as synonyms, antonyms, and hyphenation; or a science subtest could be broken down into life science, physical science, earth science, and research skills. The classroom teacher can use this information to identify more specific areas where a student or the class has difficulty.

However, one caution should be noted in using this skill area information. In most cases, any single skill area will be assessed by a small number of items. A small number of items cannot be relied on to provide reliable enough information for curriculum planning or decision making. Rather, teachers should follow up the skill area information with additional information collected on their own.

Example 2: Class Performance Report

Figure 10.3 shows the overall class performance for Mr. or Ms. Ness's fourth grade on the Iowa Tests of Basic Skills. The subtests of the Iowa tests are listed across the second line of the figure, beginning with vocabulary and ending with math computation. Four different scores are reported: the standard score (SS), the average grade equivalent score (GE), the average normal curve equivalent (NCE), and the average national percentile rank. Mr. or Ms. Ness can obtain a general picture of the performance of the class as a whole by examining the national percentile ranks.

The percentile ranks indicate the combined class average on each of the subtests of the Iowa Tests. The composite score at the far right of Figure 10.3 (last shaded column) shows that class performance across all the subtests in the battery had a percentile rank of 82. This indicates that summing across all subtests, on average, the class did better than 82 percent of similar students across the nation. Overall, the average national percentile ranks indicate that the class is somewhat above the national average on the various subtests. In most cases the class performed better than 70 to 80 percent of similar fourth-graders nationwide. Note, however, that the class performance represents the average across all students in the class. While the class, on average, performed better than most students in the norm group, not all students in the class may have performed this well, and some students in the class may have performed even better.

The grade equivalent scores across the many subtests are also higher than the 4.3 one would expect of fourth-graders tested in the third month

FIGURE 10.3 Standardized Test Report for a Class

SOURCE: Copyright © 1996 by the University of Iowa. All rights reserved. Reproduced from the *Iowa Tests of Basic Skills Interpretive Guide for Teachers and Counselors*, with permission of the publisher.

Iowa Tests of Basic Skills

Service 9:
Report of Class Averages

Class/Group:	NESS
Building:	WEBER
Building Code:	304
System:	DALEN COMMUNITY
Norms:	SPRING 1992
Order No.	000-A33-76044-00-001

Grade:	4
Form:	K
Test Date:	03/93
Page:	40

AVERAGES ITBS:

Subtest	N	SS	GE OF AVG SS	NCE	PR OF AVG SS: NATL STUDENT NORMS
READING VOCABULARY	24	203/0	5.0	54.2	58
READING COMPREHENSION	24	224.3	6.5	67.1	78
READING TOTAL	24	213.6	5.8	62.5	72
LANGUAGE SPELLING	24	214.5	5.9	62.8	74
LANGUAGE CAPITALIZATION	24	255.7	9.3	78.7	91
LANGUAGE PUNCTUATION	24	249.2	8.7	76.6	88
LANGUAGE USAGE/EXPRESS	24	227.8	6.9	65.4	77
LANGUAGE TOTAL	24	236.9	7.6	75.4	88
MATHEMATICS CON-CEPTS/ESTIM.	24	214.5	6.1	65.5	77
MATHEMATICS PROBS/DATA INTERP.	24	21.64	6.0	61.8	72
MATHEMATICS TOTAL	24	21.55	6.0	63.8	74
CORE TOTAL	24	221.9	6.4	68.8	81
SOCIAL STUDIES	24	221.3	6.2	66.4	78
SCIENCE	24	228.5	6.9	69.2	81
SOURCES OF INFO. MAPS & DIAGRAMS	24	219.0	6.1	61.8	74
SOURCES OF INFO. REF. MATLS	24	227.0	6.8	71.2	84
SOURCES OF INFO. TOTAL	24	223.0	6.3	67.1	79
COMPOSITE	24	223.0	6.4	69.8	82
MATH COMPUTATION	24	213.9	5.9	66.0	78

N TESTED= 27

SS=Standard Score, GE=Grade Equivalent, NCE=Normal Curve Equivalent, NPR=Nat'l %ile Rank

THE RIVERSIDE
PUBLISHING COMPANY
a Houghton Mifflin Company

of the fourth grade. This indicates that the students in this class answered more items correctly on the fourth-grade test than did their peers nationally. Remember, grade equivalent scores do not indicate the grade level a student is achieving at or the grade she or he should be placed in. Instead, grade equivalents provide an approximation of the age of students whose performance is similar to the class average. Figure 10.3 also shows that compared with most other subject areas, the class is relatively weak in vocabulary. This is something the teacher may wish to investigate further.

Example 3: Summary Reports for Parents

Figure 10.4 shows a California Achievement Tests report that is sent home to parents to help them understand their child's performance on the test. The section marked with a boxed *A* provides parents with a general introduction to the test and its purposes. The section marked *B* shows Ken Allen's percentile ranks on the total reading, total language, and total math tests, as well as his performance on the total battery. The areas labeled "below average," "average," and "above average" give parents a general indication of how Ken did compared with his national fifth-grade peers.

The right third of the figure (labeled *C* and *D*) provides more detailed information about Ken's performance. The four boxes contain, respectively, percentile ranks for the subtests that made up the total reading, total language, total math, and remaining battery subtests. Thus, for example, Ken's percentile ranks in vocabulary and comprehension, the two subtests that make up total reading, were 47 and 68. He scored higher than 47 and 68 percent of fifth-graders nationally on vocabulary and comprehension, respectively. The boxes also show areas of Ken's strength and weakness on the skills that make up the reading, language, and math tests. This information is similar to the skill area information described in the discussion of the Metropolitan Achievement Tests (see Figure 10.2) and should be treated with the same caution.

Figure 10.5 shows another take-home report, this one for a sixth-grader, Mary Brown. Her national percentiles also are graphed, providing concise information for a number of subjects and serving as a basis for discussion between the teacher and Mary's parents. See whether you can interpret the report.

1. What subjects were assessed?
2. In your own words, interpret what the report is saying about Mary's performance in each subject.
3. What does the pattern of scores suggest about Mary?

FIGURE 10.4 *Parent Report Form*

SOURCE: Reproduced from the California Achievement Tests, 5th Edition, by permission of the publisher, CTB/McGraw-Hill, a division of McGraw-Hill School Publishing Company. Copyright © 1992 by McGraw-Hill School Publishing Company. All rights reserved.

CAT/5 Home Report

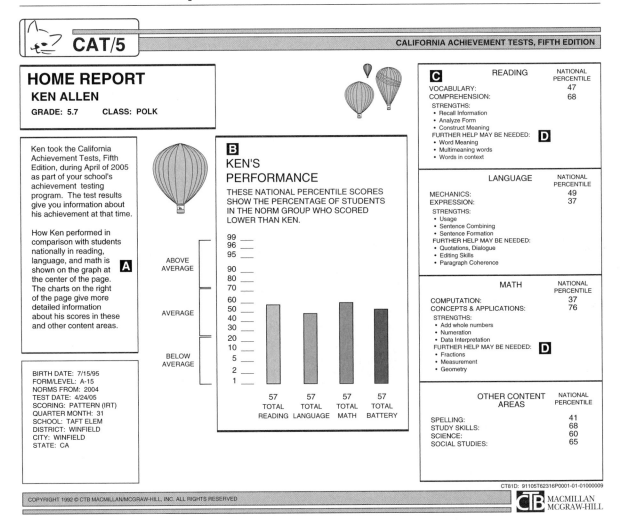

Figures 10.2 through 10.5 show the basic types of information that are returned to classroom teachers for a norm-referenced standardized test. When needed, commercial test publishers can provide scores and information in addition to that described in the preceding sections.

FIGURE 10.5 *Example of a Computer-Prepared Narrative Report on an Individual Student's Standardized Test Performance*

SOURCE: From *Teacher's Guide to TerraNova*, Figure 3, p. 150. Monterey, CA: CTB/McGraw-Hill, 1997.

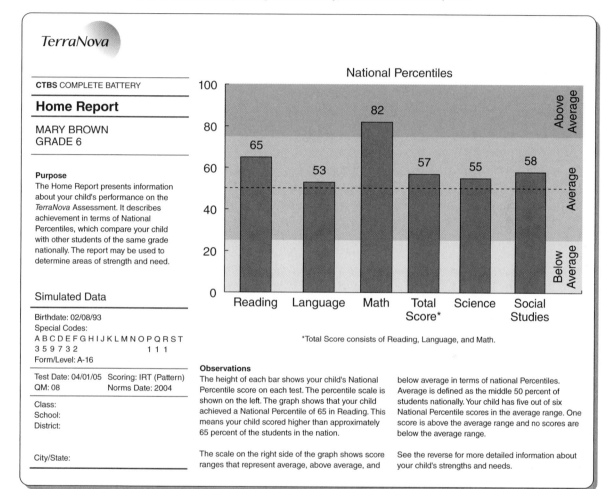

Often teachers are expected to provide information to parents about students' performance on standardized tests. This information may be shared during a parent-teacher conference or in a written description sent to the parent. Explanation is more easily done with a copy of the student's test results in hand or included in the mailing. Some useful guidelines for reporting to parents are provided in Key Assessment Tools 10.1.

Key Assessment Tools 10.1

REPORTING STANDARDIZED TEST RESULTS TO PARENTS

- Remember that the parent is not likely to be a testing expert and will basically want to know how the student performed.
- Start with some general information about the test and its purpose.
- Distinguish between a commercial standardized test and a classroom test or assessment.
- Do not tell parents all you know about standardized tests; your task is to get your message across in simple, understandable terms.
- Make your interpretations brief but accurate; you don't have to interpret every bit of information in the test report.
- Pick one or two subject areas such as math and reading, and one of the standardized scores (stanines or percentile ranks, but not grade equivalents because they are difficult to explain), and take the parent through the two subjects.
- Identify the student's strengths and weaknesses based on the test results; describe the student's overall performance.
- Do not patronize the parent; avoid comments like "You probably don't understand all of this" or "I understand that this is difficult for a parent."
- Be careful of stressing terms such as "error in testing," "flaws or imprecision in the tests," and "unreliability." Such remarks undermine the test information. It is better to say, "No single test can give an exact indication of performance" or "Although these tests are generally accurate, they can vary from time to time."
- Remember that standardized tests are "one-shot" assessments and should be interpreted in the context of the student's general classroom performance to accurately reflect the student's achievement.

THE VALIDITY OF COMMERCIAL ACHIEVEMENT TESTS

A great deal of time, expertise, and expense are put into the construction of commercial achievement tests. The most widely used tests are technically strong, with well-written items, a well-designed format, statistically sophisticated norms, and reliable, consistent student scores. More care, concern, and expertise are put into producing a standardized commercial achievement test than are typically put into constructing a teacher-prepared or textbook test.

It is still important, however, to raise the question of whether a commercial achievement test provides the information needed to make valid decisions about student achievement. Teacher-prepared and textbook tests are judged mainly in terms of whether they provide a fair assessment of how well students have learned the things they were taught. Commercial achievement tests are judged on this basis too, but on other bases as well. Regardless of the test, if it does not provide the desired information about student achievement, its use will lead to decisions with low validity. When considering the validity of a commercial achievement test, it is important to first consider what decisions will be made based on the test scores. Once this question is addressed, one can then consider whether the information provided by the test will help inform those decisions.

For commercial achievement tests, four factors influence validity and reliability: (1) the appropriateness of the content and objectives tested, (2) the representativeness of the norming sample, (3) the conditions under which the test is administered, and (4) misinterpretations of test results. This section examines these issues and their potential effect on the validity of standardized achievement tests.

Appropriate Coverage

Standardized tests are not constructed to assess every classroom teacher's unique instructional objectives. Rather they are designed to assess the core objectives that *most* classroom teachers cover in their instruction. By selecting a common set of objectives, commercial test constructors seek to ensure that most students have had exposure to the objectives tested. Of course, this does not mean that every commercial test is equally relevant to the curriculum in a given classroom where some of the topics taught are not included on standardized tests.

Commercial tests are designed to assess the core objectives that most classroom teachers at that grade level cover in their instruction.

While most classroom teachers find that the objectives tested on commercial achievement tests reflect their own instruction, few teachers find *all* of the topics included in a commercial test. Teachers whose classroom instruction deviates greatly from the text or who consistently introduce supplementary materials and concepts often find that the topics covered by the national tests are different from those they have been teaching. The time of year when testing takes place and the teacher's sequencing of topics also influence students' opportunities to learn the objectives being assessed.

A commercial test cannot be valid for a particular class if it does not match the instruction given in that class.

Virtually all commercial achievement tests rely heavily on multiple-choice test items. Restricting items to the multiple-choice format means that some topics or objectives may be tested differently from the way they were taught or tested in the classroom. For example, to assess spelling, most teachers give a weekly spelling test in which students have to spell each word correctly. In commercial achievement tests, spelling is often assessed by presenting students with four or five words and asking them to identify the one that is spelled incorrectly. Most students are not taught spelling this way.

This and the preceding factors discussed can reduce the match between the content of a standardized achievement test and the content of classroom instruction, thus lowering the test's validity. It is the responsibility of each

Each school or district must decide whether the content of a commercial achievement test matches its own objectives.

local school district to determine whether the content of a commercial achievement test is valid for students in that district. If, after inspecting the test items and the publisher's description of what is tested, the test content appears to be different from what students were taught, judgments about students' achievement may not be valid and should be made with caution.

Representative Norms

Commercial test publishers strive to obtain norming samples that are representative of national groups of students. However, several factors can undermine the appropriateness of test norms and thereby reduce test validity: (1) Norms go out of date; (2) the curriculum in a subject area changes; (3) textbooks are revised and new instructional materials appear; and (4) the same test is often administered in a school district over a number of years so teachers and students become familiar with its content and items. Inappropriate or out-of-date test norms reduce the validity of comparisons and decisions made from standardized achievement tests. While there is no hard-and-fast rule concerning the period within which standardized achievement test norms should be revised, 7 to 9 years is a generally accepted time period used by the publishers of the most widely used standardized tests. Obviously, the older the test norms, the less representative they are of instructional content and national student performance. Specific information about test norming procedures and the age of the norms should be provided in the publisher's test manual.

When commercial test norms do not match the characteristics of the local students, valid decisions cannot be made from the test results.

Conditions of Administration

Deviating from test administration directions reduces the validity of test results.

It was emphasized earlier that valid interpretations of students' standardized test performance depend on students taking the test under the conditions recommended by the test publisher. Deviations from the test administration directions—allowing students more time than specified, helping students while they are taking the test, coaching students before the test on specific items they will be asked, and generally not following the directions provided—all reduce the validity of the test results and the decisions based on those results.

Of course, students who require accommodations in testing should be provided with the appropriate resources and conditions, as noted earlier in the chapter.

Potential Misinterpretations

Two common problems in interpreting commercial standardized test scores are misinterpretation and overinterpretation. Because the types of scores that are used to describe student performance on standardized achievement tests are different from those teachers commonly use, the likelihood of misinterpretation is heightened. The most common misinterpretations involve the percentile rank, which is mistaken for the percentage of items a student answered correctly, and the grade equivalent score, which is mistakenly thought to indicate the curriculum level at which a student is performing in a subject area. Percentile ranks indicate the percentage of students in the norm group that a student scored above. Grade equivalent scores indicate how well a student performs on grade-level objectives compared with other students in that grade.

The main problem in interpreting commercial test scores is *overinterpretation,* not misinterpretation. Because commercial standardized tests are constructed by professionals and tried out on nationwide samples of students, and provide numerical indices that describe a student's performance compared with students nationwide, there is a widespread belief that they give precise, accurate descriptions of student achievement. Certainly parents and the public at large put more faith in commercial test results than they place in teacher-made assessments gathered over time in the day-to-day classroom setting. But while the information provided by the 40 or so multiple-choice items found in a typical commercial subtest is useful, it can never match the information a teacher accumulates through daily instruction and assessment of students. As one publisher has stated:

> . . . test scores represent achievement in basic skills areas at only one particular time and must be reviewed together with the student's actual classroom work and other factors. Parents should also understand that the test measures the basic content skills that are most common to curricula throughout the country. It cannot possibly measure, nor should it attempt to measure, the full curriculum of a particular classroom, school, or district. (CTB/McGraw-Hill, 1986b, 100)

Even when there are no problems with test content, norms, and administration, standardized test scores still are overinterpreted. For example, it is common for teachers and parents to treat small differences in commercial test scores as if they are significant and indicate real performance differences. A percentile rank difference of 6 to 8 points or a 2- to 5-month grade equivalent difference between students rarely indicates important or meaningful differences in their achievement or development. There is sufficient unreliability in any test score, whether standardized or teacher-made, to make small scoring differences meaningless as indicators of true differences among students. Commercial standardized test constructors try to decrease overinterpretation of small score differences by warning against them in their test manuals and by presenting scores as percentile or stanine bands (see Figure 10.2), but they are not always successful. Teachers should guard against treating small score differences as if they are meaningful.

Overinterpretation also occurs when teachers put too much faith in achievement-ability comparisons. These comparisons provide at best a general indication of how a student compares with other students of similar ability. Before a teacher acts on standardized test information of this type, he or she should reflect on personal knowledge of the student's work

The main problem in interpreting commercial test scores is overinterpretation.

Information gained from commercial tests may not be as revealing as information gathered through daily instruction and assessment by the classroom teacher.

Teachers should guard against treating small differences in commercial test scores as if they were reliable indicators of real differences among students.

habits, personality, and achievement gained by daily exposure to the student in the classroom.

Finally, the smaller the number of items that make up a test, the less reliable its results and the less trustworthy its score. This can be a particular problem in commercial standardized achievement tests that include a few performance-based, open-ended items. While performance-based items can assess areas not tested by multiple-choice items, one must interpret performance-based items cautiously because there are relatively few such items. Normally, the subtest scores on standardized test batteries are quite reliable and consistent. However, when a subtest is further broken down into specific topics, skills, or objectives, with separate scores given for each, one must be cautious about how much one reads into the scores. Often such information is used to diagnose a student's strengths and weaknesses, and while such information may provide a basis for further exploration of student performance, it should be reviewed critically because of the very few items on which it is typically based.

Information from commercial achievement tests usually corroborates a teacher's perceptions of students.

While commercial achievement tests can give teachers useful assessment information that they cannot gather themselves, such information should be used in conjunction with information gathered from their own assessments. For the most part, the information from commercial achievement tests corroborates perceptions the teacher has already formed about students. When the two types of evidence do not corroborate each other, the teacher should look again at his or her perceptions to be sure the student is not being misjudged.

CHAPTER SUMMARY

olc

CHAPTER REVIEW

Visit the Online Learning Center at **www.mhhe.com/ russell7e** to review the case study referenced in the chapter.

- Commercial achievement test batteries can be used to compare an individual student's performance with that of a larger group of students beyond the local classroom or district, usually a national sample of students in the same grade. They can also provide information about a student's areas of strength and weakness.
- Commercial standardized assessment instruments must be administered, scored, and interpreted in the same way no matter where or when they are used. Otherwise, valid interpretations of their scores are difficult.
- Although teachers have little voice in the selection and scoring of either type of commercial test, pressures are often exerted on them to ensure that their students do well on such tests.
- Commercial, norm-referenced tests are constructed and scored differently from teacher-made classroom assessments. The steps in construction are (1) identifying objectives that are common to most classrooms at a given grade level, (2) pilot testing many items to find ones that will spread out the scores of test takers for the final version of the test, (3) administering the final version to a large,

national norm group of students, and (4) using the performance of the norm group as a basis for comparing the performance of students who subsequently take the test.

- Four criteria are used to judge the adequacy of commercial standardized test norms: sample size, representativeness, recency, and description of procedures.
- Commercial standardized achievement tests usually come in the form of a test battery containing subtests in a variety of subject areas. Scores are provided for each subtest and a composite score is provided for the overall test. The scores for a student or a class can be compared across subtests to identify strengths and weaknesses.
- To make valid interpretations from a commercial achievement test, you must follow its directions strictly.
- Student performance on commercial achievement tests is described through scores that indicate how a student compares with other students. The most commonly used scores are (1) the percentile rank, which indicates the percentage of similar students nationwide that a given student scored above, (2) the stanine, which uses the scores 1 to 9 to indicate whether a student is below average (stanines 1, 2, and 3), average (stanines 4, 5, and 6), or above average (stanines 7, 8, and 9) compared with students nationwide, and (3) the grade equivalent score, which is a developmental score that indicates whether a student is above, below, or at the level of similar students in his or her grade nationwide.
- A student's test performance may appear quite different depending on the norm group (e.g., national, state, local, high- or low-achieving) to which he or she is being compared.
- Caution should be exercised when interpreting small differences in norm-referenced test scores, especially percentile ranks and grade equivalent scores. Since all tests have some degree of error in them, it is best to think of a score not as a single number, but as a range of numbers, any one of which indicates the student's true performance. Small differences in test scores are usually insignificant.
- Interpretation and use of commercial, norm-referenced achievement tests should be guided by a number of concerns: how well the tested content matches classroom instruction, whether the information agrees or disagrees with the teacher's own perceptions of students, the recency of the test norms, the extent to which administrative directions were followed, and the understanding that no score is exact or infallible.
- A mismatch between test and classroom objectives, old or nonrepresentative norms, or failure to follow prescribed administrative conditions can reduce the validity of decisions based on the test results.
- Test users must be cautious about assuming that commercial test scores are error-free. Small score differences should not be overinterpreted, because they rarely indicate meaningful performance differences.

- Commercial achievement tests provide useful comparative and developmental information that teachers cannot get for themselves. However, teachers should always use such information in conjunction with their own assessments when making decisions about students. Usually, the two types of information corroborate each other.

QUESTIONS FOR DISCUSSION

1. Are standardized tests fair to all students? Why or why not? What personal characteristics could influence how a student does on a standardized test? Would these same characteristics influence how he or she performs on a teacher-prepared test? Why?
2. What can a teacher do to help make students less anxious about taking standardized tests? Would the same actions help students when they take teacher-prepared tests?
3. If you could select only one scoring format from a norm-referenced standardized test to explain to parents, which would you choose? Why? What are the limitations of your choice?
4. What factors should influence the use of commercial standardized test results for assessment by classroom teachers?
5. What are the differences in the information provided by a norm-referenced and a criterion-referenced standardized test?
6. What are some validity issues concerning commercial standardized tests?
7. How should results be communicated to parents?

ACTIVITY

Read the standardized test home report for Ken Allen, a fifth-grade student, in Figure 10.4. Your task is to write a one-page letter to Ken's parents explaining the results of his performance on the California Achievement Tests. The following suggestions should guide your letter.

- Ken's parents will receive a copy of the test report sheet.
- Ken's parents are not standardized testing experts and basically want to know how their son performed.
- You should start with some information about the test and its purpose.
- You should describe the information in the test report sheet.
- You should interpret the information about Ken's performance.
- You should identify Ken's overall strengths and weaknesses. How can the parents see these on the test report form?
- You should describe Ken's overall performance to the parents.
- You should indicate what the parents should do if they have questions.

Your letter will be judged on the accuracy of the information about Ken's performance you convey to the parents *and* the extent to which you make the information understandable to them. You do not have to convey every bit of information in the test report. You must identify the most important information and convey it in a way that parents can understand. A letter full of technical terms will not do. Remember, parents can always arrange to visit you in school if more information is desired.

REVIEW QUESTIONS

1. What is a commercial standardized test? What information can such a test provide a teacher that a teacher-made or textbook test cannot? What is a test battery? What are subtests? How does the construction of a standardized achievement test differ from that of a teacher-made achievement test? Why do these differences exist?
2. What are test norms? What information do they provide a teacher about a student's performance? How are the following norms interpreted: percentile rank, stanine, and grade equivalent score? How do test norms differ from raw scores? Why are norms used instead of raw scores?
3. What are fall and spring norms? Why do standardized tests provide them?
4. What factors should teachers consider when they try to interpret their students' standardized test scores? That is, what factors influence the results of standardized tests and thus should be thought about when interpreting scores?

REFERENCES

CTB/McGraw-Hill. (1986a). *California achievement tests forms E and F: Test coordinator's handbook.* Monterey, CA: CTB/McGraw-Hill.

CTB/McGraw-Hill. (1986b). *California achievement tests forms E and F: Class management guide.* Monterey, CA: CTB/McGraw-Hill.

Heaney, K. J., and Pullin, D. C. (1998). Accommodations and flags: Admission testing and the rights of individuals with disabilities. *Educational Assessment, 5*(2), 71–93.

Plake, B. S., Impara, J. C., and Spies, R. A. [Eds.] (2003). *The fifteenth mental measurements yearbook* (15th ed.). Lincoln, NE: Buros Institute of Mental Measurements.

The Psychological Corporation. (1984). *Stanford Achievement Test technical review manual.* New York: The Psychological Corporation.

Riverside Publishing Co. (1986). *Iowa Tests of Basic Skills: Preliminary technical summary.* Chicago: Riverside.

COMPUTER–BASED TECHNOLOGY AND CLASSROOM ASSESSMENT

KEY TOPICS

- *Growth of Educational Technology*

- *Computers and the Instructional Process*

- *Computers Are Toolboxes*

- *Computers and Planning for Instruction*

- *Early Assessment*

- *Computers and Assessment during Instruction*

- *Computers and Summative Assessment*

- *Classroom Assessment: Summing Up*

After reading this chapter, you will be able to:

- Describe the evolution of computer use in the classroom
- Provide examples of how computers are used to support classroom instruction
- Identify several uses of computers during early assessment
- Describe strategies teachers can use to collect formative information from students using computers
- Describe how computers can be used to make summative assessment more efficient

THINKING ABOUT TEACHING

How are computers and the Internet changing what students are able to do inside and outside of the classroom? What new opportunities for teaching and learning are enabled by the presence of computers and the Internet in schools?

GROWTH OF EDUCATIONAL TECHNOLOGY

The presence of computer-based technologies in schools has increased dramatically over the past twenty years. In the mid-1980s, schools had approximately one computer for every 100 students. Today, that ratio has decreased to approximately one computer for every four students. At last count, more than 1,000 schools had introduced laptop programs in which every student and teacher is provided with a portable computer. And nearly every public school in the United States has access to the Internet.

The widespread availability of computers in schools creates opportunities for teachers to increase the efficiency, accuracy, and scope of the assessments they conduct during all phases of the instructional process. Computers can be used to help teachers get to know their students, to collect formative information during instruction, to assess outcomes of instruction, and to communicate with parents and guardians. Computers can also help provide students with greater access to test items, maintain records, and explore data. And the Internet can provide access to a wide variety of lesson plans, resources, and assessment instruments.

The increasing availability of computers in schools creates opportunities for teachers to increase the efficiency, accuracy, and scope of the assessments they conduct during all phases of the instructional process.

This chapter provides an introduction to many of the computer-based tools and resources currently available to teachers. This review is not exhaustive. Instead, it is intended to provide examples of some of the ways in which computers can be used to assist with the assessment process during each phase of instruction. The chapter ends with a brief review of the major ideas discussed in this book.

COMPUTERS AND THE INSTRUCTIONAL PROCESS

The prevailing conception of education is that of a process that helps change students in desirable ways. To define the ways in which teachers are expected to help students change, schools develop a curriculum. The curriculum describes the skills and knowledge students are expected to learn in school. To help students develop the skills and knowledge described by the curriculum, teachers employ a variety of instructional strategies.

In this model of education, teaching and learning begin with a curriculum that is delivered through instruction. Earlier, we divided the instructional process into three interrelated components: planning instruction, delivering instruction, and assessing student learning. Teachers refer to the curriculum during the planning phase to determine what they are to teach, and then select instructional methods they believe will best help foster desired changes in students. These methods are then applied while delivering instruction.

During and following the delivery of instruction, teachers assess students to determine whether they have mastered the desired curriculum goals. Figure 11.1 depicts the relationships between the curriculum and the three parts of the instructional process.

FIGURE 11.1
*A Model of the
Instructional Process*

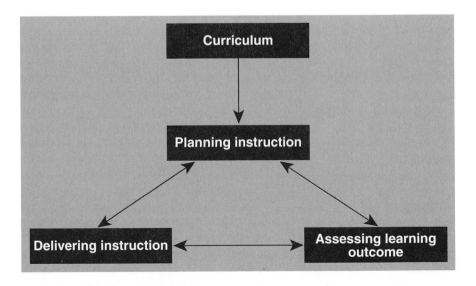

Defining Aspects of the Curriculum

When schools first acquired computers, their primary impact was felt at the curriculum level. To prepare students for computer-related jobs, the curriculum was expanded to include learning outcomes related to computer programming and the development of business-related skills such as keyboarding, use of spreadsheets and databases, and related workplace productivity skills (Fisher, Dwyer, and Yocam, 1996). In this way, computer-based tools enter the instructional process primarily at the curriculum level. These new curricular goals drive instruction. And during instruction computers are used to help students reach specific computer-related curricular goals.

Within the instructional process, computer-based tools play three primary roles. These roles include (1) defining aspects of the curriculum, (2) providing instructional tools, and (3) supporting productivity and communications.

Computer-Based Instructional Tools

During the past decade, many observers have argued that simply making computers part of the curriculum fails to capitalize on the instructional powers of computers. As deGraaf, Ridout, and Riehl (1993) explain, "Rather than computing and technology as a new subject which will take its place alongside mathematics, reading, social studies, language arts, and science as curriculum subjects . . . some educators believe that the computer should be viewed as a tool which should act invisibly in all curriculum areas" (p. 850). From this perspective, computer-based tools are viewed as instructional and assessment tools that teachers use to help students obtain curricular goals in language arts, mathematics, science, social studies, and other subject areas. In the model of instructional process depicted in Figure 11.1, this concept of computer-based tools affects the planning and delivery of instruction. During instruction, teachers select and use computer-based tools that they believe will help students develop subject area curricular goals.

As this concept of computers as tools takes hold in schools, it is becoming clear that pedagogy alone does not lead to effective use of technology. Unless students have developed the essential computer-related skills that enable them to use instructional technology to meet specific subject area curricular goals, the impact of computer-based instructional tools is limited. To help students develop these skills, technology skills are once again becoming a part of the curriculum. The reemergence of technology in the curriculum is reflected in the technology standards developed by the International Society for Technology in Education (ISTE). Unlike the stand-alone technology curriculum from a decade ago, the ISTE standards connect technology-related skills with the content included in the broader curriculum (International Society for Technology in Education, 2000).

Recently, teachers have also begun using computers to assess student learning. As will be described more fully below, a variety of computer-based tools have been developed to help teachers diagnose problems students are having within a specific area of the curriculum. Computer-based tools are also used to efficiently collect information about students' current state of knowledge and understanding of a specific content area and provide immediate feedback that teachers can use to modify instruction. Increasingly, state testing programs are also using computer-based tests to assess the outcomes of instruction.

Productivity and Communication

In addition to having an impact on curriculum and instruction, computer-related tools are also used by teachers and administrators to support communication and productivity. While planning instruction, teachers use Web browsers to access information over the Internet and develop worksheets or other instructional materials using a word processor. To communicate with parents, teachers use e-mail and create newsletters using word processors or graphic layout software. And to develop individual education plans, teachers access students' records through a database program and correspond with counselors via e-mail. Rather than fitting neatly into any one part of the model of education, the use of computer-based tools to support communication and productivity surrounds the model. The many ways in which computer-based tools fit into the model of instruction are depicted in Figure 11.2.

FIGURE 11.2 *How Computer-based Tools Fit into the Model of Instruction*

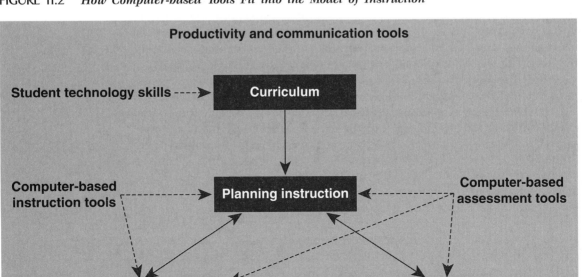

COMPUTERS ARE TOOLBOXES

Computers are often referred to as a tool that can enhance instruction. In reality, a computer is more like a toolbox than a single tool. A computer is capable of running a wide variety of software applications. Computers can also provide access to a vast array of resources and applications available on the Internet. Whether they reside on the Internet or on a computer's hard drive, these resources and applications are the tools teachers can use to enhance assessment.

Computers are often referred to as a tool that can enhance instruction. In reality, computers are more like a toolbox than a single tool.

Most tools are designed to meet specific needs. For example, a hammer is designed to pound and remove nails. But a hammer can also be used to split a rock, pry apart two objects, break glass, or shape metal. The same holds for computer software applications. Most software applications are designed to meet a limited number of specific purposes. However, with creativity, many software applications can be used for a variety of purposes. As an example, a word processor, which is designed to assist with recording and editing writing, can be used to create templates for multiple-choice tests, create electronic questionnaires, provide feedback on student writing directly in electronic papers, insert often-used comments into student work, or track revisions and edits students make as they refine an essay.

Professional development and training often focus on the technical aspects of educational software. While it is important to learn how to use the menus, icons, and features of a piece of software, it is equally important to develop the ability to think about the variety of ways in which that piece of software can be used to meet multiple needs. Often, software that is already available in the classroom can be used by a teacher to fulfill a specific assessment need. For example, several electronic grade books are available. Some of these programs are expensive and are only affordable if an entire school commits to using them. However, most teachers have easy access to a spreadsheet program (e.g., Microsoft Excel). With minimal effort a spreadsheet can be used to create an electronic grade book. While computers can be intimidating for some people, with a little time for experimentation and creativity, solutions to a teacher's assessment needs can often be found in the tools that are within easy reach.

The sections below explore specific ways in which computer-based tools can be used during each phase of assessment. The phases examined include planning for instruction, assessment during instruction, and summative assessment.

COMPUTERS AND PLANNING FOR INSTRUCTION

Planning instruction involves three important components. First, teachers must determine what content and skills they want to help students master, expressing these goals as learning outcomes or objectives. Second, once clear learning objectives are established, a teacher must develop a plan that specifies the learning activities in which students will engage to develop the desired content and skills. Together, these first two components form the lesson plan we examined in Chapter 3. However, before learning objectives and lesson plans can be defined and developed, it is important for teachers to develop an understanding of their students' current state of knowledge and skills, preferred learning styles, typical classroom behaviors, interests and dislikes, and working relationships with fellow classmates. This third component of planning instruction, which we referred to previously as early assessment, typically occurs at the start of the year.

Several computer-based tools exist to assist teachers with each of these three components of planning instruction. In the sections that follow, we will look at a few examples of how computers can be used for each component.

Defining Learning Outcomes

As we saw in Chapter 3, nearly all states have developed content standards. Content standards define the knowledge and skills students are expected to develop within each grade level. Many states make their content standards available on the Internet. In many cases, the documents available on the Internet also contain examples of test items that are designed to measure the content standards. As an example, the Web site for the Virginia Department of Education includes a section that allows teachers (or anyone for that matter) to access the state standards for specific grade levels. A separate section provides access to all test items used since 2000 that have been released to the public. These test item documents display the actual test question, show the correct response, and state which content standard the item was intended to measure.

In addition to providing teachers with access to state content standards and examples of test items used to measure the achievement of the standards, some states have created Web sites that allow teachers to share specific learning objectives they have developed for a given content standard. Given that content standards are often general statements about what students should know and be able to do, the teacher-created learning objectives provide examples of the discrete skills and knowledge students must develop in order to achieve a given content standard. As an example, the Massachusetts Department of Education has invested several years in developing and enhancing a site called Virtual Education Space. Through this site, teachers can select a given state standard and gain access to lesson plans that are designed to help students achieve the standard. By examining multiple lesson plans for a given standard, the many subskills or learning objectives related to the standard are revealed.

The Web site for your state's department of education is a good place to learn more about what your students are expected to learn and how these expectations are measured by the state test.

Although the resources available on each state department of education Web site differ across the states, your state's Web site is a good place to learn more about what your students are expected to learn and how these expectations are measured by the state test. Table 11.1 provides the URL or Internet address for each state's department of education Web site.

In addition to state-developed Web sites, many textbooks now have accompanying Web sites. These Web sites often contain additional information about the learning objectives covered within each chapter. Again, while the resources available for textbooks vary, it is often useful to explore the Web site that accompanies the textbook you use.

Developing Lesson Plans

The teacher's editions of most textbooks include lesson plans that accompany each chapter. Many textbooks now provide additional lesson plans on their companion Web site. As noted above, some state Web sites also provide examples of lesson plans that are designed to help students develop mastery of a specific content standard. But these two resources are just the tip of the iceberg.

Today, thousands of lesson plans are available on the Internet. Perhaps one of the more popular Web sites for accessing lesson plans and other instructional resources is a Web site originally developed by Kathy Schrock called *Kathy Schrock's Guide for Educators* (http://school.discovery.com/schrockguide/). Ms. Schrock began developing this site in 1995 while working as a school library media specialist. The site is designed to help educators quickly find resources on the Internet. Over the past decade, the site has expanded to include a vast collection of Web sites that contain a wide variety of lesson plans and other instructional resources. The thousands of lesson plans available on Kathy Schrock's site are organized by grade level (i.e., K–5, 6–8, and 9–12) and by subject.

Several other Web sites also provide easy access to lesson plans. The Public Broadcasting Service's (PBS) TeacherSource Web site contains a large collection of lesson plans, many of which are directly related to television programs produced by PBS. National organizations such as the National Council of Teachers of Mathematics and the National Science Teachers Association provide access to a substantial number of lesson plans that are organized by specific topics. Other sites, such as the Lesson Plans Page and the Lesson Plan Search, also contain large collections of lesson plans. Table 11.2 lists several sites that provide direct access to lesson plans.

Although the Internet makes it easy to quickly find interesting and creative lesson plans for many different content standards and learning objectives, it is important to examine the lesson plan carefully before adopting it for your classroom. When reviewing lesson plans, ask yourself these questions: "Does the lesson focus on the content and skills I want my students to develop? Does the lesson plan assume that students have knowledge and skills, and is this assumption appropriate for my students? Does the lesson plan require materials or resources that are not available in my classroom? Is the lesson plan at the correct level for my students?

Although the Internet makes it easy to quickly find interesting and creative lesson plans for many different content standards and learning objectives, it is important to examine the lesson plan carefully before adopting it for your classroom.

TABLE 11.1 STATE DEPARTMENT OF EDUCATION WEB SITES

State	DOE url	State	DOE url
ALABAMA	www.alsde.edu/html/home.asp	MISSOURI	www.dese.mo.gov/
ALASKA	www.eed.state.ak.us/	MONTANA	www.opi.state.mt.us/
ARIZONA	www.ade.az.gov/	NEBRASKA	www.nde.state.ne.us/
ARKANSAS	http://arkansased.org/	NEVADA	www.doe.nv.gov/
CALIFORNIA	www.cde.ca.gov/	NEW HAMPSHIRE	www.ed.state.nh.us/education/
COLORADO	www.cde.state.co.us/	NEW JERSEY	www.state.nj.us/education/
CONNECTICUT	www.state.ct.us/sde/	NEW MEXICO	http://sde.state.nm.us/
DELAWARE	www.doe.k12.de.us/	NEW YORK	www.nysed.gov/
District of Columbia	www.k12.dc.us/dcps/home.html	NORTH CAROLINA	www.dpi.state.nc.us/
FLORIDA	www.fldoe.org/	NORTH DAKOTA	www.dpi.state.nd.us/
GEORGIA	www.fldoe.org/	OHIO	www.ode.state.oh.us
HAWAII	http://doe.k12.hi.us/	OKLAHOMA	www.sde.state.ok.us/home/defaultns.html
IDAHO	www.sde.state.id.us/Dept/	OREGON	www.ode.state.or.us/
ILLINOIS	www.isbe.state.il.us/	PENNSYLVANIA	www.pde.state.pa.us//
INDIANA	www.doe.state.in.us/	RHODE ISLAND	www.ridoe.net/
IOWA	www.iowa.gov/educate/	SOUTH CAROLINA	http://ed.sc.gov/
KANSAS	www.ksbe.state.ks.us/	SOUTH DAKOTA	http://doe.sd.gov/
KENTUCKY	www.education.ky.gov/KDE/Default.htm	TENNESSEE	www.state.tn.us/education/
LOUISIANA	www.doe.state.la.us/lde/index.html	TEXAS	www.tea.state.tx.us/
MAINE	www.state.me.us/portal/education/k12.html	UTAH	www.usoe.k12.ut.us/
		VERMONT	http://education.vermont.gov/
MARYLAND	www.marylandpublicschools.org/MSDE/	VIRGINIA	www.pen.k12.va.us/
		WASHINGTON	www.k12.wa.us/
MASSACHUSETTS	www.doe.mass.edu	WEST VIRGINIA	http://wvde.state.wv.us/
MICHIGAN	www.michigan.gov/mde	WISCONSIN	www.dpi.state.wi.us/index.html
MINNESOTA	http://cfl.state.mn.us/mde/index.html	WYOMING	www.k12.wy.us/
MISSISSIPPI	www.mde.k12.ms.us/		

TABLE II.2   A SAMPLE OF LESSON PLAN WEB SITES

The Lesson Plan Page	www.lessonplanspage.com
Discovery Education	http://school.discovery.com/lessonplans
The Educator's Reference Desk	www.eduref.org/Virtual/Lessons
Lesson Plan Search	www.lessonplansearch.com
Teachers.Net	http://teachers.net/lessons
PBS TeacherSource	www.pbs.org/teachersource
SmithsonianEducation	www.smithsonianeducation.org/educators/index.html
National Science Teachers Association	www.nsta.org
National Council of Teachers of Mathematics	http://illuminations.nctm.org
National Council of Teachers of English	www.ncte.org
National Council for the Social Studies	www.socialstudies.org/lessons

How does the lesson build on what I have been doing recently with my students?" Based on your answers to these questions, the lesson plan may be very appropriate, it may need to be modified, or you may decide that, while interesting, it is not suitable.

EARLY ASSESSMENT

Teachers conduct early assessments to learn about their students' interests, behaviors, and prior knowledge. Several computer-based tools exist to help teachers efficiently collect information about the interests and knowledge their students bring with them into the classroom. These resources include electronic surveys, online state test reports, and online tests and quizzes. Below is a brief description of how each of these tools can be used to gather information about your students.

Several computer-based tools exist to help teachers efficiently collect information about the interests and knowledge their students bring with them into the classroom.

Electronic Surveys

A well-constructed survey or questionnaire is an efficient tool for collecting information about students' backgrounds, prior experiences, interests, and beliefs. While it is possible to create a paper-based version of a survey or questionnaire, electronic surveys can save considerable time otherwise spent organizing and summarizing student responses. As an

TABLE 11.3 ONLINE SURVEY TOOLS	
Company	**Web Site**
Survey Monkey	www.surveymonkey.com
Zoomerang	http://info.zoomerang.com
Cool Surveys	www.coolsurveys.com
Poll Cat	www.pollcat.com

example, Survey Monkey allows you to quickly create a survey that can contain a variety of item types, including forced-choice or short-answer items. Your students then complete the survey online. Their responses are recorded directly into a database and a summary report is automatically generated. Depending on the item, the report displays the mean (average) response for students in your class and/or the percentage of students selecting each response. If you are interested in exploring the responses further, the database can also be downloaded to your computer as a Microsoft Excel file (a description of Excel and different uses appears below). Table 11.3 lists of several online survey tools.

In addition to an online survey, Microsoft Word and Adobe Acrobat can be used to create electronic surveys. Both programs allow teachers to create fields in which students either type in their answers or check "boxes" to record their response to a given question. Electronic surveys created with these applications can be e-mailed directly to students (or their parents) or can be posted on a Web site for students to download and complete outside of class. Although surveys created with Word or Acrobat cannot be automatically summarized, they can reduce a teacher's paper load, ensure that students' responses are recorded clearly, and ensure that students provide only one response to each question.

Tests and Quizzes

To learn about students' cognitive skills and knowledge at the start of the school year, teachers can turn to two sources of information. By reviewing students' past test scores, particularly on end-of-year state tests, much can be learned about students' strengths and weaknesses. Most state testing programs and standardized tests make efforts to return test results to teachers prior to the start of a new school year so that teachers can use this information to identify areas in which a student may need additional instruction. In addition to formal test scores, a short quiz or test given during the first weeks of school can also provide valuable information about students' current state of knowledge and understanding. Computers can be useful in analyzing past test scores and administering tests or quizzes.

Computer-based test information systems allow teachers to access student scores on state tests. In most cases, the test information system provides information about students' total test performance and their performance on specific test items. In some cases, the system will also provide information about students' performance on subcontent areas. As an example, for an eighth-grade mathematics test containing algebra, geometry, probability, and measurement items, the total test score and the student's performance on each of these subsets of items are available.

The Test Analysis and Preparation System developed by Nimble Assessment Systems allows teachers to access and view their students' test scores in a variety of ways. As seen in Figure 11.3, teachers can view a table that lists their students' names, their total test scores, and their performance on each individual item. By clicking on an item number, teachers can view the actual test question and see the percentage of students who selected each response option. Similar information can also be viewed graphically. As shown in Figure 11.4, a teacher can select a class and then view how the students' performance on the total test and on each subcontent area

The Test Analysis and Preparation System, developed by Nimble Assessment Systems, allows teachers to access and view their students' test scores in a variety of ways.

FIGURE 11.3   *Test Analysis and Preparation System Tabular Report*

Report – Ability for 1st Period

http://corvus.bc.edu/projects/algMis/teacher/SAMPLEability_sum.html#   Q▾ Google

Apple (204) ▾   Amazon   eBay   Yahoo!   News (1012) ▾

Class Organizer | Algebra Study Home | Log Out

Algebra Ability Results

Teacher: **Sample Teacher**
Class Name: **1st Period**
Class Average: **50.0%**

1st Period Students	Correct	Test Questions – click number to view item																			
		5001	5002	5003	5004	5005	5006	5007	5008	5009	5010	5021	5012	5013	5014	5015	5016	5017	5018	5019	50
All	50.0%	60%	80%	70%	70%	70%	60%	70%	60%	70%	60%	40%	70%	60%	50%	40%	20%	10%	20%	20%	1(
Mike Russell	100%	C	C	C	C	C	C	C	C	C	C	C	C	C	C	C	C	C	C	C	
Jessica Yue	35%	X	C	X	X	C	X	C	X	X	X	X	C	X	X	C	X	X	C	C	
Tom Hoffmann	15%	X	C	X	X	X	X	X	X	X	X	X	X	C	C	C	X	X	X	X	
Helena Miranda	15%	X	X	X	C	X	X	X	X	X	X	X	C	X	C	C	C	X	X	X	
Joanne Douglas	10%	X	X	C	X	X	X	X	X	X	X	X	C	C	C	C	X	X	X	X	
Jennifer Higgins	50%	C	C	C	C	C	C	C	C	C	C	X	X	X	C	C	X	X	X	X	
Rachael Kay	70%	C	C	C	C	C	C	C	C	C	C	X	C	C	C	C	X	X	X	X	
Kevon Tucker-Seeley	75%	C	C	C	C	C	C	C	C	C	C	C	C	C	C	C	X	X	X	X	
Octavio Suarez Munist	70%	C	C	C	C	C	C	C	C	C	C	C	C	C	C	X	X	X	X	X	
Wei Tao	60%	C	C	C	C	C	C	C	C	C	C	C	C	X	X	X	X	X	X	X	

C = correct
X = incorrect
O = open, did not attempt

Download
Reading the
Teachers'
Reports
PDF

FIGURE 11.4 *Test Analysis and Preparation System Visual Report*

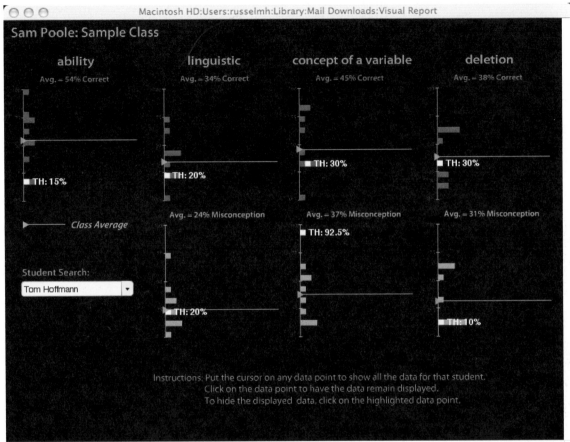

is distributed. In addition, a teacher can select an individual student within the class, and that student's performance will be highlighted on the graphs. The system also allows teachers to display the mean score for the school, the district, and the state. These displays allow teachers to compare the performance of an individual student with the whole class across each subcontent area and allows the teacher to identify areas of relative strength and weakness for an individual student or for a whole class.

In addition to providing access to past test scores, many states provide access to past test items. These items can be downloaded directly from the state department of education Web site and are often formatted as tests. In a few cases, students can work on released test items directly on the computer. As an example, Florida's FCAT (Florida Comprehensive Assessment Test) Explorer allows students to practice test items online and then view how well they have done on a sample of items. Going one step further,

Nimble Assessment Systems Test Analysis and Preparation System allows teachers to select a past test or to select specific items from all past tests, generate a test, assign it to their class, and then see how well their students performed on these items. By reviewing students' past test scores and then having students perform specific test items at the start of the year, teachers can pinpoint areas that individuals or groups of students may need to develop further. This information provides a solid foundation for developing lesson plans early in the school year.

COMPUTERS AND ASSESSMENT DURING INSTRUCTION

Computers are used in a wide variety of ways during instruction. Teachers use computers connected to LCD projectors to present information, demonstrate procedures, and develop concepts. Teachers have students use computers to find information on the Internet, write reports, create presentations, work with simulations, learn through tutorials, and solve complex mathematical problems. These teacher and student uses are intended to help students learn content and skills. But computers can also help teachers learn about their students while students are developing new knowledge and skills.

There are at least five ways in which computers can assist teachers with formative assessment during instruction. These uses include diagnosing students' misconceptions, polling the class about their knowledge, recording students' writing process, providing formative feedback on student products, and observing students as they work on assignments. Each of these functions is described below.

Diagnosing Students' Misconceptions

As students learn new concepts, they can develop misconceptions that interfere with their ability to apply a concept. Teacher-developed and standardized tests provide useful measures of whether or not a student understands a given concept. However, for students who perform poorly, these tests generally do not provide useful information about why students have performed poorly. Recently, several organizations have begun developing computer-based tests that are designed to help teachers diagnose students' understanding and misunderstandings. These assessment tools are often referred to as diagnostic assessments.

Recently, several organizations have begun developing computer-based tests that are designed to help teachers diagnose students' understanding and misunderstandings.

As an example, the Technology and Assessment Study Collaborative (inTASC) at Boston College has developed a series of diagnostic algebra tests http://www.bc.edu/research/intasc/researchprojects/DiagnosticAlgebra/

daa.shtml. inTASC's diagnostic assessment begins by having students perform an algebra ability test that is designed to provide an initial assessment of students' understanding of several algebraic concepts. Students are then presented with a small set of items that are designed to test the presence of specific algebraic misconceptions. These misconceptions involve concepts such as the difference between a variable and a constant, equality and inequality, redistribution, and graphic representation of functions. After students have completed the diagnostic test for a given misconception, teachers receive immediate feedback on students' performance and the system identifies students who are likely to hold the misconception.

Similar systems have been developed for other subject areas. As an example, Diagnoser helps teachers identify misconceptions in the area of physics (tutor.psych.washington.edu). The Interactive Multimedia Exercise (IMMEX) System provides complex problems in chemistry, biology, physics, earth sciences, and mathematics that are designed to track students' problem-solving strategies and identify students who lack knowledge or may hold misconceptions related to a given concept (www.immex.ucla). Similarly, Soliloquy Reading Assistant can track students' development of reading fluency skills (www.soliloquylearning.com). The system presents reading passages that the student reads aloud into a microphone attached to a computer. Using speech recognition technology, Reading Assistant is able to diagnose problems students may have with pronunciation or fluency. These and other related diagnostic tools allow teachers to collect information about students' current state of knowledge and intervene before a unit or lesson is completed.

Polling Students

The diagnostic assessment tools described above provide teachers with valuable information about student learning in a timely manner, but they require teachers to take time away from instruction so that students can spend 10 to 30 minutes performing a given assessment. At times, however, a quick assessment of student understanding is needed during instruction. As discussed in Chapter 4, one strategy for assessing how well students are understanding a new concept or are acquiring new knowledge is to pose a question to the class and select one or two students to respond. Although this strategy is commonly used, a major limitation is that it depends on a small sample of students to represent the entire class. It would be far better to know how the entire class would respond than only the few students who are called on. Electronic polling tools enable teachers to do just this.

Electronic polling tools consist of either a set of PalmPilots or small handheld devices, similar to a television remote control, which communicate wirelessly with software running on a teacher's computer. A teacher poses a question and presents students with answer choices, and students then respond using their handheld devices. The software tabulates the students' responses and provides teachers with an immediate summary. Electronic polling systems are often used with an LCD projector, which displays the question and response options, although the use of a projector is not required.

Electronic polling tools are useful for learning about students' understanding or knowledge. By taking a few minutes to pose a problem that students must solve or asking a series of questions about the book or historical event that the class has been discussing, electronic polling tools allow teachers to quickly collect assessment information from all students. Depending on the teacher's preference, this information can be collected anonymously or each individual student's response can be recorded.

In addition to assessing students' cognitive skills, electronic polling tools can also be used to learn about students' beliefs and opinions. By systematically recording and summarizing students' beliefs, a teacher can use this information as a springboard for further discussion or can make decisions about whether there is a sufficiently high interest level to continue a discussion. Table 11.4 lists several companies that make electronic polling tools.

Formative Assessment of Writing

Writing is a process that involves idea generation, drafting, revising, and editing. Research indicates that the use of a word processor throughout the writing process leads to the production of higher-quality writing (Bangert-Drowns, 1993; Goldberg, Russell, and Cook, 2003). Students' use of computers during the writing process also allows teachers to capitalize on three features of Microsoft Word that facilitate formative assessment during the writing process. These features are Track Changes, Comments, and AutoText.

TABLE 11.4 ELECTRONIC POLLING SYSTEMS	
Product	**Internet Address**
ACTIVote	www.activboard.com
eInstruction Classroom Performance System	www.einstruction.com
InterWrite PRS	www.gtcocalcomp.com
iRespond	www.revealtechnologies.com
Qwizdom	www.quizdom.com
SmartTRAX	www.learnstar.com/smartTRAX.htm
Assessa	www.eyecues.com/assessa

Track Changes

Track Changes is a feature that records changes students make to their writing as they work on multiple drafts. When Track Changes is activated, teachers can observe how students develop ideas in an outline as they produce a first draft. As students revise the first draft, every word or sentence that is deleted, replaced, added, or moved is recorded by Word. These changes can then be highlighted on screen or in a printed document. Similarly, as new drafts are developed, additional changes are tracked. By examining changes made between drafts, insight into the aspects of writing on which a student focuses becomes visible. For example, a teacher can see whether the student is primarily focused on correcting punctuation, grammar, and spelling during early drafts or waits until the final version to address these aspects. Similarly, Track Changes allows teachers to observe the extent to which students add details or restructure their ideas during each stage of the writing process. While much of this information can be collected by requiring students to submit each draft they produce and then comparing each version, Track Changes automatically highlights these changes, thus saving considerable time and effort.

Commenting

To help students improve their writing, teachers write comments on a student's paper. Comments can focus on a wide variety of aspects of a student's written work, including mechanical errors, organization of ideas, accuracy of arguments, need for clarification or additional details, logic of an argument, or believability of a character. Most often, comments are recorded on a printed version of a student's paper. Using Word's Insert Comment feature, comments can also be embedded directly into an electronic version of the student's paper.

Recording comments electronically has several advantages. First, for many people, it is faster to type comments than to write them by hand. Second, entire sections of an essay can be highlighted and commented on, allowing teachers to focus the student's attention on the specific block of text in need of revision or editing. Third, students often have an easier time reading typed text than handwritten (often cursive) comments. Fourth, and perhaps most important, when a student revises a paper in which comments are inserted, the comments are preserved. This preservation allows teachers to view their previous comments as they read the new version, saving considerable time otherwise spent looking back and forth between multiple drafts printed on paper.

AutoText

When recording comments electronically, teachers can also save considerable amounts of time by using Word's AutoText feature. AutoText allows a teacher to create a list of commonly used comments. Such comments may be general and be used across a wide variety of papers, such as "run on sentence," "incomplete sentence," "can you provide more details," or "this is an important point." Or they may be specific to the topic on which students are writing, such as "Were there other factors that contributed to Lincoln's decision?" "Is this really a metaphor, or is it an example of a simile?" or "Are there examples in Shakespeare's other plays that support your argument?" Once a list of commonly used comments is created, a custom menu of comments can be generated. Rather than typing a given comment, the teacher can select it from the menu so that it is inserted automatically. When providing formative feedback on an entire set of papers, combining Word's commenting and AutoText features can increase the efficiency with which teachers provide feedback on students' writing.

Observing Students While They Are Working

When students work on a computer, it can be difficult to monitor their activity. Whether students are working on desktop computers in a computer laboratory or on laptop computers in the classroom, screens can block eye contact with students and require teachers to look over students' shoulders in order to observe their work. Several products, however, have been created to help teachers view students working on computers without having to peer over their shoulders.

Tools such as Apple Remote Desktop (http://www.apple.com/remote desktop/), SynchronEyes (http://www2.smarttech.com/st/enUS/Products/SynchronEyes+Classroom+Management+Software/), and Vision (www.genevalogic.com) allow teachers to monitor students' work by having a student's screen displayed on the teacher's computer. With these tools, a teacher can view the content of the screen and can observe each mouse movement or keystroke. These tools also enable a teacher to easily "move" among students' screens without leaving her or his desk.

Teachers can use these tools to check whether students are on task or to observe specific students to see if they are experiencing difficulty with the assignment. If students are not on task or are experiencing difficulty, the teacher can then physically move to the student to provide assistance. By asking students to record their thinking about a topic or issue, these tools can also be a useful way to quickly view students' responses and to use these responses to launch a discussion about the topic.

When using tools that enable teachers to monitor student work on a computer, it is important to inform students that their work may be monitored. While students are expected to follow their school's technology use policies and to be on task, informing them that their work may be observed builds trust and helps improve the effort they put forth while working on a computer during class time.

When using tools that enable teachers to monitor student work on a computer, it is important to inform students that their work may be monitored.

COMPUTERS AND SUMMATIVE ASSESSMENT

At last count, at least 24 states are actively piloting or are actually administering computer-based testing for the state-mandated testing program. For a statewide testing program, computer-based testing offers several advantages. Computer-based testing eliminates the cost of shipping, receiving, and scanning paper-based tests. It allows results to be returned to teachers in a more timely manner. In some cases, computer-based testing can also reduce the amount of time needed for testing by adapting the items presented to a student so that they are neither too difficult nor too easy for the student. In the area of writing, computer-based tests also allow students to use the same writing tool on the test that they use when completing classroom assignments, namely a word processor. For a state testing program, computer-based tests also open up new possibilities such as allowing the computer to read aloud mathematics items to students who have reading disabilities or including simulations in a science test. As Randy Bennett (2002) describes, these are a few of the many reasons that computer-based testing is inevitable for state and national testing programs.

In addition to creating and administering online tests using the tools described earlier, computer-based tools can be used to create and manage portfolios, find performance assessments, generate scoring rubrics, grade essays, and manage grades.

The use of computers for summative assessment, however, is not limited to large state or national testing programs. Computers can aid summative assessment within the classroom in several ways. In addition to creating and administering online tests using the tools described earlier, computer-based tools can be used to create and manage portfolios, find performance assessments, generate scoring rubrics, grade essays, and manage grades. Each of these uses is described below.

Electronic Portfolios

Portfolios are an effective tool for documenting changes in student learning over time. They can also provide evidence that students have acquired a range of closely related skills or learning objectives. When students are involved in selecting material to be included in a portfolio, they are also developing the ability to critically examine and assess their own work. In addition, portfolios can be used to help communicate with parents by providing concrete evidence of a student's strengths and areas needing further improvement.

Portfolios, however, can be cumbersome to maintain, particularly for a teacher who teaches several classes. For each student, there must be a place where work is collected during the year. At times, the teacher or the students must access this collection of work and select samples they want to retain. When it is time to review the portfolios or share them with parents, the portfolios may need to be transported to a new location, and there must be room to view the collection of work.

Electronic portfolios overcome several of these limitations. Electronic portfolios can contain a wide range of material including essays, recordings of audio performances such as a student reading, videos of presentations or performances, photographs taken by the student or of projects, and artwork produced electronically or scanned into a digital format. By storing work samples in a digital format, the need for physical folders, dedicated file cabinets, or other storage devices is eliminated.

While it is important to be selective about what goes into a portfolio, electronic portfolios can hold a large sample of student work without requiring more storage space or causing clutter in the classroom. With digital files, the teacher no longer must move large stacks of paper or sets of folders when reviewing a set of portfolios. Instead, the portfolios can be accessed anywhere a computer is available.

When an electronic portfolio is stored on the Web, parents and other family members can access and view a student's work at any time. And, depending on the teacher's policies, parents and students can view the portfolios of everyone in the class. Viewing an entire set of portfolios is an effective way to develop an understanding of the range of performances and how the quality of an individual's work compares with that of other students. To learn more about electronic portfolios, Helen Barrett has created a Web site that displays several examples of electronic portfolios and provides answers to many frequently asked questions (www.electronicportfolios.com). Table 11.5 also lists several electronic portfolio systems that are available for teachers to use in their classrooms.

Viewing an entire set of portfolios is an effective way to develop an understanding of the range of performances and how the quality of an individual's work compares with that of other students.

While displaying portfolios or other work samples on the Web is an effective way to share students' work and may bolster students' confidence in their work, teachers must be cautious about revealing personal information about students. Many schools have developed policies about displaying students' names and photographs on the Web. It is important to follow these rules and to think carefully about the type of information and work samples that are displayed so that important personal information about students is protected.

TABLE 11.5   ELECTRONIC PORTFOLIOS

Product Name	Internet Address
Chalk & Wire	www.chalkandwire.com
Talk Stream Electronic Portfolio	www.taskstream.com/pub/electronicportfolio.asp
Grady Profile	www.aurbach.com/gp3/index.html
Toot!	www.aurbach.com/Toot/index.html
FolioLive	www.foliolive.com
Folio	www.eportaro.com
iWebfolio	www.nuventive.com/index.html
e-Portfolio	www.opeus.com/default_e-portfolios.php
MyPortfolio	www.myinternet.com.au/products/myportfolio.html

Performance Assessments and Scoring Rubrics

Just as the Internet can be a valuable resource for lesson plans, many examples of performance assessments and rubrics are available online. Developing performance assessments and rubrics is time-consuming. Often, the first time a performance assessment or a rubric is used, several shortcomings are revealed. The directions for a performance assessment may be unclear, some students may need access to additional materials or resources in order to complete the task successfully, or students may benefit by seeing examples of previous performances so they can develop a better sense of what the end product should look like or what expectations the teacher holds. Similarly, a rubric may need additional details in order to produce reliable scores, or an additional scoring category may be needed to accurately reflect student performances. By adopting or making slight modifications to a performance assessment or rubric that has been used previously, teachers can spend less time trying and revising these tools.

Several sites on the Internet provide free access to performance assessments and rubrics. In addition, tools are available to help teachers develop their own rubrics. As an example, with funding from the National Science Foundation, Stanford Research International has created a Web site that provides links to a wide variety of performance assessments for science (www.pals.sri.com). This site also contains several rubrics that teachers can use for science projects.

Table 11.6 lists several sites that provide samples of performance assessments and rubrics. As with lesson plans found on the Internet, it is important to carefully review a performance assessment or rubric to ensure that it is aligned with your learning objectives and is appropriate for your students before using it in the classroom. For performance assessment, it is also important to consider whether there is easy access to the materials, equipment, and resources required to perform the task. Students must also be able to use the equipment required for a given task. When students lack easy access to materials or operate unfamiliar equipment, the validity of decisions about student learning is weakened.

When students lack easy access to materials or operate unfamiliar equipment, the validity of decisions about student learning is weakened.

Essay Grading

Grading students' writing is a time-consuming task. Often, the time required to read essays results in substantial delays in providing feedback to students about their work. By the time feedback is provided, its value may be decreased because students have moved on to other assignments. To increase the speed with which students' written work is scored, several methods of using computers to analyze written responses have been developed.

Work on computer-based scoring of writing dates back to the work of Ellis Page during the late 1960s. Since Page's pioneering efforts, four

TABLE 11.6   PERFORMANCE ASSESSMENT AND RUBRIC SITES

Site	Internet Address
Performance Assessment Links in Science	www.pals.sri.com
Performance Assessment for Science Teachers	www.usoe.k12.ut.us/curr/science/Perform/Past5.htm
Performance Assessment for Language Students	www.fcps.edu/DIS/OHSICS/forlang/PALS
Sample Assessment Tasks	www.educ.state.ak.us/tls/frameworks/langarts/41task.htm
Performance Assessment for Reading	http://teacher.scholastic.com/professional/assessment/readingassess.htm
SCORE History/Social Science	http://score.rims.k12.ca.us/standards/performanceassessment
Rubistar	http://rubistar.4teachers.org
Teachnology Rubric Maker	www.teach-nology.com/web_tools/rubrics/
MidLink Magazine Teacher Tools—Rubric and Evaluation Resources	www.ncsu.edu/midlink/ho.html
Rubric Builder	http://landmark-project.com/classweb/tools/rubric_builder.php
Rubric Bank	http://intranet.cps.k12.il.us/Assessments/Ideas_and_Rubrics/Rubric_Bank/rubric_bank.html
Rubrics Activity Bank	www.sdcoe.k12.ca.us/score/actbank/trubrics.htm

approaches to computer-based scoring have evolved. These approaches are Project Essay Grading (PEG), Latent Semantic Analysis (LSA), e-Rater, and Bayesian Essay Test Scoring System (BETSY). The techniques used by these approaches range from simple frequency counts of words, punctuation, and errors to advanced statistical models. Although many educators bristle at the idea of having a computer score something as personal and qualitative as writing, all four of these systems have been shown to provide reliable scores for various types of student writing (Foltz, Gilliam, and Kendall, 2000; Page, 1995; Rudner and Liang, 2002).

At least three states and several other large-scale testing programs are exploring the use of these approaches for scoring essays. But these systems are also proving valuable in classrooms. As Page (1995) and McCollum (1998) describe, computer analysis of writing can be useful in two contexts. First, when working with younger writers, systems like PEG

TABLE 11.7   AUTOMATED ESSAY SCORING TOOLS

Scoring Tool	Internet Address
Criterion Online Writing Evaluation	www.criterion.ets.org
SAGrader	www.ideaworks.com/sagrader/index.html
BETSY	www.edres.org/betsy/
Project Essay Grader	www.measinc.com/Default.aspx?Page=AutomatedEssayScoring
Quantum Assessment Advisors—Chemistry	www.quantumsimulations.com/assessment.html

can provide feedback about mechanical aspects of a student's writing. For subject-specific courses such as U.S. history, LSA essay scoring systems that base scores on how words are combined to form ideas can provide students with preliminary feedback, including identifying pieces of information that have been omitted.

Clearly, automated essay scoring has the potential to save time and provide students with more immediate feedback. Nonetheless, in its current form, there are a few notable shortcomings. First, since most systems require teachers to train the system by first scoring a number of essays and then submitting them for analysis by the system, the use of computer scoring may only be practical for assignments that are given to large numbers of students or are repeated each year. Second, while the feedback provided to students is highly reliable, it is also limited to specific aspects of a student's writing, in no way approximating the thoughtful and thorough comments that a teacher can make. Third, computer scoring of writing requires that writing passages be submitted in an electronic format. Despite these limitations, computer scoring of writing can save substantial amounts of time while providing students with important preliminary feedback.

Table 11.7 lists a few automated essay-scoring tools that are currently available for use in K-12 schools.

Managing Grades

Awarding term or course grades is an important component of classroom assessment. Grades provide students and parents with a summative statement about how well a student has performed over a period of time. Grades also help form a record of student progress and achievement over time that is used to make decisions about student placement, graduation, employment, and acceptance into institutions of higher education.

Many teachers maintain a grade book in which they record information about classroom attendance, behavior, completion of homework, and performance on assignments, quizzes, and tests. At the end of a term, teachers condense this information into a single grade. To do this, teachers often develop formulas that give different weight to each piece of information. As an example, a teacher might count homework as 20 percent of the term grade, written assignments as 30 percent, tests as 40 percent, and attendance/participation as 10 percent. Managing all the information used to inform term grades and the process of actually calculating grades can be tedious and time-consuming.

To aid in managing and calculating grades, several computer-based tools are available. For teachers who have strong computer skills, Microsoft Excel can be used to create a custom grade management system. For those who prefer a commercially developed product, several software packages have been created. Whether you are developing your own grading system or using commercially developed grade management software, computers can be used to create classroom rosters and to record information about individual student performance.

As an example, Excel is a spreadsheet application that allows a teacher to create a custom grade book that lists all assignments, quizzes, tests, papers, and projects for a term. A separate section of the spreadsheet can also contain a tally of classes that a student missed and record information about homework assignments. For each of these categories of information, a built-in formula can be used to calculate the average performance during the semester. These averages can then be weighted and combined to form a term grade. While it takes some time to create a custom grade book using Excel, once it is complete, all calculations are performed automatically and are updated whenever new information is entered. Automatic calculation of category averages and the term grade saves a considerable amount of time and allows a teacher to easily update a student on his or her current standing in a course.

Excel is a spreadsheet application that allows a teacher to create a custom grade book that lists all assignments, quizzes, tests, papers, and projects for a term.

Commercially available grade books perform similar functions but generally offer less flexibility than does Excel. Commercial grade books, however, offer other advantages. First, they are generally easy to use and do not require a working knowledge of Excel. Second, some commercial grade books have built-in reports and can integrate with a school's student information system. These reports and integration features save time otherwise spent filling out report forms or submitting grades. Third, some commercial grade books enable students and their parents to access student's grades online. Providing students and parents with accurate and easy-to-access data can improve communication and increase awareness of how well a student is performing during the marking period. Table 11.8 lists several commercially available electronic grade books.

TABLE 11.8   COMMERCIALLY AVAILABLE ELECTRONIC GRADE BOOKS

Electronic Grade Book	Internet Address
Easy Grade Pro	www.easygradepro.com
Learner Profile	www.learnerprofile.com
GradeQuick	www.gradequick.com
GradeSpeed	www.gradespeed.com
E-Z Grader	www.ezgrader.com
MyGradeBook	www.mygradebook.com

CLASSROOM ASSESSMENT: SUMMING UP

As a way of summing up this book, let's revisit its central idea: Assessment is not an end in itself. Instead, it is a means to an end: classroom decision making. The decision-making process itself is made up of three steps: (1) collecting information, (2) interpreting information, and (3) making a decision based on the interpretation. The validity of decisions depends on both the quality of the information collected and the quality of the interpretation. Information is the raw material of classroom decision making, and meaning is added to this raw material when the teacher answers the question "What is this information telling me?" Because the decisions that teachers make can affect students and teachers in important ways, teachers are responsible for the quality of the assessment information they collect and the interpretations they make from that information.

Collecting Assessment Information

Good decisions are based on good information, and three factors determine the quality of assessment information:

1. The conditions under which information is collected, including the physical and emotional context during assessment, the opportunity provided to students to show their typical behavior, and the quality of instruction provided prior to assessing achievement.
2. The quality of the instruments used to collect the information, including factors such as the clarity of test items or performance criteria, the relationship of an assessment procedure to the characteristic being assessed, and the appropriateness of the language level of items.
3. The objectivity of the information, including unbiased scoring.

If efforts are not made to minimize pitfalls, the assessment information that teachers rely on in their decision making will be seriously flawed. Consider, for example, the following factors that can lower the validity and reliability of the report card grades a teacher assigns:

- Portions of a teacher's achievement tests might assess things the students were not taught. (validity lowered)
- The items a teacher writes might be ambiguous, poorly written, or too complex for the students. (validity lowered)
- The sample of behavior observed might be too small to provide information about the students' typical behavior. (reliability lowered)
- Scoring of the assessment information might be careless and subjective. (validity and reliability lowered)
- Informal information about student interest, motivation, and attitudes might be based on inappropriate indicators. (validity lowered)

Most teachers will interpret whatever information they have as if it were valid and reliable. If it is not, decisions will be faulty, and the resulting grades will not be a valid indication of student learning. The same is true for all other teacher decisions.

Interpreting Assessment Information: Five Guidelines

The second step in decision making is interpreting the available assessment information. It is not until information is interpreted that decisions about classroom organization, discipline, planning, teaching, learning, and grading can be made. Although it is not reasonable to expect teachers to always interpret information correctly, it is reasonable to expect them to improve their interpretations as a result of conscientious practice.

Teachers are most likely to misinterpret assessment information early in the school year, when a student's behavior changes abruptly, or when new information about the student becomes available. In general, the less a teacher knows about a student, the more interpretation is required, and the more likely that subsequent interpretations will tend to be based on earlier ones.

Key Assessment Tools 11.1 presents five general principles that should guide interpretation of classroom assessment information. These principles cut across all assessment purposes and types that have been discussed. These principles are described below in greater detail.

1. Assessment information describes students' learned behaviors and their present status. The behaviors and performances observed during assessment represent what students have learned to do, think, feel, and say. For a variety of reasons (e.g., cultural, societal, economic, familial), some students learn more, retain more, and have more opportunities to learn than others. Whatever the cause of these learning differences, the information provided by classroom assessment tells only about what students have learned to do.

> ### Key Assessment Tools 11.1
> ### PRINCIPLES FOR INTERPRETING ASSESSMENT INFORMATION
>
> 1. Assessment information describes students' learned behaviors and their present status.
> 2. Assessment information provides an estimate, not an exact indication, of student performance.
> 3. Single assessments are a poor basis for making important decisions about students.
> 4. Assessments do not always provide valid information.
> 5. Assessment information describes performance; it does not explain the reasons for it.

Assessment also describes how students currently perform, not necessarily how they will perform in the future. Students can change. They can have sudden developmental spurts, become more interested in some things and less interested in others, and reach a point when they "bloom" academically after many years of poor performance or "hit the wall" and experience a decline in academic performance. Thus, when teachers or parents use words like *potential* and *capacity* to describe students, they are making assumptions that assessments do not always support. Discussion of a student's "capacity" suggests a fixed amount of ability, interest, or motivation that places a limit on a student's performance. Assessments cannot gauge such limits, and interpretations along these lines should be avoided. Interpretations focused on "potential" and "capacity" can be especially damaging to poor or disadvantaged students who may have had fewer opportunities to learn than other students, but who often perform quite well given sufficient opportunity and practice.

But isn't assessment information used to predict student success and adjustment? Aren't scores on the SAT and the ACT used by college admissions officers to predict students' performance in college? Don't the grades students receive in one school year often predict the grades they receive in future years? Aren't students in the lowest first-grade reading group usually still in that group at the end of elementary school? Although these examples seem to suggest that assessments can provide information about students' potential or capacity, such a conclusion is faulty.

The chief reason that many students maintain the same subject grades or reading group placement over time has less to do with their "potential" or "capacity" than with the stability of their school and classroom environment. If we take a student at the start of first grade, place him or her in the lowest reading group, and provide objectives and instruction that are less challenging than those for other groups, we should not be surprised if the student fails to move out of that reading group by the end of the school year. This is an example of the self-fulfilling prophecy that was described in Chapter 2. It suggests that the reason assessments often remain stable over time has more to do with the nature of classroom expectations and instruction than with our ability to assess students' potential or capacity. Thus, assessment information should be interpreted as indicating a student's current level of performance, which can change.

2. *Assessment information provides an estimate, not an exact indication, of student performance.* Under no condition should assessment information be treated as if it were infallible or exact. There are always numerous sources of error that can influence students' performances. A single observation or test result has limited meaning and provides, at best, an approximation of a student's performance. Commercial achievement test publishers explicitly recognize this fact and use score bands to indicate the range of scores within which the student's true performance is likely to fall if tested many times. In all assessments, small differences or changes in students' performances should not be interpreted as real or significant. Placing Marcie in the top reading group and Jake in the middle reading group based on a 3- or 4-point test score difference in reading performance is an overinterpretation of the assessment information.

Although informal assessments are rarely expressed numerically, they too are best treated as estimates of student performance. Individual assessments should always be interpreted with the above cautions in mind. The larger the sample of behavior obtained and the more varied the assessments used, the more confident a teacher can be when interpreting the information. In all cases, however, it is best to interpret assessments as if they provided an estimate of performance, not an exact indication of it.

3. *Single assessments are a poor basis for making important decisions about students.* Many teacher decisions can substantially affect the lives and opportunities of students. Consequently, such decisions should not be based on a single assessment. Also, a by-product of single-assessment decision making is the tendency to ignore additional information about students that might contribute to improving the validity of important decisions.

Unfortunately, in our fast-paced, bureaucratic world, there is strong pressure to rely on the results of a single assessment when making decisions. The growing use of scores from state-based tests to determine who will be promoted, receive a high school diploma, or require remedial education is one example of this pressure. Using a single score or rating seems objective and fair to people who do not understand the limitations of assessment information. Although reliance on single assessments makes decision making quicker and easier than collecting more broadly based information, it also increases the likelihood of making invalid decisions. Most teachers are sensitive to this danger and collect varied kinds of assessment information before making a decision regarding grading, promotion, or placement of a student.

4. *Assessments do not always provide valid information.* Validity pertains to the interpretations made from assessment information. It deals with whether or not the information being collected is pertinent to the characteristics the teacher wishes to assess. Consequently, before interpreting assessment information, the classroom teacher should understand precisely what characteristic is being assessed. It is important to know this because students are often described in terms of the general characteristics teachers think they have assessed, not in terms of the actual student behaviors observed. Thus, they describe a student as "unmotivated" as a result of receiving messy homework papers from that student; or they classify a student as a "poor learner" as a result of doing poorly on a classroom "achievement" test that was badly constructed and covered material not taught. Because the behavior actually observed is quickly replaced by more global labels like "unmotivated," "poor learner," "unintelligent," "self-confident," and "hard worker," it is very important that assessment information be a valid indicator of the desired student characteristic. Otherwise, improper interpretations and incorrect labeling will result.

5. *Assessment information describes performance; it does not explain the reasons for it.* An assessment describes student performance at a particular point in time: Jack was observed hitting Paul, Lisa performed poorly on the math test, Bart's oral speech was not well prepared, Ed acted up in class all day, or Mary's astronomy project was the best in the class. When teachers observe students, they usually interpret their observations in terms of underlying causes they use to explain what they have seen. Jack hit Paul because he is aggressive. Lisa performed poorly on the math test because she is lazy. Bart has no interest in public speaking. Ed acted out because he is a defiant, spiteful child. Mary did the best work because she is the most motivated student in the astronomy class. Such interpretations of student behavior are typical, but often they are also incorrect and incomplete.

It is rarely possible to determine with reasonable certainty why students performed as they did just by examining the assessment itself. To explain student performance, teachers must look beyond the immediate assessment information. Did Paul provoke Jack into hitting him? Did Paul hit Jack first? Were they just horsing around? Was Lisa up all night working on a term paper? Did her grandmother recently die? The answers to these questions cannot be found in the original assessment information; new information must be collected to answer them. Teachers must be cautious when interpreting student performance because, more often than not, failure to look beyond the assessment information at hand leads to incorrect interpretations about students and their characteristics.

This caution is especially appropriate for minority students who have poor English fluency, limited out-of-school opportunities, or cultural behaviors different from those of the majority group. When a student is confronted by an unfamiliar language, new situations, or expectations that are alien to his or her culture, the underlying causes of that student's

---

Key Assessment Tools 11.2

GUIDELINES FOR INTERPRETING ASSESSMENT INFORMATION

- **Do** base interpretations on multiple sources of evidence.

- **Do** recognize cultural and educational factors that influence and explain student performance.

- **Do** determine whether the information collected provides a valid description of a student's characteristics.

- **Do** recognize that any single assessment provides an estimate of a student's present status, which can change with changes in the environment.

- **Do** consider contextual factors that might provide alternative explanations for student behavior or performance.

- **Don't** use assessment results to draw conclusions about a student's capacity or potential.

- **Don't** treat small score or rating differences as if they were meaningful and important; scores and ratings that are similar, though not identical, should be treated the same.

- **Don't** rely on a single assessment when making a decision that has important consequences for students.

- **Don't** confuse information provided by an assessment with explanations of what caused the performance; explanations must be sought outside the bounds of the original assessment information.

- **Don't** uncritically assume that an assessment procedure provides valid information about the desired characteristic.

---

performance may be very different from those that underlie performance among majority group students. Teachers must be sensitive to such differences when interpreting students' performances. Key Assessment Tools 11.2 lists some specific guidelines for interpreting assessment information.

Assessment: A Tool to Be Used Wisely

Assessment is a chain of many links that imposes numerous responsibilities on teachers because it is such an integral part of what goes on in classrooms. It is not expected that teachers will always assess correctly, interpret information appropriately, and decide infallibly. However, it is expected that teachers will recognize their responsibilities in these areas and strive to carry them out as best they can. Remember, how teachers collect, interpret, and use assessment information has many important consequences for their students.

An analogy is an appropriate way to conclude. The automobile is a useful tool that enables us to accomplish a great many activities. When operated properly and with an understanding of its dangers and limitations, it saves much time and energy. However, if operated carelessly and improperly, the automobile also has the potential to inflict serious injury. When it was time for you to apply for your driver's license, your parents were apprehensive about the prospect of your driving. They knew the advantages of obtaining a license, but they also knew the dangers. They did not deny you the privilege of driving despite the dangers, but they probably explained to you both its benefits and its dangers. They also no doubt impressed on you the responsibility that accompanies being in control of an automobile. They said, "Get your license, drive, and take full advantage of the many benefits an automobile provides. But also be aware of the consequences of its misuse and of your responsibilities as a driver." The same advice is appropriate for your use of classroom assessment.

CHAPTER SUMMARY

olc

CHAPTER REVIEW
Visit the Online Learning Center at **www.mhhe.com/ russell7e** to review the case study referenced in the chapter.

- Increased access to computers in schools creates many opportunities for teachers to increase the efficiency, accuracy, and scope of classroom assessments conducted during all phases of the instructional process.
- Computers provide teachers with tools to help plan instruction, deliver instruction, examine the effects of instruction, and communicate with colleagues, administrators, parents, and students.
- The Internet provides teachers with access to curriculum standards and a variety of lesson plans linked to those standards.
- Online and in-class testing and survey tools enable teachers to collect information from their students about interests, opinions, and conceptual understanding that can be used to inform classroom management and instruction.
- Word processing and automatic text analysis programs can be effective and efficient tools for assessing students' writing process and for providing quick formative feedback to students about their writing.
- Electronic portfolios can simplify the process of collecting, storing, and sharing samples of student work collected over time or intended to document achievement of specific learning goals.
- A large collection of performance tasks and scoring rubrics are available on the Internet for teachers to adapt and use in their classrooms.
- Electronic grade books increase the efficiency with which assessment information is combined to determine term and course grades and assist in helping teachers and students keep track of their performance in the classroom.

- Assessment plays important roles throughout the instructional process and describes students' learned cognitive, social, affective, and psychomotor behaviors.
- Assessment information provides an estimate, not a precise indication, of student performance.
- Important decisions about students should be based on multiple pieces of information rather than a single assessment.
- When using assessment information to make a decision, one must always consider the validity of the information and the resulting decision.

QUESTIONS FOR DISCUSSION

1. In what ways can computer-based tools enhance assessment in the classroom? In what ways can the use of computer-based assessment tools complicate planning and assessment in the classroom?
2. What characteristics of students might affect the validity of computer-based assessment tools? What can a teacher do to decrease the effect of these factors on the validity of assessment?
3. What are some content areas and skills that are better assessed through the use of paper-based methods? Which content areas and skills are better assessed through the use of computer-based tools?

ACTIVITIES

1. Access the Department of Education Web site for your state. What type of assessment information and tools are available? Can you find the state standards or curriculum frameworks? Information about the state test? Sample test items or reports? Are there online tools students can use to prepare for the state test? What are your state's policies regarding the use of computers during the state test?
2. Use the Internet to find a sample online test. Take this test, and as you work on the test identify problems your students might encounter if they were taking the test. Is it easy to move between questions? Is it easy to access directions? Is it easy to record and change answers? How difficult is it to read the test questions and supporting material such as graphs, tables, or pictures? Is the test universally designed to provide appropriate access to all students?

REVIEW QUESTIONS

1. In what ways are students and teachers using computers for instruction in the classroom?

2. How can computers be used during early assessment to help teachers make decisions about the focus of instruction or the organization of the classroom?

3. In what ways can computers be used to assess student writing? What skills do you need to develop in order to make use of these methods?

4. How can computer-based tests and assessment tools be used to provide formative or diagnostic information about students?

5. How can computer-based tools be used to prepare students for state-mandated tests?

6. What do teachers need to consider about their students and the purpose of assessment when deciding whether or not to use a computer-based assessment tool?

REFERENCES

Bangert-Drowns, R. L. (1993). The word processor as an instructional tool: a meta-analysis of word processing in writing instruction. *Review of Educational Research, 63*(1), 69–93.

Bennett, R. E. (2002). Inexorable and inevitable: The continuing story of technology and assessment. *Journal of Technology, Learning, and Assessment, 1*(1).

deGraaf, C., Ridout, S., and Riehl, J. (1993). Technology in education: Creatively using computers in the language arts. In N. Estes and M. Thomas (Eds.), *Rethinking the Roles of Technology in Education* (Vol. 2). Cambridge, MA: Massachusetts Institute of Technology.

Fisher, C., Dwyer, D., and Yocam, K. (1996). *Education and technology: Reflections on computing in classrooms.* San Francisco: Apple Press.

Foltz, P., Gilliam, S., and Kendall, S. (2000). Supporting content-based feedback in online writing evaluation with LSA. *Interactive Learning Environment, 8*(2), 111–129.

Goldberg, A., Russell, M., and Cook, A. (2003). Effects of computers on student writing: A meta-analysis of research, 1992–2002. *Journal of Technology, Learning and Assessment, 2*(1), http://www.bc.edu/research/intasc/jtla/journal/v2n1.shtml.

International Society for Technology in Education. (2000). *National Educational Technology Standards for Students: Connecting Curriculum and Technology.* Eugene, OR: Author.

McCollum, K. (1998). How a computer program learns to grade essays. *The Chronicle of Higher Education,* September 4, 1998, http://chronical.com/weekly/v45/i02/02a03701.htm.

Page, E. (1995). *Computer grading of essays: a different kind of testing?* Address for APA Annual Meeting, August 13, 1995. Session 3167.

Rudner, L. M., and Liang, T. (2002). Automated essay scoring using Bayes' theorem. *Journal of Technology, Learning, and Assessment, 1*(2), http://www.jtla.org.

APPENDIX A
Standards for Teacher Competence in Educational Assessment of Students

The professional education associations began working in 1987 to develop standards for teacher competence in student assessment out of concern that the potential educational benefits of student assessments be fully realized. The committee[1] appointed to this project completed its work in 1990 following reviews of earlier drafts by members of the measurement, teaching, and teacher preparation and certification communities. Parallel committees of affected associations are encouraged to develop similar statements of qualifications for school administrators, counselors, testing directors, supervisors, and other educators in the near future. These statements are intended to guide the pre-service and in-service preparation of educators, the accreditation of preparation programs, and the future certification of all educators.[2]

A standard is defined here as a principle generally accepted by the professional associations responsible for this document. Assessment is defined as the process of obtaining information that is used to make educational decisions about students; to give feedback to the student about his or her progress, strengths, and weaknesses; to judge instructional effectiveness and curricular adequacy; and to inform policy. The various assessment techniques include, but are not limited to, formal and informal observation, qualitative analysis of student performance and products, paper-and-pencil tests, oral questioning, and analysis of student records. The assessment competencies included here are the knowledge and skills critical to a teacher's role as educator. It is understood that there are many competencies beyond assessment competencies that teachers must possess.

By establishing standards for teacher competence in student assessment, the associations subscribe to the view that student assessment is an essential part of teaching and that good teaching cannot exist without good student assessment. Training to develop the competencies covered in the standards should be an integral part of pre-service preparation. Further,

Standards developed by the American Federation of Teachers, the National Council on Measurement in Education, and the National Education Association. Copyright © 1990 by the National Council on Measurement in Education. Reprinted by permission of the publisher.

such assessment training should be widely available to practicing teachers through staff development programs at the district and building levels. The standards are intended for use as:

- A guide for teacher educators as they design and approve programs for teacher preparation
- A self-assessment guide for teachers in identifying their needs for professional development in student assessment
- A guide for workshop instructors as they design professional development experiences for in-service teachers
- An impetus for educational measurement specialists and teacher trainers to conceptualize student assessment and teacher training in student assessment more broadly than has been the case in the past

The standards should be incorporated into future teacher training and certification programs. Teachers who have not had the preparation these standards imply should have the opportunity and support to develop these competencies before the standards enter into the evaluation of these teachers.

Approach Used to Develop the Standards

The members of the associations that supported this work are professional educators involved in teaching, teacher education, and student assessment. Members of these associations are concerned about the inadequacy with which teachers are prepared for assessing the educational progress of their students, and thus sought to address this concern effectively. A committee named by the associations first met in September 1987 and affirmed its commitment to defining standards for teacher preparation in student assessment. The committee then undertook a review of the research literature to identify needs in student assessment, current levels of teacher training in student assessment, areas of teacher activities requiring competence in using student assessments, and current levels of teacher competence in student assessment.

The members of the committee used their collective experience and expertise to formulate and then revise statements of important assessment competencies. Drafts of these competencies went through several revisions by the committee before the standards were released for public review. Comments by reviewers from each of the associations were then used to prepare a final statement.

Scope of a Teacher's Professional Role and Responsibilities for Student Assessment

There are seven standards in this document. In recognizing the critical need to revitalize classroom assessment, some standards focus on classroom-based competencies. Because of teachers' growing roles in education and policy decisions beyond the classroom, other standards address assessment competencies underlying teacher participation in decisions related to assessment at the school, district, state, and national levels.

The scope of a teacher's professional role and responsibilities for student assessment may be described in terms of the following activities. These activities imply that teachers need competence in student assessment and sufficient time and resources to complete them in a professional manner.

- **Activities occurring prior to instruction.** (a) Understanding students' cultural backgrounds, interests, skills, and abilities as they apply across a range of learning domains and/or subject areas; (b) understanding students' motivations and their interests in specific class content; (c) clarifying and articulating the performance outcomes expected of students; and (d) planning instruction for individuals or groups of students

- **Activities occurring during instruction.** (a) Monitoring student progress toward instructional goals; (b) identifying gains and difficulties students are experiencing in learning and performing; (c) adjusting instruction; (d) giving contingent, specific, and credible praise and feedback; (e) motivating students to learn; and (f) judging the extent of student attainment of instructional outcomes

- **Activities occurring after the appropriate instructional segment (e.g., lesson, class, semester, grade).** (a) Describing the extent to which each student has attained both short- and long-term instructional goals; (b) communicating strengths and weaknesses based on assessment results to students and parents or guardians; (c) recording and reverting assessment results for school-level analysis, evaluation, and decision making; (d) analyzing assessment information gathered before and during instruction to understand each student's progress to date and to inform future instructional planning; (e) evaluating the effectiveness of instruction; and (f) evaluating the effectiveness of the curriculum and materials in use

- **Activities associated with a teacher's involvement in school building and school district decision making.** (a) Serving on a school or district committee examining the school's and district's strengths and weaknesses in the development of its students; (b) working on the development or selection of assessment methods for school building or school district use; (c) evaluating school district curriculum; and (d) performing other, related activities

- **Activities associated with a teacher's involvement in a wider community of educators.** (a) Serving on a state committee asked to develop learning goals and associated assessment methods; (b) participating in reviews of the appropriateness of district, state, or national student goals and associated assessment methods; and (c) interpreting the results of state and national student assessment programs

Each standard that follows is an expectation for assessment knowledge or skill that a teacher should possess in order to perform well in the five areas just described. As a set, the standards call on teachers to demonstrate skill at selecting, developing, applying, using, communicating, and evaluating student assessment information and student assessment practices. A brief rationale and illustrative behaviors follow each standard.

The standards represent a conceptual framework or scaffolding from which specific skills can be derived. Work to make these standards operational will be needed even after they have been published. It is also expected that experience in the application of these standards should lead to their improvement and further development.

1. *Teachers should be skilled in choosing assessment methods appropriate for instructional decisions.* Skills in choosing appropriate, useful, administratively convenient, technically adequate, and fair assessment methods are prerequisite to good use of information to support instructional decisions. Teachers need to be well acquainted with the kinds of information provided by a broad range of assessment alternatives and their strengths and weaknesses. In particular, they should be familiar with criteria for evaluating and selecting assessment methods in light of instructional plans.

Teachers who meet this standard will have the conceptual and application skills that follow. They will be able to use the concepts of assessment error and validity when developing or selecting their approaches to classroom assessment of students. They will understand how valid assessment data can support instructional activities such as providing appropriate feedback to students, diagnosing group and individual learning needs, planning for individualized educational programs, motivating students, and evaluating instructional procedures. They will understand how invalid information can affect instructional decisions about students. They will also be able to use and evaluate assessment options available to them, considering, among other things, the cultural, social, economic, and language backgrounds of students. They will be aware that different assessment approaches can be incompatible with certain instructional goals and may impact quite differently on their teaching.

Teachers will know, for each assessment approach they use, its appropriateness for making decisions about their students. Moreover, teachers will know where to find information about and/or reviews of various assessment methods. Assessment options are diverse and include text- and curriculum-embedded questions and tests, standardized criterion-referenced and norm-referenced tests, oral questioning, spontaneous and structured performance assessments, portfolios, exhibitions, demonstrations, rating scales, writing samples, paper-and-pencil tests, seatwork and homework, peer and self-assessments, student records, observations, questionnaires interviews, projects, products, and others' opinions.

2. Teachers should be skilled in developing assessment methods appropriate for instructional decisions. While teachers often use published or other external assessment tools, the bulk of the assessment information they use for decision making comes from approaches they create and implement. Indeed, the assessment demands of the classroom go well beyond readily available instruments.

Teachers who meet this standard will have the conceptual and application skills that follow. Teachers will be skilled in planning the collection of information that facilitates the decisions they will make. They will know and follow appropriate principles for developing and using assessment methods in their teaching, avoiding common pitfalls in student assessment. Such techniques may include several of the options listed at the end of the first standard. The teacher will select the techniques that are appropriate to the intent of the teacher's instruction.

Teachers meeting this standard will also be skilled in using student data to analyze the quality of each assessment technique they use. Since most teachers do not have access to assessment specialists, they must be prepared to do these analyses themselves.

3. Teachers should be skilled in administering, scoring, and interpreting the results of both externally produced and teacher-produced assessment methods. It is not enough that teachers are able to select and develop good assessment methods; they must also be able to apply them properly. Teachers should be skilled in administering, scoring, and interpreting results from diverse assessment methods.

Teachers who meet this standard will have the conceptual and application skills that follow. They will be skilled in interpreting informal and formal teacher-produced assessment results, including students' performances in class and on homework assignments. Teachers will be able to use guides for scoring essay questions and projects, stencils for scoring response-choice questions, and scales for rating performance assessments. They will be able to use these in ways that produce consistent results.

Teachers will be able to administer standardized achievement tests and be able to interpret the commonly reported scores: percentile ranks, percentile band scores, standard scores, and grade equivalents. They will have a conceptual understanding of the summary indexes commonly reported with assessment results: measures of central tendency, dispersion, relationships, reliability, and errors of measurement.

Teachers will be able to apply these concepts of score and summary indexes in ways that enhance their use of the assessments that they develop. They will be able to analyze assessment results to identify students' strengths and errors. If they get inconsistent results, they will seek other explanations for the discrepancy or other data to attempt to resolve the uncertainty before arriving at a decision. They will be able to use assessment methods in ways that encourage students' educational development and that do not inappropriately increase students' anxiety levels.

4. *Teachers should be skilled in using assessment results when making decisions about individual students, planning teaching, developing curriculum, and school improvements.* Assessment results are used to make educational decisions at several levels: in the classroom about students, in the community about a school and a school district, and in society, generally, about the purposes and outcomes of the educational enterprise. Teachers play a vital role when participating in decision making at each of these levels and must be able to use assessment results effectively.

Teachers who meet this standard will have the conceptual and application skills that follow. They will be able to use accumulated assessment information to organize a sound instructional plan for facilitating students' educational development. When using assessment results to plan and/or evaluate instruction and curriculum, teachers will interpret the results correctly and avoid common misinterpretations, such as basing decisions on scores that lack curriculum validity. They will be informed about the results of local, regional, state, and national assessment and about their appropriate use for student, classroom, school, district, state, and national educational improvement.

5. *Teachers should be skilled in developing valid student grading procedures that use student assessments.* Grading students is an important part of professional practice for teachers. Grading is defined as indicating both a student's level of performance and a teacher's valuing of that performance. The principles for using assessments to obtain valid grades are known and teachers should employ them.

Teachers who meet this standard will have the conceptual and application skills that follow. They will be able to devise, implement, and explain a procedure for developing grades composed of marks from various assignments, projects, in-class activities, quizzes, tests, and/or other assessments that they may use. Teachers will understand and be able to articulate why the grades they assign are rational, justified, and fair, acknowledging that such grades reflect their preferences and judgments. Teachers will be able to recognize and to avoid faulty grading procedures such as using grades as punishment. They will be able to evaluate and to modify their grading procedures in order to improve the validity of the interpretations made from them about students' attainments.

6. *Teachers should be skilled in communicating assessment results to students, parents, other lay audiences, and other educators.* Teachers must routinely report assessment results to students and to parents or guardians. In addition, they are frequently asked to report or to discuss assessment results with other educators and with diverse lay audiences. If the results are not communicated effectively, they may be misused or not used. To communicate effectively with others on matters of student assessment, teachers must be able to use assessment terminology appropriately and must be able to articulate the meaning, limitations, and implications of assessment results. Furthermore, teachers will sometimes be in a position that will require them to defend their own assessment procedures and their interpretations of them. At other times, teachers may need to help the public to interpret assessment results appropriately.

Teachers who meet this standard will have the conceptual and application skills that follow. Teachers will understand and be able to give appropriate explanations of how the interpretation of student assessments must be moderated by the student's socioeconomic, cultural, language, and other background factors. Teachers will be able to explain that assessment results do not imply that such background factors limit a student's ultimate educational development. They will be able to communicate to students and to their parents or guardians how they may assess the student's educational progress. Teachers will understand and be able to explain the importance of taking measurement errors into account when using assessments to make decisions about individual students. Teachers will be able to explain the limitations of different informal and formal assessment methods. They will be able to explain printed reports of the results of student assessments at the classroom, school district, state, and national levels.

7. Teachers should be skilled in recognizing unethical, illegal, and otherwise inappropriate assessment methods and uses of assessment information. Fairness, the rights of all concerned, and professional ethical behavior must undergird all student assessment activities from the initial planning for and gathering of information to the interpretation, use, and communication of the results. Teachers must be well-versed in their own ethical and legal responsibilities in assessment. In addition, they should also attempt to have the inappropriate assessment practices of others discontinued whenever they are encountered. Teachers should also participate with the wider educational community in defining the limits of appropriate professional behavior in assessment.

Teachers who meet this standard will have the conceptual and application skills that follow. They will know those laws and case decisions that affect their classroom, school district, and state assessment practices. Teachers will be aware that various assessment procedures can be misused or overused resulting in harmful consequences such as embarrassing students, violating a student's right to confidentiality, and inappropriately using students' standardized achievement test scores to measure teaching effectiveness.

Notes

[1]The committee that developed this statement was appointed by the collaborating professional associations. James R. Sanders (Western Michigan University) chaired the committee and represented NCME along with John R. Hills (Florida State University) and Anthony J. Nitki (University of Pittsburgh). Jack C. Merwin (University of Minnesota)

represented the American Association of Colleges for Teacher Education, Carolyn Trice represented the American Federation of Teachers, and Marcella Dianda and Jeffrey Schneider represented the National Education Association.

[2]The associations invite comments that may be used for improvement of this document. Comments may be sent to: Teacher Standards in Student Assessment, American Federation of Teachers, 555 New Jersey Avenue NW, Washington, DC 20001; Teacher Standards in Student Assessment, National Council on Measurement in Education, 1230 Seventeenth Street NW, Washington, DC 20036; or Teacher Standards in Student Assessment, Instruction and Professional Development, National Education Association, 1201 Sixteenth Street NW, Washington, DC 20036.

Please note that this document is not copyrighted material and that reproduction and dissemination are encouraged.

APPENDIX B
Taxonomy of Educational Objectives: Major Categories

Major Categories in the Cognitive Domain[1]

1. Knowledge
2. Comprehension
3. Application

4. Analysis
5. Synthesis

6. Evaluation

Major Categories in the Affective Domain[2]

1. Receiving
2. Responding
3. Valuing

4. Organization
5. Characterization by a Value or Value Complex

Major Categories in the Psychomotor Domain[3]

1. Perception
2. Set
3. Guided Response
4. Mechanism
5. Complex Overt Response

6. Adaptation
7. Origination

---

[1]From Benjamin S. Bloom et al., *Taxonomy of Educational Objectives: Book 1, Cognitive Domain.* Published by Allyn & Bacon, Boston, MA. Copyright © 1999 by Pearson Education.
[2]From David R. Krathwohl, Benjamin S. Bloom, & Bertram B. Masia, *Taxonomy of Educational Objectives: Book 2, Affective Domain.* Published by Allyn & Bacon, Boston, MA. Copyright © 1984 by Pearson Education.
[3]From *The Classification of Educational Objectives in the Psychomotor Domain,* by E. J. Simpson, 1972, Washington, DC: Gryphon House.

APPENDIX C
Sample Individual Education Plan

This is one example of an IEP form, used by a team of educators and a parent to plan the teaching of an individual student with a disability.

I. DEMOGRAPHIC INFORMATION

	Date (MM/DD/YY)	_____
Print Student's Name (Last) (First) (M.I.) _____	Student ID No.	_____

Address	Telephone	Date of Birth
Home School Name	Assigned School Name (Complete After Section X)	

II. CONFERENCE INFORMATION

Conference Date: _____   ☐ Interim Review Date: _____
            (MM/DD/YY)   (MM/DD/YY)

Conference Type: ☐ Initial   ☐ Annual Review   ☐ Temporary Assignment   ☐ Reevaluation

(Check all that apply.)

☐ Consideration to/from Alternative Education Program ☐ Region Staffing ☐ District Placement Committee

Parent Notification:	Type	Date (MM/DD/YY)	Response
*Required	*(1) Written (Attach to IEP) *(2)		

Model/Language of Communication of Parent/Guardian _____

III. SIGNATURES AND POSITIONS OF PERSONS ATTENDING CONFERENCE

☐ Procedural Safeguards Available to Parents of Exceptional Students has been received by and was explained to the parent(s) or guardian(s) of the student.

☐ Parent was not in attendance.

_____ (LEA Representative)	_____ (	)
_____ (Parent)	_____ (	)
_____ (Parent)	_____ (	)
_____ (Evaluation Specialist)	_____ (	)
_____ (Teacher)	_____ (	)
_____ (Student)	_____ (	)

IV. EXCEPTIONAL STUDENT EDUCATION (ESE) PROGRAM ELIGIBILITY

The student has been determined eligible for the following ESE programs: _____

_____

_____

V. PRESENT PERFORMANCE LEVELS/NARRATIVE

(Do not complete if addressed on Individual Transition Plan insert.)

Area Assessed	Date (MM/YY)	Instrument	Level/Ability

Narrative: _____

_____

_____

_____

VI. DIPLOMA OPTION (Grades 8–12 only)

☐ Standard Diploma   ☐ Special Diploma

VII. PROGRAMS FOR LIMITED ENGLISH PROFICIENT (LEP) EXCEPTIONAL STUDENTS
(Complete this section only if the student is LEP.)

Home Language of Student _____

Language Dominance/Proficiency Assessment: _____
                                    (MM/DD/YY)   (Test Used)   (ESOL Level)

ESOL Entry Date _____   Test Used _____   Raw Score _____
        (MM/DD/YY)

ESOL Exit Date _____   Test Used _____   Raw Score _____
        (MM/DD/YY)

Results of Most Recent Standardized Achievement Test (if applicable): _____

Type and Location of LEP Services: (Check all that apply based upon present performance levels, behavioral observations, and the language dominance/proficiency assessment.)

	Regular Program*	ESE Program**
☐ English for Speakers of Other Languages (ESOL)	☐	☐
☐ Curriculum Content in English Using ESOL Strategies	☐	☐
☐ Curriculum Content in the Home Language (Elementary Schools)	☐	☐
☐ Bilingual Curriculum Content (Secondary Schools)	☐	☐
☐ Home Language Arts or ☐ Home Language Strategies	☐	☐
	*LEP Plan Required	**Attach Goals and Objectives.

Post Reclassification Monitoring (for exited students who continue to participate in an ESE program.)

Please Note: Monitoring procedures do not require parent notification or signature.

For use by IEP committee only:

1. Date: _____   ☐ No change in status   ☐ Refer to IEP committee
     (MM/DD/YY)
Signature:_____

☐ reclassify
Date:_____
    (MM/DD/YY)

2. Date: _____   ☐ No change in status   ☐ Refer to IEP committee
     (MM/DD/YY)
Signature:_____

☐ reclassify
Date:_____
    (MM/DD/YY)

3. Date: _____   ☐ No change in status   ☐ Refer to IEP committee
     (MM/DD/YY)
Signature:_____

☐ reclassify
Date:_____
    (MM/DD/YY)

VIII. EDUCATIONAL AND RELATED SERVICES

1. The committee has determined that the attached annual goals and short term objectives (K-8) or Individual Transition Plan (9–12 or earlier if appropriate) is necessary to provide appropriate education.

2. The committee has determined that the student be enrolled in:

   ☐ Regular Physical Education   ☐ ESE Physical Education   ☐ Not Applicable
   (Attach goals and objectives)

3. The committee has determined that the student requires the following related services to access an educational program:

   ☐ Physician's Request for In-School Nursing and/or Respiratory Therapy Services submitted. Implementation contingent upon review by the Office of Exceptional Student Education.

   ☐ Authorized   ☐ Not Authorized   ☐ Date: _____   Initial: _____

   ☐ Special Transportation: (specify)   ☐ Individual PickUp   ☐ Lift Bus   ☐ Safety Vest

   ☐ Other: _____

   ☐ No Related Services Required at this time.

IX. OTHER PERTINENT INFORMATION

☐ Medication(s): _____

☐ Other (e.g., allergies, restrictions): _____

☐ Board Approved Physical Restraint Procedures may be used if student presents a danger to self and/or others, or property.

☐ Student will participate in State Assessment Programs (e.g., Florida Writes, High School Competency Test). Modifications may include:

   ☐ Flexible Scheduling   ☐ Flexible Setting   ☐ Recording of Answers   ☐ Revised Format   ☐ Auditory Aids

☐ Student will participate in other assessment programs (e.g., Stanford Achievement Test, Scholastic Aptitude Test). Modifications may be requested prior to testing.

X. LEAST RESTRICTIVE ENVIRONMENT (LRE) PLACEMENT

Considerations: Some of the factors considered in selecting the student's placement and ensuring that it is in the least restrictive environment include the following: (Check all that apply.)

☐ Student frustration and stress
☐ Student self-esteem and worth
☐ Disruption of students in regular classes

☐ Disruption of students in special education classes

☐ Distractibility
☐ Need for lower pupil-to-teacher ratio
☐ Time required to master educational objectives
☐ Need for instructional technology

☐ Mobility problems in a large school setting
☐ Safety concerns due to physical conditions
☐ Health and safety concerns requiring adaptive equipment
☐ Emotional control causing harm to self and others
☐ Social skills causing increased isolation
☐ Difficulty completing tasks
☐ Other(s):_____
_____

Placement(s):   The following placement decision is based upon a review and consideration of former placements, current performance levels, parent comments, behavioral observations, goals and objectives, previous educational modifications, the extent to which the student can participate in the regular education program, and/or other information delineated on this IEP. The committee believes that for each program listed below, the student requires special education from an ESE teacher for the specified amount of hours/periods per week.

Program*	Hours/Periods per Week
_____	_____
_____	_____
_____	_____
_____	_____

* For Speech, Language, Occupational Therapy, and Physical Therapy, time may be expressed as a range of minutes within 30 minute blocks (e.g., 30–60 min./wk.).

(Check if applicable.) ☐ The student will be removed from the regular education program for more than 50% of the school day because this is the least restrictive environment.

Program Location:
Will the student be educated in the school he or she would attend if non-handicapped?   ☐ Yes   ☐ No

The goals and objectives of the IEP can be appropriately met at: _____
                                                                                        (Name of School)

XI. REGULAR EDUCATION PARTICIPATION

(Regular/vocational education teacher(s) should be included in, or informed of, results of IEP development.)

Description of participation (e.g., specific subjects, art, assemblies, yearbook, lunch, field trips, fund-raising, recess, etc.): _____

_____

_____

Modification required:

(select as appropriate) ☐ Increase/decrease instructional time   ☐ Use of special communication system

☐ Vary instructional methodology   ☐ Modification of tests

☐ Consultation   ☐ Other(s): Specify below

Mainstream Cost Factor (specify):

(1) Services, aids and/or equipment   (2) Applicable subject(s)   (3) Amount of time per week

_____

_____

_____

XII. IEP IMPLEMENTATION

Persons responsible for the implementation of this IEP include:

☐ ESE Teacher   ☐ Occupational   ☐ Physical Therapist   ☐ Orientation and   ☐ Speech/Language
                      Therapist   Mobility Specialist   Pathologist

☐ Other(s):_____

_____

XIII. INITIATION/DURATION DATES

Services delineated on the IEP, unless otherwise indicated:

• Will initiate _____.
                    (MM/DD/YY)

• and have an anticipated duration through _____.
                                                (MM/DD/YY)

XIV. PARENT(S)/GUARDIAN(S) COMMENTS

Parent(s)/Guardian(s), if present, please indicate: ☐ Agreement or ☐ Disagreement

Comments: _____

_____

_____

_____

_____

Notes: _____

_____

_____

_____

_____

_____

_____

_____

SOURCE: Vaughn, S., Bos, C., Schumm, J. (2000). *Teaching Exceptional, Diverse, and At-Risk Students in the General Education Classroom,* 2nd edition. Boston, MA: Allyn & Bacon.

APPENDIX D
Statistical Applications for Classroom Assessment

This appendix describes some of the basic statistical information classroom teachers can use in scoring and interpreting their students' test performance. It contains a basic introduction to four areas: (1) raw scores and score distributions, (2) the mean and standard deviation, (3) item difficulty and discrimination, and (4) the normal distribution and standardized test scores.

Raw Scores and Score Distributions

A **raw score** indicates the number of points a student got on a test. For example, Joe took a 70-item multiple-choice test and got 42 items correct. If 1 point is given for each correct answer, his raw score is 42. Jemma took a 20-item short-answer test on which each item counted 5 points. She got 17 items correct and thus received a raw score of 85 (17 items × 5 points each). Most frequently, raw scores are converted to percentage scores using this formula: raw score/highest possible score × 100 = percentage score. Thus, Joe's percentage score is 60 (42/70 × 100 = 60), and Jemma's percentage score is 85 (85/100 × 100 = 85).

Either raw or percentage scores can be arranged into a **test score distribution** that shows how the class as a whole performed. The raw and percentage scores for a class of 15 students who took a math test that had 10 problems worth 5 points each appear in Table D.1.

The performance of this class can be represented in a test score distribution by listing scores from highest to lowest. Test score distributions can be based on either raw scores or percentage scores. To construct a distribution, start by listing the possible scores students could have earned. For example, the class above took a 10-item test on which each item counted 5 points. Thus, the only raw scores possible ranged from 50 to 0 in 5-point increments (i.e., 50, 45, 40, 35, . . ., 15, 10, 5, 0). Similarly, since percentage scores are based on a 100-point scale, the only percentage scores possible on the 10-item test ranged from 100 to 0 in 10-point increments (i.e., 100, 90, 80, . . ., 20, 10, 0). The test score distributions in Table D.2 show how the class did. "Number" indicates the number of pupils who got a particular score; for example, three students got a raw score of 50, four got 40, and none got 10.

TABLE D.1

Name	Raw Score (Number Right × 5)	Percentage Score (Raw Score/50 × 100)
Lloyd	25	50
Chris	35	70
Jennifer	50	100
Kristen	40	80
Gail	25	50
Marta	35	70
Marita	40	80
David	40	80
Juan	45	90
Mike	20	40
Ted	30	60
Charles	50	100
Christina	35	70
Heather	40	80
Sara	50	100

TABLE D.2

Raw Score Distribution		Percentage Score Distribution	
Raw Score	Number	Percentage Score	Number
50	3	100	3
45	1	90	1
40	4	80	4
35	3	70	3
30	1	60	1
25	2	50	2
20	1	40	1
15	0	30	0
10	0	20	0
5	0	10	0
0	0	0	0

The two test score distributions show the same information on two different scales. The raw score scale is based on the total number of points on the test, 50, while the percentage score scale is based on a test of 100 total points. Teachers often transform the raw score distribution into a percentage score distribution to keep all of their tests on a 100-point scale. Recall from Chapter 9 that Ms. Fogarty did this with her test, quiz, and project scores so there would be comparability across them.

Notice also that the above example is intended to be mathematically simple to convey the basic ideas of test score distributions. For practice, redo this example assuming that the students' raw scores remained the same but that the test had 12 items worth 5 points each.

Summarizing Test Scores

The Mean

Test score distributions are useful, but often teachers want to summarize the information they provide into a single score that represents the performance of the class. There are many ways to summarize scores, but the most common is the **mean.** The mean, also commonly called the **average,** is calculated by adding together the students' test scores and dividing the total by the number of students. One can calculate the mean of either raw scores or percentage scores.

The original raw and percentage scores for our hypothetical class appear in Table D.3. The sums of the raw and percentage scores are shown at the bottom of the table. If these sums are divided by the total number of students, 15, the raw and percentage score means are 37.33 and 74.67, respectively. These means provide a single-number description of the class's performance. The mean raw score for the class is 37.33 out of 50, and the mean percentage score is 74.67 out of 100.

TABLE D.3

Name	Raw Score	Percentage Score
Lloyd	25	50
Chris	35	70
Jennifer	50	100
Kristen	40	80
Gail	25	50
Marta	35	70
Marita	40	80
David	40	80
Juan	45	90
Mike	20	40
Ted	30	60
Charles	50	100
Christina	35	70
Heather	40	80
Sara	50	100
Sum of scores	560	1120

TABLE D.4

Raw Score	Number
50	3
45	1
40	4
35	3
30	1
25	2
20	1
15	0
10	0
5	0
0	0

Two additional, though less frequently used, indices of the average performance of a class are the median and the mode. The **median** is the middle score in the test score distribution, after the scores have been arranged in order from highest to lowest. The **mode** is the score that more students got than any other. Medians and modes are best determined after constructing a test score distribution. For example, consider the score distribution in Table D.4.

The median is the middle score in the distribution. Because 15 students took the test, the middle score is the eighth from the top. Three students had raw scores of 50, one had a raw score of 45, and four had a score of 40. Thus, the eighth score from the top is a 40, and this is the median. Note that if there is an even number of scores in the distribution, the median would be determined by taking the average of the two middle scores. The mode is the score (or scores, as there can be more than one mode) that more students received than any other. The distribution shows that the score more students got than any other was 40, so the mode is 40. In this case, the median and the mode were the same, although this is not always the case.

The Standard Deviation

Suppose that two classes were tested with the same test and that the mean score in each class was 74. Could we conclude that performance in the two classes was identical? No, we could not, because the mean does not tell us how the scores of the two classes are distributed from high to low. Table D.5 compares the scores of students in two classes, each of which has a mean of 74. Construct two score distributions to

TABLE D.5

Student	Class A	Class B
1	727	4
2	76	64
3	74	84
4	75	50
5	73	98
6	74	60
7	77	88
8	71	59
9	72	89
10	76	74
Sum	740	740
Mean	74	74

compare the classes. Would you say that the performance in the two classes was identical?

Comparing the performance of the two classes indicates that the students in class A performed much more alike than the students in class B. The **range,** or the difference between the highest and lowest score, was 6 (77–71) in class A and 48 (98–50) in class B. In other words, students in class A were much more similar, or homogeneous, in their performance than students in class B, who were quite heterogeneous. The mean score for each class, though the same, does not indicate how similar or dissimilar the scores within the classes were. Note how a sense of the spread of scores could be obtained by examining the score distribution for each class.

When we describe a test score distribution, we also must consider the extent to which the scores are spread out around the mean. To find out about this characteristic of scores, we use another statistic called the **standard deviation.** The standard deviation provides information about score variability—that is, how similar or dissimilar a class's test scores are. Usually, test scores are described by both their mean and standard deviation. The mean tells about the average performance of a class, and the standard deviation tells how homogeneous or heterogeneous scores were within the class.

Mathematically, the standard deviation (σ) is represented as:

$$\sigma \text{ (standard deviation)} = \sqrt{\frac{\text{sum of } (x^2)}{n}}$$

where x is the difference of a student's score from the mean (score minus the mean) and n is the number of students who were tested. Calculating the standard deviation for class A's scores would be done as shown in

Pupil	Class A	(Pupil's Score − Mean Score)^2
1	72	$(72 - 74)^2 = 4$
2	76	$(76 - 74)^2 = 4$
3	74	$(74 - 74)^2 = 0$
4	75	$(75 - 74)^2 = 1$
5	73	$(73 - 74)^2 = 1$
6	74	$(74 - 74)^2 = 0$
7	77	$(77 - 74)^2 = 9$
8	71	$(71 - 74)^2 = 9$
9	72	$(72 - 74)^2 = 4$
10	76	$(76 - 74)^2 = 4$

TABLE D.6

Table D.6, given that the mean score for class A was 74. Adding up the squared difference of each student's score from the mean equals 36. Thus, according to the formula, the standard deviation of the scores in class A is equal to the square root of 36 divided by 10 (the number of students who were tested), or 3.6. The square root of 3.6 is equal to 1.89, which is the standard deviation for class A. Calculate for yourself the standard deviation for class B, which also has a mean of 74. You should get a standard deviation of 14.81 [square root of $(2194/10) = 14.81$]. Notice that the larger the standard deviation, the more spread out the scores are around the mean. Although class A and class B had the same mean score, the standard deviation of class B was much larger than that of class A, indicating greater heterogeneity in class B.

Item Difficulty and Discrimination

As we noted in Chapter 11, the difficulty index of a test item is indicated by the proportion or percentage of students who got the item correct. Thus, if 20 out of 25 students in a class answered an item correctly, the difficulty of that item would be $(20/25) \times 100 = 80$ percent. Thus, somewhat confusingly, the higher the "difficulty," the easier the item.

The difficulty of test items is related to the spread of test scores. If all items on a test are very easy, most students will get high scores and there will be few differences among students. The same is true if all the test items are very difficult, except that all students will get low scores. When the difficulty of test items is around 50 percent, meaning that about half the students pass and half fail each item, the resulting test scores will be maximally spread out from low to high. This is an important result for the construction of commercial standardized *norm-referenced* tests, which are intended to compare the relative achievement of students. The more students' scores differ, the better for making comparisons and distinctions among them. Thus, in standardized norm-referenced test construction, it is necessary to have items that have difficulties in the middle (35 to 65 percent) range to ensure a spread of scores.

In classroom assessment, which is generally *criterion-referenced* and focuses on individual student mastery (not differentiation among students), item difficulty is not a major concern. Classroom assessment items usually have higher difficulties (i.e., are easier) than standardized, norm-referenced test items. This would be expected as long as classroom tests reflect classroom instruction.

Also as we noted in Chapter 7, a test item's discrimination index compares the difference in performance of high and low test scores on an item. An item is said to have **positive discrimination** if more students who do well on the test as a whole answer it correctly than students who do poorly on the test as a whole. Thus, if 85 percent of the class with the highest overall test scores got an item correct compared with only 55 percent of those with the lowest overall test scores, the item discrimination would be 85 percent − 55 percent = 30 percent. In determining item discrimination, the lower group's percentage is always subtracted from that of the higher group. The higher the discrimination, the greater the difference between the high and low test scorers on that item. Notice that it is possible to get **negative discriminations.** For example, if 40 percent of the top scorers and 60 percent of the bottom scorers got the item correct, the discrimination index would be 40 percent − 60 percent = −20 percent. In such a case, one might want to check the scoring key or look at the options in the item to try to identify the ones that the top group is selecting incorrectly.

Item discrimination, like item difficulty, is important in the construction of commercial standardized tests. It is necessary that each item in such tests have high positive discrimination. While it is also desirable for classroom tests to have items with positive discrimination, it is less important than for commercial tests because classroom tests are usually scored in a criterion-referenced way and their higher item difficulties reduce the differences between high and low scorers.

Normal Distributions

The *normal distribution* is the familiar "bell-shaped" curve shown in Figure D.1. This curve is extremely important in commercial standardized achievement testing because norms such as the percentile rank and stanine are derived from it.

Normal distributions can be used to describe scores when a large group of people take a well-designed standardized test. As indicated along the bottom of the curve, the lowest possible scores correspond to the far left portion of the curve, while the highest possible scores correspond to the far right portion. Other scores fall at regular increments between the two extremes. The height of the distribution at any given point represents the

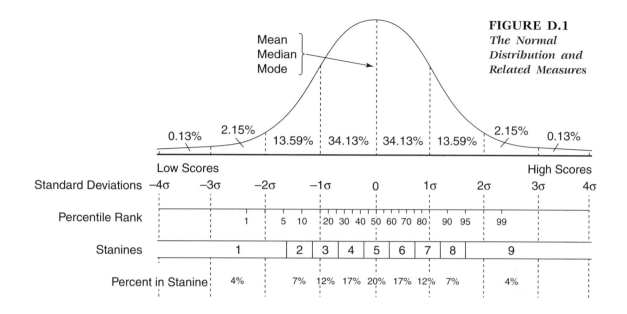

FIGURE D.1
*The Normal
Distribution and
Related Measures*

number of students who got the score that corresponds to that point. Notice that the distribution is highest in the middle and lowest at the two ends, indicating that most test takers score near the middle and very few score at either end.

As we noted, when a well-designed test with many items is given to a large number of students, the resulting scores tend to distribute themselves according to this "normal" pattern. As Figure D.1 shows, the normal distribution has three important properties:

- The mean score is exactly in the middle of the distribution, and half of all scores fall above it and half below it.
- The median and mode scores are the same as the mean.
- The standard deviation divides the normal distribution into sections as follows:
  1. About 68 percent of all the students' scores fall between 1 standard deviation below the mean and 1 standard deviation above the mean.
  2. About 95 percent of all the students' scores fall between 2 standard deviations below the mean and 2 standard deviations above the mean.
  3. Almost 100 percent of all the students' scores fall between 3 standard deviations below the mean and 3 standard deviations above the mean.

The following is a concrete illustration of these properties and how they are used in obtaining norm-referenced scores on standardized achievement tests. Assume you are a standardized-test constructor who has produced a

FIGURE D.2
Normal Distribution of Scores with Mean of 13 and Standard Deviation of 3

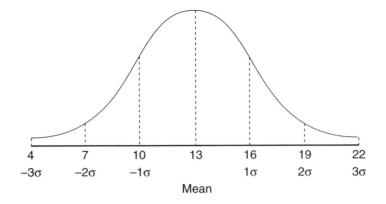

4	7	10	13	16	19	22
−3σ	−2σ	−1σ		1σ	2σ	3σ

Mean

30-item norm-referenced mathematics computation test for seventh-graders. To do this, you followed the steps described in Chapter 11: Select common objectives, write items to assess these objectives, and try the items out on many seventh-graders to identify the items with moderate difficulties and high discriminations to include on the final test version. You have identified the 30 items for your test and have but one additional step to complete: administering the test to a representative sample of 10,000 seventh-graders from across the country in order to develop test norms. These norms will be the comparative scores that will be used to interpret future test takers' performance.

You administer the test to the 10,000 seventh-graders who are meant to represent all seventh-graders across the country, and you score each student's test. You now have 10,000 scores. Because you selected items of moderate difficulty and high discrimination and because you tried out the final version of the test on a large number of seventh-graders, the distribution of scores on your test will be similar to the normal curve; many students will score near the middle of the score range and few will score very low or very high. Because 10,000 individual scores is a large number to deal with, you decide to summarize them by calculating the mean and standard deviation, using the procedures described previously. Let's assume that when your computer finishes these calculations on the math computation test scores, the mean score is 13 and the standard deviation is 3. You have a normal distribution with a mean score of 13 and a standard deviation of 3. This distribution is shown in Figure D.2.

Notice that the score of 13, which is the mean score for the group, is at the center of the distribution. Note also how the standard deviation has been used to mark off other score points on the distribution. The scores that correspond to 1 standard deviation below the mean, 10 (13 − 3 = 10), and to 1 standard deviation above the mean, 16 (13 + 3 = 16), are shown, along with the scores corresponding to 2 standard deviations below (13 − 6 = 7) and above (13 + 6 = 19) the mean and 3 standard deviations below (13 − 9 = 4) and above (13 + 9 = 22) the mean.

Suppose a student got a raw score of 13 items correct on your test. What percentage of the 10,000 students who represent all seventh-graders did she perform better than? (*Hint:* Compare Figure D.2 with Figure D.1) If her score was 13, she was exactly at the mean of the norm group and, according to the first property of the normal curve, the mean divides the normal curve into two equal halves. Thus, she performed better than about 50 percent of seventh-graders in the norm group. Notice how using the normal curve allows one to turn a raw score (13) into a percentile rank (50th) (see Chapter 11).

Suppose another student had a raw score of 16 items correct. What is that student's percentile rank? Look back at Figure D.2 for a clue. Remember that 68 percent of all the students are between the score corresponding to the mean minus 1 standard deviation (10) and the score corresponding to the mean plus 1 standard deviation (16). Because the mean (13) divides the normal curve in half, 34 percent of the students are between the mean (13) and 1 standard deviation below the mean (10), and 34 percent are between the mean (13) and 1 standard deviation above the mean (16). So, if a student had a score of 16, she was higher than all the 50 percent of pupils who were below the mean and also higher than just about all the 34 percent who were between the mean (13) and 1 standard deviation above the mean (16). Thus, a raw score of 16 on the math computation test corresponds to a percentile rank of 84 (50 + 34 = 84). The student scored higher on the test than 84 percent of the norm group. Now see if you can find the percentile ranks that correspond to a raw score of 10 and a raw score of 19.

The above example was designed to illustrate how the normal curve can be used to change raw scores into the comparative scores that can give meaning to standardized norm-referenced test performance. The example did not indicate how to change scores that are not exactly 1, 2, or 3 standard deviations above or below the mean into percentile ranks. Most introductory statistics books provide examples of how to do this, and you should refer to one if you wish further information.

APPENDIX E
Some Resources for Identifying Special Needs

Friend, M., and Bursuck, W. D. (2005). *Including students with special needs: A practical guide for classroom teachers,* 4th ed. Boston: Allyn & Bacon.

Hallahan, D. P., Lloyd, J. W., Kauffman, J. M., and Weiss, M. P. (2004). *Learning disabilities: foundations, characteristics, and effective teaching,* 3rd ed. Boston: Allyn & Bacon.

McLoughlin, J. A., and Lewis, R. B. (2004). *Assessing students with special needs,* 6th ed. Upper Saddle River, NJ: Pearson Education.

Spinelli, C. G. (2001). *Classroom assessment for students with special needs in inclusive settings.* Upper Saddle River, NJ: Prentice-Hall.

Swanson, H. L., Harris, K. R., and Graham, S. (2005). *Handbook of learning disabilities.* New York: Guilford.

Venn, J. J. (2006). *Assessing students with special needs,* 4th ed. Upper Saddle River, NJ: Pearson Education.

Ysseldyke, J. E., and Algozzine, B. (2006). *Effective assessment for students with special needs: A practical guide for every teacher.* Thousand Oaks, CA: Corwin Press.

Resources for Universal Design

Software

Built-in Accessibility of Operating Systems
Apple Special Needs www.apple.com (search for special needs)
Microsoft Enable www.microsoft.com/enable
Text-to-Speech Software Programs
CAST eReader www.cast.org
Kurzwell 3000 www.kurzweiledu.com
ReadPlease 2003 www.readplease.com
TextHELP! www.texthelp.com
Write: OutLoud www.donjohnston.com
WYNN www.freedomscientific.com
Speech-to-Text Software Programs
Dragon Naturally Speaking www.scansoft.com
IBM ViaVoice www.306.ibm.com

Accessible Multimedia
HiSoftware www.hisoftware.com

Hardware

Portable Word Processors
AlphaSmart www.alphasmart.com
CalcuScribe www.calcuscribe.com
DreamWriter www.brainium.com
LaserPC6 www.perfectsolutions.com
QuickPad www.quickpad.com

Handwriting Recognition Technologies
InkLink www.siibusinessproducts.com
Inkwell www.apple.com/macosx/features/inkwell
Logitech io Personal Digital Pen www.logitech.com
PenReader www.smarttech.com

Electronic Whiteboards
Mimio www.mimio.com
SMARTBoard www.smarttech.com

Online Resources

Digital Text
American Library Association Great Sites for Children
    www.ala.org/parentspage/greatsites/lit.html
Berkeley Digital Library SunSite http://sunsite.berkeley.edu
The Children's Literature Web Guide www.ucalgary.ca/%7Edkbrown
Internet Public Library www.ipl.org
Project Gutenberg www.gutenberg.org
University of Virginia Library Electronic Text Center
    http://etext.lib.virginia.edu/ebooks

Organizations

Technology in Education
Association for the Advancement of Computing in Education (AACE)
    www.aace.org
Association for Educational Communications and Technology (AECT)
    www.aect.org
International Society for Technology in Education (STE) www.iste.org
Network of Regional Technology in Education Consortia www.rtec.org
U.S. Department of Education Office of Educational Technology
    www.ed.gov/Technology

Accessibility
CPB/WGBH National Center for Accessible Media
    http://ncam.wgbh.org

SOURCE: Curry, C. (2003). Universal design accessibility for all learners. *Educational Leadership*, (61), 2, 55–60.

GLOSSARY

Ability   What one has learned over a period of time from both school and nonschool sources; one's general capability for performing tasks.

Achievement   What one has learned from formal instruction, usually in school.

Affective domain   Involves behaviors related to feelings, emotions, values, attitudes, interests, and personality; nonintellectual behaviors.

Analytic scoring   An essay scoring method in which separate scores are given for specific aspects of the essay (e.g., organization, factual accuracy, and spelling).

Anecdotal record   A short, written report of an individual's behavior in a specific situation or circumstance.

Aptitude   One's capability for performing a particular task or skill; usually involves a narrower skill than ability (e.g., mathematics aptitude or foreign language aptitude).

Assessment   The broad process of collecting, synthesizing, and interpreting information to aid classroom decision making; includes information gathered about students, instruction, and classroom climate.

Average   The number derived by adding up all the test scores and dividing the total by the number of students who took the test.

Bias   A situation in which assessment information produces results that give one group an advantage or disadvantage over other groups because of problems in the content, procedures, or interpretations of the assessment information; a distortion or misrepresentation of performance.

Checklist   A written list of performance criteria associated with a particular activity or product on which an observer marks the student's performance on each criterion using a scale that has only two choices.

Classroom assessment   The process of collecting, synthesizing, and interpreting information to aid in classroom decision making.

Cognitive domain   Encompasses intellectual activities such as memorizing, interpreting, applying knowledge, solving problems, and thinking critically.

Commercial achievement test   Typically a norm-referenced test that compares a student's score to a national group of similar students.

Conceptual knowledge   Knowledge that demonstrates understanding of general concepts.

Content standards   Used to define the knowledge and skills students are expected to develop in a given subject area and grade level.

Convergent question   A question that has one correct answer.

Criterion-referenced grading   Determining the quality of a student's performance by comparing it to preestablished standards of mastery.

Curriculum   The skills, performances, attitudes, and values students are expected to learn from schooling; includes statements of desired student outcomes, descriptions of materials, and the planned sequence that will be used to teach students.

Cut score   A predetermined score used to differentiate levels of student performance, given usually in statewide assessment.

Difficulty index   Indicates the proportion or percentage of test takers who answered a test item correctly.

Direct indicators   Information or perspectives provided by a firsthand observer or source.

Discrimination index   Indicates the extent to which students who get a particular test item correct are also likely to get a high score on the entire test.

Distractor   A wrong choice in a selection test item.

Divergent question   A question that has more than one acceptable answer.

Early assessments   Assessments used by teachers in the first weeks of school to get to know students so that they can be organized into a classroom society with rules, communication, and control.

Educate   To change the behavior of students; to teach students to do things they could not previously do.

Educational objectives   Statements that describe a student accomplishment that will result from instruction—specifically, the behavior the student will learn to perform and the content on which it will be performed.

Educational standards   Used to set common goals for instruction and criteria for performance to which all schools and students are held.

Evaluation   Process of judging the quality or value of a performance or a course of action.

Form   The particular version of a commercial test that has more than one equivalent version.

Formative assessment   The process of collecting, synthesizing, and interpreting information for the purpose of improving student learning while instruction is taking place; assessment for improvement, not grading.

Global objectives   Very broad statements of intended learning that require years to accomplish.

Grade   Symbol or number used by teachers to represent a student's achievement in a subject area.

Grade equivalent score   A standardized test score that describes a student's performance on a scale based on grade in school and month in grade; most commonly misinterpreted score; indicates student's level of performance relative to students in his or her own grade.

Grading   The process of judging the quality of a student's performance.

Grading curve   In norm-referenced grading, the system that sets up quotas for each grade.

Grading system   The process by which a teacher arrives at the symbol or number that is used to represent a student's achievement in a subject area.

Higher-level cognitive behavior   Cognitive behaviors that involve more than rote memorization and recall.

Holistic scoring   An essay scoring method in which a single score is given to represent the overall quality of the essay across all dimensions.

Individual Education Plan (IEP)   A special education plan developed for a student after extensive assessment of the student's special educational needs.

Instruction   The methods and processes by which students' behaviors are changed.

Instructional assessment   The collection, synthesis, and interpretation of information needed to make decisions about planning or carrying out instruction.

Instructional objectives   Specific objectives used to plan daily lessons.

Interpretive exercise   A test situation that contains a chart, passage, poem, or other material that the student must interpret in order to answer the questions posed.

Items   Questions or problems on an assessment instrument.

Key   A list of correct answers for a test.

Level   The grade level(s) at which a particular commercial test should be administered to students.

Levels of tolerance   The extent to which a teacher can tolerate different noise levels, activities, and student behavior.

Local norms   Norms that are confined to students in a specific school district.

Logical error   The use of invalid or irrelevant assessment information to judge a student's status or performance.

Lower-level cognitive behavior   Rote memorization and recall.

Mean   The average of a group of scores.

Measurement   The process of assigning numbers or categories to performance according to rules and standards (e.g., scoring a test).

Median   The middle score when all scores are listed from lowest to highest.

Mode   The score that is obtained by more students in a group than any other; there can be more than one mode in a group of scores.

Negative discrimination   When a test item is answered incorrectly more frequently for high scorers on the test than for low scorers, the item discriminates in a different direction from the total score of the test.

Nonstandardized assessment   An assessment approach intended to assess a single group of students, such as a class.

Norm group   The group of students who were tested to produce the norms for a test.

Norm-referenced grading   Determining the quality of a student's performance by comparing it to the performance of other students.

Norms   A set of scores that describes the performance of a specific group of students, usually a national sample at a particular grade level, on a task or test; these scores are used to interpret scores of other students who perform the same task or take the same test.

Numerical summarization   Use of numbers to describe performance on an assessment.

Objective   Agreement among independent judges, scorers, or observers.

Observation   Watching and listening to students carry out specific activities or respond to given situations.

Official assessments   Assessments, such as grading, grouping, placing, and promoting students, that teachers are required to carry out as part of their official responsibilities.

Opportunity to learn standards   Focus on the quality of teachers, availability of resources, and condition of facilities.

Options   Choices available to select from when answering a multiple-choice test item.

Percentile bands   The range of percentile ranks in which a student is expected to fall on repeated testing; a way to indicate the error in scores to avoid overinterpretation of results.

Percentile rank   A standardized test score that describes the percentage of the norm group a given student scored higher than (e.g., an 89th percentile rank means that a student scored higher than 89 percent of the norm group).

Performance assessment   Observing and judging a student's skill in actually carrying out a physical activity (e.g., giving a speech) or producing a product (e.g., building a birdhouse).

Performance criteria   The aspects of a performance or product that are observed and judged in performance assessment.

Performance standards   The levels of achievement students must reach to receive particular grades in a criterion-referenced grading system (e.g., higher than 90 receives an A, between 80 and 90 receives a B, etc.).

Performance tasks   Include book reports, journal entries, portfolios, science experiment, and class projects.

Portfolio   A well-defined collection of student products or performances that shows student achievement of particular skills over time.

Positive discrimination   When a test item is answered correctly more frequently for high scorers on the test than for low scorers, the item discriminates in the same direction as the total score of the test.

Practical knowledge   The beliefs, prior experiences, and strategies that enable a teacher to carry out classroom duties and activities.

Prejudgment   Inability to make a fair and objective assessment of another person because of interfering prior knowledge, first impressions, or stereotypes.

Premise   The stem or question part of a matching item.

Psychomotor domain   Physical and manipulative activities such as holding a pencil, buttoning buttons, serving a tennis ball, playing the piano, and cutting with scissors.

Range   The difference between the highest and lowest test scores in a group; obtained by subtracting the highest test score from the lowest test score.

Rating scale   A written list of performance criteria associated with a particular activity or product on which an observer marks a student's performance on each criterion in terms of its quality using a scale that has more than two choices.

Raw score   The number of items correct or the total score a student obtained on an assessment.

Reliability   The extent to which an assessment consistently assesses whatever it is assessing; if an assessment is reliable, it will yield the same or nearly the same information on retesting.

Response   The answer choices given for a matching item.

Scoring rubric   A rating scale based on written descriptions of varied levels of achievement in a performance assessment; also called a descriptive rating scale.

Selection item   A test item to which the student responds by selecting the answer from choices given; multiple-choice, true-false, and matching items.

Self-fulfilling prophecy   The process in which teachers form perceptions about student characteristics and treat students as if the perceptions are correct, and students respond as if they actually have the characteristics, even though they might not have originally had them; an expectation becomes a reality.

Specific determiners   Words that give clues to true-false items; *all, always, never,* and *none* indicate false statements, while *some, sometimes,* and *may* indicate true statements.

Standard deviation   A measure of the variability or spread of scores for a group of test takers.

Standardized assessment   An assessment that is administered, scored, and interpreted the same for all students taking the test, no matter when and where it is used.

Standards-based test   A test used to measure performance standards.

Stanine   A standardized test score that describes student performance on a 9-point scale. Scores of 1, 2, and 3 are often interpreted as being below average; 4, 5, and 6 as being average; and 7, 8, and 9 as being above average.

Stem   The part of a multiple-choice item that states the question to be answered.

Subjective   A lack of agreement among judges, scorers, or observers.

Subtests   Sets of items administered and scored as a separate portion of a longer, more comprehensive test.

Summative assessment   The process of collecting, synthesizing, and interpreting information for the purposes of determining student learning and assigning grades; assessments made at the end of instruction or teaching.

Supply item or **supply question**   A test item to which the student responds by writing or constructing his or her own answer; short-answer, completion and essay.

Test   A formal, systematic, usually paper-and-pencil procedure for obtaining a sample of students' behavior; the results of a test are used to make generalizations about how students would perform on similar but untested behaviors.

Test battery   A group of subtests, each assessing a different subject area but all normed on the same sample; designed to be administered to the same group of test takers.

Test norms   A set of scores that describe how a national sample of students who are representative of the general population perform on a test.

Test score distribution   The listing of test scores from lowest to highest; the spread of students' scores.

Testwise skills   The test taker's ability to identify flaws in test questions that give away the correct answers; used during tests to outwit poor item writers.

Validity   The extent to which assessment information is appropriate for making the desired decision about students, instruction, or classroom climate; the degree to which assessment information permits correct interpretations of the desired kind; the most important characteristic of assessment information.

CREDITS

Chapter opener 1: © Creatas/PunchStock

Chapter opener 2: © Creatas

Chapter opener 3: © Ingram Publishing/AGE Fotostock

Chapter opener 4: © BananaStock/PictureQuest

Chapter opener 5: © BananaStock/PictureQuest

Chapter opener 6: © Dynamigraphics/Jupiterimages

Chapter opener 7: © image100 Ltd

Chapter opener 8: © Royalty-Free/CORBIS

Chapter opener 9: © Andersen Ross/Getty Images

Chapter opener 10: © Frederick Bass/Getty Images

Chapter opener 11: © BananaStock/AGE Fotostock

NAME INDEX

SUBJECT INDEX